Envisioning the Arab Future

Decades before 9/11 and the "Arab Spring," U.S. and Arab elites contended over the future of the Middle East. Through unprecedented research in Arabic and English, *Envisioning the Arab Future* details how Americans and Arabs – nationalists, Islamists, and communists – disputed the meaning of modernization within a shared set of Cold War–era concepts. Faith in linear progress, the idea that society functioned as a "system," and a fascination with speed united officials and intellectuals who were otherwise divided by language and politics. This book assesses the regional implications of U.S. power while examining a range of topics that transcends the Arab–Israeli conflict, including travel, communities, gender, oil, agriculture, Iraqi nationalism, Nasser's Arab Socialism, and hijackings in both the United States and the Middle East. By uncovering a shared history of modernization between Arabs and Americans, *Envisioning the Arab Future* challenges assumptions about a "clash of civilizations" and profoundly reinterprets the antecedents of today's crises.

Nathan J. Citino is an Associate Professor of History at Rice University.

Global and International History

Series Editors

Erez Manela, *Harvard University*
John McNeill, *Georgetown University*
Aviel Roshwald, *Georgetown University*

The Global and International History series seeks to highlight and explore the convergences between the new international history and the new world history. Its editors are interested in approaches that mix traditional units of analysis such as civilizations, nations, and states with other concepts such as transnationalism, diasporas, and international institutions.

Titles in the Series

Envisioning the Arab Future

Modernization in U.S.–Arab Relations, 1945–1967

NATHAN J. CITINO

Rice University

CAMBRIDGE
UNIVERSITY PRESS

University Printing House, Cambridge CB2 8BS, United Kingdom

Cambridge University Press is part of the University of Cambridge.

It furthers the University's mission by disseminating knowledge in the pursuit of education, learning and research at the highest international levels of excellence.

www.cambridge.org
Information on this title: www.cambridge.org/9781107036628

© Nathan J. Citino 2017

First published 2017

Printed in the United States of America by Sheridan Books, Inc.

A catalogue record for this publication is available from the British Library

Library of Congress Cataloging-in-Publication data
Names: Citino, Nathan J., author.
Title: Envisioning the Arab future: modernization in U.S.–Arab relations, 1945–1967 / Nathan J. Citino.
Description: Cambridge, United Kingdom: Cambridge University Press, 2017. |
Series: Global and international history |
Includes bibliographical references and index.
Identifiers: LCCN 2016024241 | ISBN 9781107036628 (hardback)
Subjects: LCSH: Arab countries – Foreign relations – United States. |
United States – Foriegn relations – Arab countries. |
Arab countries – Foreign relations – 20th century. |
United States – Foreign relations – 1945–1989. |
BISAC: HISTORY / United States / General.
Classification: LCC DS63.2.U5 C55 2016 | DDC 327.73017492709/045–dc23
LC record available at https://lccn.loc.gov/2016024241

ISBN 978-1-107-03662-8 Hardback

Cover credit: Gourna with Hathor, with plans and elevations in mountainous landscape with trees; Portrait golden tone gouache on scratchboard; 58h × 46w. © Rare Books and Special Collections Library, The American University in Cairo, Egypt

For Sharon

For there's no such thing as the present: there is only a past, and a future at its beck and call. In our subconscious minds we are forever constructing our futures.

– Ahmet Hamdi Tanpinar, *The Time Regulation Institute*

Contents

Figures

Maps

Acknowledgments

Researching and writing this book took more than a dozen years. It began with a trip to Egypt in 2002 funded by the College of Liberal Arts and the History Department at Colorado State University. The Earhart Foundation helped me to continue my research by awarding me a Fellowship Research Grant. In 2008, I participated in the summer institute "Rethinking America in Global Perspective" sponsored by the National Endowment for the Humanities and the National History Center, which gave me access to the Arabic resources available in the African and Middle Eastern Reading Room of the Library of Congress. Stephen Holden, a former student, generously supported my work through a donation to the Colorado State University History Department. A research fellowship from the American Council of Learned Societies enabled me to begin writing the book in 2011–12. I finished drafting the manuscript in 2014 at Durham University in England, where I was fortunate to have an in-residence fellowship at the Institute of Advanced Study. At Rice University, my new academic home, I revised and completed this book with support from the School of Humanities and the Department of History.

Some of the topics examined in this book I first addressed in articles that appeared in the *Arab Studies Journal, Business History Review, International Journal of Middle East Studies, Cold War History*, and *Journal of Cold War Studies*. The feedback I received about these articles and from invited talks at the Graduate Seminar in International History at Ohio State University, the Yale Colloquium in International Security Studies, the Georgetown International History Seminar, and the Center for American Studies and Research at the American University of Beirut helped me to formulate the arguments found in this book. I also benefited from giving a workshop presentation at the European Institute at Columbia University and from participating in conference panels at annual meetings of the Society for Historians of American Foreign Relations and the American Historical Association.

I owe particular thanks to Robert Vitalis, James Jankowski, and Ussama Makdisi, each of whom read the entire manuscript and offered numerous helpful suggestions and criticisms. This is a much better book because of them, but responsibility for any remaining errors of fact or judgment lies entirely with me. James Lindsay offered wisdom and friendship over many years. Numerous colleagues shared sources, suggestions, and experience, including Nick Cullather, Peter Hahn, Tareq Ismael, Guy Laron, Mark Atwood Lawrence, Douglas Little, Martha Mundy, Tammy Proctor, Thomas Zeiler, and William Zeman. The Rare Books and Special Collections Library at the American University in Cairo graciously gave permission to use images from the Hassan Fathy Collection. Drew Beja offered lodging and good food during a research trip to Boston, Nadya Sbaiti showed me around Beirut, and Todd Kenreich and Amy Wei provided companionship during numerous trips to Washington, DC. I am especially grateful to the Global and International History Series editors, Erez Manela, John McNeill, and Aviel Roshwald, for supporting this project and to Deborah Gershenowitz at Cambridge University Press for her help in bringing it to completion.

My family deserves the biggest thanks. My mother, Mary, and late father, David, siblings Dominic and Maria, and in-laws Lee and Jane Flower offered encouragement over many years. Grandparent childcare made this book possible. I have received the greatest support from my daughters, Helen and Katherine, and from my wife, Sharon. For her love and for all of the adventures we've shared, including a move to Texas, I dedicate this volume to her.

Note on Transliteration and Translation

Arabic titles and names are spelled according to a simplified version of the transliteration system used by the *International Journal of Middle East Studies*. Familiar names such as "Nasser" appear in their commonly used spellings. All translations from Arabic are the author's unless otherwise indicated.

Abbreviations

ADP	Allen Dulles Papers
ASIIA	Records of the Adlai Stevenson Institute of International Affairs
BNA	British National Archives
CBP	Chester Bowles Papers
CFR	Records of the Council on Foreign Relations
CHMP	Charles Habib Malik Papers
CIA	Central Intelligence Agency
DDEL	Dwight D. Eisenhower Library
DDRS	Declassified Documents Reference System
DHP	Donald Hawley Papers
EDP	Everette DeGolyer Sr. Papers
FBI	Federal Bureau of Investigation
FRUS	*Foreign Relations of the United States*
HFA	Hassan Fathy Archive
HIA	Hoover Institution Archives
HSTL	Harry S. Truman Library
JFKL	John F. Kennedy Library
JMD	John Marshall Diary
LBJL	Lyndon B. Johnson Library
MBP	Max Ball Papers
MMAUK	*Muhakamat al-Mahkamah al-ʿAskariyah al-ʿUlya al-Khassah*
NARA	National Archives and Records Administration
NSF	National Security File
NYT	*New York Times*
RFC	Rockefeller Foundation Collection
RG	Record Group
SML	Seeley G. Mudd Library
WEM	William E. Mulligan Papers
WEP	William Eddy Papers
WLP	Walter Levy Papers

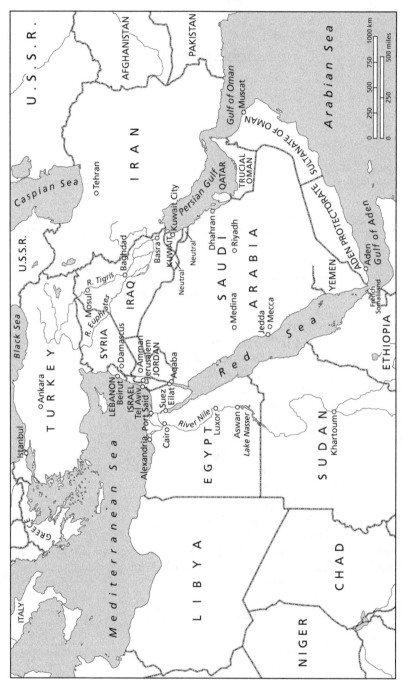

MAP 1. The Middle East prior to 1967.

Introduction

The "History of the Future"

"[I]t is only the history of the future which can resolve the basic question of what kind of modernity the Middle East is to have."
  – U.S. Ambassador to Egypt John Badeau, May 26, 1962[1]

"[Developing] peoples are now firmly determined to compensate for the past and catch up with the future under circumstances of rapid progress."
  – Egyptian President Gamal 'Abd al-Nasser, July 9, 1962[2]

This book examines modernization as a theme in U.S. relations with the Arab Middle East between the end of World War II and the June 1967 Arab–Israeli War. It analyzes not only economic development policies, but also the ideas elites used to explain social change. Rather than being fundamentally divided by culture, I argue, Americans and Arabs contended over the aims and meanings of modernization within a shared set of widely held concepts from the postwar era about how societies advance. This study also focuses attention on the dialogue between regional and global influences in the politics of postwar Arab modernization. As the two quotations that open this introduction indicate, officials situated Arab development within both a Middle Eastern and a universal framework. On one hand, Arab countries experienced movements for social progress as part of a distinct regional history encompassing past Ottoman imperial reforms, a modern renaissance in Arabic letters and thought, European colonialism and anticolonialism, and the struggle against Zionism. On the other hand, those same countries joined a world of decolonizing states after 1945 engaged in the universal pursuit of economic development on the basis of competing ideological

---

[1] Paper by Badeau, "Prospects and Problems in United States–UAR Relations," May 26, 1962, folder: Egypt (UAR), box 215, Policy Planning Council, Subject Files, 1954–1962, RG 59, NARA.
[2] Brubeck to Bundy, July 11, 1962, with speech attached, folder: UAR General 7/62–8/62, box 168A, NSF, JFKL.

prescriptions. As part of the third world, Arab states became a focus of the global Cold War rivalry between the United States and the Soviet Union. Some Arab leaders associated their governments with other Afro-Asian and nonaligned countries, and many implemented policies administered by international experts in areas such as industry, agriculture, housing, and population control. The politics of modernizing the Arab world therefore synthesized regional factors including the Ottoman legacy, competition among Arab anticolonial movements, and rivalries between Arab regimes, with global factors such as Cold War ideological conflict, third world solidarity, and technological advances. This book studies the different ways in which Arabs and Americans defined regional underdevelopment in historical terms, as well as their alternative strategies for helping the Arab Middle East "to compensate for the past and catch up with the future," as Nasser put it.

A regional emphasis in the study of international development provides a much-needed complement to the prevailing globalism of Cold War studies. In *The Global Cold War*, historian Odd Arne Westad featured the superpowers' struggle to "prove the universal applicability of their ideologies" by persuading the leaders of newly independent states to adopt either a capitalist or a communist development strategy.[3] Westad's *tour de force* not only refocused Cold War studies outside of Europe, but also established a model for writing global history in which the superpowers, states from their respective blocs, and elites from developing countries interacted on the world stage. Global history has thrived recently by helping scholars to understand the phenomena that created the modern world, including capitalism, empires, migrations, and anticolonialism.[4] This approach has influenced historians such as Guy Laron, Paul Thomas Chamberlin, Craig Daigle, and Roham Alvandi, who usefully place the Middle East into a global context.[5] Framing development as part of the Cold War's global clash of modernities portrays

[3] Odd Arne Westad, *The Global Cold War: Third World Interventions and the Making of Our Times* (New York: Cambridge University Press, 2007), 4.

[4] See C. A. Bayly, *The Birth of the Modern World: 1780–1914* (Malden, MA: Blackwell Publishing, 2004); Erez Manela, *The Wilsonian Moment: Self-Determination and the International Origins of Anticolonial Nationalism* (New York: Oxford University Press, 2007); *A World Connecting: 1870–1945* (A History of the World), ed. Emily S. Rosenberg, et al. (Cambridge, MA: Belknap Press, 2012); Jürgen Osterhammel, *The Transformation of the World: A Global History of the Nineteenth Century*, trans. Patrick Camiller (Princeton, NJ: Princeton University Press, 2014); and Sven Beckert, *Empire of Cotton: A Global History* (New York: Knopf, 2014).

[5] See Guy Laron, *Origins of the Suez Crisis: Postwar Development Diplomacy and the Struggle over Third World Industrialization, 1945–1956* (Baltimore, MD: Johns Hopkins University Press, 2013); Paul Thomas Chamberlin, *The Global Offensive: The United States, the Palestine Liberation Organization, and the Making of the Post–Cold War Order* (New York: Oxford University Press, 2012); Craig Daigle, *The Limits of Détente: The United States, the Soviet Union, and the Arab–Israeli Conflict, 1969–1973* (New Haven, CT: Yale University Press,

it as a universal problem and highlights connections among third world countries.

A global perspective employed by itself, however, carries certain disadvantages. First, emphasizing the superpowers' clashing modernities tends to neglect regional and religious ideologies – such as Arab nationalism and Islamism – and to marginalize their importance in a historical narrative dominated by Washington and Moscow. Westad compares such ideologies to Marxism using the collective term "nativist," but concedes that "[t]he Marxist and nativist labels used here are of course only crude and imprecise pointers to movements that emerged on different continents and among widely varying cultures."[6] As a consequence, Islamists are not well integrated into postwar international history and are abruptly introduced into accounts of the 1970s and '80s, when they confronted the superpowers in Iran and Afghanistan.[7] As will be shown, however, Islamists participated in postwar modernization debates and were subject to the same global trends that affected secular reformers. Second, presenting third world countries as equivalent objects of superpower competition neglects how varied experiences with European colonialism and anticolonialism prior to 1945 influenced the postwar politics of development. In the case of the Arab Middle East, the Ottoman legacy also held significance for the empire's successor states into the late twentieth century. By emphasizing distinctions among Arab countries and between the Arab Middle East and other third world regions, this book joins recent criticism by scholars such as Heonik Kwon and Masuda Hajimu questioning whether the Cold War can plausibly be described as a unified global event or as a "single, encompassing geopolitical order."[8] Third, Cold War globalism corresponds to the official American account of communism as a total threat. It therefore legitimizes a global response and accepts the need for a *grand* strategy. Chamberlin observes that the proliferation of global revolutionary movements during the 1960s "suggested that American fears of the domino theory were perhaps not entirely off base."[9] While a global perspective is essential for understanding postwar development, disaggregating the third world offers a critical approach to analyzing American power by exposing gaps between sweeping U.S. doctrines and the diverse circumstances faced by postcolonial societies.

2012); and Roham Alvandi, *Nixon, Kissinger, and the Shah: The United States and Iran in the Cold War* (New York: Oxford University Press, 2014).

[6] Westad, *The Global Cold War*, 82.

[7] See, for example, Amin Saikal, "Islamism, the Iranian Revolution, and the Soviet Invasion of Afghanistan," in *The Cambridge History of the Cold War*, ed. Melvyn P. Leffler and Odd Arne Westad, 3 vols. (New York: Cambridge University Press, 2010), 3:112–34.

[8] Heonik Kwon, *The Other Cold War* (New York: Columbia University Press, 2010), 7. See also Masuda Hajimu, *Cold War Crucible: The Korean Conflict and the Postwar World* (Cambridge, MA: Harvard University Press, 2015).

[9] Chamberlin, *The Global Offensive*, 27.

Numerous scholars have analyzed how the Cold War combined with regional struggles for decolonization and economic progress. Those who have provided the most historically rich accounts work in regional languages and literatures to understand the reciprocal influences of Cold War development formulas and regional politics. They examine encounters between U.S. policies and experts on one hand, and the ideas and historical experiences of their third world counterparts on the other. These encounters often produced results that were not entirely consistent with the objectives of any single actor, in which the outcome emerged instead from a collision of ideas, historical circumstances, and power relations. In his two-volume history of the Korean War, Bruce Cumings described the intersection between competing U.S. foreign policy agendas in postwar Asia and the history of Korean struggles first against Japanese colonialism and then against control by other powers.[10] Gregg Brazinsky built on Cumings' approach by examining how South Korea's colonial experience, and the ideas of Buddhism and Confucianism, influenced its postwar campaigns of modernization and state-building.[11] David Biggs places Cold War development in the Mekong Delta within a long-term historical context that encompasses precolonial, colonial, and postcolonial periods of Vietnamese history.[12] In Latin America, Greg Grandin similarly interprets Cold War–era violence in terms of a century-long conflict between Guatemalan elites and indigenous peoples.[13] Historians studying other parts of the globe have therefore demonstrated the value of combining regional and Cold War histories, and in some cases decenter the Cold War by examining relations between third world regions.[14]

---

[10] Bruce Cumings, *The Origins of the Korean War*, 2 vols. (Princeton, NJ: Princeton University Press, 1981, 1990). For indications of Cumings' influence, see Laron, *Origins of the Suez Crisis*; and Bradley Simpson, *Economists with Guns: Authoritarian Development and U.S.–Indonesian Relations, 1960–1968* (Stanford, CA: Stanford University Press, 2008), 40.

[11] Gregg Brazinsky, *Nation Building in South Korea: Koreans, Americans, and the Making of a Democracy* (Chapel Hill: University of North Carolina Press, 2007).

[12] David A. Biggs, *Quagmire: Nation-Building and Nature in the Mekong Delta* (Seattle: University of Washington Press, 2010). For an account that emphasizes South Vietnam's distinct religious and social politics, see Jessica M. Chapman, *Cauldron of Resistance: Ngo Dinh Diem, the United States, and 1950s Southern Vietnam* (Ithaca, NY: Cornell University Press, 2013).

[13] Greg Grandin, *The Last Colonial Massacre: Latin America in the Cold War* (Chicago: University of Chicago Press, 2004). See also Thomas C. Field Jr., "Ideology as Strategy: Military-Led Modernization and the Origins of the Alliance for Progress in Bolivia," *Diplomatic History* 36 (January 2012): 147–83; and Jason C. Parker, *Brother's Keeper: The United States, Race, and Empire in the British Caribbean, 1937–1962* (New York: Oxford University Press, 2008). For a regional history of the Cold War in Latin America, see Tanya Harmer, *Allende's Chile and the Inter-American Cold War* (Chapel Hill: University of North Carolina Press, 2011).

[14] See Piero Gleijeses, *Conflicting Missions: Havana, Washington, and Africa, 1959–1976* (Chapel Hill: University of North Carolina Press, 2002); and Zach Levey, *Israel in Africa, 1956–1976* (Dordrecht, Netherlands: Martinus Nijhoff /Republic Of Letters, 2012).

This historical literature has helped to inspire the present study. It uses modernization to reinterpret postwar U.S.–Arab relations beyond conventional accounts of the Arab–Israeli conflict. By the end of World War II, American Arabists had already lost debates within the policy establishment about whether the United States would support Zionism. Pro-Zionist voices in Congress and the White House overruled objections from some State Department and Pentagon figures to the creation of a Jewish state in Palestine. Meanwhile, individuals such as intelligence officer William A. Eddy (1896–1962), and institutions such as the American University of Beirut, embodied a transition in the U.S. campaign to uplift the Middle East from that of a religious mission in the Holy Land to one of secular modernization. As a result, Americans came to see the region's distinctive importance in terms of oil interests at the same time that it became part of a global third world. American perceptions of Arab societies shifted as the older, Orientalist tradition of studying Islamic civilization textually met the latest social science approaches concerned with universal problems of development. After Israel's establishment in 1948, a new generation of Middle East experts and petroleum industry figures worked "within the constraints" created by the evolving U.S. relationship with Israel to incorporate Arab countries into Cold War strategy, protect oil interests, and promote economic progress.[15] Doing so presented them with difficulties given the obstacle Israel posed to U.S.–Arab cooperation. Although clashes between competing development policies served as one expression of the conflict over Zionism, and a focus on development never really succeeded in transcending it, the theme of modernization also reveals that U.S. relations with the Arab world encompassed more than just battles over Israel. The efforts of Americans concerned with modernizing the Middle East brought them into contact not only with the region's past, but also with Arab elites who authored their own agendas against the global backdrop of decolonization and the Cold War.

This book uses the official archives of the United States and Great Britain, numerous private manuscripts, postwar development literature, and a wide range of Arabic-language materials to examine how Americans and Arabs contested the meaning of modernization in a variety of settings. It explains U.S. officials' conflicts over development strategy toward the Arab world

---

[15] Matthew F. Jacobs, *Imagining the Middle East: The Building of an American Foreign Policy, 1918–1967* (Chapel Hill: University of North Carolina Press, 2011), 237. See also Hugh Wilford, *America's Great Game: The CIA's Secret Arabists and the Shaping of the Modern Middle East* (New York: Basic Books, 2013), 54–65; and Parker T. Hart, *Saudi Arabia and the United States: Birth of a Security Partnership* (Bloomington: Indiana University Press, 1998), 41–42. On U.S. missionaries, see Ussama Makdisi, *Artillery of Heaven: American Missionaries and the Failed Conversion of the Middle East* (Ithaca, NY: Cornell University Press, 2008); and Hans-Lukas Kieser, *Nearest East: American Millennialism and Mission to the Middle East* (Philadelphia: Temple University Press, 2010).

and the ways in which contrasting readings of regional history informed their competing policies. Among Arab leaders, it considers conflicts between secular revolutionary modernizing agendas, such as those of Nasser and Iraqi prime minister 'Abd al-Karim Qasim, and those of non-revolutionaries such as Jordan's King Husayn. This study also incorporates Islamists such as Egyptian Sayyid Qutb as well as communists and Palestinian *fida'iyin* into its account of postwar Arab development. This book explores Cold War and third world influences on Arab modernization debates and on the policies of individual Arab countries. But it also places those debates within a regional context. Area studies, in the Middle East as in other regions, have been criticized as a creation of the U.S. national security state and as beholden to its agenda of sowing capitalist development across the post-colonial world.[16] Nevertheless, there are compelling historical reasons for studying Arab modernization in a regional setting. Recent scholarship has portrayed development policies on the part of some Arab governments as attempts to counter encroachment on their sovereignty by other Arab states.[17] Additional reasons include the Ottoman legacy, the history of anti-colonialism and anti-Zionism, the implications of oil development, and the ideal of pan-Arab unity. Such factors argue against subsuming the politics of Arab modernization entirely within the global Cold War. At the same time, regional factors confronted postwar modernizers with the fundamental problem of how to translate development formulas into distinctive contexts. Understanding this issue requires greater attention to regional particularities and their relationship to universalizing ideologies. This book therefore investigates postwar Arab history and its intersections with American power at multiple registers, inserting regionalism as an intermediate frame of reference between the nation-state (diplomatic historians' traditional focus) and the world.

Studying encounters between American modernizers and their Arab contemporaries yields important criticisms of the U.S. foreign policy literature about modernization. As historian Nick Cullather has written, that literature analyzes "modernization" as a set of ideas belonging to the Cold War era. Recent scholarship "puts the framework inside the frame," he explains,

[16] See Zachary Lockman, *Contending Visions of the Middle East: The History and Politics of Orientalism* (New York: Cambridge University Press, 2004), 126–28; Bruce Cumings, "Boundary Displacement: Area Studies and International Studies During and After the Cold War," in *Universities and Empire: Money and Politics in the Social Sciences During the Cold War*, ed. Christopher Simpson (New York: The New Press, 1998), 159–88; and Mark T. Berger, "Decolonisation, Modernisation and Nation-Building: Political Development Theory and the Appeal of Communism in Southeast Asia, 1945–1975," *Journal of Southeast Asian Studies* 34 (October 2003): 421–48.

[17] See Cyrus Schayegh, "1958 Reconsidered: State Formation and the Cold War in the Early Postcolonial Arab Middle East," *International Journal of Middle East Studies* 45 (August 2013): 421–43.

"and treats development *as* history."[18] These studies have concentrated not simply on policies intended to promote development – improving poor economies with respect to growth, productivity, and other measures – but also on the ideas that constituted modernization theory, the social science framework that influenced American strategy. Historian Michael Latham offers the best summary of modernization theory's basic assumptions:

(1) "[T]raditional" and "modern" societies are separated by a sharp dichotomy; (2) economic, political, and social changes are integrated and interdependent; (3) development tends to proceed toward the modern state along a common, linear path; and (4) the progress of developing societies can be dramatically accelerated through contact with developed ones.[19]

According to Latham, modernization theory provided an academic rationale for the Vietnam War and other U.S. interventions in the third world by updating the American exceptionalist ideology of Manifest Destiny. Other historians have described modernization theory as the overseas edition of twentieth-century American liberalism. Nils Gilman associates it with Talcott Parsons's structural-functionalist sociology. Modernization theory derived its optimistic account of social progress from postwar America, Gilman notes, and rested on assumptions of political consensus and elite dominance. It provided "a high-concept version of Americanism" promising "materialism without class conflict" and "democracy without disobedience."[20] Both Gilman and Latham interpret Cold War modernization as a discourse of power and criticize its proponents for promising to remake third world societies according to an idealized image of the United States.[21] David Ekbladh describes American development projects as the export of the New Deal liberalism embodied in the Tennessee Valley Authority.[22] These scholars trace modernization in U.S. foreign policy to the history of domestic American reforms.

But defining modernization as a set of ideas formulated in the United States and exported abroad constitutes its own form of American

---

[18] Nick Cullather, "Modernization Theory," in *Explaining the History of American Foreign Relations*, ed. Michael J. Hogan and Thomas G. Paterson, 2nd ed. (New York: Cambridge University Press, 2004), 214.

[19] Michael Latham, *Modernization as Ideology: American Social Science and "Nation Building" in the Kennedy Era* (Chapel Hill: University of North Carolina Press, 2000), 4.

[20] Nils Gilman, *Mandarins of the Future: Modernization Theory in Postwar America* (Baltimore, MD: Johns Hopkins University Press, 2003), 13.

[21] For an earlier version of this argument, see Irene L. Gendzier, *Managing Political Change: Social Scientists and the Third World* (Boulder, CO: Westview Press, 1985).

[22] David Ekbladh, *The Great American Mission: Modernization and the Construction of an American World Order* (Princeton, NJ: Princeton University Press, 2010). For a larger discussion, see Nathan J. Citino, "Modernization and Development," in *The Routledge Handbook of the Cold War*, ed. Artemy M. Kalinovsky and Craig Daigle (New York: Routledge, 2014), 118–30.

exceptionalism. Many postwar Arab elites shared the assumptions that Latham attributes to American modernizers. For instance, Nasser's statement cited earlier assumes that developing countries would progress along a common, linear path. The Egyptian president justified a disastrous military campaign in Yemen, also known as "Nasser's Vietnam," by arguing that intervention on the part of a more advanced country could help to accelerate the progress of a backward one. This book offers numerous examples of Arab modernizers – nationalists, Islamists, and communists – who objected to U.S. foreign policy but who described social change using ideas similar to those American cold warriors employed. A more interesting story remains to be told about how elites engaged in political conflict through a shared language of structure and change, society and development. These concepts circulated globally after 1945, when thousands of Arabs and others from the third world studied in Europe, the United States, and the Soviet Union, and the United Nations defined common standards for measuring development.[23] In this debate, American claims about the exemplary character of U.S. development were judged by postcolonial elites in light of their own societies' historical experiences. Moreover, it is problematic to claim that American ideas about modernization were created wholly out of domestic liberalism. Development strategies cannot be fully understood apart from American engagements with Middle Eastern and other peoples, because those strategies were made and remade at the points of contact. American liberalism also took on varied meanings when it encountered other reform legacies across the third world, such as the inheritance of the nineteenth-century Ottoman *Tanzimat* reforms in the old empire's Arab successor states.

Any reinterpretation of U.S.–Arab relations cannot ignore the preponderant global power the United States wielded after World War II. In the Middle East, America's military strength was reinforced by that of its ally Great Britain, which, despite conflict over Suez, participated in coordinated Anglo-American military interventions during 1958. Officials in Washington frequently resorted to covert operations to bring about desired political changes in Middle Eastern countries.[24] The United States also exerted formal and informal economic power, including huge investments in oil. It held a permanent seat on the UN Security Council, granting it leverage over UN policies toward the Arab–Israeli conflict. The United States contributed more funding to international development agencies such as the World Bank, and thereby exercised more authority over them, than any other country. Private American philanthropies such as the Rockefeller and Ford Foundations helped to set third world development agendas. Arab and American elites

---

[23] See UN Department of Economic Affairs, *Measures for the Economic Development of Under-Developed Countries* (New York: UN Department of Economic Affairs, 1951).

[24] See Douglas Little, "Mission Impossible: The CIA and the Cult of Covert Action in the Middle East," *Diplomatic History* 28 (November 2004): 663–701.

therefore conducted their debates over modernizing the Middle East on decidedly unequal terms. Yet for all of its might, the United States was at best only partially successful in imposing its vision of the future on Arab and other third world countries. Explaining why requires an understanding of how American power intersected with distinct regional circumstances. Through its examination of those intersections in the Arab world, this study combines Middle East regional history with the history of Cold War–era U.S. foreign policy.

Analyzing U.S. policies from the perspective of Middle Eastern history represents a departure from recent trends in American foreign relations. Douglas Little, Melani McAlister, Michelle Mart, and Matthew F. Jacobs have emphasized American cultural perceptions of the Middle East.[25] Their critical interpretations reveal that cultural stereotypes, rather than strictly rational, strategic considerations, helped to define U.S. approaches to the region. These scholars have adapted the insights of Edward Said's *Orientalism* to the study of U.S. foreign policy. Said's influential work described a European cultural discourse about Middle Eastern peoples that portrayed them as the opposite and inferior "Other" to Western civilization.[26] In following Said, however, the U.S. scholarship shares some of *Orientalism*'s limitations. Just as Said portrayed Orientalism as a closed Western discourse, recent works about American foreign policy have turned inward to examine U.S. images of the Middle East and the network of American experts who influenced policy. This inward focus has come at the expense of understanding American and Arab perceptions of one another as being mutually constituted. Cultural images of other societies as "modern" or "backward" were the products of particular encounters, which must be studied from both Arab and American perspectives. As historian Ussama Makdisi writes: "It is one thing to criticize American representations of foreign cultures; it is an entirely different matter to study American engagements with them."[27] Another problem is that neither Said nor those he inspired convincingly explains how Americans reconciled the cultural essentialism about the Middle East that they inherited from European Orientalism with the universal claims of their global development model. As will be seen, various American officials and experts attempted to show how U.S. modernization formulas could solve unique regional problems. They used their knowledge of the Middle East to argue

[25] Douglas Little, *American Orientalism: The United States and the Middle East since 1945*, 3rd ed. (Chapel Hill: University of North Carolina Press, 2008); Melani McAlister, *Epic Encounters: Culture, Media, and U.S. Interests in the Middle East since 1945*, Rev. ed. (Berkeley: University of California Press, 2005); Michelle Mart, *Eye on Israel: How America Came to View Israel as an Ally* (Albany: State University Press of New York, 2006); and Jacobs, *Imagining the Middle East.*

[26] Edward Said, *Orientalism* (New York: Vintage Books, 1979).

[27] Ussama Makdisi, "After Said: The Limits and Possibilities of a Critical Scholarship of U.S.–Arab Relations," *Diplomatic History* 38 (June 2014): 659.

that U.S. policies could overcome the particular historical circumstances of its underdevelopment. Evaluating their arguments requires some familiarity with Middle East historiography. This is necessary to identify how the interpretations on which those arguments were based have since been challenged. It also makes it possible to detect when Americans applied their expertise selectively to serve the needs of U.S. strategy.

In seeking to relate the regional to the global, this study is consistent with recent scholarship on the modern Middle East. Several important works have attempted to break out of an area studies model and challenge assumptions of regional exceptionalism by incorporating the Middle East into global history.[28] This book considers how American development strategies and the superpower rivalry combined with patterns in Arab history. It also examines the ways in which Arab elites sought to appropriate the ideas of Cold War modernization and use the promise of development for their own political advantage. Studies of earlier periods in Middle Eastern history offer some guidance about how to understand this dynamic. In *Ottoman Brothers*, for example, Michelle U. Campos examines the responses of different groups living in Palestine to the 1908 revolution in Istanbul that reinstated the Ottoman constitution.[29] Central to her study is analyzing different interpretations of political liberalism within Palestine and the contested idea of "liberty [*hurriya*]" among Christians, Muslims, and Jews. Through competing invocations of "liberty," members of these groups sought to reform the empire's community-based conception of rights and to redefine Ottoman citizenship. Conflicts over the meaning of *hurriya* were ultimately struggles to determine who would benefit from the revolution. Arab modernizers from half a century later similarly contended over the meaning of such universal terms as "development [*tanmiya*]," "progress [*taqaddum*]," and "modernization [*ta'sir* or *tajdid*]." After 1945, debates about modernization became the language of political conflict. Perhaps the postwar era's most important analogue to "liberty" was the term "system [*nizam*]."[30] Arab officials and intellectuals applied this term not only to capitalism and communism, but also to Islamist and other models for regional development that they preferred to either of the superpowers' prescriptions. The term *system* stands, in the first place, for the set of assumptions shared

---

[28] See, for instance, Robert Vitalis, *America's Kingdom: Mythmaking on the Saudi Oil Frontier* (Stanford, CA: Stanford University Press, 2007); Cemil Aydin, *The Politics of Anti-Westernism in Asia: Visions of World Order in Pan-Islamic and Pan-Asian Thought* (New York: Columbia University Press, 2007); and Ilham Khuri-Makdisi, *The Eastern Mediterranean and the Making of Global Radicalism, 1860–1914* (Berkeley: University of California Press, 2010).

[29] Michelle U. Campos, *Ottoman Brothers: Muslims, Christians, and Jews in Early Twentieth-Century Palestine* (Stanford, CA: Stanford University Press, 2011).

[30] Other common postwar Arabic terms used for discussing development policies and that denote a systematic understanding of society include "model [*namudhaj*]," "program [*barnamaj* or *minhaj*]," and "method [*uslub*]."

by Arab and American leaders, as well as by many others around the globe who were concerned with third world development: that society was an integrated structure whose progress could be directed and managed by elite authority. In the second place, its use across a political spectrum indicates the intense conflict over the Arab future waged within a common set of Cold War–era concepts.

Technology is another important aspect of modernization that held particular implications for the Arab Middle East. Just as steam-powered ships and trains facilitated global mobility in the nineteenth century, the automobile and jet airplane gave rise to new experiences of speed in the twentieth.[31] Historian On Barak has described the relationship between the technologies of speed and temporality in nineteenth-century Egypt.[32] In her scholarship on the automobile in interwar Lebanon, anthropologist Kristin V. Monroe has observed that "practices of mobility not only reflect, but also shape social relations of power."[33] Historian Yoav Di-Capua has argued that the cosmopolitan Egyptian elite used aviation to "give shape and authority to its own modern enterprise" while preserving its leadership role over the Westernized middle class or *effendiyya*. During the interwar period, the Egyptian upper class "treated the airplane metaphorically and impregnated it with its own values of universal equality, liberty, progress, and harmony." Advances in the technology of speed were therefore linked to social politics within colonial society. These conflicts over authority only intensified in the face of Arab decolonization and revolution, and as the "age of speed" identified by Di-Capua accelerated with the proliferation of aerospace technologies.[34] Speed influenced Arab modernization debates at a time when conflicts over development emphasized gender as well as class and challenges to existing forms of privilege coincided with growing opportunities for global travel.

Regional histories can provide new perspective on world-historical trends, in this case the rise and decline of modernization as a widely held postwar concept. According to Makdisi, however, American foreign relations scholars "have traditionally not been interested in seriously studying the worlds beyond American shores, let alone qualified to evoke them." To be fair, he also criticizes some Arab historians for narrowly interpreting missionary and other encounters on the basis of nationalist or sectarian agendas.[35] With respect to researching in languages other than English, Makdisi's criticism of American diplomatic historians has diminishing validity given the

---

[31] On travel during the nineteenth century, see Bayly, *The Birth of the Modern World*, 315, 354.

[32] On Barak, *On Time: Technology and Temporality in Modern Egypt* (Berkeley: University of California Press, 2013).

[33] Kristin V. Monroe, "Automobility and Citizenship in Interwar Lebanon," *Comparative Studies of South Asia, Africa, and the Middle East*, vol. 34, no. 3 (2014): 520.

[34] Yoav Di-Capua, "Common Skies, Divided Horizons: Aviation, Class and Modernity in Early Twentieth Century Egypt," *Journal of Social History* 41 (Summer 2008): 934.

[35] Makdisi, *Artillery of Heaven*, 8.

multi-archival basis of many recent foreign policy studies.[36] More legitimate, however, is the argument that diplomatic historians should pay closer attention to non-U.S. historiographies. Integrating other literatures into the study of American diplomacy demands not merely consulting them to provide fuller context or to paint a more vivid backdrop against which to feature the roles of American actors. Rather, it requires assessing the regional or local implications of U.S. power by considering historical questions borrowed from other relevant fields. This study offers just such an appraisal of postwar American influence in the Arab Middle East.

This book is organized according to significant issues addressed by scholars of the Middle East. Rather than coinciding with shifts in U.S. global strategy or changes in presidential administration, its seven chapters address aspects of modernization in U.S.–Arab relations that correspond to subjects in regional historiography. The structure is therefore topical and not strictly chronological. Nor does this book attempt to give a comprehensive account of U.S. development programs in the Arab world. Given the pervasive concern with economic and social progress after 1945, this book can present merely an evocative, rather than an exhaustive, set of topics selected for their relevance at both the global and regional levels. It seeks to demonstrate not only that the meanings of modernization in U.S.–Arab relations were contested as part of the Cold War, but also that they depended on contingent historical circumstances across the Middle East and within particular Arab countries. This study features the intersections between global and regional politics as the basis for exploring the range and depth of postwar U.S.–Arab relations. Such an approach offers a more substantial framework for understanding the past than either focusing exclusively on the Arab–Israeli conflict as a problem for U.S. diplomacy or assuming that inherent cultural differences determine the course of Arab relations with the West.

The first two chapters reconstruct how Arabs and Americans respectively imagined modernizing the Middle East and situated the region within a global context. Chapter 1 ("The Age of Speed") examines the ways that jet-age speed affected Arab travelers' perceptions of the world and influenced Arab political debates; Chapter 2 ("Imperial Legacies") studies the relationship between U.S. oil interests in Arab countries and Americans' historical interpretations of reforms in the Ottoman Empire and the Turkish republic, whose experience with modernization many cold warriors came to see as a model first for the Arab Middle East and then for the third world. The next four chapters examine cases in which Arabs and Americans contested the meaning of modernization in direct encounters. Chapter 3 ("City of

---

[36] In addition to works already cited, see Lien-Hang T. Nguyen, *Hanoi's War: An International History of the War for Peace in Vietnam* (Chapel Hill: University of North Carolina Press, 2012); and Piero Gleijeses, *Visions of Freedom: Havana, Washington, Pretoria and the Struggle for Southern Africa, 1976–1991* (Chapel Hill: University of North Carolina Press, 2013).

the Future") compares regional cases of community-building and gendered development; Chapter 4 ("Yeoman Farmers") considers regional land reform policies and how previous Ottoman and colonial reforms influenced an important U.S. agricultural project in Jordan; Chapter 5 ("The People's Court") explains how Cold War debates about modernizing Iraq were inseparable from an existing conflict between competing definitions of Iraqi nationalism; and Chapter 6 ("New Men") analyzes U.S.–Egyptian relations and the ideology of Nasser's regime. Chapter 7 ("Changing Course") reconsiders the decline of postwar modernization by comparing the American and Arab experiences of the late 1960s. It features the crisis of Palestinian statelessness and interprets the phenomenon of airline hijackings in both the United States and the Middle East as signifying an end to the "age of speed" described at the beginning. Late 1960s crises including the Arab–Israeli and Vietnam Wars not only challenged postwar elites' power, but also discredited their optimistic accounts of modernization as an integrated process of economic, social, and political change that they could manage effectively. When elites' promises to improve society on the basis of developmental systems went unfulfilled, new agendas emerged for confronting the authority of states and the oppressive structure of postwar societies.

The appearance of certain individuals in multiple contexts throughout this book reveals a circulation of ideas among U.S. and Arab elites and reflects their shared belief that modernization was a holistic process affecting various aspects of society simultaneously. It also serves to provide a layered account of modernization in U.S.–Arab relations and to knit the chapters together. Each chapter incorporates the global setting for those relations, but this book's topical organization foregrounds aspects of Arab history to reinforce the point that the Cold War held distinctive meanings within and among third world regions.

In more ways than one, the "History of the Future" is an apt phrase with which to introduce this book. At the most basic level, it is a historical study of conflicts from the previous century over the future of the Arab Middle East. Those conflicts frequently took the form of arguments about the past. As Daniel T. Rodgers writes, postwar American intellectuals described societies as driven along a historical path by the influences of structural change: "The forces of history swept over them."[37] Through historical research, this book also challenges popular misconceptions about its topic. One fallacy is that U.S.–Arab clashes over modernity are the inevitable consequence of timeless cultural differences. As this book shows, however, Arab and American modernizers differed most often over the aims rather than the desirability of progress, while sharing a Cold War context and common ideas about how societies evolve. Another is the claim that Arab "underdevelopment" is the

---

[37] Daniel T. Rodgers, *Age of Fracture* (Cambridge, MA: Belknap/Harvard University Press, 2011), 4.

result of isolation from the influences of globalization. The development debates examined in this book occurred as part of an ongoing Arab engagement with global politics and the world economy, of which the postwar era represented only the latest historical phase. Among Cold War scholars, this book questions the empiricist faith that it is even possible to fit different case studies together into a universal history about the clash between opposite paths to modernity. As historian Jürgen Osterhammel prescribes, this book "shuns the illusory neutrality of an omniscient narrator or a 'global' observation point" and "plays consciously on the relativity of ways of seeing."[38] Recovering the meanings of the Cold War across diverse postcolonial settings requires analyzing discrete instances of political conflict and using these to complement and criticize the Olympian narrative about the superpower struggle. Finally, and most importantly, this study revisits the antecedents of today's U.S.–Arab relations in the determined hope that understanding them better will contribute to a more humane future.

[38] Osterhammel, *The Transformation of the World*, xx.

I

The Age of Speed

"As for the distances, they are not so important today, for modern methods of communication have shortened them greatly. Baghdad is nearer to Damascus than Aleppo, Hama, Homs, and Beirut were in the past. If these distances did not prevent unity in the age of the camel, they will not do so in the age of the train, the automobile, and the plane. The distances between our countries are small when compared to those in the United States."
– Musa Alami, "The Lesson of Palestine."[1]

"[T]he governing classes and students of underdeveloped countries are gold mines for airline companies. African and Asian officials may in the same month follow a course on socialist planning in Moscow and one on the advantages of the liberal economy in London or at Columbia University."
– Frantz Fanon, *The Wretched of the Earth*.[2]

For growing numbers of Arabs in the postwar era, the experience of travel linked Middle Eastern politics with global debates about modernization. This basic fact is apparent from their writings, which are thick with descriptions of planes, airports, trains, ships, hired cars, and even rickshaws, as well as hotels, tourist sites, and showcase development projects. Global travel was nothing new for Arabs with the means to undertake it, and Arab debates about modernity had long incorporated accounts of experiences abroad. But travel assumed particular significance after 1945. As will be seen from the examples presented in this chapter, the increasing speed of travel reinforced the tendency to draw prolific comparisons among development models as a defining feature of postwar politics. Arab elites translated encounters with other peoples into terms that could be employed in ideological conflicts back home. Many also used the experiences of traveling by

[1] Musa Alami, "The Lesson of Palestine," *Middle East Journal* 3 (October 1949): 393.
[2] Frantz Fanon, *The Wretched of the Earth* (New York: Grove Press, 1963), 83.

plane, train, ship, or automobile as metaphors for characterizing their own societies as structures undergoing rapid change and for contesting who had the right to set society's course. Accounts of trips abroad and depictions of others, whether positive or negative, had helped previous Arab travelers to construct reform agendas and envision what modernity could mean for their own societies. During the era of superpower conflict, swift modes of travel to the United States and elsewhere influenced Arab depictions of modernization. Speed inspired modernizers to represent society's development over time as acceleration through space.

This chapter focuses on travel in order to understand how the Cold War affected Arab modernization debates. It examines Arab memoirs and political writings to make three related arguments. The first is that after 1945, Arab elites used travel experiences to other third world regions, the United States, and the Soviet Union to formulate ideas about modernization. These Cold War travel experiences built on the long-established practice in Arabic letters of using encounters with Europe to imagine modernity. The second argument is that the bipolar competition between the superpowers intersected with an existing, multisided rivalry among anticolonial ideologies within the Arab world. Appropriating Cold War terminology, some Arab elites reconfigured anticolonial movements from the early twentieth century – including Islamism – as modernizing "systems" modeled on those of Washington and Moscow. The third argument is that as Arab modernizers grew accustomed to traversing the globe, many employed speed metaphors to characterize their preferred paths to development. The metaphor of "takeoff," popularized by economist and presidential advisor Walt Rostow in *The Stages of Economic Growth*, is the most famous use of speed to represent modernization.[3] Rostow held up the "high mass-consumption society" of the United States as a universal development model. But his modernizing formula shared imagery and assumptions with those of Arab elites who rejected U.S. policies. The presence of similar elements in Arabic writings points to shared concepts among otherwise dissimilar modernizers, including their structural interpretation of society, concern for elite authority, comparative methodology, and use of speed to represent progress.

Following World War II, Arab travelers observed America and other societies in a global context defined by rapid mobility. For instance, Jordanian diplomat 'Abd al-Munim al-Rifa'i (1917–1985) served the Hashemite kingdom in Cairo, Damascus, Athens, Tunis, and Tehran before becoming ambassador to Washington. He summered in Maine, wintered in Miami, and motored by causeway to Key West. From these experiences, he found American society "incompatible with intellectual complexity [*ba'id 'an al-ta'qid al-fikri*]." In 1959, he accompanied King Husayn to Taiwan and across

---

[3] Walt Rostow, *The Stages of Economic Growth: A Non-Communist Manifesto* (Cambridge, England: Cambridge University Press, 1960).

the Pacific to Hawaii and the continental United States, where they appealed for economic and military aid. The pair flew from Amman to Dhahran, Karachi, Bangkok, Taipei, Wake Island, and Honolulu before arriving in San Francisco.[4] Egyptian Islamist Sayyid Qutb (1906–1966) visited America between 1948 and 1950.[5] Qutb cruised by ship from Alexandria to New York and then traveled to Washington, DC; Denver; Palo Alto; and San Francisco. He studied education in Greeley, Colorado, where the sight of adolescents dancing at a church social to the tune "Baby, It's Cold Outside" confirmed his belief in America's sexual immorality.[6] In a lament written from the United States, whose material wealth he both admired and criticized, Qutb longed to discuss something other than "dollars, film stars, and car models."[7] Qutb returned by plane to Cairo, where members of the Muslim Brotherhood met him at Faruq airfield. He soon took off again for Saudi Arabia on the Muslim pilgrimage.[8] Syrian foreign minister Khalid al-'Azm (1903–1965), scion of a notable family and known as the "Red Pasha," arrived in New York in 1955 following a route that had taken him from Damascus to Beirut, Istanbul, Munich, Paris, and Boston. Al-'Azm had been invited to San Francisco to commemorate the tenth anniversary of the United Nations but felt snubbed by President Dwight D. Eisenhower. Instead, al-'Azm met Soviet foreign minister Vyacheslav Molotov, an encounter captured by a photographer from *Life* magazine. Playing the tourist, al-'Azm ricocheted between destinations on the two coasts by plane and train, seeing only Chicago in the heartland. From the Empire State Building, al-'Azm observed how Broadway staggered across Manhattan's grid like a "drunk," and in Los Angeles he studied the movie stars' handprints pressed into the cement outside Grauman's Chinese Theater. He marveled that his flight from L.A. to Washington, DC, which reached 650 kilometers per hour, matched the airspeed record for 1955. From Washington, he took a "fast train" that delivered a smooth ride without any "vibration [*al-ihti-zaz*]," despite reaching New York in just three and a half hours. Two years later, al-'Azm would undertake a similar tour of Soviet Eurasia.[9] Despite

4 'Abd al-Munim al-Rifa'i, *Al-Amwaj: safahat min rihlat al-hayah* (Amman: Wizarat al-Thaqafa, 2001), 91, 131–34.

5 John Calvert, *Sayyid Qutb and the Origins of Radical Islamism* (New York: Columbia University Press, 2010), 139–55. See Yusuf al-'Azm, *Al-Shahid Sayyid Qutb: Hayatuhu wa madarasatuhu wa atharuh* (Damascus and Beirut: Dar al-Qalam, 1980), 34–35.

6 See Calvert, *Sayyid Qutb and the Origins of Radical Islamism*, 151.

7 Quoted in Salah 'Abd al-Fattah al-Khalidi, *Amrika min al-dakhil bi-minzar Sayyid Qutb* (Jidda, Saudi Arabia: Dar al-Manarah, 1986), 154. See also Calvert, *Sayyid Qutb and the Origins of Radical Islamism*, 145.

8 Calvert, *Sayyid Qutb and the Origins of Radical Islamism*, 157.

9 Khalid al-'Azm, *Mudhakkirat Khalid al-'Azm.* 3 vols. (Beirut: Dar al-Muttahida li-l Nashr, 1973), 2:411–39. Quotations on pp. 421, 438. On Khalid al-' Azm and his elite family background, see Jane Hathaway with Karl Barbir, *The Arab Lands under Ottoman Rule, 1516–1800* (Harlow, England: Pearson/Longman, 2008), 87–90.

their political differences, these three figures shared the experience of fast movement across the globe. Speed gave postwar Arab travelers compressed encounters with America and other societies, which they could then compare as alternative models for development.

Twentieth-century speed empowered Arabs to judge other societies comparatively, a prerogative previously claimed by European colonizers and one that would become U.S. cold warriors' stock in trade. Global travel helped to make Arab and other third world elites active participants in conflicts over development, which for them, as much as for the Americans and Soviets, served as a vehicle for achieving power. "Speed," writes Enda Duffy, "has been the most empowering and excruciating new experience for people everywhere in twentieth-century modernity." Not only should speed be regarded as political, Duffy argues, "but speed, it turns out, *is* politics: the expression of a new order of the organization of global space."[10] The ubiquity of speed metaphors to represent modernization reflects the shared structuralist concepts that underlay global development debates following World War II. Assumptions about the interdependence of social, economic, and political changes, which formed the basis for Keynesian economics and modernization theory, gained currency even among modernizers who did not share American agendas of liberal capitalism and anticommunism.[11] Speed metaphors also served as arguments for the necessity of elite authority over development. Just as the airplane, train, or automobile operated on the basis of a complex system managed by technical skill, so too did society advance according to a complicated process requiring leadership by those who understood how the parts functioned in relation to the whole. Anthropologist James C. Scott has observed how reformers attempt to "cash in on the symbolic capital" of the term "streamlining" to evoke the "bureaucratic equivalent of a sleek locomotive or jet."[12] Such references to advanced modes of transportation indicate a shared understanding of development as a process of interdependent change and correspond to descriptions of postwar modernizing ideologies as "systems."

As travel sped up after 1945, mass education and multiplying connections opened the world to an ever wider cross section of Arab society. Arabs with opportunities to travel included not only sons of the Ottoman-era elite such as al-'Azm and Westernized state functionaries (the *effendiyya*) such as Qutb, but also a larger group of educated professionals including doctors and engineers, military and police officers, party cadres, students, and

[10] Enda Duffy, *The Speed Handbook: Velocity, Pleasure, Modernism* (Durham, NC: Duke University Press, 2009), 1, 19.

[11] See Nick Cullather, *The Hungry World: America's Cold War Battle Against Poverty in Asia* (Cambridge, MA: Harvard University Press, 2010), 146–50; and Rodgers, *Age of Fracture*, 1–14.

[12] James C. Scott, *Seeing Like a State: How Certain Schemes to Improve the Human Condition Have Failed* (New Haven, CT: Yale University Press, 1998), 237.

university professors.[13] Official and semiofficial Cold War initiatives, including student exchanges and the Fulbright and Foreign Leader programs, would bring thousands of students, journalists, academics, and military and civilian officials to American shores.[14] Private interests such as the Arabian American Oil Company also sponsored Arab students in the United States.[15] According to the Institute of International Education's *Open Doors* report on international exchange, 2,514 of 14,485 total students from the top ten countries sending students to the United States in 1948–49 came from Near Eastern and South Asian nations.[16] A State Department document citing the same source reported that the number from Near Eastern and South Asian countries had increased to 9,277 by 1960, though most of these students came from non-Arab states.[17] Another State Department source indicated that in 1960 more than 1,000 students from Iraq alone were studying in the United States, while a British diplomat put the total number of Iraqis studying at colleges in Western countries at 2,000 compared with 1,500 studying in the Soviet bloc.[18] In 1961, the Organization of Arab Students claimed to represent 5,000 Arabs studying at U.S. institutions.[19]

As the superpowers hosted students, officers, and intellectuals from the third world, Arab societies experienced a postcolonial crisis of authority. The postwar years witnessed a succession of military coups, including those in Syria beginning in 1949, the 1952 revolution in Egypt led by 'Abd al-Nasser and other Free Officers, and the 1958 revolution that brought 'Abd al-Karim Qasim to power in Iraq. This political upheaval intensified battles over who was best suited to direct Arab development among the Ottoman-era elite, ideological parties, and military officers, all of whom

[13] See Michael Eppel, "Note about the Term *Effendiyya* in the History of the Middle East," *International Journal of Middle East Studies* 41 (August 2009): 535–39.

[14] See Kenneth Osgood, *Total Cold War: Eisenhower's Secret Propaganda Battle at Home and Abroad* (Lawrence: University Press of Kansas, 2006), 304–10. On the Foreign Leader program, see Giles Scott-Smith, "The US State Department's Foreign Leader Program in France During the Early Cold War," *Revue Française d'études Américaines* 107 (2006): 48–49.

[15] See Malik to Duce, May 19, 1953, Folder: Duce, James Terry, 1946–60, box 13, CHMP, Library of Congress Manuscript Division, Washington, DC.

[16] See Table 4.2 in Teresa Brawner Bevis and Christopher J. Lucas, *International Students in American Colleges and Universities: A History* (New York: Palgrave Macmillan, 2007), 118.

[17] Sims to Meyer, March 9, 1961, Chron Inter-office Memorandum [folder 2 of 2], box 3, Bureau of Near Eastern and South Asian Affairs/Office of Near Eastern Affairs, Records of the Director, 1960–1963, RG 59, NARA.

[18] Trevelyan to Lloyd, October 22, 1959, FO 481/13, BNA. See the table "Arab Students in the Soviet Union 1960–1980" in Constantin Katsakioris, "Soviet Educational Aid towards Arab Countries after 1956," *Journal of Modern European History* vol. 8, no. 1 (2010): 95.

[19] Meyer to Jones, March 16, 1960, Inter-agency Group on Iraq, box 3; letter by Tarjouman, July 20, 1961, Cairo – 1961, box 4, Bureau of Near Eastern and South Asian Affairs/Office of Near Eastern Affairs, Records of the Director, 1960–1963, RG 59, NARA.

competed for support from the *effendiyya* and promised to liberate subaltern groups such as peasants, women, and workers. One strategy by which cosmopolitan elites could establish their authority was to point to the knowledge of other societies that they argued familiarized them with the mechanism of social change. Arab nationalists barnstormed the past searching for relevant examples of other people's national consolidation in the way that travelers comparing development models did the globe, illustrating how rapid mobility compressed conceptions of historical time as well as perceptions of space. As Arab politics came to focus on development, political language incorporated increasing numbers of abbreviated comparisons drawn between the superpowers and among many other societies.

Speed altered the politics of intercultural encounters. Edward Said associated the writings of nineteenth-century Western travelers in the Middle East such as Richard Burton, François-René Chateaubriand, and Wilfrid Blunt with a new phase in the tradition of Western cultural representations of the Middle East. Although Europeans could convert disparaging "textual and contemplative" representations of the region into "administrative, economic, and even military" control of it, Middle Eastern travelers during the "age of steam and print" could also scrutinize Western societies firsthand. In doing so, they reinterpreted Western ideas and disputed Europeans' superiority and right to rule other peoples.[20] The speed of post-1945 travel, however, offered Arabs a range of experiences that included opportunities to assess the competing Western development models of capitalism and communism. Anthropologist Johannes Fabian criticized Western travelers' cultural perceptions of others on the basis of "*temporalization*," the sense that experiences of underdeveloped societies across spatial distance were really journeys back in time.[21] From the perspective of Arab travelers, encounters with "free" and communist societies afforded glimpses of possible rather than inevitable futures. These development alternatives enabled them to identify desirable and undesirable outcomes and to define for literate Arab audiences what form the future should take.

This chapter interprets travel as "a quintessential feature of the twentieth century's globalizing world," one in which Arab societies participated.[22] It seeks to dispel misperceptions that Arab "underdevelopment" is the result of isolation from global change. As recently as 2002, the UN Arab Human Development Report simplistically opposed "traditional Arab culture and

---

[20] Said, *Orientalism*, 210. See James Gelvin and Nile Green, eds., *Global Muslims in the Age of Steam and Print* (Berkeley: University of California Press, 2013). See also Marwa Elshakry, *Reading Darwin in Arabic, 1860–1950* (Chicago: University of Chicago Press, 2013).

[21] Johannes Fabian, *Time and the Other: How Anthropology Makes Its Object* (New York: Columbia University Press, 1983), 28.

[22] Christopher Endy, *Cold War Holidays: American Tourism in France* (Chapel Hill: University of North Carolina Press, 2004), 3.

values" against "those of the globalizing world."[23] The examples compiled later in this chapter expose such a dichotomy as ahistorical and represent a new phase in the ongoing dialogues between global and regional influences that have long characterized Arab reform debates. This chapter describes the historical importance of travel in contesting the meaning of modernity in the Middle East. It next examines Arabs' Cold War travel experiences and how these were invoked in ideological conflicts back at home. Finally, it focuses on Arab modernizers' use of speed metaphors in debates about development. Such representations illustrate not only how Arabs were influenced by global conflicts over modernization, but also how they adapted Cold War concepts to the regional circumstances of a decolonizing Middle East.

During the colonial period, travel by Middle Eastern elites served reformers in the Ottoman Empire and Egypt as one strategy for acquiring knowledge with which to confront growing European power.[24] Their experiences provide a crucial precedent for understanding Cold War travelers. Among the most famous nineteenth-century Arab sojourners was Rifaʻa al-Tahtawi (1801–1873), who worked in the translation office of Egyptian ruler Muhammad ʻAli Pasha and visited Paris in 1826. From this experience, he wrote *Takhlis al-ibriz fi talkhis bariz* [*An Extraction of Pure Gold in a Summary of Paris*], whose purpose, according to historian Lisa Pollard, was "to tell the Egyptians as much as possible about European society and its customs, and to give suggestions ... for how Egypt might shape its institutions in the French image."[25] Also among al-Tahtawi's comments were critical observations about French women that were not far removed from those Qutb made more than a century later about American women. "Among their bad qualities is the lack of virtue of many of their women," al-Tahtawi wrote. "Fornication among them is a secondary sin (especially among those who are not married)," he observed, "rather than a major one."[26] Historian Carter V. Findley, writing about the 1889 trip by Ottoman intellectual Ahmed Midhat to see the Exposition Universelle in Paris, observes that nineteenth-century technologies complicated notions of cultural difference: "[I]nventions such as telegraphy and photography enhanced the effect

[23] UN Development Programme, Arab Fund for Social and Economic Development, *Arab Human Development Report 2002: Creating Opportunities for Future Generations*, p. 8, http://www.arab-hdr.org/publications/other/ahdr/ahdr2002e.pdf, accessed September 17, 2015.

[24] See Ibrahim Abu-Lughod, *The Arab Rediscovery of Europe: A Study in Cultural Encounters*, Rev. ed. (London: Saqi Books, 2011). See the description of Paris in the nineteenth-century novel and travelogue by Ahmad Faris al-Shidyaq, *Leg over Leg, or the Turtle in the Tree, Concerning the Fariyaq, What Manner of Creature Might He Be*, ed. and trans. Humphrey Davies, 4 vols. (New York: New York University Press, 2014), 4:249–69.

[25] Lisa Pollard, *Nurturing the Nation: The Family Politics of Modernizing, Colonizing, and Liberating Egypt, 1805–1923* (Berkeley: University of California Press, 2005), 34.

[26] Ibid., 38.

of immediacy, while the railroad and steamship hastened travel between the 'represented' and the 'real.' " Midhat was an "explorer in red fez rather than pith helmet," Findley writes, and he "did not fault the natives for staring as he studied fine Parisian buildings with binoculars in one hand and guidebook in the other." The Ottoman's account followed the Occidentalist practice of portraying "the West as feminine and its greatest danger to the East as its libidinousness." At the Exposition, Midhat encountered a jumble of Orientalist elements incorporated into the facsimile of a Cairo street but objected most of all to the belly dancers.[27]

As historians have shown, non-Europeans depicted others and appropriated their ideas in the course of pursuing agendas of modernization and reform. Hybridization and borrowing thus belied the stark cultural differentiation found in writings by European and non-European travelers alike. Cemil Aydin has examined the intersection between pan-Islamic and pan-Asian movements, as illustrated by the journey of Russian-born pan-Islamist Abdurreşid Ibrahim "from Central Asia, to Mongolia, China, Korea, and Japan, and then back to Istanbul by way of China, Singapore/the Malay Islands, India, and Mecca." Ibrahim was among "the most traveled Muslim activists in modern times," who sought inspiration from Japanese and other non-European reformers.[28] Ussama Makdisi has described Ottoman elites' own "Orientalism," which "implicitly and explicitly acknowledged the West to be the home of progress." Such elites interposed themselves between European modernity and the Arab and other peoples whom they depicted in terms of a "temporal subordination," and sought to civilize through imperial reforms.[29] In *Artillery of Heaven*, Makdisi similarly describes the liberalism that Christian Arab scholar Butrus al-Bustani synthesized from Ottoman reforms and the ideals brought by American missionaries, a commitment to intellectual freedom that neither of these sources could have formulated by itself.[30] In contrast to later years, early twentieth-century America could serve anticolonial reformers as a modern symbol and democratic foil to European imperialism. A distant power with imperial ambitions focused elsewhere, the United States could play this role for Arabs as well as for others such as Indian visitor Rabindranath Tagore.[31] Following World War I, America also came to stand for the homogenization and mediocrity that

[27] Carter V. Findley, "An Ottoman Occidentalist in Europe: Ahmed Midhat Meets Madame Gülnar, 1889," *American Historical Review* 103 (February 1998): 16, 26, 27, 39. See also Timothy Mitchell, *Colonising Egypt* (Berkeley: University of California Press, 1988), 1–5.

[28] Aydin, *The Politics of Anti-Westernism in Asia*, 84.

[29] Ussama Makdisi, "Ottoman Orientalism," *American Historical Review* 107 (June 2002): 769.

[30] Makdisi, *Artillery of Heaven*.

[31] See Ussama Makdisi, "'Anti-Americanism' in the Arab World: An Interpretation of a Brief History," *Journal of American History* 89 (September 2002): 538–57; and Manela, *Wilsonian Moment*, 91–92.

some self-appointed cultural guardians associated with a globalizing consumerism.[32] Taking the measure of other societies, creating representations of them, and assimilating their ideas were therefore central to debates about modernity during the "age of steam and print."

During the First World War, Britain and France partitioned the Ottoman Empire's Arab territories. The League of Nations later assigned France mandates over Lebanon and Syria, while Britain governed mandates in Iraq, Transjordan, and Palestine, and effectively controlled Egypt. Travel to Europe by Arab elites helped to circulate the liberal ideals used both to justify and oppose imperial rule. Studying in Paris, the blind Egyptian intellectual Taha Husayn (1889–1973) faced the familiar moral dangers:

How could Egyptian youths expect to live in France and frequent cafés and clubs and celebrations without love coming into the picture, to tease and tempt them, and from time to time tax them hardly?

An introvert in the world, he declared, "I was a stranger in my homeland and I was a stranger in France," at least until experiencing true *amour*.[33] As Egyptian education minister, Husayn would later become Sayyid Qutb's boss, although Qutb did not share Husayn's esteem for European civilization. The Lebanese Druze Amir Shakib Arslan (1869–1946) visited Geneva, London, and Rome in his anticolonial campaign before visiting both the United States and the Soviet Union in 1927.[34] Egyptian Huda Sha'rawi (1879–1947) participated in a global network of women activists. Her public unveiling at the Cairo train station following her return from one international women's meeting in Rome helped to introduce feminism into Egypt's public consciousness.[35]

Debates over the postwar settlement and purpose of the mandate system brought a new politics of representation based on the projection of legitimizing images by colonial authorities and the subversion of those images by anticolonial nationalists. Scholars have described Arab leaders' anti-imperial strategy of seizing on the liberal ideals Western countries used to represent themselves. Erez Manela incorporates Egypt into a "Wilsonian moment," when anticolonial elites such as Sa'd Zaghlul embraced the ideal

---

[32] See Harry Harootunian, *Overcome by Modernity: History, Culture, and Community in Interwar Japan* (Princeton, NJ: Princeton University Press, 2001), 47–65; and Emily Rosenberg, "Consuming Women: Images of Americanization in the 'American Century,'" *Diplomatic History* 23 (Summer 1999): 479–97.

[33] Taha Husayn, *The Days*, trans. E. H. Paxton et al. (Cairo: American University in Cairo Press, 1997), 325, 355.

[34] Nazik Saba Yared, *Arab Travellers and Western Civilization*, trans. Sumayya Damluji Shahbandar, ed. Tony P. Naufal and Jana Gough (London: Saqi Books, 1996), 138.

[35] See Leila Rupp, *Worlds of Women: The Making of an International Women's Movement* (Princeton, NJ: Princeton University Press, 1997), 58, 59; and Margot Badran, *Feminists, Islam, and Nation: Gender and the Making of Modern Egypt* (Princeton, NJ: Princeton University Press, 1996).

of self-determination that they associated with President Woodrow Wilson.[36] Through repeated missions to Geneva and a campaign of "bombard[ing] the League with a stream of petitions, letters and memoranda on the theme of Syrian independence," Arab nationalist Riyadh al-Sulh sought political leverage by using appeals to liberal values.[37] Historian Elizabeth Thompson describes how subaltern leaders in Lebanon and Syria, including trade unionists and feminist Nazira Zayn al-Din, sought to claim their rights as citizens on the basis of the very republicanism that France cited to justify its rule.[38] Arabs struggling for independence used their knowledge of the great powers as a political weapon, a tactic that would take on new meanings during the Cold War.

Another feature of interwar Arab politics with implications for the future was ideological diversity and competition, as mass political movements arose to challenge discredited notables who had inherited their authority from the Ottoman era. Historians' debates about interwar politics have focused on the limits of Arab liberalism under colonial rule. One version of this debate has examined the "crisis" of intellectuals, who either abandoned modern, secular ideals to take up Islamic themes in the years prior to World War II, or else expressed those ideals using popular literary forms to reach a mass audience.[39] Another version considers the degree to which Arabs embraced fascism and Nazism, an argument too often characterized by what historian Marc David Baer calls the "tendentious politics of history and memory produced by the Israeli–Palestinian struggle."[40] The growth of anticolonial movements across a political spectrum during the first postwar

---

[36] See Manela, *Wilsonian Moment*.

[37] Patrick Seale, *The Struggle for Arab Independence: Riad el-Solh and the Makers of the Modern Middle East* (New York: Cambridge University Press, 2010), 188. See also Susan Pedersen, "Getting Out of Iraq – in 1932: The League of Nations and the Road to Normative Statehood," *American Historical Review* 115 (October 2010): 975–1000.

[38] Elizabeth Thompson, *Colonial Citizens: Republican Rights, Paternal Privilege, and Gender in French Syria and Lebanon* (New York: Columbia University Press, 2000).

[39] See Charles D. Smith, "The 'Crisis of Orientation': The Shift of Egyptian Intellectuals to Islamic Subjects in the 1930s," *International Journal of Middle East Studies* 4 (October 1973): 382–410; and Israel Gershoni, "The Theory of Crisis and the Crisis in a Theory: Intellectual History in Twentieth-Century Middle Eastern Studies," in *Middle East Historiographies: Narrating the Twentieth Century*, ed. Israel Gershoni, et al. (Seattle: University of Washington Press, 2006), 131–82.

[40] Marc David Baer, "Muslim Encounters with Nazism and the Holocaust: The Ahmadi of Berlin and the Jewish Convert to Islam Hugo Marcus," *American Historical Review* 120 (February 2015): 141. See also Israel Gershoni and James Jankowski, *Confronting Fascism in Egypt: Dictatorship versus Democracy in the 1930s* (Stanford, CA: Stanford University Press, 2010); Peter Wien, *Iraqi Arab Nationalism: Authoritarian, Totalitarian, and Profascist Inclinations, 1932–1941* (New York: Routledge, 2006); and Peter Wien, "Coming to Terms with the Past: German Academia and Historical Relations between the Arab Lands and Nazi Germany," *International Journal of Middle East Studies* 42 (May 2010): 311–21.

period established a pattern of ideological competition that would domi-nate the politics of independent Arab states during the second postwar period. In 1928, Egyptian Hasan al-Banna formed the Muslim Brotherhood, whose organizing efforts confronted those of communists and other rival movements that sought to mobilize the *effendiyya* during the Depression. Historians Joel Beinin and Zachary Lockman have also studied attempts by the Egyptian nationalist Wafd Party, the Muslim Brotherhood, and com-munists to appeal to the country's laboring classes during the 1930s and 1940s. In Egypt as elsewhere in the Arab world, the inability of notables, such as the Wafd leaders, to achieve real independence stoked the competi-tion among more ideologically militant successors. "As the liberal political principles of the Wafd appeared to be incapable of providing the basis for achieving Egypt's national objectives," these authors explain, "the Muslim Brothers and the communists posed two diametrically opposed alternative visions for Egypt's future."[41] Thompson has similarly observed that in man-date Syria and Lebanon, "the labor movement and Islamic populists sought to recruit the same constituency of the urban lower classes."[42]

In the 1930s, Arab ideological polarization mirrored that in Europe, whose societies anticolonial travelers could sample as a kind of political bazaar. In Paris, Syrian students Salah al-Din al-Bitar (1912–1980) and Michel 'Aflaq (1910–1989) encountered the socialist and nationalist ideas on which they would base the Ba'th Party.[43] Fascism inspired the Phalange in Lebanon and various paramilitary "shirt" organizations across the region. The Syrian National Party of Antun Sa'ada (1904–1949) promoted a greater Syrian nationalism, as opposed to pan-Arabism, predicated on geographical determinism. Born to a Greek Orthodox family in Lebanon, Sa'ada spent his youth in the United States and Brazil and traveled to Germany before launching his party in Beirut.[44] Iraqi diplomat and former prime minister Tawfiq al-Suwaydi (1892–1968), who represented his country at the League of Nations, met Italian dictator Benito Mussolini during a 1934 mission to Rome. Suwaydi told *il Duce* that he wished to study European countries with differences in their "varieties of systems and regimes [*alwan anzimatiha wa hukmiha*]" in order to derive lessons for the benefit of his own country. Suwaydi admired Italian fascists for defeating communism and develop-ing Italy but criticized the view held by some Arabs that Hitler's Germany

---

[41] Joel Beinin and Zachary Lockman, *Workers on the Nile: Nationalism, Communism, Islam, and the Egyptian Working Class, 1882–1954* (Cairo, Egypt: American University in Cairo Press, 1998), 376.

[42] Thompson, *Colonial Citizens*, 111.

[43] See Philip S. Khoury, *Syria and the French Mandate: The Politics of Arab Nationalism, 1920–1945* (Princeton, NJ: Princeton University Press, 1987), 627.

[44] See Seale, *Struggle for Arab Independence*, 375–77; and Adel Beshara, ed., *Antun Sa'adeh: The Man, His Thought, An Anthology* (Reading, England: Ithaca Press, 2007).

could be an ally against Zionism and Anglo-French imperialism.[45] Ahmad Husayn (1911–1982), a leader of the Young Egypt movement, came away from a 1938 trip admiring fascist governments in Italy and Germany. Their economic achievements impressed Husayn, who argued that Egypt "must imitate the German example, so that all work together in all types of work for the good of the country."[46]

Ideological competition led a younger generation of Arab leaders, many of them born after 1900, to define their prescriptions by negation, contrasting their programs with those of rival movements and grouping ideological enemies together. During the Spanish Civil War, Syrian communist Khalid Bakdash (1912–1995), an ethnic Kurd trained in Moscow, warned Arabs about how General Francisco Franco recruited Moroccan Islamists to fascism by promising to "save Islam" from communism. Bakdash likewise criticized Syrian nationalists for mistakenly believing that they could win concessions from the French right. He urged all Arabs to join the Soviet Union and France's popular front in the antifascist struggle.[47] Postwar rhetoric would draw contrasts between modernizing systems even more starkly.

Ideological conflict in the Arab world after 1945 would be multisided, because it emerged from this earlier experience with competitive anticolonialism. But Arab politics would evolve to address the new contexts of decolonization and the Cold War. Just as previous Arab leaders had used travel experiences and appropriated European self-representations for their anticolonial struggles, images of the superpowers' societies would figure prominently in postcolonial conflicts over development. Competing American and Soviet campaigns to recruit allies would give Arab elites power, through their role in interpreting the "free" and communist worlds for Arab audiences. Greater opportunities for travel brought elites into direct contact with a wide range of development possibilities. As they returned home full of observations about the world, Arab elites waged battles to modernize their own societies on a global stage.

Speed enabled travelers to overcome spatial distances as well as to peer into the alternative futures represented by competing development models. These experiences constituted a form of privilege and helped Arab leaders to justify paternalism toward the elements within their own societies that were characterized temporally as "*mutakhallif* [retarded, backward, underdeveloped]." Similar to the Ottoman statesmen of a century earlier, peripatetic Arab elites imposed a "temporal subordination" on the social and geographic peripheries of their world. Unlike those imperial reformers,

---

[45] Tawfiq al-Suwaydi, *Mudhakkirati: nisf qarn min ta'rikh al-Iraq wa-l qadiya al-'Arabiya* (Beirut: Dar al-Katib al-'Arabi, 1969), 249, 283.

[46] Quoted in Gershoni and Jankowski, *Confronting Fascism in Egypt*, 250.

[47] Khalid Bakdash, *Al-'Arab wa al-harb al-ahliyya fi Isbaniya* (Damascus: n.p., 1937).

postwar Arab elites were constrained by a pan-Arab revolutionary environment that limited the degree to which they could distance themselves from their laggard brethren. As a result, even those from notable families such as al-'Azm sought to base their leadership on worldly experience and ideological sophistication. Travel within the Arab world and to other third world regions proved useful in this regard. As Roxanne L. Euben has written about Muslim travel literature, "otherness is defined not just against the West but also by regional, racial, ethnic, linguistic, sexual, and other differences somewhat closer to home."[48]

Travel to the Arab periphery furnished one set of images Arab elites used to imagine underdevelopment. In 1944, al-'Azm accompanied other Syrian officials to Saudi Arabia. They began their journey to Riyadh by riding the train to Aleppo and then to Baghdad and Basra; from there, they boarded cars sent for their use by the Saudi king 'Abd al-'Aziz and specially outfitted for desert travel, because no regular flights stopped in the central Arabian city. After passing through Kuwait, the caravan navigated the desolate desert region of al-Dahna'. The bumpy ride and frequent stops to push cars out of the sand led many in the party to regard the journey as a "hardship [*mashaqqa*]." Nevertheless, al-'Azm writes of sitting around the campfire tended by Bedouin servants at night and listening to Arabic poetry recited under the beautiful desert moonlight (afraid of snakes, he slept in the car). King 'Abd al-'Aziz and his sons held court in an earthen palace that failed to impress al-'Azm, who was even more dismayed by his accommodation outside Riyadh given its stinking, open-pit toilet. What especially appalled the Syrian, however, was the fact that the king's impoverished people were forced to live amid filth in the streets and clouds of flies. Such sights did not at all match his expectations for the Saudis' traditional capital, which al-'Azm disparaged by comparing it to a small Syrian village. He could not reconcile such squalor with "the vast extravagance [*al-israf al-wasi'*]" found inside the palace, including the gifts lavished on visitors and "the numerous banquets [*al-ma'adib al-'adida*]." Conditions (including the quality of the food) had improved by the time of his next trip to Saudi Arabia in 1950, changes al-'Azm attributed to the growing role of U.S. petroleum companies.[49]

About a decade following al-'Azm's trip, the speed of air travel had made the journey to Riyadh a different experience.[50] Waiting for his delayed flight from Jidda to Riyadh to take off, Jordanian 'Abd al-Munim al-Rifa'i composed a *qasida*, or traditional Arabic verse, inspired by the birthplace of

[48] Roxanne L. Euben, *Journeys to the Other Shore: Muslim and Western Travelers in Search of Knowledge* (Princeton, NJ: Princeton University Press, 2006), 14.

[49] al-'Azm, *Mudhakkirat*, 1:267–70.

[50] On the use of Landrovers, see undated memo by Hawley, "The Six with No Oil," HAW 10/3/6, DHP.

Islam. Once airborne, his plane traversed the "sky of the Arabian desert [*sama' al-sahara' al-'Arabiya*]," and he felt humbled "by the greatness which had come from its heart [*lil-'azama allati akhrajat min qalbiha*]," including "the conquest, the civilization, and the religion [*al-fath, al-hadara, wa al-din*]."[51] In their regard of the Arab periphery, elites of the generation who achieved independence combined exoticism with paternalism toward those whom they regarded as their backward cousins. During the age of flight, Arab and other postcolonial elites could literally look down on peoples with whom they supposedly shared a national identity. After a trip to the United States in 1957, followed by a voyage on the *Queen Elizabeth* east across the Atlantic and a train ride to London, Iraqi diplomat al-Suwaydi flew to Morocco to visit King Muhammad V. Landing at Rabat, his party took a four-hour car trip through picturesque villages before arriving at Marrakesh, whose history as the capital of the medieval Almoravid dynasty stirred al-Suwaydi's imagination. In the Atlas mountains, the Iraqis were treated to a royal banquet under a tent and enjoyed "singing and dancing performed by men and women" from among the colorful local Berbers. Later, al-Suwaydi condescended to tell Muhammad V that he should rename his kingdom "Marrakesh," to avoid geographic confusion and evoke past glories. The king graciously agreed to consider this advice. But following a series of flights home to Baghdad over Algeria, Tunis, and Malta, and a diversion from Istanbul to Athens because of ice, al-Suwaydi heard a report that the king had officially adopted "Morocco" as the name of his country.[52]

As Egyptian leader 'Abd al-Nasser aspired to lead the Arab world and forge ties with Afro-Asian countries, global mobility gave Arab elites first-hand experiences of other decolonizing regions. Consequently, they could formulate their ideas about development not only in a pan-Arab, but also in a more expansive third world context. The 1955 meeting of Afro-Asian countries at Bandung, Indonesia proved especially important in expanding their horizons. It was in the Rangoon airport on the way to Bandung that Indian prime minister Jawaharlal Nehru, along with Burma's prime minister, U Nu, first introduced Nasser to Chinese foreign minister Zhou Enlai.[53] Khalid al-'Azm, along with Arab leaders including Prince Faysal of Saudi Arabia, Charles Malik of Lebanon, and Fadl al-Jamali of Iraq, followed Nasser to Indonesia. Flying via Abadan and Karachi, al-'Azm and other Syrians stopped off in Calcutta, where they stayed as guests of the Bengali governor-general. Al-'Azm slept in a room of the governor's palace that had once belonged to Lord Curzon but lacked air conditioning. In the city streets,

[51] al-Rifa'i, *al-Amwaj*, 97.

[52] al-Suwaydi, *Mudhakkirati*, 560–63.

[53] See Mohamed Hassanein Heikal, *The Cairo Documents: The Inside Story of Nasser and His Relationship with World Leaders, Rebels, and Statesmen* (New York: Doubleday & Co., 1973), 47.

he and other Syrians commandeered seventeen rickshaws, which followed one another closely to form a miniature train. Joking and laughing, they called out to the white cows that snarled the crushing traffic. But Calcutta's poor were no laughing matter, and al-'Azm's descriptions of them are some of the most visceral in his three-volume memoir. Their emaciated, sunburned bodies were naked except for loincloths. They evoked the Arabic verse that describes man as "flesh and blood [*lahm wa dam*]," except in this case, the men consisted of "desiccated [*mujaffaf*] flesh" and hardly any blood at all. Bereft of vitality, they sprawled on the pavement like the "ewes [*ni'aj*]" seen in Syrian villages. Al-'Azm commended Nehru's population control measures, which he hoped would curb the increasing numbers of poor. Al-'Azm's trip to east Asia brought him face to face with poverty outside of the Arab world. As the result of a glitch with the airline, which could not send all of the Arab travelers and their luggage home on the same plane, al-'Azm found himself temporarily stranded in Bangkok. There he encountered foul-smelling rice paddies and watched animals and children frolic in the water where women scrubbed clothes.[54] During a later stopover in east Asia while flying from Jordan across the Pacific to the United States, 'Abd al-Munim al-Rifa'i gained a new perspective on the questions of development facing his kingdom. The ambassador not only admired the powerful Taiwanese military but also carefully noted how farmers on the island utilized every available inch of cultivable land and took full advantage of the three growing seasons the warm climate afforded.[55] "Underdevelopment" took on meaning for Arab elites through travel experiences not only to the *maghrib* and Arabian peninsula, but also to the global periphery of the third world.

For Egyptian architect Hassan Fathy (1900–1989), travel likewise enlarged the context for understanding underdevelopment from a strictly Arab to a larger third world setting. Born to a family that owned several country estates but raised in the city, Fathy could glimpse the rural landscape only "from the windows of the train as we went from Cairo to Alexandria for the summer holidays." It was not until he was twenty-seven years old that Fathy visited any of the family's rural property, which he hoped would offer "a simpler, happier, and less anxious life than the city could." Rather than a paradise, however, he found "clouds of flies" and streams "muddy and infested with bilharzia and dysentery." This awakening inspired him to study architecture and to specialize in the problem of sanitary rural housing (see Chapter 3). Supervising the construction of a school in a small village, Fathy became

disgusted at the sight and smell of the narrow streets, deep in mud and every kind of filth, where all the garbage from the kitchens – dirty water, fish scales, rotting vegetables, and offal – was regularly thrown.

---

[54] al-'Azm, *Mudhakkirat*, 2:366–69, 384–85 [quotations on p. 369]. On al-'Azm's experience at Bandung, see Gardiner to Rose, May 4, 1955, FO 371/115051, BNA.

[55] al-Rifa'i, *al-Amwaj*, 132.

Worse, he sensed the "hopeless resignation" of peasants, their "cramped and stunted view of life, their abject acceptance of the whole horrible situation." Their apathy, he wrote, "seized me by the throat; my own help-lessness before such a spectacle tormented me. Surely something could be done?"[56] Fathy displayed more compassion than al-'Azm but also evinced paternalism toward the poor. During the 1940s and 1950s Fathy worked on rural settlements in Egypt, Iraq, and Saudi Arabia, but a fact-finding tour of Africa undertaken for the Athens development firm Doxiadis Associates led him to the realization that the problems he had first encountered in the Nile Valley were universal. In 1961, he was able to crisscross the continent by air, touching down in Khartoum, Kano, Lagos, Accra, Ouagadougou, Bamako, Dakar, Guinea, Togo, Dahomey, Cameroon, and Tripoli. As Fathy later wrote to Nasser, Africa shared with Latin America and Asia a common legacy of colonialism and the staggering challenge of housing millions of the poor.[57]

The Arab elites who were most international in outlook were communists. Travel by Arab communists helped to link their struggles for inde-pendence and development to those of other peoples within a global Cold War context. Their doctrine provided a historical explanation for the relationship between imperial and feudal oppression. Arab communist parties attempted to implement the prescription for an ideological vanguard to organize workers and peasants. Communism faced troubled relations, however, with Arab nationalist movements. The region's communist par-ties had non-Arab minorities – Jews, Kurds, and Armenians – among their early leaders, and Arabization efforts undertaken after 1945 to broaden the appeal of communism encountered difficulty in part because of unpopu-lar positions taken by Bakdash. These included his politically disastrous decision to endorse Soviet support at the United Nations for partitioning Palestine and an uncompromising Stalinist opposition to cooperating with bourgeois nationalist parties. But after Bakdash's election to the Syrian par-liament in 1954, his Communist Party of Syria and Lebanon, as well as those in Iraq and other Arab states, formed limited alliances with nationalist movements opposing the anti-Soviet Baghdad Pact sponsored by the United States and Britain.[58] Seeing Soviet and other communist societies firsthand

---

[56] Hassan Fathy, *Architecture for the Poor: An Experiment in Rural Egypt* (Chicago: University of Chicago Press, 1973), 1–3.

[57] See Fathy to Kamal Rif'at, undated, binder III, number 66; and Fathy to Nasser, March 23, 1963, binder IV, number 106, HFA.

[58] See Tareq Y. Ismael and Jacqueline S. Ismael, *The Communist Movement in Syria and Lebanon* (Gainesville: University Press of Florida, 1998); and Tareq Y. Ismael, *The Rise and Fall of the Communist Party of Iraq* (New York: Cambridge University Press, 2008). See also Khalid Bakdash, "For the Successful Struggle for Peace, National Independence, and Democracy, We Must Resolutely Turn toward the Workers and the Peasants," *Middle East Journal* 7 (Spring 1953): 206–21.

during this period gave Arab comrades a vision of modern society that they could promote at home, although their experiences abroad included direct observations of escalating Sino–Soviet tensions and did not necessarily reinforce Marxist-Leninist teachings.[59]

Returning from a mission to Moscow in 1946, Bakdash's deputy Niqula Shawi (1912–1983) visited Iran, attended meetings of Iranian trade unions, and toured the country. He recounted his experiences in a series of articles for the official communist newspaper *Sawt al-Sha'b* [*The People's Voice*], published as the book *Sha'b 'azim yakharaj min qafas – Iran fi ghamra al-nidal wa matla' al-hurriya* [*A Great People Escapes Its Cage: Iran in the Exuberance of Struggle and the Dawn of Freedom*]. Shawi not only returned to Moscow in 1956 for the Twentieth Congress of the Communist Party of the Soviet Union, but his later travels would also take him to Poland, Hungary, Czechoslovakia, Bulgaria, the German Democratic Republic, and Cuba.[60] Jordanian communist Nabih Rushaydat, who had worked in Paris and London as a physician employed by the World Health Organization, described himself in 1956 as feeling an "intense desire [*shadid al-shuq*]" to see Moscow, "a great dream [*hulman kabiran*]." Rushaydat visited the Kremlin and attended a performance of *Swan Lake*, his first ballet. His disappointment was evident, however, when he told one of his handlers that after five days he had seen "tsarist Russia [*Rusiya al-Qaysiriya*]" but not "the accomplishments of socialism [*munjazat al-ishtirikiya*]." Returning to Moscow after attending a world youth congress in Sofia, Bulgaria, Rushaydat got into a heated argument with a white South African woman who criticized the Soviets for erasing Leon Trotsky from Bolshevik history and for displaying Lenin's embalmed corpse. The Jordanian doctor helped to set up Arabic-language radio services in Moscow and Beijing, where he credulously informed Arab audiences about the successes of Mao Zedong's Great Leap Forward. He left China as the result of growing Sino–Soviet conflict, however, after he and Bakdash resolved to oppose Chinese broadcasts attacking the Soviet Union. Later, Rushaydat traveled to Cuba where he toured the Museum of the Cuban Revolution, visited Ernest Hemingway's former home, and heard Fidel Castro give a lengthy speech. To reach the Caribbean island, Rushaydat boarded a Soviet plane in Cyprus bound for Moscow. Two days later, another flight departed Moscow on a fifteen-hour odyssey to Havana that took him over the North Pole.[61] When Iraqi communist Salah Mahdi Daklah traveled to Beijing to celebrate the tenth

---

[59] See Constantin Katsakioris, "The Soviet-South Encounter: Tensions in the Friendship with Afro-Asian Partners, 1945–1965," in *Cold War Crossings: International Travel and Exchange across the Soviet Bloc, 1940s-1960s*, ed. Patryk Babiracki and Kenyon Zimmer (College Station: Texas A & M University Press, 2014), 134–65.

[60] Niqula Shawi, *Tariqi ila al-hizb* (Beirut: Dar al-Farabi, 1984), 339–43.

[61] Nabih Rushaydat, *Awraq Laysat Shakhsiya: Mudhakkirat* (Damascus: Dar al-Yanabi', 2001), 134–38, 143–59, 177–80 [quotations on pp. 134, 135].

anniversary of the Chinese communist revolution, it was the first time that he and his journalist wife had ever boarded a plane. They flew by way of Karachi, where they survived a harrowing bus ride to their first-class hotel, gawked at snake charmers, and met Kashmiri refugees. After taking a Dutch propeller plane to Rangoon, Daklah was driven around the Burmese city in a bicycle cart and observed local rickshaw drivers, who he felt embodied the "injustices and oppression in some third world societies [*alam wa zulm fi ba'd mujtama'at al-'alam al-thalith*]." On the flight to the People's Republic, he greeted Arabic-speaking Indonesians of Yemeni origin, and, after arriving, participated in talks with Chinese officials who maneuvered to draw the Iraqi Communist Party away from Moscow.[62]

The relatively small Arab communist movements, which attracted little support beyond select groups of workers and intelligentsia, were less important to Soviet diplomacy than courting uncommitted leaders from the decolonizing world.[63] In the contest to win over nonaligned third world elites, the Soviets achieved a breakthrough with Khalid al-'Azm's 1957 tour of the U.S.S.R. At the center of his account is the experience of flying to Moscow aboard an advanced Soviet jet and descriptions of the Soviets' economic and cultural achievements. Although al-'Azm eschews communist doctrine, he employs descriptions of his travels in the U.S.S.R. to justify the decision to accept Soviet and reject American aid. After trips to Rome and Bonn, where he concluded that any Western aid would come with unacceptable political conditions, al-'Azm stopped over in Prague en route to Moscow. On July 24, the Syrian party boarded the deck of a "gigantic model of Russian airplane [*al-ta'ira al-Rusiya al-jabara min tiraz*]," "the greatest jet plane in the world [*a'azm ta'ira naffatha fi al-'alam*]," with places for seventy-two passengers, sixteen of them sleeper seats. It could reach a speed of 1,000 kilometers per hour and a height of 16,000 meters, although on his flight, al-'Azm traveled at 580 kilometers per hour and at a height of 10,500 meters. When the plane soared above the cirrus clouds, al-'Azm felt neither vibration, nor constriction of breath, nor nausea. For him, "the invention of this plane proves the greatness of Soviet production [*'azma al-intaj al-Sufyiti*] and its advance [*taqaddamihi*] over that of any other country in the world." Not until 1960, he wrote in retrospect, would the United States produce anything similar to it. Once in Moscow, al-'Azm met with Defense Minister Georgy Zhukov and was put up in a guest house on Tolstoy Street outfitted with a billiard room and cinema. The Syrian foreign minister then embarked on a tour that took him from Tashkent to Stalingrad, Kiev, Leningrad, and Sochi on the Black Sea. His hosts made an Ilyushin plane available to cover the great distances,

---

[62] Salah Mahdi Daklah, *Min al-Dhakira (sira hiyat)* (Nicosia, Cyprus: Al Mada, 2000), 62–66 [quotation p. 64].

[63] See Yevgeny Primakov, *Russia and the Arabs: Behind the Scenes in the Middle East from the Cold War to the Present*, trans. Paul Gould (New York: Basic Books, 2009), 57–70.

though al-'Azm also traveled by car, ship, and train. During a steamer trip on the Volga, he visited a hydroelectric dam with twenty-two turbines, each of which could generate 100,000 kilowatts of electric power. The Syrians marveled at the forty-four outlets that delivered water to the turbines at 700 meters per second, which al-'Azm compared to the three-meter-per-second flow of the Barada River through Damascus. This dam, his Soviet minders told him, was just one of seven under construction. In Leningrad, he visited the tsars' Winter Palace, renamed the Hermitage Museum, with "the most marvelous oil paintings by world-famous artists" and hundreds of rooms that so exhausted the Syrian traveler that he had to request a wheelchair. Al-'Azm arrived back in Moscow on a night train that, while frustratingly slow, consisted of luxury cars that "surpassed the most beautiful of European cars." In short order, his negotiations with Alexei Kosygin, the first deputy chairman of the council of ministers (al-'Azm would have preferred a higher-ranking interlocutor), resulted in a trade agreement and principles for Syria's acceptance of Soviet economic aid and technical assistance. Al-'Azm focuses most of his account on superlative descriptions of traveling to and across the Soviet Union, rather than on his talks with Soviet officials. This emphasis, particularly on the achievements of Soviet aviation and transportation, as well as on the rich natural and cultural resources of Soviet Eurasia, was intended to convince Syrians and other Arabs that his foreign policy of accepting aid from Moscow had been the correct one.[64]

Arab countries opposed U.S. support for Zionism and recognition of Israel in May 1948. But leading Arab modernizers were as concerned with using the idea of America to advance their particular development agendas as they were with criticizing Washington's policies. At first challenging the official U.S. insistence that it offered a universal model for developing the third world, postcolonial Arab elites advanced sweeping claims of their own for what they held up as superior ideological alternatives. Islamists and Arab nationalists drew authority from their observations of American society, a claim Qutb staked early on in the title of his article series "The America I Have Seen."[65] As anticommunist policies such as the Baghdad Pact and the Eisenhower Doctrine projected American power across the Arab Middle East, U.S. propaganda sought to promote American values as the basis for Arab development. It starkly presented the Cold War to Muslims as a conflict "between a society in which the individual is motivated by spiritual and ethical values and one in which he is the tool of a materialistic state."[66]

[64] al-'Azm, *Mudhakkirat*, 3: 9–27 [quotations on pp. 13, 22].

[65] See *America in an Arab Mirror: Images of America in Arabic Travel Literature, An Anthology*, ed. Kamal Abdel-Malik (New York: St. Martin's, 2000), 9–27; and al-Khalidi, *Amrika min al-dakhil bi-minzar Sayyid Qutb*, 90–91.

[66] "Inventory of U.S. Government and Private Organization Activity Regarding Islamic Organizations as an Aspect of Overseas Operations," May 3, 1957, p. 1, OCB 000.3

Rarely, if ever, were such messages accepted uncritically. Instead, Arab modernizers crafted one-dimensional representations of America that served to burnish their own preferred agendas. While they accepted the premise that knowledge of America's past and present was crucial to mapping Arab societies' futures, most rejected the idea that the United States had blazed a trail that Arab countries ought to follow. After World War II, attempts by the United States to position itself as a model for developing countries made America into a useful and protean concept for an assortment of Arab ideological movements.

The political strategy of contrasting Islamist or Arab nationalist agendas against America's Cold War promises emerged at a time of growing opportunities for Arabs and other non-Europeans to travel to the United States. The presence of Arab students tended to confirm the centrality of the conflict over Zionism in U.S.–Arab relations, however, which undermined the supposed propaganda value of hosting them. A Jewish-American war veterans' group sent information to the Justice Department about the activities of the Organization of Arab Students (OAS) and demanded that the organization be required to register under the Foreign Agents Registration Act.[67] Justice officials complied with the veterans' request to investigate, though the matter was eventually settled through negotiations in which the OAS agreed to limit the scope of its political activities. The FBI took a similar approach to the Iraqi Students' Society.[68] "There are problems in the exchange programs" with Arab countries, diplomat Parker Hart told the Council on Foreign Relations in 1961, "and perhaps some of the students will return from here to lead revolutions against Western interests, but we must hope that some constructive residue of their American experience remains."[69]

Overscheduled official guests hastily shuttled between far-flung sites were as likely to come away exhausted as impressed by the American way of life. On his first trip to the United States as crown prince, Sa'ud had endured a "thirty-day tour of the country" that included "visits to agricultural experiment stations, industrial installations, and places of historic and scenic interest from New York to California."[70] Lebanese supreme court judge Hassan

(Religion) File #2 (4) Jan.–May 1957, box 2, OCB Central File Series, NSC Staff Papers, DDEL.

[67] Thatcher to Jones, November 14, 1960, 1960 Chron, Inter-office memos [folder 1 of 2], box 1, Bureau of Near Eastern and South Asian Affairs/Office of Near Eastern Affairs, Records of the Director, 1960–1963, RG 59, NARA.

[68] Meyer to Jones, February 8, 1960, Baghdad 1960, box 1, Bureau of Near Eastern and South Asian Affairs/Office of Near Eastern Affairs, Records of the Director, 1960–1963, RG 59, NARA. See also SAC Chicago to FBI Director, March 31, 1959; and Yeagley to FBI Director, February 4, 1960, documents obtained under the Freedom of Information Act.

[69] Transcript of sixth meeting of the study group on Arab foreign policy, May 17, 1961, folder 7, box 160, series 3, CFR, SML.

[70] "The Life of King Sa'ud," November 15, 1953, p. 5, folder 34, box 2, WEM.

Kabalan traveled by bus, train, and plane during a 1959 tour sponsored by the Foreign Leader Program that visited Oklahoma City, Los Angeles, San Francisco, Denver, Detroit, Buffalo, Princeton, New York, and Washington, DC.[71] In 1961, a Jordanian parliamentary delegation came for an official visit whose itinerary took them from New York to Detroit, Chicago, Kansas City, San Francisco, Los Angeles, Phoenix, Dallas, and Knoxville. A State Department official warned the group that they would face "a formidable schedule" that included "visiting everything from automobile assembly lines in Detroit and farms in Missouri, to educational facilities in California and American Indian residential communities in our southwest."[72] The negatives of postwar American society interfered with efforts at portraying it in a positive light. Former CIA officer Miles Copeland proposed plans to have President Nasser's son attend a summer camp in the United States with Copeland's own son. The camp experience was meant to counter a visit by Nasser's daughter to the Soviet Union. But an official hinted at one possible reason why the plan was never carried out: "the camp should be located outside of racially difficult areas, since Nasser's son is slightly dark in color."[73] Whether such policies were successful from Washington's perspective, expanding contacts held significance for Arab debates about development. As knowledge of American society became valuable in such debates, those travelers who could claim direct exposure to the United States sought to translate their firsthand observations into a form of authority back at home.

During the Cold War, the earlier practice in which Arab anticolonialists had subverted the legitimizing images projected by European powers shifted to the United States. *Ruz al-Yusuf*, the influential Egyptian weekly that disseminated pan-Arabism and Cold War neutralism to educated Arab readers, registered this shift following the war. Instead of its wartime travel pieces about taking the train to Hollywood, the magazine published more serious content scrutinizing American society and U.S. plans for the postwar world.[74] One macabre political cartoon (Figure 1.1) published in December 1947 questioned the moral legitimacy behind the late President Franklin D. Roosevelt's call for the "four freedoms," first issued during a 1941 speech to Congress.[75]

---

[71] See itinerary, May 1959, frames 406–410, reel 49, series 833, Record Group 2 – 1959, RFC, RAC.

[72] Strong to Jones, April 12, 1961, 1961 Chron Inter-office Memorandum [folder 2 of 2], box 3, Bureau of Near Eastern and South Asian Affairs/Office of Near Eastern Affairs, Records of the Director, 1960–1963, RG 59, NARA.

[73] Barrow to Badeau, June 10, 1963 and Badeau to Barrow, June 1, 1963 (with attachment), POL – Political Affairs & Rels POL – 7. Visits. Meetings. 1963 (Miscellaneous), box 3, NEA Bureau Office of the Country Director for the United Arab Republic (NEA/UAR) Records Relating to the United Arab Republic Affairs, 1961–1966, RG 59, NARA.

[74] "al-Qahira ... Hollywood 'an tariq London, New York," *Ruz al-Yusuf*, June 29, 1944, pp. 2, 19.

[75] *Ruz al-Yusuf*, December 10, 1947, p. 19.

من جثث الزنوج ، ومن فوق قبور الهنود الحمر ..

تطالب أمريكا بالحريات الأربع ! ! !

FIGURE 1.1. *Ruz al-Yusuf*, December 10, 1947.

The image depicts Uncle Sam holding an olive branch while standing over the body of a dead American Indian. In the background, a dark-skinned corpse hangs by the neck from a tree while armed figures huddle in the distance. The caption reads: "Over the bodies of Negroes, and atop the tombs of Red Indians, America demands the Four Freedoms!!!" Economist Dr. Rashid al-Barawi, in an article published the following spring, noted the myriad of books about American democracy indicating its "advantages [*fada'iliha*]" and "lessons [*amthila*]," which we must "imitate [*nahtadha*]." But al-Barawi distinguished between democracy as a "system [*nizam*]" and American society, where practices such as the poll tax restricted the franchise for some 15 million blacks. He notes that in Mississippi, which counted 2.5 million residents, half of whom were black, Senator Theodore G. Bilbo won election to his seat in 1944 with support from only 85,000 white voters. The U.S. Congress, he concluded, cannot possibly be said to represent public opinion.[76] As American recognition of Israel tarnished Arab perceptions of

[76] Rashid al-Barawi, "Firaq al-dimurqratiya fi Amrika," *Ruz al-Yusuf*, May 12, 1948, p. 10.

the United States, social scientist Hasan 'Amr explained in an article titled "The city of New York ... America's Jewish quarter [*hara yuhud Amrika*]" how the subversion of American democracy affected U.S. foreign policy. As New York governor, 'Amr writes, Franklin D. Roosevelt grew to rely on influential Zionists such as Bernard Baruch and Henry Morgenthau, and his successor as president, Harry Truman, ignored his advisors and recognized Israel out of concern for his reelection campaign. 'Amr's byline explains that during three years spent earning his doctorate in the United States, he was able to study American life "up close [*'an kathab*]."[77] 'Amr rests his authority on personal experience in the United States, which offers the only way, he implies, to grasp the antidemocratic reality hidden behind America's lofty Cold War rhetoric.

Qutb offers the most important example of an Arab intellectual who drew on his encounter with America to formulate a third-way, modernizing "system," in his case, Islamism. He goes further than any other member of the Arab elite in relying on authority derived from seeing the United States firsthand. In a letter written from Colorado to his colleague Anwar al-Ma'dawi, for instance, Qutb substitutes his own authority for that of Egyptians who had previously been to the "vast workshop [*al-warsha al-dakhma*]" of America, and to Europe as well. "I know now, the extent of the propaganda with which America floods the world," he writes, "in which Egyptians who come to America and return take part." Such people "inflate [*tadkhim*]" America, Qutb asserts, "deriving their self-worth from it."[78] Qutb's retrospective writings about his time in America similarly emphasize his direct observations of society, whose attributes he imperiously lays bare for less well-traveled Egyptians and Arabs. In one self-important statement, he declares:

And as for America: those who have not lived in it and have not seen it cannot talk about anything except its treachery toward us in our affairs before the UN Security Council, and in the Palestine War. But those who have lived in it and who have seen how its press and broadcasting stations and film companies defile our honor and our reputation and how it disseminates this clear, deliberate contempt far and wide, or feels this harsh enmity toward everything that is Islamic and Eastern in general, or knows how Americans regard colored skin generally and the extent of their scorn, such people know what America is.[79]

Disparaging America's level of development, Qutb refers to the "primitivism [*bada'iya*]" that characterizes the society's films, athletics, and jazz music. For him, racial hatred and violence offer the most direct refutation of American democratic claims, and so the Egyptian feels obligated to bear witness. He describes the "conscience [*damir*]"

---

[77] "Madinat New York ... hara yahud Amrika," *Ruz al-Yusuf*, November 2, 1948, p. 13.
[78] al-Khalidi, *Amrika min al-dakhil bi-minzar Sayyid Qutb*, 157–58.
[79] Ibid., 177–78.

which I saw with my own eyes in America, when the whites gathered around a lone Negro youth to strike him and kick him and trample him with the heels of their shoes until they mingled his bones with his flesh in the public road, and the police did not show up at all except after the crime was committed, and the barbarous crowd had scattered like jungle beasts.[80]

Reprising the Occidentalist theme of the West as libidinous, Qutb draws on his personal experience to portray America as a sick society. He argues, contradicting Freud by name, that sexual freedom leads to "mental illnesses and complexes [al-amrad al-nafsiya wa al-'uqad]":

Yes ... I have seen in the country which does not have in it one single constraint on bodily exposure, and mixing of the sexes, in all its types and forms, that all of this does not lead to refining the sexual impulse or taming it! Rather, it leads to an insane voracity that is not satisfied and assuaged until it returns to thirst and exuberance![81]

As witness to America, Qutb offers his personal experiences as uncompromising testimony against the notion that the United States should serve as the model for developing countries.

Puncturing U.S. pretensions to offer such an example is less important to Qutb, however, than creating a contrasting image of America against which to define his own, modernizing Islamic ideology. American racism is therefore significant to Qutb because it offers a helpful foil to the universal appeal of Islam. He wrote in *Social Justice in Islam*:

Islam became free of tribal and racial partisanship – besides being free of partisanship based on family and lineage, so that it attained a level which Western "civilization" has not reached even in our day. For this is the civilization which permits the American conscience to engage in an organized extermination of the Red Indian race while the rest of the world looks on, just as it permits that miserable discrimination between white and black, a loathsome savagery, and it is the civilization which permits the government of South Africa to make open racial laws against the colored and permits the governments of Russia, China, India, Ethiopia, Yugoslavia and others to exterminate all their Muslims.[82]

The experience of the Turkish soldiers who fought in the Korean War served Qutb's purposes as a cautionary tale about U.S. discrimination against third world peoples. According to him, the Americans found Turks acceptable non-Western allies only because they had white skin, but even so deprived them of air support and of adequate food and ammunition during combat.[83]

---

[80] Ibid., 182.

[81] Ibid., 174.

[82] William Shepard, *Sayyid Qutb and Islamic Activism: A Translation and Critical Analysis of Social Justice in Islam* (Leiden, Netherlands: E. J. Brill, 1996), 59–60.

[83] Sayyid Qutb, *Ma'rakat al-Islam wa al-ra'smaliyah*, 4th ed. (Beirut: Dar al-Shuruq, 1975), 33; and al-Khalidi, *Amrika min al-dakhil bi-minzar Sayyid Qutb*, 178.

After returning to Egypt from his pilgrimage in Saudi Arabia, where he "networked with Muslims from around the world," Qutb published *Ma'rakat al-Islam wa al-ra'smaliya* [*The Battle of Islam and Capitalism*].[84] In *Ma'rakat*, he criticized prevailing economic conditions in Egypt and attempted to devise an Islamic "system [*nizam*]" superior to either of the superpowers' materialistic prescriptions. Qutb's approach would remove impediments not simply to economic growth, but also to "social and human growth [*al-nama al-ijtima'i wa al-insani*]," addressing human beings' spiritual as well as material needs.[85] While imitating the United States would be "a human catastrophe [*karitha*] without doubt," Qutb wrote, communism was "possessed of a small idea unworthy of respect among anyone who contemplated a human thought higher than food and drink."[86] Communism, moreover, was a vehicle for "domination [*saytara*]" by the Russian state.[87] Qutb's approach reflects the advent of the Cold War as well as the long-standing rivalry within Egypt between Islamists and communists. *Ma'rakat* borrows a Marxist critique linking Egyptian landowners and capitalists to U.S. economic imperialism. Justice for Egypt's rural masses required breaking landowners' stranglehold on land, credit, and water, and establishing a state monopoly over exports. For him, U.S. assistance under the Point Four program merely disguised imperialism as development. At the same time, Qutb described Islam as a potential "third bloc [*kutla thalatha*]," holding in its hands the "balance [*tawazun*]" between the superpowers and representing "a special social philosophy [*falsafa ijtima'iya khassa*]" based on the "totality of Islam [*al-Islam al-kuliya*]." Indeed, it was the unity of the spiritual and material under Islam that made it a formidable rival to capitalism and communism. Such a philosophy could aim for the "highest horizons [*afaq a'la*]" and "universal justice [*'adala ashmal*]."[88]

To promote his vision of Islamism over capitalism and communism, Qutb conflated the two superpowers on the basis of their common materialism. In this way, he updated Arab politics from the 1930s, when the proponents of mass movements had grouped ideological enemies together in a competitive bid to recruit workers and other urban groups. The Cold War raised the stakes in the battle among modernizing visions, however, as the superpowers pitched their solutions in universal terms to Afro-Asian countries. Qutb formulated his vision of political Islam accordingly as a response to the superpowers' ideological appeals. Biographer John Calvert writes: "Qutb's definition of Islam as a corporate entity in competition with other ideologies reflected the sharply polarized categories of the Cold War."[89] His journey to

[84] Calvert, *Sayyid Qutb and the Origins of Radical Islamism*, 157.
[85] Qutb, *Ma'rakat*, 5; see also 56–57.
[86] al-Khalidi, *Amrika min al-dakhil bi-minzar Sayyid Qutb*, 156; Qutb, *Ma'rakat*, 21.
[87] Qutb, *Ma'rakat*, 111.
[88] Ibid., 54; see also 61.
[89] Calvert, *Sayyid Qutb and the Origins of Radical Islamism*, 162.

America gave Qutb authority to argue for his third way and convinced him that Islam could play a balancing role in global politics between the United States and the Soviet Union. Qutb wrote in *Ma'rakat*: "Christians knew and it was said plainly among them – I heard it in America with my own ears – that Islam was the one religion that was a threat to them."[90]

Qutb was not the only writer to couch modern Islam in Cold War terms as a "corporate entity in competition with other ideologies." This line of argument depended on knowledge of the other systems with which Islam was in competition. Al-Bahi al-Khuli, a propagandist for the Egyptian Muslim Brotherhood, defined an Islamic path to modernity by means of just such an explicit contrast in his tract *Islam: La shuyu'iya wa la ra'smaliya* [*Islam: Neither Communism nor Capitalism*]. Using the metaphor of God's creation as a great table to which all are invited, al-Khuli commends Islam to Egyptian youth as a social and economic system against the "crush [*zahma*]" of rival ideologies and theories. Islam is older than the two Western ideologies, he argues, and so Muslims should not simply look within their religion for what bears resemblance to either of them. He writes:

when the Muslim cuts his path between these two ideologies, he can measure only against prospective unbelief and the ugliness of abiding evil, without seeing in modern idols any advantage over ancient ones![91]

In his later work, *Al-Ishtirakiya fi al-mujtama' al-Islami* [*Socialism in Islamic Society*], al-Khuli would walk a fine line between arguing for Islam's transcendent superiority over other paths to modernity and defining its social justice aspects using Western categories.[92] Islamists thus joined the theoretical discussion of Cold War development in which different modernizing systems were compared abstractly on the basis of their presumed merits. Egyptian social scientist Muhammad Shawqi Zaki examined the structure and ideology of the Muslim Brotherhood in a study that began as a Cairo University doctoral thesis supervised by a Brotherhood official. In it, Zaki credits al-Banna with reinterpreting Islam as a

total social system [*nizam ijtima'i shamil*], structuring the affairs of the people and their relations with one another in all aspects of life, just as democracy and communism do, and having whatever is attributable to them as social systems in equal measure.

In his analysis of the Brotherhood's program, Zaki incorporates a temporal dimension comparable to the linear historical change envisioned by

---

[90] Qutb, *Ma'rakat*, 95.

[91] Al-Bahi al-Khuli, *Al-Islam: La shuyu'iya wa la ra'smaliya* (Kuwait: Maktaba al-Falah, [1948]1981), 11, 14.

[92] Al-Bahi al-Khuli, *Al-Ishtirakiya fi al-mujtama' al-Islami: bayna al-nazariya wa al-tatbiq* (Cairo, Egypt: Maktabat Wahbah, 1964).

both Soviet and American ideologies. "As for the Brotherhood's means of building the Islamic society," he explains, "it is possible to summarize it in four stages [*marahil*]: (1) the Muslim individual; (2) the Muslim family; (3) the Muslim nation [*al-umma*]; (4) the Muslim government."[93] The most sustained argument for the superiority of Islam's logic over those of the superpowers' ideologies came from Iraqi cleric Muhammad Baqir al-Sadr (b. 1931), who helped to establish the Islamic Da'wa Party to counter communist appeals to Iraq's poor Shi'a.[94] In *Falsafatuna* [*Our Philosophy*], al-Sadr characterized capitalism as "a materialistic system, even though it is not based on a clearly outlined materialistic philosophy." Communism, on the other hand, "is based on a specific materialistic philosophy which adopts a specific understanding of life that does not admit any of the moral ideals or values of life." In contrast to both, "the goal that Islam set up for human beings in their lives is the divine satisfaction" that constitutes "a spiritual and moral doctrine from which a complete system for mankind proceeds."[95]

The Cold War built on Arabs' earlier experiences with ideological conflict and fostered a new global setting in which Middle Eastern reformers constructed their agendas. The most important postwar Islamist, Qutb initially used accounts of his travels in America to impeach its Cold War claims and then gradually to fashion an alternative ideology based on Islam. As capitalism and communism came to be regarded as abstract "systems," critical knowledge of them provided the basis for arguments in favor of an equivalent Islamic "system." The Cold War thus amplified and shifted the interwar competition among anticolonialisms in the Arab world.

As part of the ideological debate, secular Arab nationalists formulated third ways of their own by critically analyzing other societies. Islamists, communists, and nationalists clashed over modernization within particular countries and on the basis of competing international solidarities, incorporating concepts borrowed from the superpowers. Patrick Seale describes an early version of this multisided conflict as experienced in the schoolyard by the young Syrian Hafiz al-Asad, a member of the 'Alawite minority who would enlist in the air force and later join other military officers and Ba'th Party members in seizing political power:

In the late 1940s Asad's school and others like it throughout Syria were noisy with political argument. To distinguish friend from foe, one boy might ask another, "*Shu dinak?*" literally, "What's your religion?" but meaning "Where do you stand?" One of three answers could be expected: Communist, Ba'thist or Syrian Nationalist, rival ideological movements which competed with each other for young minds, while all

---

93 Muhammad Shawqi Zaki, *Al-Ikhwan al-Muslimun wa al-Mujtama' al-Misri* (Cairo, Egypt: Dar al-Ansar, [1952] 1980), 52, 72.
94 See Laurence Louër, *Transnational Shia Politics: Religious and Political Networks in the Gulf* (London: Hurst & Company, 2008), 84.
95 Muhammad Baqir al-Sadr, *Our Philosophy*, trans. Shams C. Inati (New York: Muhammadi Trust, KPI, 1987), 10, 17, 27, 31.

opposed the ruling establishment of city notables and the religious zealots of the Muslim Brotherhood. Young men from minority backgrounds, who were uncomfortable with the identification of Arab nationalism with Islam, found the secular doctrines of the ideological parties especially seductive.[96]

Postwar ideological competition in the Arab world was multipolar, while the Cold War context helped to fuse regional issues of identity and nationhood with universal questions of modernity.

Just as Islamists and other reformers traded on their knowledge of the superpowers to help sell their agendas, Arab intellectuals debating the nature of national identity displayed familiarity with the histories of the United States, Soviet Union, and other societies. In fact, their rapid-fire use of historical examples matched the speed with which Arab travelers canvassed the globe. Antun Sa'ada's Syrian National Party (SNP) was among the ideological contestants on Asad's schoolyard. Sa'ada's interest in the pre-Islamic history of the Mediterranean served to legitimize a definition of the Syrian people not linked to religion. In *The Genesis of Nations*, completed in 1936 while imprisoned by French authorities, Sa'ada launched into a comparative study of human communities encompassing the Nile, Euphrates, and Huang-Ho Valleys; Rome, Athens, and Sparta; pre-Columbian America; and what he identifies as Syria's Carthaginian and Phoenician antecedents. Associating nationhood with community life rooted in a particular place rather than with inherent characteristics, Sa'ada exhibits the outsider perspective of one who spent his youth exiled in the New World:

The traveler knows the community before knowing its interests, features and characteristics.... Similarly, he who moves from his own country into another realizes that he is now in a new community, while he may or may not know what language the inhabitants speak or what kind of character they have.[97]

Soon after returning from a decade-long absence in Latin America, Sa'ada delivered a speech to the SNP in which he rehearsed Greater Syria's genealogy. It amounted to a whirlwind tour of the ancient Holy Land:

Indeed, the history of the ancient Syrian empires – Akkadian, Chaldean, Assyrian, Hittite, Canaanite, Aramaean, Amorite – points, all of it, toward one direction: the political, economic, and social unity of the Syrian Fertile Crescent.[98]

In another speech, Sa'ada set off his concept of a greater Syrian nation forged through geographic and environmental determinism against the individualism

---

[96] Patrick Seale with assistance of Maureen McConville, *Asad of Syria: The Struggle for the Middle East* (Berkeley: University of California Press, 1988), 25–26.

[97] Antoune Sa'ade, *The Genesis of Nations* (Beirut: Syrian Social Nationalist Party, 2004), 256.

[98] Antun Sa'ada, "Al-muhadara al-rabi'a," February 1, 1948, http://www.ssnp.com/new/library/saadeh/10_lectures/10_lectures_04.htm, accessed September 17, 2015.

instilled in Americans because of the vast and rich North American continent. He explained that after the American Revolution:

Americans never restored the feelings of a collectivity, a community into being and life, because America found itself after independence a very great, huge body rich in material resources, in iron, coal, oil, grain, livestock, in everything that humanity needs. And it possessed this wealth very far removed from any other collectivity that could be a hostile rival for the resources and territories.[99]

A Greek Orthodox Christian, Sa'ada claimed Greater Syria as his homeland and rejected the linguistic nationalism on which rivals sought to base a much bigger pan-Arab state, presumably dominated by Sunni Muslims. For him, America's revolution and separation from Britain offered proof that geography played a larger role in the historical processes of nation building and development than did a common language.

A pan-Arab response to Sa'ada came from Abu Khaldun Sati' al-Husri (1881–1968), who was born in Yemen to an Ottoman official from Aleppo.[100] Al-Husri's historical counterarguments to essays published in Sa'ada's periodical *al-'Amal* became required reading for pan-Arabists in the age of Nasser. In *Al-'Aruba bayna du'atiha wa mu'aridiha [Arabism: Between Its Propagandists and Its Opponents]*, al-Husri ransacked the past for evidence of language-based nationhood, repeatedly invoking his favorite example of Germany, as well as others ranging from the Austro-Hungarian Empire and its successor states to Yugoslavia, Greece, and the Soviet Union.[101] Not surprisingly, his interpretation of American history differed markedly from Sa'ada's. In his works *Difa' 'an al-'Aruba [Defense of Arabism]* and *Ma hiya al-qawmiya [What Is Nationalism]?*, al-Husri contrasted Arabs with Americans but to different effect. Rejecting the criticism that America's separation from Britain invalidated linguistic nationalism, al-Husri cites the ratio of nine-to-one non-English- to English-speaking immigrants entering the United States during the years 1820–1940 to portray the United States as a polyglot society. For this reason, there was "a tremendous difference [*ikhtilafan kabiran*]" between Arab countries and the United States.[102] Still, al-Husri notes, compared with Latin America the United States witnessed much less intermarriage between Europeans and native peoples, who faced either "extinction [*fana'*]" or confinement to "tightly enclosed

99 Antun Sa'ada, "Al-muhadara al-sadisa," February 22, 1948, http://www.ssnp.com/new/library/saadeh/10_lectures/10_lectures_06.htm, accessed September 17, 2015.
100 See William L. Cleveland, *The Making of an Arab Nationalist: Ottomanism and Arabism in the Life and Thought of Sati' al-Husri* (Princeton, NJ: Princeton University Press, 1971).
101 Sati' al-Husri, *Al-'Aruba bayna du'atiha wa mu'aridiha* (Beirut: Dar al-'Ilm lil-malayin, 1961).
102 Sati' al-Husri, *Difa' 'an al-'uruba*, 2nd ed. (Beirut: Dar al-'Ilm li-Malayin, [1956] 1961), 151–65 [quotation on p. 164]. See also al-Husri, *Ma hiya al-qawmiyya? Abhath wa dirasat 'ala daw' al-ahdath wa al-nazariyyat* (Beirut: Markaz dirasat al-wahda al-'Arabiyya, [1959] 1985), 92–93.

regions [*manatiq mahdud jiddan*]."[103] In *Ma hiya al-qawmiya?*, al-Husri rambled across Europe between the Napoleonic wars and World War I to understand the rise of national states, making excursions to Germany, Italy, Austria, and Russia. Like Qutb and the Islamists, al-Husri referenced the two superpowers to chart his independent course. Refuting Josef Stalin's "Marxism and the National Question," which identified an economic basis for bourgeois nationalism, al-Husri notes that the United States had to overcome great economic differences among the states, which established a union in spite of divisive issues such as the tariff. Al-Husri cites alleged Luddite attacks on Robert Fulton's steamboats as illustrating divergent economic interests within American society.[104] Salah al-Din al-Bitar, whose Ba'th Party pursued a more revolutionary pan-Arabism than that of al-Husri's generation, described the Cold War not merely as a clash between the United States and the Soviet Union, but "between two different understandings of democracy [*bayna mafhumayn mukhtalifayn lil-dimurqratiya*]" produced by a dialectical process within Western history. The turning point came when the development of "the railroad and heavy industry placed the reins of control [*zimam al-hukm*] into the hands of the capitalist owning class," destroying individual equality and justice and prompting the rise of labor movements. For Arabs, al-Bitar explained, the challenge was to learn from this process and create a socialist society that could "end exploitation without acts of murder and terror [*yaqada 'ala al-istighlal duna a'mal al-qatl wa al-irhab*]."[105] Though al-Husri and al-Bitar understood history's driving mechanism differently, both referenced comparisons among societies and the rise of new transport technologies to show it at work.

In the conflict between different Arab nationalist agendas, opponents furiously cited America and other examples to demonstrate their facility with the forces of historical change and to bolster arguments about how such forces would remake the Arab Middle East. Their representation of other societies in rapid succession replicates the physical sensation of velocity, not only in the number of societies experienced quickly, but also in the lack of context and complexity apparent during such brief "visits." The effect is similar to that of flying in to inspect a development project or model village, and then just as quickly returning to the airport to depart again for the next destination. In a superficial manner, the intellectual takes the measure of another society as a means of validating his own modernizing agenda. Yet, whether he hurtles at such speeds through space or time, his authority rests on the virtuosity with which he compares the others whom he has come to "know" through his experiences as a traveler.

---

[103] al-Husri, *Ma hiya al-qawmiyya*, 94–95.
[104] Ibid., 132–33.
[105] Salah al-Din al-Bitar, *Al-siyasa al-'Arabiya bayn al-mabda' wa al-tatbiq* (Beirut: Dar al-Tali'ah lil-Tiba'ah wa-al-Nashr, 1960), 28, 30, 33.

Iraqi legal scholar and diplomat 'Abd al-Rahman al-Bazzaz (1913–1973) cited evidence from both his historical investigations and overseas travels in expounding a constitutional vision for a pan-Arab state. Al-Bazzaz addressed the bitter conflict among Iraqis regarding their relationship to the Egyptian-Syrian union, the United Arab Republic (1958–1961), led by Nasser (see Chapter 5). The dispute concerned whether Arab amalgamation should come in the form of a unitary [*muwahhad*] or a federal [*ittihadi*] state. The author provides historical examples of both, analyzing differences among the unitary states Britain, France, and Belgium, as well as those among federal states Switzerland, West Germany, the U.S.S.R., and the United States. As with other advocates of a third way, al-Bazzaz sets the Arab course by referencing both superpowers. On one hand, he writes, the Soviet Union's constitution provided for an authoritarian state while masquerading as a federation of sovereign republics. On the other hand, the more desirable form of American federalism emerged only through a historical process that overcame the emphasis on states' rights and their tendency to regard themselves as states in the international [*duwal*] rather than the federal [*wilayat*] sense. The difference between a federal and a unitary state is therefore "one of degree and not of kind [*fi al-daraja wa la fi al-nau'*],"[106] and as America's experience demonstrates, historical forces can transform a loose federation into a strong state. As proof, al-Bazzaz cites his own firsthand familiarity with the United States. Aside from the "color problem [*mushkilat al-malunin*]" and animosity left over from the Civil War, he explains, federalism had helped to foster national homogeneity, leaving only minor regional differences. "These observations came to light," he declares in a footnote, "from experience."

I had the opportunity on my second visit to the United States of America (which lasted more than five months) to work in it and I lectured in some of its universities and I spoke at some of its clubs, and I translated all of this into a study of its conditions. I have prepared a book – not yet published – about this trip.[107]

The same historical forces that shaped federalism and ultimately society in the United States, he argues, might eventually reconcile states' sovereignty with unity in the Arab world. In this manner, al-Bazzaz maps a pan-Arab state onto America's past and present, citing his own travels as evidence. Like his contemporaries, however, he places the U.S. example alongside other societies stretching to the geographic and temporal horizon.

Arab elites, like cold warriors in the United States, conceived of modernization as linear, structural change pursued according to a developmental

---

[106] 'Abd al-Rahman al-Bazzaz, *Al-dawlah al-muwahhada wa-al-dawlah al-ittihadiya*, 2nd ed. (Cairo: Dar al-Qalam, 1960), 78.
[107] Ibid., 87, 88n1.

"system." These similarities extended to the use of speed metaphors to represent progress. Qutb and Bakdash each characterized his prescription as a "system [*nizam*]" in the sense that Daniel Lerner employed when he wrote in *The Passing of Traditional Society* that "the conditions which define modernity form an interlocking 'system.'"[108] Of course, the former two contemporaries would have disagreed with one other, and with Lerner, over what sort of modernity Arabs needed. Like Arab modernizers, Rostow defined his vision in *The Stages of Economic Growth* through negation, contrasting it against "traditional" societies and Marxism. For Rostow, too, as for Ba'thists and Arab communists, the 1930s had been formative in pushing him to study the structure of societies:

The book fulfills, at least *ad interim*, a decision made when I was an undergraduate at Yale, in the mid-1930s. At that time I decided to work professionally on two problems: the relatively narrow problem of bringing modern economic theory to bear on economic history; and the broader problem of relating economic to social and political forces, in the workings of whole societies. As a student and teacher these two questions have engaged me ever since.[109]

A Rhodes scholar and wartime analyst of the Allies' aerial bombing campaign against Germany, Rostow developed his ideas while teaching U.S. history abroad at Oxford and Cambridge. *The Stages of Economic Growth* is likewise concerned with establishing the authority with which to define the future – "articulating new ideas briefly and simply to an intelligent nonprofessional audience." It attempts to do so through a profusion of historical examples. Rostow concedes:

any way of looking at things that pretends to bring within its orbit, let us say, significant aspects of late eighteenth-century Britain and Khrushchev's Russia; Meiji Japan and Canada of the pre-1914 railway boom, Alexander Hamilton's United States and Mao's China; Bismarck's Germany and Nasser's Egypt – any such scheme is bound, to put it mildly, to have certain limitations.

As a result, glib representations of other peoples substitute for evidence:

One need look no farther than the primacy colonial peoples give to independence over economic development, or the hot emotions Arab politicians can generate in the

---

[108] Daniel Lerner, *The Passing of Traditional Society: Modernizing the Middle East* (New York: The Free Press, 1958), 55. See Qutb, *Ma'rakat*; and Khalid Bakdash, *Al-Hizb al-shuyu'i fi al-nidal li-ajli al-istiqlal wa-al-siyada al-wataniya* (Damascus: Dar al-Taqaddum, n.d.), 24. On Islam as a "System of Life," see Sayyid Qutb, *Islam: The Religion of the Future* (Beirut: Dar al-Kalam Press, 1971). See also Omnia El Shakry, *The Great Social Laboratory: Subjects of Knowledge in Colonial and Postcolonial Egypt* (Stanford, CA: Stanford University Press, 2007), 13–14; and James Toth, *Sayyid Qutb: The Life and Legacy of a Radical Islamic Intellectual* (New York: Oxford University Press, 2013), 163.

[109] Rostow, *The Stages of Economic Growth*, ix.

street crowds, to know that economic advantage is an insufficient basis for explaining political behavior.[110]

Scholar Gilbert Rist criticized both Rostow and Marx, but could just as easily have been referring to postwar Arab elites, when he wrote that they "*replace history with a philosophy of history.*"[111] Arab modernizers may have differed politically with one another and with their American counterparts, but close intellectual combat drew otherwise dissimilar thinkers closer together conceptually.

Just as speed and mobility influenced the ideas of postwar modernizers, metaphors of modern travel furnished the descriptive images that they used to represent societal change. According to Rist, Rostow's evocative use in *Stages* of the jet-age term *takeoff* to illustrate a country's achievement of self-sustaining economic growth "partly accounted for the book's success."[112] Rostow borrowed this metaphor from the report *The Objectives of United States Economic Assistance Programs* compiled by MIT's Center for International Studies.[113] For him, the metaphor illustrated how, instead of narrowly serving military strategy, U.S. aid to poor nations could accelerate the preconditions for takeoff that already industrialized countries had built up in the course of becoming "airborne." As Gilman notes, Rostow conceived linking U.S. aid to a "theory of history," even before incorporating the conceptual distinction between tradition and modernity that Gilman associates with "full-blown modernization theory."[114]

In the early 1960s, Rostow's *Stages* was serialized in the Egyptian paper *al-Ahram*, but postwar Arabic political writings already featured metaphors of speed tailored to particular regional concerns about development.[115] For Arab elites, such images served different purposes than validating specific strategies for fostering economic growth. Instead of the thrust and lift evoked by "takeoff," such metaphors in Arabic literature feature linear motion and a concern with trajectory. This emphasis speaks to the competition among ideologies as well as to Arab elites' interest in garnering the social authority needed to chart a course to the future. If a society's members are collectively bound for a common destination, such metaphors imply, then its

[110] Ibid., x, 1, 152.
[111] Gilbert Rist, *The History of Development: From Western Origins to Global Faith*, trans. Patrick Camiller, Rev. ed. (New York: Zed Books, 2002), 102. Emphasis in original.
[112] Ibid., 95.
[113] Ibid., 95n8. See U.S. Congress, Senate, Special Committee to Study the Foreign Aid Program, *The Objectives of United States Economic Assistance Programs* [Study Prepared by the Center for International Studies, Massachusetts Institute of Technology], 85 Cong., 1 Sess. (Washington, DC: Government Printing Office, 1957), 70.
[114] Gilman, *Mandarins of the Future*, 177, 181.
[115] See Polk to Battle, November 16, 1965, POL 7 Visits. Meetings. UAR 1965, box 2, NEA Bureau, Office of the Country Director for the United Arab Republic (NEA/UAR) Records Relating to United Arab Republic Affairs, 1961–1966, RG 59, NARA.

most capable leaders must be at the controls to ensure a safe arrival. Like
Rostow, Arab modernizers featured speed images to depict development as
a multifaceted historical process. Unlike the MIT economist, however, they
accentuated questions of social authority – of who had the right to guide
development, and on the basis of what values. Through their references to
modern travel, Arab elites chose symbols of worldly experience to evoke
societal progress guided by intellectual sophistication, moral righteousness,
and technocratic expertise.

Speed metaphors mingled with Orientalist imagery expressed anxieties
about Arabs' temporal lag behind other peoples. In a cartoon featured on
the cover of the September 7, 1944 edition of *Ruz al-Yusuf* (Figure 1.2), the
Egyptian everyman Misr Effendi, wearing a *tarbush* and clutching prayer
beads, sits atop a visibly exhausted mule resting beside some train tracks.
The diminutive, nearsighted rider glances anxiously at a locomotive racing
by at full steam and labeled "The World After the War." Misr Effendi is
holding his own sign that reads "Egypt after the War." The image ironically
references a familiar association between speed and progress to raise concerns about the state of Egypt's middle classes. As On Barak writes about
Egypt's nineteenth-century elite: "They experienced modernity as moving
swiftly ahead yet always remaining one step behind."[116] In this case, the
caption proclaims the postwar era as "The Age of Speed [*'asr al-sur'a*]."[117]

This image not only employs the train as a symbol of progress, but it also
identifies speed and modes of transportation as standards for comparing
levels of development. In *Ma'rakat al-Islam wa al-ra'smaliya*, Qutb employs
similar Orientalist imagery but reconfigures it to indicate the possibilities
of a non-Western, Islamic path to modernity. Qutb rejects the stereotypical
image of Arabs riding camels in the desert for implying Islam's incompat-
ibility with 1,400 years of technological innovation. Instead, Qutb's metaphor associates Islam with forward progress. Rather than trailing in the
"caravan's train [*dhayl al-qafila*]," he declares, Muslims should seize the
camel's "reins [*al-zimam*]."[118] Islam, he suggests, accepts the need for material advances while also redefining the meaning of progress in moral terms.
Another example comes from secular Arab nationalist al-Bazzaz. He accuses
Iraq's monarchical regime prior to the 1958 revolution of a slavish devo-
tion to the Baghdad Pact that excluded Iraq from the "caravan of Arab
riders [*qafila al-rakb al-'Arabi*]."[119] Magdi Hasanayn, a military officer who
directed Egypt's Tahrir Province desert reclamation project in the 1950s,

---

[116] Barak, *On Time*, 2.
[117] *Ruz al-Yusuf*, September 7, 1944, p. 1. Yoav Di-Capua dates the phrase to 1930 in a statement made by Egypt's transportation minister. See Di-Capua, "Common Skies, Divided
Horizons," 937 n27.
[118] Qutb, *Ma'rakat*, 54. See also ibid., 65.
[119] al-Bazzaz, *Al-dawlah al-muwahhada*, 29.

FIGURE I.2. *Ruz al-Yusuf*, September 7, 1944.

wrote in his memoir that "all of us, in our country are riding horses galloping to catch up with the procession of the age and civilization ... if we know the language of the age and its spirit, means, and laws, then we can exchange this horse for cars or airplanes."[120]

Across the spectrum of Arab politics, modernizers described societal development as a journey whose success demanded competent navigation.

[120] Magdi Hasanayn, *Al-Sahara'... al-thawra wa al-tharwa: qissa mudiriya al-tahrir* (Cairo: Al-Hay'a al-Misriya al-'Ama lil-Kitab, 1975), 363.

Refitting the ship-of-state metaphor for an era of contending ideologies, Iraqi cleric Muhammad Baqir al-Sadr wrote in *Falsafatuna*:

for we know the destination where humanity must eventually land, and the natural shore for which the ship sets its course and anchors to arrive at peace and goodness, and returns to a stable life, filled with justice and happiness, after long struggle and hardship, and after wandering far and wide in various directions and on different courses [*al-ittijahat*].[121]

Lebanese communist Niqula Shawi weaves his personal story of becoming a party member with a Marxist history of Lebanon and the Middle East compiled according to socialist principles. His is therefore not a conventional political memoir characterized by nostalgia for youth, he writes, nor one "that strikes a pose of distress and regret that any one of us expresses upon missing the train or ... the airplane when an opportunity is irretrievably lost." Rather, Shawi portrays history as moving inexorably according to a fixed plan accessible only to the historian steeped in dialectical materialism. He imagines great events as "stations [*mahattat*]" from which to glimpse the historical forces rushing past.[122] Syrian Ba'thist Zaki Arsuzi (1899–1968), who studied philosophy at the Sorbonne, evaluated the same political "orientations [*ittijahat*]" that competed on Asad's schoolyard. In *Mashakiluna al-Qawmiya* [*Our Problems of Nationalism*], he identified industry as a principal basis for comparing societies' levels of development in the "parade of civilization [*mawkib al-hadara*]." Arsuzi described industrialization as transforming the people from a condition of dependency to one of mastery, "the mastery of the driver [*saytara al-sa'iq*] (chauffeur) over the machine," by which the car reaches its destination and the nation takes its place among industrialized countries.[123] Even Nasser, in *The Philosophy of the Revolution*, wrote that Egypt did not enjoy the long centuries in which to develop as did Europe, which "crossed the bridge between the Renaissance at the end of the Middle Ages and the Nineteenth Century step by step."[124]

Speed could represent development gone awry. In a cartoon published in the Iraqi magazine *Qarandal*, and reprinted in "What the Arabs Think" (1952) by Arabist William Polk, a Stalin-faced locomotive labeled "communism" advances over a bridge supported by figures representing feudalism, poverty, ignorance, exploitation, sickness, and schism (Figure 1.3).[125]

---

[121] Muhammad Baqir al-Sadr, *Falsafatuna* (Beirut: Dar al-Fakr, 1969), 12.

[122] Shawi, *Tariqi ila al-hizb*, 20, 21.

[123] Zaki Arsuzi, *Mashakiluna al-Qawmiya*, (Damascus: Mu'assasa al-Thaqafiya lil-nushr wa al-tawziy', 1958), 114–15.

[124] Gamal 'Abd al-Nasser, *The Philosophy of the Revolution* (Buffalo, NY: Economica Books, 1959), 50.

[125] William R. Polk, "What the Arabs Think," *Foreign Policy Association, Headline Series* 96 (November–December 1952): 23.

The magazine *Qarandal* of Baghdad on April 9, 1952 printed the above cartoon on its cover. At the lower left Qarandal explains to an American how
communism enters the Middle East: "These are the supports for the bridge
of communism." The supports are labeled (right to left) "Feudal Landlords," "Poverty," "Exploitation," "Ignorance," "Sickness," "Schism." The
locomotive is labeled "Communism."

FIGURE 1.3. *Qarandal*, April 9, 1952.

Tawfiq al-Suwaydi, condemning the 1958 Iraqi revolution led by Brigadier
'Abd al-Karim Qasim, wrote:

the military track, the proper and sound one, is that which stretches between the
barracks and the front. Whenever any army leaves this track, the country overturns
just as the train overturns which leaves its rails.

Al-Suwaydi reaches this conclusion at the end of a lengthy memoir detailing
his diplomatic and international experience, a rebuke to what he regarded as
the provincial, uneducated soldiers who had seized power. Far from overseeing progress, al-Suwaydi declares in a conflation of the spatial and temporal,
Qasim was responsible for the "retrogression [*taqahqur*] of the country by
fifty years."[126]

In his most important work, Qutb evoked speed to represent moral progress according to his Islamist system. He identified a moral leadership, "the
vanguard [*al-tali'a*]," needed to navigate Islamic society through a world
disoriented by dead-end, materialist ideologies. Prior to his temporary

[126] al-Suwaydi, *Mudhakkirati*, 627, 613.

release from Nasser's prisons in 1964, Qutb authored *Ma'alim fi al-Tariq* [*Signposts Along the Road*], which proclaimed: "Democracy in the West has become infertile to such an extent that it is borrowing from the systems of the Eastern bloc," while "Marxism is defeated on the plane of thought, and if it is stated that not a single nation in the world is truly Marxist, it will not be an exaggeration."[127] At the same time, Qutb associated present-day Muslim societies with the *jahiliyya*, the historical era of moral ignorance prior to the revelation of Islam. Borrowing this concept from the south Asian Islamist Abu l-A'la Mawdudi, Qutb redefines underdevelopment in moral terms.[128] He therefore represents spiritual advancement in terms of temporal and spatial progress. The title of Qutb's work is sometimes translated as *Milestones*. This rendering may not convey his message, however, because milestones are universally accessible and require no interpretation. They are clearly and easily recognizable markers that trusted authorities have placed at regular intervals along a road to guide each and every traveler. By contrast, Qutb concedes that his comments in *Ma'alim fi al-Tariq* are characterized by "their disconnectedness, [*tafarruqiha*]" just as "it is the nature of signs along the road to be disconnected."[129] For him, the most important markers are the Qur'an and the generation of the prophet Muhammad, who made the most significant journey, the *hijra* from Mecca to Medina that established a new, Islamic community. Qutb explicitly addresses his work to the vanguard charged with interpreting the moral landscape and navigating the way toward recreating such a society:

It is necessary that there should be a vanguard which sets out with this determination and then keeps walking on the path, marching through the vast ocean of Jahiliyyah which has encompassed the entire world.... It is necessary that this vanguard should know the landmarks and the [signs] of the road toward this goal so that they may recognize the starting place, the nature, the responsibilities and the ultimate purpose of this long journey.... I have written *Ma'alim fi al-Tariq* for this vanguard, which I consider a waiting reality about to be materialized.[130]

Qutb identified different markers of progress from those employed by communism, capitalism, or Nasser's regime.[131] *Ma'alim fi al-Tariq* reflects its Cold War context at the same time that it addresses conflicts over political and social authority within Egypt. As Euben writes, Qutb's "project – its language, symbols and focus – is defined as much by his contemporary

[127] Sayyid Qutb, *Milestones* (Damascus: Dar al-Ilm, 1990), 1.

[128] Calvert, *Sayyid Qutb and the Origins of Radical Islamism*, 158.

[129] Qutb, *Milestones*, 13. For the Arabic text, see Sayyid Qutb, *Ma'alim fi al-Tariq* (Cairo: Dar al-Shuruq, 1982), 13.

[130] Qutb, *Milestones*, 12; Qutb *Ma'alim fi al-Tariq*, 12. I have quoted the cited English translation but substituted "signs" for "milestones."

[131] See Qutb, *Milestones*, 124.

interlocutors as by the 'origins' of Islam."[132] In formulating his Islamic vision, Qutb incorporates the same concern for technological achievement and social justice that characterized the alternatives his secular rivals promoted. Qutb should therefore be considered a modernizer, even though he claims to reject the materialist and rationalist foundations of the ideologies to which his prescription is a response. His metaphor representing development as speeding along the road is consistent with the imagery his post-war contemporaries employed. This positive depiction of spatial movement as moral progress supplanted Qutb's earlier, negative association between "speed" and "haste."[133] *Ma'alim* could only have been written in a setting characterized by ideological pluralism and global mobility. In conceiving the struggle to reestablish Islamic society as a global journey, Qutb derived a philosophy of history from his formative experiences traveling across the United States and making the pilgrimage to Saudi Arabia.

If Huxley is correct that speed is the "only new pleasure invented by modernity," writes Duffy, then traveling by car, train, or airplane "was the moment at which individual people were allowed to feel modernity in their bones."[134] Demonstrating mastery over the technology of speed appears in some accounts to stake a claim to modern political leadership. From his interviews with Hafiz al-Asad, Patrick Seale describes how the future Syrian leader

narrowly escaped death on the eve of his graduation as a pilot officer in 1955. At the rehearsal two formations of four aircraft were due to fly past and land in turn. As Asad's formation wheeled to allow the planes behind to come in, it entered a dense cloud over Aleppo. Flying blind required skill which he did not yet possess, but he knew that he must match his instruments and not trust to his senses. He noticed he was losing speed and opened the throttle: to his surprise the speedometer needle continued to fall. Any moment now the engine would stall and he would crash. He felt the engine vibrating and dust falling in his eyes. Only then did he realize he was flying upside down. He shot out of the cloud and found himself heading straight for earth. "Just in time I managed to climb to safety, grazing the tops of the olive trees. Other cadets watching me said, 'Has he gone mad?' They thought I was playing games but I wasn't." On the following day Asad graduated and collected his cup for aerobatics.[135]

In King Husayn's memoir, *Uneasy Lies the Head*, Jordan's young monarch flaunts his proficiency as a daredevil pilot and racer of sports cars

---

[132] Roxanne L. Euben. *Enemy in the Mirror: Islamic Fundamentalism and the Limits of Modern Rationalism, a Work of Comparative Political Theory* (Princeton, NJ: Princeton University Press, 1999), 84.
[133] See Barak, *On Time*, 148–49.
[134] Duffy, *The Speed Handbook*, 4.
[135] Seale, *Asad of Syria*, 40.

FIGURE 1.4. King Husayn. © Bettmann/Corbis.

(Figure 1.4). He describes evading two attacking Syrian MiGs while at the controls of his De Haviland Dove, "putting the plane into a dive at about 240 air-miles an hour," and "playing tig [tag] in the air at fantastic speeds."[136] This near-death incident occurred in 1958 as Husayn was attempting to overfly Syrian territory of the United Arab Republic and so encapsulates the clash between the king's Hashemite modernity and Nasser's revolutionary pan-Arabism. Arguments about modernizing the Arab Middle East evoked speed at a time when aerospace represented the newest technology. For Arabs and Americans alike, fascination with the cutting-edge technologies of speed influenced the dominant postwar descriptions of societal progress.

Revisiting "the age of speed" provides needed perspective on the meaning of the Cold War in the Arab Middle East. If travel, creating representations of other societies, and assimilating foreign ideas had for more than a century been crucial to constructing regional reform agendas, then circumstances after 1945 accelerated the tempo and broadened the scope of such activities. Arabs collected wider and compressed experiences of the world just as the United States and Soviet Union were competing to demonstrate the

[136] H.M. King Hussein of Jordan, *Uneasy Lies the Head* (London: Heinemann, 1962), 181, 183.

universal validity of their ideologies. Arab development debates shifted as intellectuals built upon the interwar competition among anticolonial movements by reformulating regional ideologies as alternatives to capitalism and communism. The superpower rivalry provided the language for escalating battles over social authority, while Cold War junkets gave travelers what they depicted to Arab audiences as previews of alternative futures. American and Soviet appeals to Arab and other postcolonial elites provoked a fierce argument about the meaning of development in which participants shared assumptions about the integrated nature of societies. In these exchanges, political rivals similarly described antithetical ideologies as "systems" and sought to validate them using a myriad of historical and present-day examples. A race to master the comparative study of societal change united those otherwise divided by ideology, language, and politics. The sensation of speed characterized postwar arguments about development, as Arab and other modernizers translated their conquest over spatial distance into visions of the future.

2

Imperial Legacies

"Jess Heroy, who spent a few days with us not long ago, told us that you and Nell were visiting the McGhees. We hope you found them all well and enjoying Turkey. That's one country I want to visit someday, especially Istanbul, but before I do I want to read at least a dozen books to resaturate myself with its history."
— Max W. Ball to Everette L. DeGolyer, August 27, 1952.[1]

"Sir Hamilton is professor of Middle Eastern studies at Harvard University and is also the most outstanding and well known Middle Eastern scholar. I want to add my voice to those of others urging you to make a special effort to attend the dinner in his honor."
— James Terry Duce to Everette L. DeGolyer, February 8, 1956.[2]

If global travel and the superpower conflict influenced Arab development politics, then American encounters with the Middle East helped to define modernization in U.S. strategy. This chapter shows how American ideas about modernizing the Middle East emerged from successive reinterpretations of Ottoman history. Through this dialogue with the past, Americans drew on the legacy of previous Ottoman imperial reforms as they pursued their economic interests. Although modernization served as a discourse of power in U.S. foreign policy, it was neither simply the export of domestic liberalism nor a fixed development model. It also arose from American engagements with the histories of postcolonial societies and evolved in response to changing policy needs. After 1945, Americans were forced to redefine their relationship to imperial legacies across the third world. In the Middle East, they had to reckon not only with British and French colonialism, but also with the much longer and more complicated history of the Ottoman Empire, which dated to the fourteenth century. The Ottomans had

[1] Folder 5044, box 97, EDP.
[2] Folder 360, box 4, EDP.

reigned over the Balkans, Anatolia, and North Africa, as well as the Levant, the Arabian Peninsula, and the Gulf. During the empire's last 200 years, sultans, bureaucrats, and intellectuals pursued reforms to preserve the empire against internal challenges and European imperialism. Following World War I, an Ottoman military officer, Mustafa Kemal, later known as Atatürk, founded the Turkish republic and attempted to transform its society, culture, and language. Numerous Americans would define their strategies for modernizing the Middle East by seeking to assimilate this legacy of reform.[3]

American oilmen and diplomats engaged in intense historical debates about the Ottoman imperial and Kemalist legacies. Through reinterpretations of the past, cold warriors advanced self-serving definitions of modernization meant to protect the American economic stake in the region's petroleum. Like their Arab counterparts, U.S. elites emphasized the role indigenous leaders could play in fostering changes within traditional societies. But the American preference for authoritarian modernization served mainly to preempt alternative visions for developing the Middle East through the reinvestment of oil wealth. By cultivating a usable history of the region, in which Americans would help to complete the process begun by a modernizing imperial elite, Western petroleum companies could respond to demands made by producing governments for a greater share of profits. In a running dialogue with the past, Americans argued that U.S. policies would fulfill the unrealized promise of Ottoman-Turkish reforms whose defects they criticized. Ironically, however, these discussions about modernizing the Middle East adapted Ottoman reformers' older accounts of imperial decline and paternalism toward the empire's Arabic-speaking periphery. Americans repurposed the ideas of Ottoman reform to portray Arab societies as backward and to argue that Arab modernization would require behavioral modification rather than a more equitable distribution of resources.

This chapter examines how Americans sought to assign positive historical meanings to the rise of U.S. power in the Middle East. It describes debates about the past in which many of the participants were motivated by a desire to preserve the favorable terms under which U.S. companies extracted Arab countries' oil. In these debates, oil geologists and economists, along with historians, philologists, and social scientists, excavated and refined the region's rich historical raw materials. Their noncommunist version of modernization, validated by selective readings of Ottoman-Turkish history, gained currency just as oilmen and diplomats maneuvered to defeat a UN plan for reinvesting oil company profits in Arab development. Through their

---

[3] See *Imperial Legacy: The Ottoman Imprint on the Balkans and the Middle East*, ed. L. Carl Brown (New York: Columbia University Press, 1996). On Nazi uses of Turkish history and Atatürk, see Stefan Ihrig, *Atatürk in the Nazi Imagination* (Cambridge, MA: Belknap/ Harvard University Press, 2014). On the Kemalist appropriation of Ottoman history, see Nick Danforth, "Multi-purpose Empire: Ottoman History in Republican Turkey," *Middle Eastern Studies* 50 (July 2014): 655–78.

historical portrayal of U.S. policy as fulfilling Ottoman reforms and emphasis on Turkey's contemporary role as regional leader, Americans sought to confront the economic threat that many recognized in Arab nationalism.

Viewing modernization through a regional lens offers a critical alternative to existing accounts describing it as a development formula derived from American liberalism and Parsonian sociology. In fact, cold warriors' enthusiasm for studying the Ottoman-Turkish past contradicts David Engerman's statement that "[h]istory mattered less than sociology" in postwar modernization.[4] A regional approach helps to explain the exact nature of the exchange between Orientalists and modernization theorists, a working relationship previously characterized in ambiguous terms. Said wrote that "the social scientist and the new expert" inherited Orientalism but rendered it "scarcely recognizable," while historian Zachary Lockman observes that the two fields shared assumptions of Western superiority but "divided up the world in different ways."[5] The oilmen, diplomats, and scholars examined in this chapter may have taken a paternalistic approach to developing the Middle East, but they could not portray the region's peoples as lacking history. Rather, they positioned themselves regionally as historical actors to whom the torch of earlier reforms had passed. Although American engagement with the Middle East contributed to birthing modernization theory, a similar analysis could be written about how Cold War elites made use of East Asian and Latin American history to defend interests in other regions. In addition to Ottoman-Turkish reformers, for instance, U.S. social scientists studied those from Meiji-era Japan to understand modernization in a non-Western society.[6] Looking through the opposite end of the telescope makes it possible to see how U.S. modernizers attempted to assimilate previous reform movements from different parts of the non-European world into a coherent global strategy of American-administered change. In this neglected aspect of the U.S. rise to world power, Americans' attempts to portray themselves as heirs to previous reform movements and to align their

---

[4] David C. Engerman, *Modernization from the Other Shore: American Intellectuals and the Romance of Russian Development* (Cambridge, MA: Harvard University Press, 2003), 280.

[5] Said, *Orientalism*, 290; Zachary Lockman, *Contending Visions of the Middle East: The History and Politics of Orientalism* (New York: Cambridge University Press, 2004), 139.

[6] See Masamichi Inoki's interpretation of the Meiji-era civil bureaucracy as a "modernizing oligarchy" in *Political Modernization in Japan and Turkey*, ed. Dankwart A. Rustow and Robert E. Ward (Princeton, NJ: Princeton University Press, 1964), 283–300. On the place of Japan in Ottoman understandings of modernization, see Renée Worringer, *Ottomans Imagining Japan: East, Middle East, and Non-Western Modernity at the Turn of the Twentieth Century* (New York: Palgrave Macmillan, 2014). On Eastern Europe and Latin America as "laboratories of underdevelopment," see Joseph L. Love, *Crafting the Third World: Theorizing Underdevelopment in Rumania and Brazil* (Stanford, CA: Stanford University Press, 1996). On Latin America, see also Edgar J. Dosman, *The Life and Times of Raul Prebisch, 1901–1986* (Kingston, Ontario: McGill-Queen's University Press, 2008).

interests with inherited narratives of regional progress led them to appropriate non-Western reformers' ideas.

The epigraphic quotations that opened this chapter begin to establish the group of oil industry, government, and academic figures who collaborated on developing useable historical narratives. Both come from the papers of Everette Lee DeGolyer Sr. (1886–1956), the twentieth century's premier oil geologist. Born in Kansas, DeGolyer studied geology at the University of Oklahoma, worked for the U.S. Geological Survey, and made his fortune developing Mexican oil. Mexico's nationalization of its oil industry in 1938 was the formative event of DeGolyer's professional life, a step he attributed to oil companies' neglect of the native labor force. This experience framed the issues that he would address in his subsequent career advising the U.S. government and major oil companies as head of the Dallas firm DeGolyer & MacNaughton. DeGolyer's legend as a petroleum geologist rested on his wartime role assessing the resources of the Persian Gulf for oil czar Harold Ickes' Petroleum Reserves Corporation. In his 1944 report to Ickes, DeGolyer wrote, "the conclusion is inescapable that reserves of great magnitude remain to be discovered" in the Middle East. He told a congressional committee soon after that the "center of gravity of world oil production is shifting" from the Caribbean and the Gulf of Mexico to the Persian Gulf.[7] How to maintain access to those resources on acceptable terms would consume industry leaders and officials in the postwar years.

DeGolyer's correspondent Max W. Ball (1885–1954), a lawyer and oil geologist trained at the Colorado School of Mines, headed the Oil and Gas Division of the Department of the Interior and acted as President Harry S. Truman's liaison to the industry's National Petroleum Council. Ball served on petroleum advisory boards across Truman's administration and helped to coordinate oil policies between the State Department and the CIA.[8] Together with German economist Walter Levy (1911–1988), who had provided the U.S. government with wartime estimates of Hitler's oil reserves, Ball successfully defended the interests of major companies in disputes over how to price Persian Gulf oil purchased by the European Recovery Program (ERP), or Marshall Plan.[9] In the Middle East, Ball served

---

[7] Everette DeGolyer, "Preliminary Report of the Technical Oil Mission to the Middle East," February 1, 1944, folder 3459, box 52, EDP; "Maloney to Head Senate Oil Study," *New York Times*, March 24, 1944, 11. See also Lon Tinkle, *Mr. De: A Biography of Everette Lee DeGolyer* (Boston: Little, Brown, 1970); and Karen R. Merrill, "Texas Metropole: Oil, the American West, and U.S. Power in the Postwar Years," *Journal of American History* 99 (June 2012): 197–207.

[8] See transcripts contained in folder: 060 Interdepartmental Petroleum Committee, 1946–1947, (Meetings), box 23, Records of the Department of Energy, Department of the Interior, Office of Oil and Gas, Oil and Gas Division, Office of the Director, Central Files, 1946–53, RG 434, NARA; and entry for May 19, 1952, folder: Diary, 1952, box 3, MBP, HSTL.

[9] See "Middle East Crude Oil," March 23, 1949, folder 4, box 22, WLP; and entry for March 23, 1949, folder: Diary, 1949, box 2, MBP.

as oil consultant to Israel and soon realized his dream of seeing Istanbul. Ball authored a new extractive law for the Turkish government designed to attract investment and that U.S. oilmen envisioned as a model for oil company–government relations. His role in Turkey involved dismantling Atatürk's *étatism*, or statist economic policy, which oilmen portrayed as the historical vestige of Turkey's national adolescence. Ball's relationship with DeGolyer and DeGolyer's wife, Nell, formed part of a network of oil geologists that included William B. Heroy, whose wife, Jess, Ball also mentions. The other name in Ball's note, "the McGhees," refers to DeGolyer's daughter Cecilia and son-in-law George Crews McGhee (1912–2005). McGhee, a Waco-born oil geologist educated at the University of Oklahoma and at Oxford as a Rhodes scholar, had worked for DeGolyer before marrying his daughter. Levy had recommended McGhee to succeed Ball directing the Oil and Gas Division at Interior, but McGhee pursued a diplomatic career instead, establishing America's Cold War foreign policy in the Middle East.[10] The president appointed him to administer emergency U.S. assistance to Turkey under the Truman Doctrine, and as Assistant Secretary of State for Near Eastern, South Asian, and African Affairs, McGhee helped to author the first U.S. economic aid programs in the region. Later, as ambassador in Ankara, he negotiated Turkey's membership in the North Atlantic Treaty Organization (NATO).[11]

McGhee presided over a Middle East chiefs-of-mission conference held in 1949 in Istanbul, where American diplomats identified preserving access to oil, containing Soviet influence, and promoting economic development as the top regional priorities. McGhee juxtaposed this contemporary agenda with the imperial traditions memorialized in the former Ottoman capital:

Although I have been to Istanbul many times over the years, including my visits earlier as coordinator of Greek-Turkish Aid and later as Ambassador to Turkey, I have never failed to be moved by the aura of this ancient seat of empires. Beneath its modern drab exterior, Istanbul hides more history than any other city in the world except Rome.... Although little of the Byzantine city remains, and much of the Turkish capital is in ruins or disrepair, an air of power and mystery hangs over the city.[12]

When America's regional envoys returned to Istanbul, McGhee's staff arranged side trips to acquaint them with the city's imperial heritage. These included excursions "to the Sultan's palace, with a visit to the treasury and to the Chinese porcelain collection comprising some ten thousand outstanding pieces of Ming Blue and Celadon pieces." Diplomats visited "Hagia Sophia, now a museum, and the nearby Sultan Ahmed Sulaimaniye and

---

[10] See entry for July 19, 1949, folder: Diary, 1949, box 2, MBP.

[11] See George McGhee, *The US-Turkish-NATO Middle East Connection: How the Truman Doctrine Contained the Soviets in the Middle East* (New York: St. Martin's Press, 1990).

[12] George McGhee, *Envoy to the Middle World: Adventures in Diplomacy* (New York: Harper & Row, 1983), 81.

Rustem Pasha mosques," as well as "the Dolma Bahce and Yildiz palaces on the Bosphorous," the former being the site where imperial reformers convened the first Ottoman parliament in 1877.[13] During his time as ambassador, McGhee became an avid collector of books on Ottoman and Turkish history. "I sensed that the history of Asia Minor was so complex, and the Ottoman Empire so difficult for Westerners to understand," McGhee later wrote, "that I must seek out all available sources." As a result, he recalled, "I practically preempted the Turkish market for historical books."[14] McGhee would put his historical knowledge to political use, portraying the defense of U.S. regional interests as fulfilling earlier Ottoman and Kemalist attempts at reform. At the same time, McGhee and other cold warriors hoped that Arab states would participate in U.S.-led regional defense and accept American aid in imitation of Turkey, which in the American reading of the Middle Eastern map constituted the modern, anticommunist core of the old empire. As Near East Foundation president Allen Dulles hopefully explained to McGhee in 1949, Syria's new military leader seemed to be following in Atatürk's footsteps:

Mr. Dulles stated that General [Husni] Zaim is aspiring to the role of a Mustapha Kemal. He has a military mind and tends to believe that the issuance of an order insures its implementation. However, he has succeeded in substituting a certain amount of discipline for the previous inefficiency. Mr. Dulles was unable to predict whether Zaim will become a good dictator or a bad one.[15]

McGhee and other Americans invoked the Ottoman and Kemalist legacies to articulate U.S. interests in the Arab Middle East.

DeGolyer's second correspondent, James Terry Duce (1892–1965), was yet another oil geologist. Born in England but educated at the University of Colorado, Duce was vice president of the Arabian American Oil Company (Aramco), which was owned by four major U.S. oil companies and was developing the vast oil resources of Saudi Arabia. "He had the face and figure of a kewpie doll with thinning hair," one Aramco file noted, while the "merry twinkle in his squinty, little eyes reminded one of Santa Claus."[16] Duce orchestrated the public relations campaigns touting the company's modernizing role in Saudi Arabia and, in a previous letter to DeGolyer, had insisted that "the oil companies have not exploited the Mexicans or any other group – that quite to the contrary, the exploitation has been the other

[13] Ibid., 267–68.
[14] The George C. McGhee Library, *A Catalogue of Books on Asia Minor and the Turkish Ottoman Empire*, ed. Joseph E. Jeffs (Washington, DC: Georgetown University Library, 1984), vii.
[15] Memo of conversation by Hope, June 14, 1949, folder: General – 1950, box 11, Records of NEA, Office Files of Asst. Sec'y. of State George C. McGhee, 1945–1953, Lot File 53 D468, RG 59, NARA.
[16] "Duce, James Terry," folder 17, box 1, WEM.

way."[17] Years before DeGolyer's fabled survey of the Persian Gulf, Duce wrote him: "The amounts of oil are incredible and I have to rub my eyes frequently and say like the farmer – 'There ain't no such beast.'"[18] Duce invited DeGolyer to inspect the Dhahran oil facilities in November 1943, at about the time that Duce was forced to resign as head of the foreign division of the Petroleum Administration for War. A conflict of interest generated controversy after Ickes announced his abortive plan for the government to purchase shares in Duce's company.[19] After the war, Duce conferred privately with Max Ball about the pricing of oil purchased under the ERP.[20] Duce was a frequent guest at the State Department, where he met with McGhee and other officials, served on the board of the American University of Beirut, and headed the Washington-based Middle East Institute, whose *Middle East Journal* Aramco subsidized.[21]

There was no need for Duce to introduce "Sir Hamilton" – H.A.R. Gibb (1895–1971), the British Orientalist who relocated to Harvard in 1955 – because DeGolyer was already well acquainted with him. Gibb chaired the session on economic development in which DeGolyer and McGhee had participated at the 1950 Harvard University conference "The Great Powers and the Near East."[22] In his presentation, DeGolyer had described the cunning of "the wily Turk" in pre–World War I oil negotiations before going on to praise Aramco's efforts to "assure their workers of the availability of proper housing and opportunities for self-improvement."[23] Duce had suggested material for DeGolyer's previous public appearances, and the Aramco vice president's influence was apparent on this occasion.[24]

DeGolyer complained about having to endure "a lot of college professors" at this "cloud gathering group of do-gooders" meeting in Harvard Yard.[25] But just as Duce urged DeGolyer to spend one more evening with Gibb at a Harvard Foundation dinner, historians need to revisit Gibb's importance

---

[17] Duce to DeGolyer, December 16, 1944, folder 360, box 4, EDP.

[18] Duce to DeGolyer, April 29, 1941, folder 360, box 4, EDP.

[19] Duce to DeGolyer, November 4, 1943, folder 3459, box 52, EDP. See Vitalis, *America's Kingdom*, 77.

[20] Diary entry for November 4, 1949, folder: Diary, 1949, box 2, MBP.

[21] See memo of conversation by Funkhouser, November 6, 1950, *FRUS, 1950*, vol. 5: 106–09; Meeting of the Nominations Committee of the Board of Trustees of the American University of Beirut, March 3, 1948, p. 4, Book V, 1947–52, A.U.B. Minutes of Board of Trustees, Special Collections, Jafet Library, American University of Beirut, Lebanon. See also Kathleen Manalo, "A Short History of the Middle East Institute," *Middle East Journal* 41 (Winter 1987): 66.

[22] See conference program, "The Great Powers and the Near East," August 7–9, 1950, folder 2387, box 22, EDP.

[23] *The Near East and the Great Powers*, ed. Richard N. Frye (Port Washington, NY: Kennikat Press, Inc., 1951), 126, 135.

[24] Memo of telephone call with Duce, June 2, 1947, folder 2348, box 20, EDP.

[25] DeGolyer to Funkhouser, September 5, 1950, folder 2387, box 22, EDP.

to postwar area studies and modernization theory. Lockman associates Gibb, along with Bernard Lewis of Princeton, with "mainstream Anglo-American Orientalism in the post–Second World War period" and describes Orientalists as competing against social scientists for scholarly authority.[26] Gibb's relationship with social scientists was mostly collaborative, however, and helped to bring them, along with U.S. diplomats and oilmen, into contact with the ideas of Ottoman imperial reformers. His recovery of Ottoman reformist texts not only introduced Americans to imperial history, but also made them heirs to an already long tradition of reforming the Middle East. Gibb's widely cited work coauthored with Harold Bowen, *Islamic Society and the West*, transmitted eighteenth- and nineteenth-century Ottoman reform discourses to Americans concerned with securing their interests in the twentieth-century Middle East.[27] Mining Gibb's study and other historical sources, American modernizers struck buried strata of reformist ideas dating from earlier eras. This perspective on modernization theory reveals what Orientalists – who claimed particular knowledge of Islamic civilization through the study of texts – contributed to the postwar construction of universal development models.

To understand how the Ottoman and Kemalist legacies influenced U.S. Middle East policy demands an original analysis encompassing petroleum, historiography, and modernization. Only by combining topics that scholars have previously treated separately is it possible to reconstruct postwar American ideas about the Middle East. In the standard work on post-1945 U.S. diplomacy in the Middle East, Douglas Little's *American Orientalism*, oil and modernization are literally separate chapters in America's encounter with the region.[28] Robert Vitalis' *America's Kingdom* challenges Aramco's modernizing claims, but does so within an American historical context that relates the company's labor policies in Saudi Arabia to African American civil rights and the North American frontier.[29] Scholarship on modernization describes it as the export of American liberalism without analyzing the interface between America's reform experiences and those of other societies.[30] Other development literature focuses narrowly on conflicts between free-market and statist variants within American liberalism, trade-or-aid debates

---

[26] Lockman, *Contending Visions of the Middle East*, 108. See also Said, *Orientalism*, 53, 105.

[27] H.A.R. Gibb and Harold Bowen, *Islamic Society and the West: A Study of the Impact of Western Civilization on Moslem Culture in the Near East* (London: Oxford University Press, 1950, 1957).

[28] Little, *American Orientalism*.

[29] Vitalis, *America's Kingdom*, 31–61.

[30] See Gilman, *Mandarins of the Future*; David Engerman et al., eds., *Staging Growth: Modernization, Development, and the Global Cold War* (Amherst: University of Massachusetts Press, 2003); and Michael Latham, *The Right Kind of Revolution: Modernization, Development, and U.S. Foreign Policy from the Cold War to the Present* (Ithaca, NY: Cornell University Press, 2011).

that correspond to the parsing of public–private relations featured in studies of oil diplomacy.[31]

These approaches cannot account for the contingent manner in which reformers constructed their agendas, the diverse elements they combined into seemingly unified visions, and their need to render a complex history into the prologue for their efforts. Postwar expertise blurred the distinctions separating capitalist, strategic, and scholarly interest in the Middle East. DeGolyer, Ball, McGhee, and Duce all articulated their designs on the region's petroleum using the language of historical progress, a strategy long practiced by their industry.[32] Gibb not only shared a platform with DeGolyer at the 1950 conference, but would also benefit from Duce's support for Harvard's Center for Middle Eastern Studies. "Although the University has provided most financial support for the Center," explained the *Crimson*, "American business interests – especially the oil companies – have helped substantially."[33] The Rockefeller Foundation was another major funder of Gibb's Center at Harvard, while Gibb advised the Foundation on grants supporting research on Arab modernization and the Ottoman legacy.[34] The British Orientalist would also participate in a Council on Foreign Relations study group on modern Islam that brought together diplomats and oilmen including Duce.[35] Gibb, meanwhile, became the leading guide to the Ottoman past for scholars who pioneered the study of modernization as a process of behavioral change. Their Cold War formula associating modernization with anticommunist, authoritarian leaders would function as a useful alternative to development agendas based on redistributing oil wealth. Bringing this history to the surface involves reconstructing the relationships among individuals concerned with development and oil interests in the Middle East. Uncovering the sources of their historical knowledge reveals the debt the ideas of Cold War development owed to the

[31] See Burton I. Kaufman, *Trade and Aid: Eisenhower's Foreign Economic Policy, 1953–1961* (Baltimore, MD: Johns Hopkins University Press, 1982); and Sylvia Maxfield and James H. Nolt, "Protectionism and the Internationalization of Capital: U.S. Sponsorship of Import Substitution Industrialization in the Philippines, Turkey, and Argentina," *International Studies Quarterly* 34 (March 1990): 49–81. On oil diplomacy, see Irvine Anderson, *Aramco, the United States, and Saudi Arabia: A Study of the Dynamics of Foreign Oil Policy, 1933–1950* (Princeton, NJ: Princeton University Press, 1981); and David S. Painter, *Oil and the American Century: The Political Economy of U.S. Foreign Oil Policy, 1941–1954* (Baltimore, MD: Johns Hopkins University Press, 1986).

[32] See Vitalis, *America's Kingdom*, 35.

[33] "Regional Studies: A War Baby Grows Up," Harvard *Crimson*, December 9, 1955, http://www.thecrimson.com/article/1955/12/9/regional-studies-a-war-baby-grows/, accessed September 18, 2015.

[34] See Rockefeller Foundation, *The Rockefeller Foundation Annual Report, 1956* (New York: Rockefeller Foundation, 1956), 55; and Gibb to Marshall, May 14, 1955, September 24, 1954, April 20, 1955, folder 29, box 3, series 485, RG 1.2, RFC, RAC. See also Gibb to Marshall, August 11, 1950 and December 9, 1951, folder 1, box 1, series 804, RFC, RAC.

[35] See Roster for the Discussion Group on the Middle East and Modern Islam (1958–59), and transcript of first meeting led by Gibb, November 5, 1958, folder 1, box 166, Records of Groups, 1918–1994, Series 3, CFR.

legacy of Ottoman reform. Through an indirect comparison between Ottoman and American elites, this discussion illuminates how reformers selectively consult the past to construct their historical rationalizations. Like the *bricoleur* French anthropologist Claude Lévi-Strauss described,

the reformer's first practical step is retrospective. He has to turn back to an already existent set made up of tools and materials, to consider or reconsider what it contains and, finally and above all, to engage in a sort of dialogue with it, and before choosing between them, to index the possible answers which the whole set can offer to his problem.[36]

In debates about modernizing the Middle East, Americans assembled the historical raw materials at hand that they thought most helpful for defending regional interests, rearranging them as circumstances changed. Yet some of those same materials were themselves artifacts of *bricolage* fashioned to justify older imperial reforms. Ottoman bureaucrats and intellectuals had similarly validated their own reform policies using inherited descriptions of imperial decline. Their texts, written a century or more before the Cold War, served as the basis for accounts by Gibb and other scholars from whom social scientists received their understandings of Ottoman "tradition." In an unintended consequence of postwar interdisciplinary collaboration between historians and social scientists on the problem of modernization, Orientalist scholarship by Gibb and others bridged previous regional reform movements with American policies toward the postcolonial Middle East. Cold War modernizers may have criticized the Ottomans, but American uses of the past were based on adopting the declinist narrative about the empire's institutions and paternalism toward its Arab periphery that had legitimized earlier imperial reforms. This argument therefore challenges the conventional boundaries found in accounts of modernizing the region, the most significant being the one that Orientalists such as Gibb drew between Islamic society and the West.

Aramco used claims that its investments would develop the Middle East economically in domestic political battles. These included disputes over pricing oil in ERP transactions and in sales to the U.S. Navy.[37] They also included securing export licenses for the enormous amounts of steel pipe needed by a spinoff company to construct the 1,100-mile Trans-Arabian pipeline (Tapline) from eastern Arabia to the Mediterranean. Duce boasted that Tapline would be "'a little Marshall Plan' for the Middle East" to deflect opposition from domestic oil producers concerned about competing with imported oil.[38] With Ball's assistance, Duce won the licenses, while Ball

---

36 Claude Lévi-Strauss, *The Savage Mind* (Chicago: University of Chicago Press, 1962), 18.
37 See "Arab Oil Royalty Stirs Senate Group," November 1, 1947, *NYT*, p. 2.
38 Quoted in Anderson, *Aramco, the United States, and Saudi Arabia*, 177. See "Oil Industry Expects 'Very Peaceful' World, Official Declares at Pipe Export Hearing," October 18, 1947, *NYT*, p. 22.

and Levy helped major companies to gain the upper hand in the ERP pricing controversy.[39] When President Truman, in his 1949 inaugural address, proposed offering technical assistance to developing countries, a policy subsequently known as Point Four, Duce took full advantage of the political cover it provided to Aramco. In a lavishly illustrated, seventeen-page spread published in the March 28, 1949, issue of *Life*, Aramco was portrayed as "a prototype of the kind of thing President Truman had in mind." Company executives "have tried to avoid the odium of old-style colonialism," the article gushed in language similar to that used by DeGolyer, and Aramco consequently "drills water wells for its Arabs, promotes irrigation projects, gives free medical care ... [and] provides new housing and schools."[40] The article conveyed the same message about Aramco's modernizing mission that Duce promoted relentlessly. According to William A. Eddy, the first American minister to Saudi Arabia who joined the CIA and consulted for Aramco, Duce "is very demanding" and "wants an audience every minute," often for evening screenings of his "film on irrigation, etc."[41] In a speech he shared with DeGolyer, Duce told a San Francisco audience that as a result of Aramco's investment:

the basic wage ... has multiplied ten times – hospitals have been constructed – twenty-thousand people find employment, new and sanitary towns have sprung up, railroads and ports have been built, the burdens of government financing have been eased and this year the government of the desert Kingdom of Saudi Arabia relieved the pilgrim to Mecca of the dues which they have paid from time immemorial. Further, thousands of men have been instructed in all sorts of trades and arts and have taken those skills into the remote parts of King Ibn Saud's desert kingdom – and the process has just begun.... The world must be supplied with oil – we must compete with other sources of energy and it must be done on a world scale. We must find the brains, the capital, the courage and the men to carry the work on. We must tame the jungle and the desert. This is Point IV at work – this is the way toward peace.[42]

Such claims gained Duce traction in political conflicts at home but undermined the bargaining position of Aramco and other companies as they struggled to fend off demands by producing governments for an ever-increasing share of company profits.

In 1950, McGhee cabled DeGolyer inviting his father-in-law to a September 11 meeting at the State Department, where oil company executives

---

[39] See entry for October 1, 1947, folder: Diary, Sept. 18–Dec. 31, 1947, box 1; and November 2, 1949, folder: Diary, 1949, box 2, MBP.

[40] "Aramco: An Arabian-American Partnership Develops Desert Oil and Places U.S. Influence and Power in the Middle East," *Life* (March 28, 1949): 62, 66. See also Vitalis, *America's Kingdom*, 103.

[41] William A. Eddy to Mary Eddy, August 16, 1951, folder 4, box 6, WEP.

[42] Text of speech by Duce, September 25, 1952, folder 360, box 4, EDP. See also text of speech by Duce, January 13, 1953, folder: "Duce, James Terry, 1946–60," box 13, CHMP.

assembled to discuss growing demands from producing countries.[43] The group, which also included Duce and Socony-Vacuum Director Charles Harding, considered how companies could prevent further government demands following the recent fifty–fifty profit-sharing agreement concluded in Venezuela. Those present agreed on the importance of public relations to reach "the coffee house crowd," but even Duce acknowledged the limits of this approach. "Aramco was finding itself hamstrung in its operations," Duce explained, "by an accumulation of small S[audi] A[rabian] G[overnment] moves to obtain money," which might make it "preferable to reconsider the financial terms of the contract." Indeed, "Aramco found itself building roads, railroads, [and] port facilities for the government," but "the Saudi Government was demanding that these facilities be built in addition to royalty payments." McGhee inquired whether the "sanctity of contracts could not better be maintained if financial aspects could be separated from the rest of the agreement." Companies did combat such challenges at the margins by maintaining control over oil pricing and how royalties were paid. Ball and Levy had been hired by the companies to adjudicate pricing issues in Venezuela, and DeGolyer & MacNaughton would play a similar role in Saudi Arabia in the wake of Aramco's acceptance of the fifty–fifty principle. Aramco did so at little cost because the Treasury Department permitted the company to count royalties paid to Saudi Arabia against its tax liability in the United States. The United Kingdom did not grant this privilege to the Anglo-Iranian Oil Company (AIOC), however, and that company refused to adopt fifty–fifty in Iran until it was too late. Although DeGolyer insisted that AIOC could afford to compromise given its 6¢ per barrel production costs, its clash with the Iranian government suggested to the assembled oilmen that fifty–fifty was only the beginning of governments' demands.[44]

After the Iranian *majlis* passed a measure to nationalize AIOC and nationalist leader Muhammad Musaddiq became prime minister in April 1951, McGhee reassured Duce and other oilmen that the State Department was determined "to keep Iran on the side of the West, to maintain the flow of oil, and to protect concession rights in Iran and other parts of the world."[45] When Musaddiq came to the United States to address the United Nations, the McGhees hosted him at their Virginia farm in an attempt to broker a compromise.[46] Levy, meanwhile, went to Tehran to give Iranian officials

43 McGhee to DeGolyer, September 6, 1950, folder 3682, box 61, EDP.

44 Funkhouser to McGhee, September 18, 1950, folder: Petroleum, box 18, Records of the Bureau of Near Eastern, South Asian, and African Affairs, Office Files of Assistant Secretary of State George C. McGhee, 1945–1953, Lot 53 D 468, RG 59, NARA. On Ball and Levy in Venezuela, see entries for November 4, 1949, folder: Diary, 1949; and for April 19, 1950, folder: Diary, 1950, box 2, MBP. On DeGolyer & MacNaughton in Saudi Arabia, see memo of conversation by Sturgill, June 20, 1952, *FRUS, 1952–1954*, vol. 9: 603–04.

45 Memo of conversation by Funkhouser, May 14, 1951, *FRUS, 1951*, vol. 5: 309.

46 See McGhee, *Envoy to the Middle World*, 391–92.

"their first frank detailed education on the technical aspects of how the worldwide oil business was conducted."[47] For the time being, AIOC's difficulties appeared to work to Aramco's advantage. McGhee told the House of Representatives Foreign Affairs Committee that Aramco had "precluded nationalization" in Saudi Arabia by adopting fifty–fifty, unlike AIOC, which "appeared to have been behind the game."[48] The crisis aided Duce's fight against Federal Trade Commission accusations that major oil companies had violated antitrust laws in pricing and other areas of their operations. Duce prepared Interior Secretary Oscar Chapman to put the companies' case before Truman's National Security Council, and Chapman successfully argued that the explosive charges might encourage nationalizations elsewhere and "cost us our concessions."[49] The final report by the Interior, State, and Defense Departments recommending dismissal of criminal antitrust charges echoed Duce's argument that oil company investments advanced "economic development in the backward areas."[50] But while such claims had demonstrated a political value at home, as even Duce recognized, they fueled the demands that companies were facing abroad. As is well documented, the AIOC crisis culminated in August 1953 with a CIA coup against Musaddiq that was led by Kermit "Kim" Roosevelt and that paved the way for a new U.S.-dominated oil consortium in Iran.[51]

It was against this background that Max Ball undertook the rewriting of Turkey's extractive law to protect companies investing there from government demands. Even before Ball's mission to Turkey, U.S. oilmen and officials had defined its historical significance. The problem, from their perspective, was that under Atatürk the state had played a central role in the economy, one that extended to the ownership of mineral wealth. Max Weston Thornburg (1892–1962), a former California Standard and Bahrain Oil Company executive, wrote an economic survey of the republic that the Twentieth-Century Fund had commissioned before Turkey's receipt of

[47] Harriman to State, July 17, 1951, *FRUS, 1952–1954*, vol. 10: 93.

[48] U.S. Congress, House Committee on Foreign Affairs, *Selected Executive Session Hearings of the Committee, 1951–56*, vol. 16: *The Middle East, Africa, and Inter-American Affairs* (Washington, DC: Government Printing Office, 1980), 30, 62.

[49] Memo of discussion at the 127th Meeting of the National Security Council, December 17, 1952, *FRUS, 1952–1954*, vol. 1: 1299. See Duce to Chapman with attachments, October 23, 1952, Folder: Correspondence, Nov. 1949–Jan. 1953, DR to DY, box 44, Oscar L. Chapman Papers, HSTL. Thanks to Erica Flanagan for finding the latter source.

[50] Reprinted in Burton I. Kaufman, *The Oil Cartel Case: A Documentary Study of Antitrust Activity in the Cold War Era* (Westport, CT: Greenwood Press, 1978), 149.

[51] See James F. Goode, *The United States and Iran: In the Shadow of Musaddiq* (New York: St. Martin's Press, 1997); Mary Ann Heiss, *Empire and Nationhood: The United States, Great Britain, and Iranian Oil, 1950–1954* (New York: Columbia University Press, 1997); and Mark J. Gasiorowski, *U.S. Foreign Policy and the Shah: Building a Client State in Iran* (Ithaca, NY: Cornell University Press, 1991).

aid under the Truman Doctrine.[52] According to Thornburg, "underground deposits are the property of the state" and royalties were required "in advance of development" from concessionaires limited to two-year leases. "If the Turks had designed a system to prevent private mineral development, whether foreign or domestic," he declared, "they could scarcely have done better."[53] Even worse, Turkey had accepted aid and technical assistance from the Soviet Union during the 1930s and developed a five-year economic plan modeled on Moscow's. Making Turkey into a favorable place to invest therefore required reconciling the Kemalist legacy with Americans' Cold War purposes in the Middle East.

Thornburg participated in a discussion group on the Near and Middle East (1947–48) at the Council on Foreign Relations, which became one of the main venues where oilmen, scholars, and diplomats sought to place American regional interests into a useful historical context. Chairing the group was Goldthwaite H. Dorr, a New York attorney who had supervised a previous economic survey of Turkey in 1934.[54] Members also included Eddy, Charles Harding of Socony-Vacuum, as well as Walter Livingston Wright Jr., a Princeton University professor of Turkish history and the former president of Robert College in Istanbul. Wright published the sense of the group in a *Foreign Affairs* article titled "Truths about Turkey," which argued that the United States could build on the reforms of the Kemalist period. "The United States is not dealing with the Turkish Empire," he emphasized, "but with a Turkey ... which has changed more than any other country in the world." These changes were the singular achievements of Atatürk, "a man of extraordinary acuteness, vigor, and ambition." Such admiration required a historical sleight-of-hand by which Wright sequestered Kemalist economic policies and relegated them decisively to the past. He argued that "suspicion of foreigners and foreign enterprises" might have been "justified a generation ago," but "the foreign capital and skill desperately needed for the development of the country will surely not be forthcoming unless the existing excessive regimentation and taxation of foreign activities are relaxed." The "Turkish Republic's credits far outweigh its debits," Wright concluded, reckoning its historical progress. It has "moved an almost incredible distance along the road from the Ottoman Middle Ages toward western democracy."[55]

---

[52] See Linda Wills Qaim-Maqami, "Max Thornburg and the Quest for a Corporate Foreign Oil Policy: An Experiment in Cooperation," PhD diss., Texas A&M University, 1986.

[53] Max Weston Thornburg et al., *Turkey: An Economic Appraisal* (New York: Greenwood Press, [1949] 1968), 92–93.

[54] See Roger R. Trask, "The United States and Turkish Nationalism: Investments and Technical Aid during the Atatürk Era," *Business History Review* 38 (Spring 1964): 73. See also folder 5, box 140, CFR.

[55] Walter Livingston Wright, "Truths about Turkey," *Foreign Affairs* 26 (January 1948): 349–59. On Turks' mistrust of foreign economic investment in light of the Ottoman past, see Department of State Policy Statement, "Turkey," May 5, 1949, *FRUS, 1949*, vol. 6: 1664.

Thornburg drew on Wright's account but defined business opportunities in Turkey prior to Ball's mission through a highly selective account of
Ottoman-Turkish history. Like McGhee, Thornburg used Istanbul to symbolize the half-finished work of Turkish modernization, whose completion
awaited outside help:

The traveler arriving at one of the few important ports like Istanbul (Constantinople)
will, to be sure, see minarets and mosques – but below them are the glistening new
buildings; modern architecture jostles the heavy stone of ancient fortifications. He
will find factories, power plants, railway stations, department stores, night clubs and
restaurants, beauty parlors, universities, bookshops, theaters. He will also come to
narrow streets lined with ancient bazaars where the innumerable products of immemorial handicrafts are offered for sale. American motor cars dash by villagers on
donkeys; a young Turkish girl who in dress and carriage would not be noticeable on
Fifth Avenue strides along past an old woman in baggy trousers, with a veil below
her eyes.

"The impression one carries away from Turkey is that of a thin layer of
modernity," Thornburg wrote, "imported from abroad and imposed from
above, with great will and vigor, upon a population the larger part of which
is still steeped in medieval or even ancient ways of life." The old capital
hearkened back to the Ottoman Empire, which since its zenith in the time
of sixteenth-century sultan Süleyman the Magnificent, had decayed until it
was "incapable of developing the resources of lands or people." Thornburg
also praised Atatürk, who "pulled the throttle wide open after the Republic
was founded in 1923" and "unloosed regenerative forces," yet his statist
economic policies "began more and more sharply to define two Turkeys –
the Turkey of the jet plane, and the Turkey of the oxcart." Indeed, such policies prevented Atatürk from fully transcending "the long years of Ottoman
oppression." At the same time, Thornburg defended Atatürk from charges
that he was a communist or fellow-traveler. The misguided acceptance of
Soviet help in formulating the first five-year plan "did not mean that the
Turks were converted to Bolshevism," but stemmed from an "impatience for
rapid industrialization." In fact, Atatürk's revolution "was an effort to save a
people and to *create* a nation as an instrument for doing so, since the Empire
of the Sultans had never absorbed the spirit of nationalism characteristic of
western Europe." Despite their limitations, Atatürk's achievements indicated
Turkey's potential to serve as a model for other countries in the region. "No
other Middle Eastern people," Thornburg declared, echoing Wright, "has
accomplished so much so rapidly as the Turks since their Revolution."[56]

Ball's economic reform of the Kemalist state likewise went hand in
hand with the idolization of Atatürk in the hope that Turkey's economic
liberalization could set an example for Arab countries. Duce supported

[56] Thornburg, *Turkey: An Economic Appraisal*, vii, 3, 4, 12, 14, 19, 27, 35. See also Max
Weston Thornburg, "Turkey: Aid for What?" *Fortune* 37 (October 1947): 106–07, 171–72.

Ball's consulting work for Israel, but fear of an Arab boycott prevented Aramco and the oil majors from investing there. "Terry says that as things stand now," Ball wrote in an August 1949 diary entry, "they would not dare build a line across Israel."[57] Turkey, by contrast, offered oil companies a reprieve from the Arab–Israeli conflict, as well as an opportunity to apply lessons learned from the AIOC nationalization and demands made by Saudi Arabia and other Arab oil producers. As ambassador to Ankara, McGhee identified precisely what the international companies required of the Turkish government: repeal of law 2804, enacted on June 14, 1934, which transferred all mineral rights to the Minerals Research and Development Institute, known by its Turkish acronym MTA [*Maaden Tadkik va Arama Istituti*].[58] Turkey had been in negotiations with DeGolyer & MacNaughton, but DeGolyer withdrew when his son-in-law's appointment as ambassador created a conflict of interest.[59] Ball was among the legal consultants recommended by the U.S. government and had demonstrated his usefulness in Israel, though Turkish prime minister Adnan Menderes complained to McGhee that "Mr. Ball had been very expensive."[60] Menderes told Ball that Turkey needed a domestic source of oil to preserve its foreign exchange and "would pass whatever law is necessary to bring about private exploration and development."[61] As Ball went to work drafting a new extractive law, ensuring companies favorable tax policies including the duty-free import of equipment and reorganizing MTA with help from the UN Technical Assistance Program, he asked his Turkish colleagues for a "small picture of Ataturk." He explained that he wanted "to have in my office small pictures of four modern founders of new countries: Washington, Bolivar, Weizman [*sic*], and Ataturk." Ball's Turkish hosts were happy to oblige. MTA director general Emin Iplikci, Ball wrote, even "inscribed it for me at my request."[62]

Though ostensibly employed by the Turkish government, Ball consulted closely with McGhee and with representatives from Jersey Standard, Socony-Vacuum, Caltex, Gulf, and other oil companies in drafting the law.[63] Thornburg, "keeping his activities very much sub rosa," chased down investment opportunities while Ball was still working in Turkey, and Levy was

57 Entry for August 4, 1949, folder: Diary, 1949, box 2, MBP.

58 McGhee to State, May 31, 1952, *FRUS, 1952–1954*, vol. 8: 892.

59 See DeGolyer to Ball, December 18, 1952, folder 81, box 1, EDP. On Ball's selection, see memo of conversation, March 26, 1953, folder: Memoranda of Conversations, 1950–1953, 1953, January–June, box 1 George C. McGhee Papers, HSTL.

60 Memo of conversation by McGhee, May 2, 1953, *FRUS 1952–1954*, 8: 924. See also McGhee, *The US-Turkish-NATO Middle East Connection*, 113.

61 Entry for May 14, 1953, folder: January 1–June 30, 1953, box 3, MBP.

62 Entries for May 22 and 29, 1953, folder: January 1–June 30, 1953, box 3, MBP.

63 See diary entries for June 15–16, October 16, 1953, folder: Diary, July 1–December 31, 1953; and January 14, February 3, March 9, 23, 31, 1954, folder: Diary, January 1–September 2, 1954, box 4, MBP.

"highly complimentary" about Ball's extractive law.[64] It was just the sort
of "mining law operating automatically and without favor" that DeGolyer
had argued should replace the "special, tailor-made contract" between governments and companies.[65] Jersey Standard lawyer Woodfin L. Butte proclaimed that "if the Turks pass it in substantially its present form, it will
be a model petroleum law for the world."[66] The Republican People's Party,
founded by Atatürk but now in opposition, vilified Ball and Menderes over
article 136 of the draft law, which prohibited the government from altering
the terms of any oil concession for fifty years.[67] The Turkish press attacked
Ball personally, but Menderes' government was confident enough in the passage of the new law by the Grand National Assembly that it encouraged Ball
to return to Turkey on the eve of the vote.[68]

In the United States, Ball campaigned to make Turkey into the oil companies' favorite country just as President Dwight D. Eisenhower identified
the Turkish republic as the key to Middle East regional defense. Having
sent troops to Korea and joined NATO, Turkey served as the basis for
the "northern-tier" strategy, which the administration developed because
Egypt and some other Arab states remained preoccupied with Israel and
European colonialism, making them unreliable Cold War allies. When
Eisenhower's secretary of state, John Foster Dulles, stopped in Ankara as
part of a regional tour, Turkish president Celal Bayar bargained for military
aid by arguing that "Turks had lived as neighbors with Russia for many
centuries, during which time they had fought many bloody wars." While
Arab states put forward "'puerile'" arguments opposing Western defense
schemes, Bayar explained, the Cold War was nothing new for Turkey
because "Russian policy has always played an important part in Turkish
history." Dulles told the National Security Council a few days later that the
Free Officers who had seized power in Egypt "were too ignorant and too
lacking in experience to grasp the stake of the free world in the security
of the Suez base." The secretary had shared with Bayar his hope that the
"Arabs can gradually be brought into an association with you and with
us." Acknowledging the implications of the Ottoman past for U.S. strategic
plans, however, Dulles informed the Council that "Turkey was still greatly
feared by the Arab countries which she had once controlled."[69] Eager to

---

[64] Entries for December 2, 1953, folder: Diary, July 1–December 31, 1953; and May 12, 1954,
folder: Diary, January 1–September 2, 1954, box 4, MBP.

[65] DeGolyer to Eakens, August 29, 1947, folder 3682, box 61, EDP.

[66] Entry for October 17, 1953, folder: Diary, July 1–December 31, 1953, box 4, MBP.

[67] See "Ankara to Revise Draft of Oil Law," February 15, 1954, *NYT*, p. 6.

[68] See "Anti-American Feeling in Turkey Fomented by Opposition to Bayar," February 10,
1954, *NYT*, p. 7; and entry for February 12, 1954, folder: Diary, January 1–September 2,
1954, box 4, MBP.

[69] Memo of conversation by McGhee, May 26, 1953, *FRUS 1952–1954*, 9: 150, 151, 153;
Transcript of the 147th Meeting of the National Security Council, June 1, 1953, box 4, NSC

promote oil investment in Turkey, Ball sought to capitalize on Bayar's trip to the United States for a summit with Eisenhower. At a reception held by the Turkish-American Society on February 1, 1954, at the Waldorf Astoria Hotel in New York, the oil executives whom Ball had invited greeted Bayar and the U.S. vice president, Richard Nixon. "Going through the reception line," Ball ran into the society's president, McGhee, who wanted to meet with Ball back in Washington. Bayar "patted my hand and said something fatherly," Ball wrote, "but no one was nearby to interpret."[70] Turkey's Grand National Assembly passed Ball's extractive law on March 7, with article 136 amended only slightly to reduce concessions from fifty to forty years.[71] Ball died suddenly on August 28, however, without having completed his work of making Turkey into the model for government–oil company relations. In his final recorded words, he "bemoaned the plight of the 'poor Turks.' "[72]

Just prior to Ball's death, McGhee published "Turkey Joins the West," a *Foreign Affairs* article offering what amounted to the official U.S. version of Ottoman-Turkish history.[73] That narrative, which emerged from three Council on Foreign Relations study groups on the Middle East (1947–48), the Muslim world (1948–49), and American policy in the Middle East (1951–52), placed Ottoman and Kemalist reforms in a linear relationship with U.S. Cold War diplomacy. Herbert J. Liebesny, a scholar employed by the American Independent Oil Company, had explained the shortcomings of Ottoman legal reforms to the Council and described Atatürk's Westernization of Turkey's law codes as correcting their deficiencies.[74] It was oil economist Walter Levy who put his finger on Atatürk's Cold War significance by asking "what factors caused Ataturk to be a benevolent dictator and whether we could duplicate [them] elsewhere." Princeton professor Lewis V. Thomas replied that the Kemalist reforms had "been agreed upon by the upper class" in Atatürk's infancy, "i.e., the work of the 'Young Turks,' " who authored the final phase of imperial reform.[75] Atatürk did not represent a complete break

---

Series, Dwight D. Eisenhower, Papers as President of the United States, 1953–61, DDEL. See also Little, *American Orientalism*, 127–29.

[70] Entry for February 1, 1954, folder: Diary, January 1–September 2, 1954, box 4, MBP.

[71] See "Turkey Opened to Search for Oil; Foreign Concerns Get Incentives," March 8, 1954, *NYT*, pp. 1, 3.

[72] See addendum to diary, August 28, 1954, folder: Diary, January 1–September 2, 1954, box 4, MBP.

[73] George C. McGhee, "Turkey Joins the West," *Foreign Affairs* 32 (July 1954): 617–30.

[74] See transcript of Second Meeting of Discussion Group on the Moslem World, January 24, 1949, pp. 3–6, folder 6, box 141, CFR. See also *Law in the Middle East*, vol. 1, *Origin and Development of Islamic Law*, ed. Majid Khadduri and Herbert J. Liebesny (Washington, DC: Middle East Institute, 1955), in which H.A.R. Gibb authored the opening chapter, "Constitutional Organization," pp. 3–27. The Rockefeller Foundation subsidized the volume's publication. See D'Arms to Keiser, April 10, 1953, folder 5305, box 617, series 200, RG 1.2, RFC, RAC.

[75] See transcript of Fourth Meeting of the Group on American Policy in the Middle East, March 3, 1952, p. 11, folder 4, box 148, CFR.

with the past. He too was an inheritor, and not the progenitor, of Turkey's pro-Western development.

Turkey's adherence to NATO and participation in northern-tier defense, McGhee argued, reflected a "remarkable similarity in national aims and policies" to those of the United States, making Turkey "one of our most reliable partners." This alliance was "the result of a meeting of two historical trends," the first of which was America's realization of the Russian danger to which Turks had been alive by virtue of their imperial past and the thirteen wars fought with Russia since 1677. Second, "the Turkish people, freed from the rule of the Sultans and the burdens of empire to concentrate on their adopted homeland of Asia Minor" have "entered the full stream of Western progress in the development of their natural resources and their democratic institutions." McGhee credited Atatürk, "one of the great leaders of all times," with creating the "new Turkey," but located him historically in the middle of Turks' centuries-long journey toward the West. While "it was Atatürk who was primarily responsible for the decisive turn to the West," McGhee wrote, "the seeds of Western thought and influence were actually planted much earlier." Western contacts began during the sixteenth-century reign of Süleyman, but Westernization gained momentum only as the result of the eighteenth- and nineteenth-century military reforms of Selim III and Mahmud II, the mid-nineteenth-century *Tanzimat* reforms introduced by Western-educated bureaucrats, and those of the Young Turks who were Mustafa Kemal's forerunners. Indeed, the Ottoman legacy lived on in the person of foreign minister and historian Fuad Köprülü, whose ancestors had "saved the Ottoman Empire in the seventeenth century" and who currently oversaw Turkey's participation in Cold War regional defense.

McGhee presented Atatürk's half-achieved revolution as finally on the verge of fulfillment. That Atatürk's Republican People's Party "acquiesced gracefully" after losing an election in 1950 "proved that Turkey had become a democracy in practice as well as in form." The dismantling of *étatism*, whose "limitations" had become "increasingly apparent," was being accomplished by new legislation including the extractive law. Drafted "with the assistance of an American expert, Mr. Max Ball," the law "compares favorably with the laws of other countries, such as Venezuela and Saudi Arabia." Since the liberalization of its economic policies, "the Turks have seen their faith in the free play of economic forces indicated by remarkable progress." McGhee used the Ottoman-Turkish past to construct a historical rationale for U.S. Cold War policy in the Middle East, one that encompassed regional defense, economic reforms, and, last, democratization. Like Thornburg, McGhee the oil geologist zeroed in on Turkey's extractive law (without divulging his personal role in helping Ball to rewrite it). McGhee's account uncoupled national development from resources, however, emphasizing instead the transformative role of Atatürk's leadership and that of the

Westernizing elites who preceded him. He did not try to assert, as Duce did in Aramco's public relations, that investments made for the limited purpose of extracting oil could by themselves modernize the region. On a grander historical scale, McGhee portrayed the dawn of American power in the Middle East as the culmination of a process of Westernization encompassing Atatürk's revolution but dating to Ottoman times.

Shortly after publishing his article, McGhee, along with Duce and Levy, participated in a Council on Foreign Relations study group (1954–55) that delved more deeply into historical and economic aspects of Middle East defense. The group brought together military, oil industry, and academic elites such as General Norman Schwarzkopf and Near East Foundation president, John Badeau. It also included former Office of Strategic Services analysts T. Cuyler Young, a Princeton University Persianist, and Jacob Coleman (J. C.) Hurewitz of Columbia University. The group's research secretary, whose personal fascination with Ottoman-Turkish history set its agenda, was German-born political scientist Dankwart A. Rustow.[76] The son of a political refugee from Nazi Germany, Rustow was educated in the former Ottoman capital, where his father taught at the University of Istanbul. Rustow attributed his father's move to "Atatürk's plans for rapid Westernization," which involved reforming the Ottoman *Darülfünun* into the modern university where Rustow's father was among the "thirty-odd German refugee professors who became the founders." Rustow learned Turkish auditing university courses and went on to study Turkish literature at the Galatasaray Lycée, where Ottoman educational reformers had introduced French instruction during the *Tanzimat* era three-quarters of a century earlier. He studied Ottoman Turkish script at the Academy of Fine Arts with the sultan's former calligrapher Beşiktaşlı Hacı Nuri, and his baccalaureate exam was proctored by Turkish novelist and feminist Halide Edib. After doctoral work at Yale, Rustow taught at Princeton, which was developing its Near East studies program. While Rustow was overseeing the Council group on Middle East defense, Cuyler Young recruited him for the Near and Middle East Committee cosponsored by the Social Science Research Council and the American Council of Learned Societies (SSRC-ACLS). Among those with whom Rustow worked closely on the new committee was Gibb.[77]

In a working paper produced for the Council, Rustow contrasted Turkey's anticommunist modernity with the Arab states' backwardness and

---

[76] See Roster, Study Group on the Defense of the Middle East (1954–55), folder 5, box 157, CFR.

[77] See *Paths to the Middle East: Ten Scholars Look Back*, ed. Thomas Naff (Albany: State University Press of New York, 1993), 263, 264, 267, 269, 272–73, 278. On Edib, see Carter Vaughn Findley, *Turkey, Islam, Nationalism, and Modernity* (New Haven, CT: Yale University Press, 2010), 239–44.

unwillingness to confront Soviet Russia.[78] His analysis closely paralleled the arguments Bayar had made to Dulles. "For years," Rustow declared,

no amount of Western insistence, reasoning, coaxing, and cajoling could move the Arab countries to a frank recognition of the Russian danger; the Turks, by contrast, took pride in having opposed that threat at a time when official Western diplomacy was still pursuing the will-o'-the-wisp of Big Three Unity.

The reason was that from "the sixteenth century until the First World War Turkey and Russia never were at peace for more than a few decades at a time." Turkish parents' warning, the "Moskofs will get you," was still the "scare that shushes the toddler." Turkey's modernity was mainly the product of Atatürk's Westernizing program in which the "hat revolution" in favor of European headgear, the adoption of the Latin alphabet, and Western cultural styles were meant to overcome "memories of a degrading and 'backward' Ottoman past." But Atatürk was heir to a "century of Ottoman efforts to adopt Western military technique and limited aspects of the West's legal and education system." Though Ottoman reforms ultimately failed, the "patient survived" as the result of a necessary but "painful dismemberment." Atatürk may have pursued "'wholesale, force-draft, compulsory Westernization,'" but his party "wasn't doctrinaire," and so there was "no basis for ideological purges, no thought of concentration camps." Rustow criticized Atatürk's quest for autarchy and Soviet dalliance, however understandable given the empire's experience with European extraterritorial rights. He also portrayed Atatürk's National Historical Thesis and Sun-Language Theory as "fictitious glories" that placed the Turkish people and language at the center of world history and thereby "facilitated the avid reception of Western cultural patterns." Turkey's transition to multiparty democracy with the election of 1950, "the most remarkable development in the Republic's internal policy," indicated the potential for an authoritarian program of modernization in underdeveloped states to eventually give way to democracy. Describing Turkey as the "Cornerstone of Western Defense in the Near East," Rustow surveyed the region in terms of the former empire, whose Turkish core had modernized and democratized but whose Arab periphery had not.

Writing on "Economic Aspects of Middle East Defense," Rustow explained the reasons for the Arab states' developmental lag. He noted their vast oil wealth, but insisted that Arabs' political and historical deficiencies prevented them from applying it to regional development.[79] Reversing the "military and political decline of the Middle East since the sixteenth

---

[78] Dankwart A. Rustow, "Turkey – Cornerstone of Western Defense in the Near East," December 15, 1954, Working Paper No. 2, Discussion Group on the Defense of the Middle East, folder 5, box 157, CFR.

[79] Dankwart A. Rustow, "Some Economic Aspects of Middle East Defense," March 24, 1955, Working Paper No. 5, Discussion Group on the Defense of the Middle East, folder 6, box 157, CFR.

century" required instead the "constructive adaptation of Western economic techniques and Western patterns of social organization and political solidarity," as Atatürk had shown. The "oil production of the total region," Rustow calculated, "is sufficient to cover its current trade deficits, and royalties (since the recent 50–50 agreements) could supply most or all of the capital needed for economic development." But "the benefits of petroleum accrue almost exclusively to the states surrounding the Persian Gulf," and so any development program would require "intra-regional economic cooperation" of the sort that only "the Arabs' economic boycott of Israel" had managed to inspire. He acknowledged the magnitude of oil company profits, but not the possibility that they siphoned off the region's natural and financial resources. "Returns on oil investments have been high," he admitted, estimating Aramco's net income in 1951 at "$180 million." Echoing Duce, however, Rustow insisted that "American companies have set an example for the whole industry not only by signing generous royalty agreements but also in their policy of training nationals of the host countries." Rustow explained underdevelopment in terms of the "Arabs' fear of foreign entanglements" and "suspicion of 'dollar imperialism,'" which he associated with the "one-sided acts of confiscation" Turkish economic policy had left behind. In the group's subsequent discussions, Duce himself reinforced the argument that "the financial impact" of oil was "less important than the impact western oil companies have had through their introduction of new technology, new methods and new standards." Such transfers of know-how would "speed up the development of these countries," Duce prophesied, giving rise to "a profound renaissance in our time."[80]

The shift toward nonmaterial factors – psychological, behavioral, political – in studying economic development occurred at a time when anxiety about maintaining access to Middle Eastern resources was on the rise among American oilmen and officials. In a letter written to McGhee on September 11, 1956, just after Egyptian president Gamal 'Abd al-Nasser nationalized the Suez Canal, Levy predicted "increasing pressure on the international oil companies not only relating to the profits," but also "to the control over the management of the operations of these companies." If "the impression should spread that a country, through nationalization, could improve its economic conditions or its prestige or its political power," Levy wrote, "then nationalization itself will spread."[81] Soon after, McGhee joined a Council on Foreign Relations study group examining "Human Factors in Economic Development." Its roster included oil executives Duce and Kenneth T. Young of Standard-Vacuum, Turcophile Dankwart Rustow,

---

[80] Transcript of the Fifth Meeting of the Discussion Group on the Defense of the Middle East, March 29, 1955, p. 4, folder 6, box 157, CFR.
[81] Levy to McGhee, September 11, 1956, folder: 1, Correspondence, General, A–N, 1954–1969, box 21, WLP.

and two other social scientists influential in developing the new science of modernization, Marion J. Levy Jr. and Daniel Lerner. In the invitation letter, Princeton economist Gardner Patterson wrote that the group would be "concerned with some of the psychological, social, cultural, and intellectual factors – in shorthand, the 'human factors' – that impede economic development." The group would focus on these factors "to clarify their impact and importance and relate them to the more familiar issues of resources, investment, technical training, and economic expansion." In order to "avoid the pitfalls of undue dispersion of effort, over-generalization or simply confusion from the multiplicity of facts," Gardner explained, "the study will concentrate on Turkey."[82]

McGhee's official history portraying U.S. policy as fulfilling imperial and Kemalist reforms served as the group's point of departure. Yet its deliberations also exposed emerging tensions between a globally oriented, social science approach to modernization and a regional perspective emphasizing the particular value of the Ottoman inheritance. The basis for the group's discussions were papers prepared by economist Edwin J. Cohn, a Columbia PhD who worked in Turkey for the Mutual Security Administration. Cohn praised Turkey's "strenuous efforts to become a strong, modern, national state," attributing these to Atatürk's "unique personal prestige" and "campaign of reform and national regeneration." He distinguished these reforms from the Ottomans' limited military and administrative measures going "back at least as far as the end of the 18th Century." According to Cohn, Ottoman reformers had mistakenly believed "that a modern army could be created and sustained without any corresponding reform in the political, economic, social, and cultural institutions of the Empire." Cohn's structural analysis compared unsuccessful imperial reforms with "recent efforts in underdeveloped countries to borrow industrialization and introduce it without its social and economic context." By contrast, Atatürk sought "a fundamental and far-reaching reshaping of the political and social system," a campaign that helped to "emancipate the Turks from the paralyzing influence of the Ottoman regime."[83] Princeton historian Lewis V. Thomas objected that Cohn had disregarded Atatürk's inheritance of the Ottoman reform legacy. Mustafa Kemal "was a child of his times" influenced by Westernized imperial institutions such as the School of Public Administration – "the Mulkiye" – and the "Ottoman Public Debt Administration."[84] Arabist John Badeau criticized Cohn's attempts to

[82] Letter by Patterson, September 19, 1957, folder 4, box 167, CFR.

[83] Edwin J. Cohn, "Turkish Development: 1922–57," September 16, 1957, folder 4, box 164, CFR. See also Edwin J. Cohn, *Turkish Economic, Social, and Political Change: The Development of a More Prosperous and Open Society* (New York: Praeger, 1970).

[84] Transcript of the First Meeting of the Study Group on Human Factors in Economic Development, October 14, 1957, p. 2, folder 4, box 164, CFR.

generalize from the Turkish case to those of "[u]nderdeveloped countries in general," arguing that "it was necessary to take into account various distinctions between countries" when discussing underdeveloped peoples' alleged incapacity for collective action and contempt for facts and punctuality.[85] As promised, however, the group elevated "human" over material factors, even when the talk turned to oil. Holding forth on how developing peoples acquire the modern habit of experimentation, Duce insisted that "experimentation began in Saudi Arabi[a] when the Americans went there." Aramco "gave them a push in many directions at once."[86]

These discussions addressed not only the significance of the Ottoman legacy in Turkish modernity, but also the degree to which lessons drawn from the Turkish case could be applied to Arab and other formerly Ottoman territories in the Middle East and even globally. In short, they considered whether that legacy made Turkey exceptional or whether, as Walter Levy had wondered about Atatürk's authoritarian approach, "we could duplicate it elsewhere." Interest in Turkey as a model for developing states seeped into Cold War discourse about regions other than the Middle East. Discussing Vietnam, Senator J. William Fulbright told an Eisenhower administration official:

> what you need here is a man comparable, we will say, to Ataturk in Turkey; that you cannot expect this country to respond to democratic ideas, that you have got to have a transitional period here with a real strong leader, and a native leader.[87]

Among intellectuals in the late 1950s and early '60s, Ottoman-Turkish history became the focus of interdisciplinary collaboration between historians who rewrote late Ottoman history and social scientists interested in extrapolating rules governing third world development. Rustow marked up drafts of Bernard Lewis' *The Emergence of Modern Turkey* and then heralded Turkey's example in a Council group on developing countries whose roster included MIT political scientist Lucien Pye.[88] Ottoman studies exerted an important influence on theories that envisioned development as a process of behavioral change compelled by authoritarian leadership. The state of Ottoman historiography in the late 1950s helps to explain just how that

[85] Transcript of the Fourth Meeting of the Study Group on Human Factors in Economic Development, January 15, 1958, p. 1, folder 4, box 164, CFR. See also "Questions Relating to Propositions on Human Factors in Economic Development," October 14, 1957, folder 4, box 164, CFR.

[86] Transcript of the Third Meeting of the Study Group on Human Factors in Economic Development, December 16, 1957, p. 5, folder 4, box 164, CFR.

[87] Quoted in David Schmitz, *Thank God They're on Our Side: The United States and Right-Wing Dictatorships, 1921–1965* (Chapel Hill: University of North Carolina Press, 1999), 201. I am grateful to Guy Laron for this reference.

[88] See Bernard Lewis, *The Emergence of Modern Turkey* (London: Oxford University Press, 1961), ix; and roster, Ad Hoc Group on Diplomacy in the Developing Countries, March 13, 1961, folder 3, box 171, CFR.

scholarship shaped the Cold War modernization literature. At the same moment, a new conflict erupted over the region's oil wealth that made the imperial legacy useful for defending American economic interests.

From Harvard, Gibb presided over the policy and academic branches of U.S. Middle East studies, as indicated by the dinner in his honor to which Duce invited DeGolyer, Gibb's collaboration with Rustow on the SSRC-ACLS committee, and his role at the Council on Foreign Relations. Among those who developed modernization theory, Gibb's reputation rested principally on *Islamic Society and the West*, his study of the eighteenth-century Ottoman empire co-written with Harold Bowen and published in two parts in 1950 and 1957. At the time of its publication, however, their work was already becoming methodologically obsolete. The authors based their Orientalist approach on close readings of Turkish- and Arabic-language texts at a time when scholars such as Lewis were beginning to conduct significant research in the partially opened Ottoman archives.[89] As Gibb and Bowen admitted in the preface to part 2 of their study:

> The opening of the Ottoman archives has in recent years enabled both Turkish scholars and those from other countries to investigate the institutions of the Empire on the basis of exact documentary materials; and it is evident that these newer studies will modify or correct in detail, and possibly even in principle, many of the conclusions which we have reached on the basis of the available secondary materials.[90]

This self-criticism was prescient. Rather than a reliable guide to the Ottoman eighteenth century, later analysts would regard *Islamic Society and the West* as a distillation of the authors' eighteenth- and nineteenth-century sources.[91] Such sources promoted reformist agendas that harmonized readily with American Cold War priorities in the Middle East.

Islamic Society and the West proved appealing to cold warriors because, like them, Ottoman reformers had selected historical materials that validated their own agendas for change. In the Ottoman case, the reformers whose writings Gibb and Bowen cited, such as Mouradgea d'Ohsson (1740–1807), Seyyid Mustafa Nuri Paşa (1824–1890), and Ahmed Cevdet Paşa (1822–1895), could themselves draw upon a venerable literary tradition of writing

---

[89] See Bernard Lewis, *Notes and Documents from the Turkish Archives: A Contribution to the History of the Jews in the Ottoman Empire* (Jerusalem: Israel Oriental Society, 1952); "Studies in the Ottoman Archives – I," *Bulletin of the School of Oriental and African Studies*, vol. 16, no. 3 (1954): 469–501; and *Notes on a Century: Reflections of a Middle East Historian* (New York: Viking, 2012), 88–104.

[90] Gibb and Bowen, *Islamic Society and the West*, part 2, v.

[91] See Roger Owen, "The Middle East in the Eighteenth Century – An 'Islamic' Society in Decline? A Critique of Gibb and Bowen's Islamic Society and the West," *Bulletin (British Society for Middle Eastern Studies)* vol. 3, no. 2 (1976): 110–17; and Suraiya Faroqhi, *Approaching Ottoman History: An Introduction to the Sources* (Cambridge, England: Cambridge University Press, 1999), 177–78.

about imperial decline. According to historian Carter V. Findley, d'Ohsson wrote *Tableau Général de L'empire Othman* partly to secure French support "for what would become the reforms of Selim III's New Order" military.[92] Gibb and Bowen concede that Seyyid Mustafa and Cevdet exhibit a prejudice "in favour of the reforms of the early nineteenth century" while "painting the anterior age in too sombre colours."[93] Cevdet helped to author the mid-nineteenth-century legal reforms of the *Tanzimat* and in his writings sought "its legitimation through historiography."[94] *Islamic Society and the West* reproduces the bias found in its sources. As historian Douglas A. Howard writes, Gibb and Bowen's "analysis of the 'decay of the ruling institution' repeats almost verbatim the interpretations of Ottoman Decline writers of the sixteenth and seventeenth centuries."[95] The pair associated the imperial center's decline with the reassertion of "the violence of factional spirit" among the Arabs, the "senseless and ceaseless tearing of faction against faction ... restrained neither by scruples of religion and humanity nor by consideration of economic and political consequences."[96] It was this version of Ottoman history handed down by Gibb and Bowen that cold warriors found useful. Their account reproduced the temporal and spatial dimensions of Ottoman reform discourses, which Makdisi has characterized in terms of a "temporal subordination in which an advanced imperial center reformed and disciplined backward peripheries of a multi-ethnic and multi-religious empire."[97] Such discourses served the purposes of 1950s cold warriors, who identified modern Turkey as the cornerstone of regional defense and who sought scholarly explanations for Arab backwardness. Rustow used Gibb and Bowen's account of the eighteenth-century Ottoman empire as a guide to understanding the problems of Cold War development.[98] The Istanbul-educated German scholar praised their study as a "comprehensive survey" of the "traditional structure of Near Eastern society before the concentrated impact of the modern West."[99]

---

[92] Carter V. Findley, "Mouradgea D'Ohsson (1740–1807): Liminality and Cosmopolitanism in the Author of the *Tableau Général de L'empire Othman*," *Turkish Studies Association Bulletin* 22 (1998): 34.

[93] Gibb and Bowen, *Islamic Society and the West*, part 1, 16.

[94] Faroqhi, *Approaching Ottoman History*, 157.

[95] Douglas A. Howard, "Ottoman Historiography and the Literature of 'Decline' of the Sixteenth and Seventeenth Centuries," *Journal of Asian History* 22 (1988): 76.

[96] Gibb and Bowen, *Islamic Society and the West*, part 1, 206.

[97] Makdisi, "Ottoman Orientalism," 769.

[98] See Dankwart A. Rustow, "The Army and the Founding of the Turkish Republic," *World Politics* 11 (July 1959): 514n5.

[99] Dankwart A. Rustow, "The Politics of the Near East: Southwest Asia and Northern Africa," in *The Politics of the Developing Areas*, ed. Gabriel Almond and James S. Coleman (Princeton, NJ: Princeton University Press, 1960), 378n8. See also Rustow's review in the *Annals of the American Academy of Political and Social Science* 318 (July 1958): 153–54.

Other social scientists who conceived of modernization as a universal process consulted *Islamic Society and the West* and subsequent histories of Ottoman reform as authorities on what they took to be the preeminent example of that process at work in a non-Western society. Daniel Lerner, along with Harvard scholar Richard Robinson, relied on Gibb and Bowen's account of Ottoman tradition in an article summarizing the work of the Council's "human factors" study group. Lerner and Robinson acknowledged Ottoman influences on Atatürk's reform program and portrayed his authoritarian methods as exemplary:

This is the great lesson which the Turkish Republic has to teach underdeveloped nations of the world. Its past provides a model, and its future a test, for the role of dynamic government in the critical decades of rapid growth that lie ahead – and, perhaps more fundamentally, for the supremacy of civilian authority itself.[100]

Lerner and RAND Corporation social scientist Manfred Halpern, for their respective books on Middle East modernization, each cited Gibb and Bowen on the traditional passivity of the region's peasants.[101] "H.A.R. Gibb and Harold Bowen," Halpern wrote in *Social Change in the Middle East and North Africa*, "have provided indispensable materials for the present analysis."[102] Frederick W. Frey cited *Islamic Society and the West* as an authority on the decline of Ottoman education.[103] In *The Political Systems of Empires*, Israeli sociologist S. N. Eisenstadt made heavy use of *Islamic Society and the West*, identifying the Ottoman Empire as a special case "that, while it disintegrated through secessions and rebellions, later became transformed – at its core – into a more differentiated, modern system."[104] Contributors to *Political Modernization in Japan and Turkey*, coedited by Rustow, not only relied on Gibb and Bowen as authorities on Ottoman-Islamic tradition but also directly quoted *Tanzimat* reformers Ahmed Cevdet Paşa and Midhat Paşa (1822–1884).[105] With the publication of studies on imperial reform in the

---

[100] Daniel Lerner and Richard D. Robinson, "Swords and Ploughshares: The Turkish Army as a Modernizing Force," *World Politics* 13 (October 1960): 44. See their citation of Gibb and Bowen, ibid., 19n2.

[101] Lerner, *The Passing of Traditional Society*, 129; and Manfred Halpern, *The Politics of Social Change in the Middle East and North Africa* (Princeton, NJ: Princeton University Press, 1963), 90n30. See also Daniel Lerner, "Toward a Communication Theory of Modernization: A Set of Considerations," in *Communications and Political Development*, ed. Lucian Pye (Princeton, NJ: Princeton University Press, 1963), 340n8.

[102] Halpern, *Social Change in the Middle East and North Africa*, 17n15.

[103] Frederick W. Frey, *The Turkish Political Elite* (Cambridge, MA: MIT Press, 1965), 32n8.

[104] Shmuel Noah Eisenstadt, *The Political Systems of Empires* (New York: The Free Press of Glencoe, 1963), 347.

[105] *Political Modernization in Japan and Turkey*, 11, 256, 302–05, 357–58, 414–15. On the career of Midhat Paşa, see Ali Haydar Midhat Bey, *The Life of Midhat Pasha: A Record of His Services, Political Reforms, Banishment, and Judicial Murder* (London: John Murray, 1903).

early 1960s, references to authoritarian modernization in Ottoman-Turkish history became *de rigueur* for social scientists. David E. Apter cited Şerif Mardin's study of the Young Turks to show how intellectuals could serve as "critical mediators between traditionality and modernity."[106] Paraphrasing Bernard Lewis, Lerner and political scientist Harold D. Lasswell announced that Turkey had "changed its continental identity" from Asia to Europe. Its history, they exclaimed, demonstrated how societal change could be "engineered by *intellectual* and *official* cadres!"[107]

For cold warriors, the Ottoman-Turkish past appeared to show that Western modernity resulted when authoritarian leadership rooted out traditional behaviors and attitudes. Turkey served as a supposedly successful example of how authoritarianism in a non-Western society could then culminate in democracy. Traces of imperial reform movements contained in the historical literature consumed by social scientists also reinforced a temporal dichotomy between tradition and modernity and the ethno-geographic distinction between modern Turks and backward Arabs. This Ottoman-influenced perspective subsumed a century and a half of history into a coherent process of change. It likewise portrayed Atatürk one-dimensionally and exaggerated the success of his "wholesale" Westernization. As American scholar Philip Hitti quipped to an audience at the American University of Beirut, Atatürk changed Turks' "headwear, but probably not what was under it."[108] More recent scholarship helps to illustrate the congruence between postwar Ottoman-Turkish historiography and American Cold War interests. While Thornburg, McGhee, and Rustow all portrayed Atatürk from the beginning as a secular noncommunist, in his recent biography M. Şükrü Hanioğlu writes that Mustafa Kemal initially followed the examples of both Islamists and Bolsheviks. He therefore "gave the impression of being a Muslim communist" during Turkey's war for independence.[109] Challenges to assumptions about Ottoman decline have also been accompanied by new perspectives on the eighteenth century that portray the imperial elite as the product of households throughout Ottoman lands.[110] Seeing the empire as an incipient Turkish republic, or as having distinct "Turkish" and "Arab" national components, is an anachronism that does violence to historical

---

[106] David E. Apter, *The Politics of Modernization* (Chicago: University of Chicago Press, 1965), 154. See Şerif Mardin, *The Genesis of Young Ottoman Thought: A Study in the Modernization of Turkish Political Ideas* (Princeton, NJ: Princeton University Press, 1962).

[107] "Foreword" by Lerner and Lasswell in Frey, *The Turkish Political Elite*, ix, xi. See Lewis, *The Emergence of Modern Turkey*, 3, 273, 479.

[108] Zeine to Malik, nd [1946], p. 3, folder: Zeine, Zeine, N. 1945–62, 1970, box 52, CHMP.

[109] M. Şükrü Hanioğlu, *Atatürk: An Intellectual Biography* (Princeton, NJ: Princeton University Press, 2011), 105.

[110] See Jane Hathaway, *The Politics of Households in Ottoman Egypt: The Rise of the Qazdağlıs* (New York: Cambridge University Press, 1997).

realities, as Rustow inadvertently acknowledged with his reference to the empire's "painful dismemberment."[111]

Gibb and Bowen bequeathed to Cold War social scientists an authoritative account of tradition against which they could define modernity as a state of mind and set of behaviors. Edwin E. Calverly, reviewing *Islamic Society and the West* in the *American Sociological Review*, commended the study to social scientists for its "special sociological character" and "use of Oriental sources."[112] Cold War scholarship both adopted Ottoman reformers' assumptions and portrayed the United States as completing their unfinished work. Rustow told the Council's group on Diplomacy and the Developing Countries:

Turkey [*sic*] had established school systems in the 1850s. In [the] 1870s these school systems showed no results, but during the past forty years, [they] have shown definite results and have contributed to the stabilization of Turkey. Using this country and experience as an example ... we should not expect immediate results from educational aid.[113]

As Lévi-Strauss wrote of the *bricoleur*, "in the continual reconstruction from the same materials, it is always earlier ends which are called upon to play the part of means."[114] Once justified by imperial statesmen and bureaucrats using declinist accounts they themselves had inherited, Ottoman reforms became part of historical arguments promoting American hegemony over former imperial lands. By insisting that elite leadership had modernized the Ottoman Empire into the Turkish republic, U.S. oilmen and diplomats could more effectively resist development agendas based on sharing oil wealth with the Arab successor states.

In late 1957, just when the Council on Foreign Relations was studying Turkey to promote "human factors" in social change, UN Secretary-General Dag Hammarskjöld launched a major initiative for oil-funded development of the Arab world.[115] Hammarskjöld envisioned an Arab development organization funded through "investment in the Middle East by the oil companies" and "credits made available by the oil producing countries in the area."[116] The plan's features have to be reconstructed mostly from accounts of Hammarskjöld's conversations with British and American officials, because

---

[111] See Hathaway, *The Arab Lands under Ottoman Rule*, 3–4; and Hasan Kayalı, *Arabs and Young Turks: Ottomanism, Arabism, and Islamism in the Ottoman Empire, 1908–1918* (Berkeley: University of California Press, 1997).

[112] *American Sociological Review* 15 (December 1950): 819–20.

[113] Transcript of Third Meeting, Ad Hoc Group on Diplomacy and the Developing Countries, April 10, 1961, folder 3, box 171, CFR.

[114] Lévi-Strauss, *The Savage Mind*, 21.

[115] See Dixon to Foreign Office, December 31, 1957, FO 371/133843, BNA.

[116] Dixon to Foreign Office, January 4, 1958, FO 371/133843, BNA.

the secretary-general hesitated to commit to paper the details of a plan that he knew would be controversial.[117] Hammarskjöld proposed precisely the kind of "intra-regional economic cooperation" among the Arab states that Rustow had derided in his paper on regional defense. Indeed, Hammarskjöld aimed to "bridge the gulf between the 'haves' and the 'have nots' in the Arab world."[118] Moreover, the secretary-general identified "Egypt as the fulcrum of any scheme of inter-Arab economic development."[119] Hammarskjöld's plan thus assumed a material explanation for Arab underdevelopment, which he sought to rectify through the redistribution of oil wealth from the Arab Gulf states to more populous but resource-poor Arab countries. The scheme advanced a rival account of Arab underdevelopment to that of American cold warriors by focusing on present inequalities rather than historical deficiencies. It also challenged their strategy of making Turkey the center of Middle East modernization.

Hammarskjöld's plan clashed with American priorities in the Middle East. Prior to contacting U.S. and British officials, he went to Cairo, where Nasser told the secretary-general that he "had his blessing."[120] Hammarskjöld then tried to sell it to the British, French, and Americans in Cold War terms, arguing that it would "check the present trend" of non-oil Arab states "to side with the Soviet Union" and "take the heat out of Arab nationalism."[121] But the secretary-general made clear that his plan was principally about the redistribution of regional oil wealth, which he believed could help to ameliorate the Arab–Israeli conflict:

The scheme would contribute to a solution of the problem of the Palestine refugees in that development would create a demand for labour and the refugees would thus gradually get resettled without any Arab country incurring the odium of promoting their resettlement.[122]

Although one detractor in the U.S. State Department observed that it was naïve to think "that the Arab refugee problem could be solved by economic development," Hammarskjöld believed that financial incentives could affect political calculations on both sides and expand the possibilities for an Arab–Israeli agreement.[123] Israeli prime minister David Ben-Gurion privately gave Hammarskjöld his support.[124] The UN Secretariat and World Bank would help Arab countries to manage the fund, assuring contributors

---

[117] See editorial note, *FRUS, 1958–1960*, vol. 12: 1; and Hammarskjöld to Lloyd, January 3, 1958, FO 371/133843, BNA.
[118] Dixon to Foreign Office, January 4, 1958, FO 371/133843, BNA.
[119] Dixon to Hayter, December 31, 1957, FO 371/133843, BNA.
[120] Ibid.
[121] Dixon to Foreign Office, January 4, 1958, FO 371/133843, BNA.
[122] Ibid.
[123] Caccia to Foreign Office, January 8, 1958, FO 371/133843, BNA.
[124] Dixon to Foreign Office, January 4, 1958, FO 371/133843, BNA.

that it supported viable development projects rather than individual states' political agendas. He identified the Tigris, Jordan, and Nile Valleys, as well as the Suez Canal and Syrian plains, as initial candidates for investment.[125] Hammarskjöld envisioned an institutional mechanism for applying oil wealth to Arab development. This was a significant missed opportunity, because the formation in 1960 of the Organization of Petroleum Exporting Countries (OPEC), a cartel of Arab and non-Arab oil producers, foreclosed such a possibility.[126] Thereafter, Arab oil states funded regional development on a voluntary, piecemeal basis, and Arab inequality grew apace.[127]

Hammarskjöld believed that he could win support from Western oil majors, in part because executives from "some of the American oil companies" had stated that they were "interested in the idea of re-investment in the area." The secretary-general told Britain's ambassador to the United Nations, Pierson Dixon, that U.S. companies "were already aware of his thinking and 'quite deep' in it."[128] Hammarskjöld called the bluff of Duce and others who portrayed oil company investments as regional development. As U.S. Assistant Secretary of State William Rountree observed, if the "oil companies now showed in this way that they had money to spare, there would automatically be increased pressure by the producing countries for bigger royalties."[129] The British Foreign Office similarly worried that "the exaction of more money from the companies might well mean an inroad into the 50/50 arrangements which have been the foundation of Anglo-American endeavours to put an end to Middle Eastern oil quarrels."[130] Hammarskjöld nevertheless approached John J. McCloy, president of Chase Manhattan and banker to several major oil companies, to draw up a blueprint for the development fund with input from the companies.[131] Hammarskjöld also sat down with Secretary Dulles on New Year's Day 1958 to familiarize him with the plan. The next evening, Dulles warned McCloy about

[125] See memo of conversation by Reinhardt, January 30, 1958, *FRUS, 1958–1960*, 12: 35.

[126] See Meyer to Jones, "Organization of Petroleum Exporting Countries," November 21, 1960, folder: Folder: 1960 Chron, Inter-office Memos (folder 1 of 2), box 1, Bureau of Near Eastern and South Asian Affairs, Office of Near Eastern Affairs, Records of the Director, 1960–1963, RG 59, NARA.

[127] See Nathan J. Citino, *From Arab Nationalism to OPEC: Eisenhower, King Sa'ud, and the Making of U.S.–Saudi Relations*, rev. ed. (Bloomington: Indiana University Press, 2010), 150–56.

[128] Dixon to Foreign Office, January 4, 1958, FO 371/133843, BNA. Hammarskjöld may also have been encouraged by the establishment in May 1957 of a Middle East subcommittee by members of the Bilderberg Group. See "The Formation of the Middle East Study Group," October 6, 1957, http://brd-schwindel.org/download/DOKUMENTE/Bilderberg%20Meetings,%201957,%20Official%20Report.pdf, accessed September 18, 2015.

[129] Morris to Hadow with attachment, January 11, 1958, FO 371/133843, BNA.

[130] Foreign Office to Embassy in Washington, January 9, 1958, FO 371/133843, BNA.

[131] See Kai Bird, *The Chairman: John J. McCloy and the Making of the American Establishment* (New York: Simon & Schuster, 1992).

Hammarskjöld's scheme: "Arab unity may make it more difficult for the oil companies to maintain a decent position" in the Middle East.[132] Dulles elaborated a few days later in a conversation with British ambassador Harold Caccia. The Arab organization Hammarskjöld envisioned, explained Dulles, "might attempt to negotiate as a united Arab bloc with the oil companies and blackmail them – at the time of our difficulties with Iran, it had been an advantage that no such bloc existed." Further, Dulles believed that the organization "was likely in practice to be controlled by Egypt," because it "alone of the Arab countries could provide personnel qualified to staff an organization of this kind."[133]

Three weeks later, Dulles traveled to Turkey to attend a ministerial meeting of the Baghdad Pact, the U.S.-sponsored northern-tier defense organization. Turkey remained central to U.S. regional defense strategy, although Dulles had been disappointed by Ankara's inability during the previous summer to prevent Nasser from intervening in Syria following U.S. attempts to destabilize the government there.[134] Having survived a white-knuckled landing in Ankara after a blizzard forced his pilot to abort two previous attempts, Dulles was greeted with explosions when someone tried to blow up the U.S. embassy.[135] Nevertheless, Dulles privately reassured President Bayar that he considered Turkey among America's "staunchest allies."[136] Speaking to representatives of Pact countries, Dulles addressed the issue of development:

Social and economic progress is a universal desire. It is understandably most acute among those peoples who, for various historical reasons, do not yet fully share in the benefits of modern technology and science.[137]

During a meeting held in Ankara with Secretary Lloyd, Dulles poured cold water on Hammarskjöld's plan. Though it was Dulles who had initially warned McCloy, the U.S. secretary of state reported that "Mr. McCloy had many doubts about the plan because of the inherent dangers for the oil companies in which his bank was interested." Lloyd suggested to Dulles that they not seem overtly to oppose Hammarskjöld, but their resolve to do so hardened when Nasser announced two days later that Egypt and Syria would unite to form the United Arab Republic.[138]

Contrary to Hammarskjöld's hopes, oil executives refused to cooperate with his plan. One day after Dulles' meeting with Lloyd, Harold "Tim"

---

[132] Editorial note, *FRUS, 1958–1960*, 12: 1.
[133] Caccia to Foreign Office, January 5, 1958, FO 371/133843, BNA.
[134] See Salim Yaqub, *Containing Arab Nationalism: The Eisenhower Doctrine and the Middle East* (Chapel Hill: University of North Carolina Press, 2004), 147–80.
[135] See editorial note, *FRUS, 1958–1960*, 12: 32–33.
[136] Memo of conversation by Rountree, January 26, 1958, *FRUS, 1958–1960*, vol. 10, part 2, 739.
[137] "Text of the Speech by Dulles at Baghdad Pact Meeting," January 28, 1958, *NYT*, p. 3.
[138] Memo of conversation by Reinhardt, January 30, 1958, *FRUS, 1958–1960*, 12: 35.

Wilkinson of Shell Oil Company came to the Foreign Office in London to tell officials about his consultations with representatives from Jersey Standard, Gulf, and Texaco. The U.S. companies agreed that Hammarskjöld's plan "is not attractive," that "'have' oil nations will not disgorge," and so "the oil companies are likely to be the victims."[139] Hammarskjöld was forced to abandon his plan in March when the United States announced its opposition. At the United Nations, Ambassador Henry Cabot Lodge explained that implementing the plan "would allow Nasser to 'play oil politics.'"[140] Hammarskjöld retreated to a more modest scheme, disclaiming "any intention of transferring money from the oil producing countries to the have-not countries or of levying a contribution on the oil companies."[141] Months later, when the Eisenhower administration proposed its own Arab development fund, officials did not find much support among the oil executives whom they solicited for voluntary contributions. Wilkinson informed Assistant Secretary of State Douglas Dillon that "Shell Oil Company had one major caveat and that was that there should be no connection between any contribution by the oil companies and negotiations regarding the 50–50 arrangement in the Middle East."[142]

Duce opposed the idea most of all. Dillon informed the Aramco vice president: "we have been looking into Hammarskjold's idea of a regional organization which would be tied in with the International Bank." In response, Duce expressed "doubts as to whether a project initiated from outside the area would succeed." Though he claimed to support regional development, he "thought there would not be much gratitude on the part of the Arabs if the initiative came from the West."[143] A week later, Duce reiterated that "the oil companies should not be looked to as a source of funds for a Near East development institution." By producing oil, he explained, "they are generating a great amount of foreign exchange which is finding its way into local purchases, wages and salaries – all of which contribute to the welfare of the area." Duce repeated the arguments he had previously made at the Council on Foreign Relations, emphasizing the introduction of Western expertise and practices, rather than the sharing of profits, as the greatest contribution the oil companies could make to regional development. The industry "provides and will continue to provide," he declared in a written statement,

[139] Ayers to Paul Gore-Booth, January 31, 1958, FO 371/133844, BNA.
[140] Dixon to Foreign Office, March 24, 1958, FO 371/133845, BNA.
[141] "Talks with Mr. Hammarskjold: Middle East Economic Development, Summary," March 28, 1958, FO 371/133845, BNA.
[142] Memo of conversation by Dillon, September 9, 1958, Folder: General Subject – Financial General 1958 7., box 11, General Subject Files Relating to the Middle East, 1955–1958, Lot 61 D 12 RG 59, NARA.
[143] Memo of conversation by Shaw, August 1, 1958, Folder: General Subject – Economic Dev. General 1958 6., box 11, General Subject Files Relating to the Middle East, 1955–1958, Lot 61 D 12 RG 59, NARA.

"housing, schools, training, pays good wages, maintains hospitals, does research on health problems and particularly on endemic diseases, such as trachoma, and does many other things which are so necessary to build up a standard of living in the area."[144]

The official U.S. reaction to Hammarskjöld's plan, and that of oil companies, reveals the economic interests at stake in American debates about modernizing the Middle East. Dulles himself had recognized the implications of Middle Eastern history when the administration shifted to a "northern-tier" defense concept led by Turkey and when he cited "historical reasons" at the Baghdad Pact meeting to explain the backwardness of some peoples in the region. Oilmen and diplomats defined Middle Eastern underdevelopment in terms of the past as an alternative to addressing regional inequality and revising the terms of oil concessions in the present. Invoking the Ottoman legacy validated a Turco-centric regional strategy while helping to defend oil companies against schemes for pan-Arab economic development. Imagining the postwar Middle East in terms of an Ottoman imperial geography, in which Turkey was further along in the development process than the Arab successor states, served U.S. interests. This motivation helps to explain the otherwise curious fascination with the history of imperial reforms that oil-company executives and U.S. officials shared with scholars and their successive reexaminations of that history at the Council on Foreign Relations and in other policy forums.

Early in the Cold War, oilmen, diplomats, and social scientists collaborated on a legitimizing narrative for U.S. regional power based on fulfilling the promise of imperial and Kemalist reforms. Its genealogy passed from oil industry figures such as Thornburg, Ball, and McGhee to modernization scholars such as Rustow, Lerner, and Halpern. That narrative also evolved from a specific concern with Turkey at the time of Ball's work there to a theory of development extrapolated from the Ottoman-Turkish case. A contingent set of circumstances influenced these interpretations of the past, so that economic interests alone did not determine their content. The fact that Gibb and Bowen published their study based on Ottoman reformist texts just when Turkey took center stage in oil politics and regional defense illustrates this contingency. But the rise of Arab nationalism and Nasser led to changes in the region after 1960. These changes eroded the common interest that oil executives, policy makers, and social scientists had shared in reinterpreting the Ottoman legacy. Oilmen including McGhee, Duce, and Kim Roosevelt would oppose attempts by President John F. Kennedy to come to terms with revolutionary nationalism in the Arab Middle East through appeals to Nasser. Rival officials would seek to legitimize Kennedy's policy using an

---

[144] Memo of conversation by Shaw, August 7, 1958 and attached memo by Duce, folder: General Subject Middle East Developments Arab Development Institution 1958 3., box 12, General Subject Files Relating to the Middle East, 1955–1958, Lot 61 D 12, RG 59, NARA.

alternative interpretation of regional history (see Chapter 6). Given the need to seek alliances with noncommunist nationalist leaders, the significance of Ottoman-Turkish history also shifted for social scientists. They would focus on the usefulness of "military modernizers" in general with Atatürk serving as historical archetype. In contrast to the previous decade, Mustafa Kemal took on a historical importance that was increasingly divorced from Turkey's contemporary place in American strategy. As the result of a deterioration in U.S.–Turkish relations, Americans could no longer look on Turkey as an ideal Cold War ally.

As Kennedy incorporated the Arab Middle East into a new third world strategy, oilmen who had associated their industry with progress and studied authoritarian reform in Ottoman-Turkish history found themselves marginalized. Ball's 1954 death was followed by DeGolyer's two years later and Thornburg's in 1962. McGhee temporarily left the State Department in 1953, serving as a consultant to Eisenhower's National Security Council and on the Committee to Study the Military Assistance Program, until returning to head the Policy Planning Council during the first year of Kennedy's administration. Duce retired from Aramco in 1959, but in his informal role as advisor to the State Department sounded alarm bells about Arab nationalism. He warned about nonpetroleum states' threat to Gulf oil wealth: "neighbors are hungry and frontiers are not demarcated or defended."[145] His insistent antinationalist remonstrations revealed the degree to which Kennedy's policies diverged from the paternalistic approach Aramco had pursued. As the increasingly out-of-touch Duce would splutter to former CIA director Allen Dulles:

it looks to me as though we're going to spend the next decade at least, discussing nonsense with knaves like Sukarno and our silly Panamanian and Cypriot friends who have always talked nonsense, to say nothing of the Nkrummas [sic] who are imperialists and have visions of vast black empires.[146]

At the Council on Foreign Relations, Gulf Oil consultant and CIA veteran Kim Roosevelt chaired a new group on military modernizers that focused on Ottoman-Turkish history. A fixture at the Council, Roosevelt had joined Duce for Gibb's 1958 session on modern Islam and, like Duce, had taken a turn heading the Middle East Institute.[147] Musaddiq's nemesis used his close relations with the Shah of Iran, who shared a dislike for Nasser, to press OPEC member states into compromising with the oil companies. Whereas U.S. oilmen had once sought refuge in Turkey from incessant demands by

---

[145] Polk to Rostow, January 15, 1962, Folder: W.R. Polk – Chron – Jan.–May 1962, box 237, Policy Planning Council Subject Files, 1954–1962, RG 59, NARA.
[146] Duce to Dulles, February 3, 1964, folder 3, box 16, ADP.
[147] See Manalo, "A Short History of the Middle East Institute," 66.

Arab oil producers, they could now take advantage of oil exporters' fears of revolutionary Arab nationalism during negotiations with the cartel. When the Council group met to consider J. C. Hurewitz's historical comparison between Atatürk and Nasser, Roosevelt was absent, having "unexpectedly undertaken a trip to the Middle East."[148] He dashed off in an attempt to exploit cracks in OPEC's unity and to head off sanctions against the oil companies. Meanwhile, the Council group he chaired once again reconsidered the policy implications of the Ottoman and Kemalist legacies.[149]

Hurewitz offered the group a Plutarchian study of Atatürk and Nasser intended to identify principles governing the role of military modernizers.[150] Both men came from humble social origins and distinguished themselves in battle, Mustafa Kemal at Gallipoli and in the struggle against Greece, and Nasser during the first Arab–Israeli war. Both were "disillusioned with the existing political regime," and, after seizing political authority, sought "to use the powers of state to reshape the political, economic and social system." Neither man originated his reform program. In the Ottoman Empire, "the urge to Westernize (i.e., modernize)" had "already gained currency among the Muslim Ottoman élite eighty years" before Mustafa Kemal founded modern Turkey. Nasser drew on the pan-Arab and socialist program of the Syrian Ba'th Party, while exploiting superpower competition to secure aid. For Hurewitz, "Atatürk's dedication to modernization in his day was something new," while the fact that "the Egyptian revolution has been taking place a generation later than the Turkish" helped to explain the reach of Nasser's reforms into the countryside. In Turkey, the "rural revolution" had "to await the construction of the road system in the early years of the American aid program." The main differences, however, were in foreign policy and the nature of domestic political leadership. Mustafa Kemal took over the "politics of a dying empire," and his success in consolidating modern Turkey stemmed from his willingness to renounce regional ambitions. Under Nasser, Egypt moved "in precisely the opposite political direction" by grasping for pan-Arab supremacy and influence among Afro-Asian states. As for political leadership, Hurewitz asked rhetorically, "who would question that Atatürk in his day was the most forceful, imaginative, and persistent military modernizer in the Middle East? Or was he?" While in post-1952 Egypt, none "of the officers resigned his commission in the army," Atatürk had made a "rigorous point of civilizing his regime." Hurewitz's study identified in Atatürk those attributes that the United States

---

[148] Transcript of the Second Meeting of the Group on the Role of the Military in the Middle East, November 26, 1963, p. 1, folder 3, box 174, CFR.

[149] See memo of conversation by Blackiston, December 6, 1963, *FRUS, 1961–1963*, vol. 18: 826–31.

[150] J. C. Hurewitz, "Military Modernizers: Similarity and Difference in the Turkish and Egyptian Experiences," November 26, 1963, Working Paper No. 2, Discussion Group on the Role of the Military in the Middle East, folder 3, box 174, CFR.

most desired in a military modernizer. These included a commitment to domestic Westernization and willingness to foreswear foreign adventures of the sort Nasser was pursuing. Atatürk likewise remained the prime historical example of how a military leader could fulfill an authoritarian program of modernization and then step aside in the interest of democracy.

The Council's discussion illustrates how the uses of Ottoman-Turkish history changed to serve the needs of U.S. policy. While McGhee had invoked that history earlier to justify Turkey's role in regional defense, Atatürk came to serve as an archetypal military modernizer once the focus of U.S. policy shifted to addressing Arab nationalism and Nasser. For Americans worried that Nasser would "play oil politics," an Atatürk removed from the economic context of the 1930s functioned as a useful role model. Cold warriors' interpretations nevertheless continued to reflect the "temporal subordination" toward the Arab periphery they had inherited secondhand from imperial reformers. Hurewitz portrayed Nasser as following "a generation later" the trail Atatürk had blazed in establishing the Turkish republic. As discussion leader, Rustow concluded that "Egypt was at least thirty years behind Turkey in its development." For him, Turkey represented "a new nation based on an old state with a continuous ruling tradition" where modernization dated "from the late eighteenth century" and the military served "as the guarantor of the ultimate values of society."[151] He invoked the Ottoman-Turkish legacy to portray modernization as a process that could be accelerated by authoritarian reform and in which progress was measured against a universal clock.[152]

Americans reimagined Atatürk as an ideal type of military modernizer just as Turkey itself no longer seemed to provide the most successful example of modernization in a non-Western society. While circumstances in the immediate postwar period appeared to show that military rule could culminate in democracy, officers under General Cemal Gürsel seized power in 1960 and hanged Menderes after convicting him of extra-constitutional abuses. Rustow was consequently forced to tweak his teleological account of Turkish democratization to portray the military as the "guarantor of the ultimate values of society." U.S.–Turkish relations declined as a result of Kennedy's decision to remove missiles from Turkey during the Cuban Missile Crisis and worsened with President Lyndon Johnson's opposition to Turkish policy in Cyprus.[153] What McGhee disparaged as "public investment in uneconomic enterprise" disappointed the hopes he had harbored

---

[151] Transcript of the Second Meeting of the Group on the Role of the Military in the Middle East, November 26, 1963, pp. 1, 2, 15, folder 3, box 174, CFR.

[152] See also J. C. Hurewitz, *Middle East Politics: The Military Dimension* (New York: Frederick A. Praeger [published for the Council on Foreign Relations], 1969).

[153] See Nasuh Uslu, *The Turkish–American Relationship between 1947 and 2003: The History of a Distinctive Alliance* (New York: Nova Science Publishers, 2003), 135–90.

since the Ball mission for Turkey's liberalization.[154] Turkey's threats to intervene in Cyprus and risk war with Greece showed that military leaders and ex-officers had not forsaken regional ambitions. "Adhesion to NATO, in its very essence," Johnson wrote Prime Minister Ismet Inönü in June 1964, "means that NATO countries will not wage war on each other." The United States and Turkey "have fought together to resist the ambitions of the world communist revolution," Johnson recalled. "I ask you, therefore," he implored, "to delay any decisions which you and your colleagues might have in mind."[155] Johnson referred to Turkish participation in the Korean War, but would be disappointed when Turkey broke with that precedent and declined to send troops to Vietnam.[156]

Turkey's fall from grace corresponded to a change in Atatürk's historical significance for social scientists, from the father of the Turkish example to a generic military modernizer. This Atatürk served the needs of U.S. policy in managing third world revolution. Writing in 1967 for the Brookings Institution, Rustow swept Mustafa Kemal into a historic and global comparison with other nation builders appropriately titled *A World of Nations*. Rustow addressed how, "in Latin America, Asia, and Africa, nationhood and modernity have appeared as two facets of a single transformation."[157] Leaving aside his former regionalism, Rustow measured Atatürk against Muhammad 'Ali Jinnah, Johann Fichte, Otto von Bismarck, Jawaharlal Nehru, Mohandas Gandhi, George Washington, Nasser, Charles de Gaulle, and Lázaro Cárdenas.[158] For a special 1968 issue of *Daedalus* dedicated to "Studies in Leadership," Rustow similarly attempted to use Mustafa Kemal's role following the collapse of the Ottoman Empire to elucidate Max Weber's concept of charismatic leadership.[159] Princeton historian Cyril E. Black, who cited Rustow and had spent some of his own youth in Turkey, wrote in *The Dynamics of Modernization*:

From Cromwell, Washington, and Robespierre, to Lenin, Atatürk, Mao, Ho, Nehru, Nasser, and Castro, revolutionary leaders have normally been well-educated individuals who would have made a respected place for themselves in the existing society if they had not become alienated.[160]

---

[154] McGhee, *Envoy to the Middle World*, 275.

[155] Department of State to the Embassy in Turkey, June 5, 1964, *FRUS, 1964–1968*, vol. 16: 107–10.

[156] See Harriman to Johnson, December 23, 1965, *FRUS, 1964–1968*, vol. 3: 686.

[157] Dankwart A. Rustow, *A World of Nations: Problems of Political Modernization* (Washington, DC: The Brookings Institution, 1967), 2.

[158] Ibid., 25, 37, 45–46, 160, 161–63, 168, 200, 212, 213.

[159] Dankwart A. Rustow, "Atatürk as Founder of a State," *Daedalus* 97 (Summer 1968): 793–828.

[160] Cyril E. Black, *The Dynamics of Modernization: A Study in Comparative History* (New York: Harper & Row Publishers, 1966), 65.

This global perspective on military modernization expunged the partial but nevertheless significant and unacknowledged debt social scientists owed to Ottoman studies. Initially mobilized to defend Middle Eastern petroleum interests and then proclaimed as the model for non-Western development, Ottoman-Turkish history depreciated in value until it became just another case in Cold War intellectuals' comparative study of modernization.

In any event, the individuals who had adapted the Ottoman legacy to America's Cold War needs in the Middle East did not abandon their interest in contemporary vestiges of the imperial past. Gibb retired from teaching in 1964 but until his death in 1971 continued to interpret modern Islam on the basis of Ottoman texts. As in *Islamic Society and the West*, Gibb distilled an account of "tradition" from older sources that reinforced the binary temporal logic of Cold War modernization and the role of elites. Interpreting the Islamic caliphate partly through a text written by Lutfi Pasha (b. 1488), among the earliest contributors to the Ottoman decline genre, Gibb noted:

as we survey the present Middle East in the light of its historic development, we become sharply conscious of the breach which modern nationalism, in the hands of its leaders, has created with the organic development of political institutions in Islam and with the traditional principles of the political organization of the Community.[161]

After retiring from the State Department in 1969, McGhee spent part of each year with his wife, Cecilia, at their villa "on the beautiful Mediterranean coast of southern Turkey."[162] Named "Turkish Delight," the villa was restored by the McGhees in the Ottoman Mediterranean style. "To understand the relationship between style and function in traditional Turkish homes," McGhee explained, "one must have some grasp of life during Ottoman times."[163] When not working on his Turkish villa or at his Virginia farm, McGhee served on the board of the Mobil Oil Corporation and authored a novel, *Dance of the Billions*, about oil tycoons in Houston.[164] McGhee gave Georgetown University both his Turkish villa and his library of books on

---

[161] Hamilton A. R. Gibb, "The Heritage of Islam in the Modern World (I)," *International Journal of Middle East Studies* 1 (January 1970): 16–17. See also Hamilton A. R. Gibb, "Lutfi Paşa on the Ottoman Caliphate," *Oriens* 15 (December 1, 1962): 287–95; and Howard, "Ottoman Historiography and the Literature of 'Decline' of the Sixteenth and Seventeenth Centuries," 62–63.

[162] McGhee, *The US-Turkish-NATO Middle East Connection*, 7.

[163] George and Cecilia McGhee, *Life in Alanya: Turkish Delight* (Benson, VT: Chalidze Publications, 1992), 14. McGhee recommended Raphaela Lewis's book, *Everyday Life in Ottoman Turkey* (New York: G.P. Putnam's Sons, 1971).

[164] See Adam Bernstein, "George C. McGhee Dies; Oilman, Diplomat," *Washington Post*, July 6, 2005, http://www.washingtonpost.com/wp-dyn/content/article/2005/07/05/AR200 5070501581.html, accessed December 23, 2011; and George Crews McGhee, *Dance of the Billions: A Novel about Texas, Houston, and Oil* (Austin, TX: Diamond Books, 1990).

Ottoman history.[165] As for Rustow, he participated in another Council study group on Turkey more than three decades after first chairing the one on Middle East defense. Led by diplomat Parker Hart, the group included Cyril Black and Bernard Lewis. In a throwback to the early Cold War, participants considered how Turkey's historical role as a bridge between East and West positioned the republic to help contain communism. Rustow could no longer defend the Turkish military as the "guarantor of the values of society," however, given officers' serial interventions in Turkish politics, most recently in 1980. Reversing himself entirely, he dismissed those interventions instead as the "childhood ills of democracy."[166] When Rustow published a book summarizing the Council group's work, its title indicated how far removed the 1980s were from those days in the early Cold War when Turkey had anchored American regional policy and the Ottoman imperial legacy had inspired ideas about modernization. He called it *Turkey: America's Forgotten Ally*.

In the Middle East, American visions of Cold War modernization emerged from a dialogue between the needs of U.S. policy and representations of the past. Protecting access to petroleum remained a constant concern, however, whether manifested in Aramco's portrayal of oil extraction as regional development or in the Council on Foreign Relations' elevation of "human" over material factors as the basis of progress. The successive accounts of authoritarian Westernization in Ottoman-Turkish history formulated in Council study groups and in published scholarship were more than academic exercises. They served to refute the Soviet materialist doctrine that struggles over resources drove historical change and, in practical terms, to deflect rival agendas seeking to develop the Arab Middle East through the redistribution of oil wealth. Studying the ways in which oilmen, diplomats, and scholars took possession of the Ottoman-Turkish past helps to relate the ideas of Cold War modernization to a specific economic interest. Americans' investment in petroleum led them to stake a claim to the layers of reform locked beneath the surface in the Middle East.

At the same time, their story serves as its own historical case study in how reformers construct their agendas. Selecting from among the historical materials at hand like the *bricoleur*, cold warriors constructed a legitimizing narrative, rearranging the elements as their needs shifted. A contingent set of circumstances moved Turkey to the center and then exiled it to the periphery of U.S. regional policy. Those circumstances brought oilmen, officials, and scholars together around a shared fascination with the imperial legacy

---

[165] See http://mcgheecenter.georgetown.edu/, accessed October 25, 2015; and *A Catalogue of Books on Asia Minor and the Turkish Ottoman Empire*, ed. Jeffs.

[166] Dankwart A. Rustow, *Turkey: America's Forgotten Ally* (New York: Council on Foreign Relations, 1987), 64.

before separating them on the basis of their distinct interests. Although the contexts differed markedly, cold warriors transposed their agendas onto inherited accounts of regional decline and underdevelopment, much as Ottoman imperial reformers had, and this similarity helps to explain why Americans found Ottoman-Turkish history useful. By the time of the Cold War, regional reform was already an old idea. As Findley wrote in 1989, the "Ottomans' efforts to reform and preserve their state ... mark them as pioneers of the struggle for development that has become a universal Third World theme in this century."[167] The history of modernizing the Middle East therefore does not conform to the boundaries foreign policy scholars have drawn in studying America's encounter with the region. That history also transcends the distinctions between tradition and modernity, East and West that Cold War development debates have handed down to the present.

[167] Carter V. Findley, *Ottoman Civil Officialdom: A Social History* (Princeton, NJ: Princeton University Press, 1989), 10.

3

City of the Future

"I am especially impressed by the fact that the Arab Development Society began this project on its own initiative, carried it forward with its own resources and demonstrated by action and example the tremendous potentialities of self-help projects, not only in respect of the settlement of refugees but also in pointing the way toward a general improvement of village life in the Near East."
– George C. McGhee to Musa al-'Alami, July 5, 1951.[1]

"Aramco must have a maximum possible knowledge of Arabia and the Arabs in order to operate successfully in the Arab world."
– Arabian American Oil Company, "Local Government Relations Department Program," June 1955.[2]

"Development without self-help is an impossibility."
– William R. Polk, Foreword to Fathy, *Architecture for the Poor*, xii.

"In brief, 'aided self-help' must aid peasants to build in local, virtually costless materials, using skills which they themselves already have or can easily acquire."
– Hassan Fathy, *Architecture for the Poor*, 118.

This chapter examines model communities as showplaces of development in U.S.–Arab relations. It challenges historians' insistence on drawing clear distinctions between the centralized, rational schemes of planners and the local knowledge by which particular human settlements lived and thrived. Just as American ideas about modernizing the Middle East emerged partly from a dialogue with the region's history, planners appropriated knowledge from

[1] McGhee to Alami, July 5, 1951, folder: Arab Development Society (Project of Musa Bey Alami), box 9, Office of Near Eastern Affairs Subject File Relating to Economic Affairs, 1947–1951, Lot File 55D643, RG 59, NARA.
[2] Barger to Henry, June 30, 1955, with attached paper, folder 19, box 4, WEM.

the local populations for whom they designed communities. The politics of community building make it difficult to always distinguish between schematic and local knowledge in the pursuit of development – between top-down bureaucracy and bottom-up practicality. Planners worked in revolutionary settings that compelled them to identify "indigenous" or "local" sensibilities whose preservation was an indispensable aspect of political legitimacy, even as they implemented their development visions among the poor. Postwar community building was not simply a matter of the state imposing an alien logic on society. The value placed on "self-help" reflected a belief that successful development strategies incorporated local knowledge derived from the poor themselves. As will be seen, the local knowledge planners valued most often was that related to gender and the distinct roles of women and men. This focus on gender raises questions about what constitutes "local" knowledge, however, and whether development strategies based on it could be replicated within one country, across a region, or globally. Planned communities were places where modernizers struggled to accommodate the Cold War pursuit of universal models to anticolonial demands for self-determination. Gender became central to the strategies of both Arab and American planners for reconciling these aims.

In existing accounts, the violence with which authoritarian governments pursued development signified state planners' contempt for local knowledge and conditions. "Designed or planned social order is necessarily schematic," James C. Scott writes in *Seeing Like a State*; "it always ignores essential features of any real, functioning social order."[3] Scott's influential analysis of "authoritarian high modernism" takes the collectivization of Soviet agriculture and other man-made catastrophes as illustrating the disparity between planners' abstract administrative grids and diverse local practices. He describes this relationship both as violent, with states coercing the latter into accord with the former, and as parasitic, because planned cities and model villages survived only through the initiative of locals acting outside of the formal plan. For the Arab Middle East, Timothy Mitchell offers a similar argument in *Rule of Experts*, which examines the violent implications of successive colonial and postcolonial efforts at remaking Egyptian society. These plans were predicated on a distinction between the "real" Egypt and a series of centralizing administrative tools believed to be accurate representations of it, including cadastral maps and, later, the balance sheet of the "national economy," which purported to account for "the totality of monetarized exchanges within a defined space."[4] The dominant paradigm historians use to criticize twentieth-century modernization thus pits the centralizing knowledge of increasingly powerful states against the

---

[3] Scott, *Seeing Like a State*, 6.

[4] Timothy Mitchell, *Rule of Experts: Egypt, Techno-politics, Modernity* (Berkeley: University of California Press, 2002), 4.

humanity embodied in natural communities. Historians of American foreign relations base their critiques of U.S. policy toward the third world on this same dichotomy, with some borrowing from Scott's analysis explicitly. Among them is Michael Latham, who describes America's Strategic Hamlet Program as an authoritarian effort to modernize Vietnamese villages while depriving the Vietcong of material support and recruits. By forcibly relocating peasants inside military compounds, Latham argues, this community-building program replicated the historical pattern in which "'progress' and violence went hand in hand."[5]

Many postwar communities, however, were the result of an unequal but nevertheless important exchange between state and society. In addition, communities were constructed by private philanthropies and corporations as well as by states. Not all were the products of a government acting on "a prostrate civil society," in which the preponderance of official power "tends to devalue or banish politics," as Scott writes.[6] In less extreme cases, community development involved an asymmetrical negotiation in which planners sought validation by appearing to take the wishes of locals into account and by demonstrating respect for their ways of life. Because of the narrower power disparities at play in such instances, local knowledge about human and natural environments took on political value. Far from ignoring local knowledge, planners compiled, scrutinized, and brandished it as a defense against charges of paternalism. Incorporating local knowledge into their technical data permitted community designers to claim that they were giving residents what they really needed. At the same time, planners attempted to extrapolate from local practices formulas that they argued could be replicated elsewhere. Historian Daniel Immerwahr observes correctly that "the urge to modernize and the quest for community shared space, existing alongside or even within each other."[7] By attempting to present these two agendas as distinct, however, he ultimately accepts Scott's dichotomy. The contradiction embodied in the phrase "model community" requires more direct analysis than it has previously received. It was an inherent characteristic of Cold War–era projects built in the Arab Middle East and beyond.

Precedents from the Ottoman and colonial eras set the terms in which postwar modernizers sought to legitimize their work, because planned communities in the Middle East had historic associations with authoritarian rulers and European colonialism. Historian Omnia El Shakry dates experimentation with model villages in Egypt to the early nineteenth-century reign

[5] Latham, *Modernization as Ideology*, 153, 184.

[6] Scott, *Seeing Like a State*, 5, 94. For another critique of Scott, see Huri İslamoğlu, "Politics of Administering Property: Law and Statistics in the Nineteenth-Century Ottoman Empire," in *Constituting Modernity: Private Property in the East and West*, ed. Huri İslamoğlu (New York: I.B. Tauris, 2004), 276–319.

[7] Daniel Immerwahr, *Thinking Small: The United States and the Lure of Community Development* (Cambridge, MA: Harvard University Press, 2015), 71.

of Muhammad 'Ali Pasha. She also notes that during the interwar period, when Egypt was subject to British authority, it was "the second nation (after Belgium) to commission a large-scale survey and study of rural housing."[8] As historian Mark LeVine has shown, Jaffa and the new Zionist town of Tel Aviv served as conjoined, competing enterprises in modern urban planning from the Ottoman era until Zionist forces drove most Arab residents out of Jaffa in 1948.[9] From company towns in the Nile Delta to oil workers' housing in the Persian Gulf, capitalist development likewise brought community-building experiments to the region. According to Joel Beinin and Zachary Lockman, during World War II Egyptian workers living in housing communities built by textile companies "resented management's around-the-clock supervision and the loss of their personal independence."[10] Postwar planners had to take this legacy into account. They could overcome it only by designing communities that could be portrayed as democratically conceived for the benefit of the people who inhabited them.

The case studies presented in this chapter are villages or towns rather than city neighborhoods. They demonstrate the reach of governments, capital, and urban political movements into the countryside, which became the focus of a myriad of improvement schemes in decolonizing countries.[11] "To develop viable political societies with a sound rural structure built upon or replacing the old arrangements," generalized a State Department report on village development, "requires a major effort at rural political and social reconstruction."[12] The featured communities were also products of their political and economic contexts. These factors included the displacement of refugees, growing oil production, and state policies promoting import substitution and tourism. The mechanization of agriculture also disrupted existing rural communities in many Arab countries. At a time when rural depopulation and rampant urbanization went hand in hand, the distinction

---

[8] El Shakry, *The Great Social Laboratory*, 104, 123.

[9] Mark LeVine, *Overthrowing Geography: Jaffa, Tel Aviv, and the Struggle for Palestine, 1880–1948* (Berkeley: University of California Press, 2005).

[10] See Beinin and Lockman, *Workers on the Nile*, 271; Ellis Goldberg, "Worker's Voice and Labor Productivity in Egypt," in *Workers and Working Classes in the Middle East: Struggles, Histories, Historiographies*, ed. Zachary Lockman (Albany: State University of New York Press, 1994), 120; Ian J. Seccombe and Richard I. Lawless, *Work Camps and Company Towns: Settlement Patterns and the Gulf Oil Industry* (Durham, UK: University of Durham, Centre for Middle Eastern and Islamic Studies, 1987); and Nelida Fuccaro, *Histories of City and State in the Persian Gulf: Manama Since 1800* (New York: Cambridge University Press, 2009).

[11] On India's experience, see Cullather, *The Hungry World*, 77–94; and Nicole Sackley, "Village Models: Etawah, India, and the Making and Remaking of Development in the Early Cold War," *Diplomatic History* 37 (September 2013): 749–78.

[12] Wriggins to Miniclier, April 17, 1962, folder: Wriggins, H., Chron Jan.–June 1962, box 238, Policy Planning Council Subject Files, 1954–1962, RG 59, NARA.

between "natural" settlements and "planned" communities built to cope with changing circumstances was not always clear.[13]

The four featured cases are Palestinian notable Musa al-'Alami's Arab Development Society near Jericho, supported by the U.S. government as an "Arab Boys' Town"; the Arabian American Oil Company's housing for American and Arab workers in the Eastern Province of Saudi Arabia; the Egyptian government's villages constructed for its Tahrir Province agricultural settlement; and the model village of New Gourna, designed by Egyptian architect Hassan Fathy and used as a template for subsequent communities in the Middle East and beyond. As these cases demonstrate, states were not the only entities that constructed communities, nor were new towns exclusively agricultural but could also be designed to subsist on wage labor or handicrafts. Although built for different purposes, these communities are nevertheless comparable in two significant ways. First, the community builders defined their visions as successfully reconciling modernity with humanity through careful attention to local conditions and the needs of inhabitants. They could make this claim most effectively by strategically distinguishing their own, locally focused efforts from what they portrayed as the malign influence of distant and impersonal bureaucracies. Long before *Seeing Like a State*, community builders in the postcolonial Middle East drew politically useful contrasts between local knowledge and schematic planning, in which the latter characterized the wrong kind of development.

Second, each sought to legitimize community projects by appearing to demonstrate respect for existing gender roles in local society.[14] These modernizers walked a fine line between *describing* women's roles in particular places, claiming to respect those roles in their schemes, and *prescribing* an idealized domesticity for them within modern built environments. This tension similarly characterized postwar American experiences with domesticity and consumerism. Historian Elaine Tyler May uses the famous "kitchen debate" between U.S. vice president Richard Nixon and Soviet premier Nikita Khrushchev to show how the American suburban home, equipped with shiny appliances to liberate housewives from domestic labor, became a weapon in the Cold War. The "legendary family of the 1950s," May argues, "represented something new" and was not "the last gasp of 'traditional'

---

[13] See Roger Owen and Şevket Pamuk, *A History of Middle East Economies in the Twentieth Century* (Cambridge, MA: Harvard University Press, 1998), 98–99.

[14] Historian Michael Adas notes that "communist and modernization ideologies shared a strong bias toward men as the agents and main beneficiaries of development" and that the "subordination or neglect of women's issues meant that local knowledge systems" were therefore ignored by modernizers. See Michael Adas, *Dominance by Design: Technological Imperatives and America's Civilizing Mission* (Cambridge, MA: Belknap/Harvard, 2006), 260, 266. But it was on the basis of gender that the community builders described in this chapter sought to demonstrate their respect for local knowledge.

family life with roots deep in the past." It paradoxically enshrined "traditional" gender roles within a modern "American way of life" that was "classless, homogenous, and family centered."[15] Historian Lizabeth Cohen describes New Jersey's gendered "landscape of mass consumption" in which shopping centers were "feminized public space."[16] As postwar visions combining material abundance with clearly delineated gender roles, planned communities in the Arab Middle East were not so far removed from the subdivisions of America's affluent society.

The Cold War competition among development models forced modernizers to seek legitimacy for their prescriptions as fulfilling the needs of ordinary people. By the late 1950s, authoritarian bureaucrats had already come to serve as useful villains. As illustrated by the protagonist of William J. Lederer and Eugene Burdick's *The Ugly American* (1958), whose "hands were calloused," practical knowledge was the antithesis of abstract plans drawn up by functionaries in air-conditioned offices. "The princes of bureaucracy," write Lederer and Burdick, "were the same all over the world."[17] In her sharp critique of city planning, *The Death and Life of Great American Cities* (1961), Jane Jacobs lamented how

forceful and able men, admired administrators, having swallowed the initial fallacies and having been provisioned with tools and with public confidence, go on logically to the greatest destructive excesses, which prudence or mercy might previously have forbade.[18]

In an attempt to combine planning with local initiative, official U.S. policy embraced "aided" or "guided" self-help to govern community development programs. According to a USAID training manual, based on guidelines created by an American advisor in Libya, "change can be brought about by the efforts of the people themselves." The villager is "capable of defining his own problems" and "suggesting solutions" while experts must not "dictate, drive, manage, impose," or try to "accelerate growth for the sake of acceleration."[19] Both American and Arab community builders recognized that their visions would succeed only to the degree that they could be portrayed as legitimate expressions of residents' desires, rather than as elite or bureaucratic impositions. Planners were therefore obliged to collect local

---

[15] Elaine Tyler May, *Homeward Bound: American Families in the Cold War Era* (New York: Basic Books, 1988), 11, 172.

[16] See Lizabeth Cohen, *A Consumers' Republic: The Politics of Mass Consumption in Postwar America* (New York: Alfred A. Knopf, 2003), 278–86.

[17] William J. Lederer and Eugene Burdick, *The Ugly American* (New York: Fawcett Crest, 1958), 174–75.

[18] Jane Jacobs, *The Death and Life of Great American Cities* (New York: Random House, 1961), 13.

[19] United States Agency for International Development, *Community Development: An Introduction to CD for Village Workers* (Washington, DC: USAID, 1962), 2, 4.

knowledge about the men and women whom their projects served and to cultivate a development mythology based on the concept of "self-help."

Musa al-'Alami (1897–1984) was born to one of the leading notable families of Ottoman Jerusalem and served as an official in Britain's Palestine mandate. When Arab states met in 1944 to discuss plans for what became the Arab League, al-'Alami solicited Arab governments for funds to help preserve Arab landownership in Palestine. Conceived as a successor to the Ottoman Land Bank, the Arab Development Society (ADS) would enable Arab smallholders to convert their lands into *awqaf*, or religious endowments, to prevent indebted farmers from having to sell land to Zionists. Al-'Alami also planned to teach villagers modern agricultural techniques, provide them with improved sanitation, and encourage small-scale industries. His plans received a disappointing level of financial support from Arab governments, however, and al-'Alami took them over as independent projects when rival Palestinian leader Hajj Amin al-Husayni sought to gain control over the League's welfare activities. Al-'Alami acquired land for two of three planned model villages that would plant modern Arab communities in the Palestinian countryside to counter the Zionists' *kibbutzim*.[20]

The first Arab–Israeli war upended these plans, however, and following the flight of hundreds of thousands of Palestinians from their homes, al-'Alami was forced to reinvent the ADS as a refugee relief organization. Thereafter, he mounted a public relations campaign that built on his earlier experience lobbying on behalf of the Arab League. He relentlessly petitioned the United States, Britain, Arab governments, international agencies, and private philanthropies to support the model farm he built near Jericho in the West Bank. To promote his cause, al-'Alami developed a narrative centered on the role practical knowledge had played in establishing the ADS. Al-'Alami contrasted this *savoir faire*, which exploited the know-how ordinary refugees possessed, against the pessimism he had encountered from a host of bureaucratic opponents and useless "experts" whom he managed to prove wrong time and again. Meanwhile, al-'Alami used the ADS to try to reestablish his own paternal authority within a national community torn apart by the disaster of 1948. Rather than simply rely on his elite pedigree, al-'Alami acted as a modernizer helping to fashion new productive roles for male and female Palestinians.

Al-'Alami established the basic elements of his development agenda as early as 1949 in *'Ibrat Filastin* [*The Lesson of Palestine*], a tract published in

---

[20] See Thomas Mayer, "Arab Unity of Action and the Palestine Question, 1945–48," *Middle Eastern Studies* 22 (July 1986): 335–36; Seale, *The Struggle for Arab Independence*, 291–92, 294–95, 297–98; Sir Geoffrey Furlonge, *Palestine Is My Country: The Story of Musa Alami* (New York: Praeger, 1969), 136–38; and Cecil A. Hourani, "Experimental Village in the Jordan Valley," *Middle East Journal* 5 (Autumn 1951): 497–501.

Beirut and then summarized in translation for the *Middle East Journal*. He attributed Palestinians' dispossession to Arab disunity and underdevelopment. Recounting the Arab defeats of the previous year, al-'Alami emphasized Palestinian villages' tenuous hold on the land. "And so the country fell," he wrote, "town after town, village after village, position after position, as a result of its fragmentation and lack of unity." His language portrayed the national crisis in terms of domestic disorder and sexual dishonor:

Hundreds of thousands of the Arabs of Palestine have left their houses and homes, suffered the trials and terrors of flight, died by the wayside, lived in misery and destitution, naked, unprotected, children separated from their parents, robbed, raped, and reduced to the most miserable straits.

In contrast, "the Jews mobilized not only all their young men, but also all their girls," as part of a "general mobilization and complete military organization." The way forward, al-'Alami insisted, required not merely unity but "complete modernization in every aspect of Arab life and thought." An egalitarian nationalism must be created "for the benefit of the whole people, not of a special class or specific element," and "the woman must be equal to the man, so that she may share in the formation of this new Arab society."[21] The new order would create strength through education, technical expertise, and economic development. Al-'Alami declared that we must "adapt ourselves and our ways of life" in order to meet the new situation.[22]

Al-'Alami proved adept at eliciting sympathy from a succession of American and British officials drawn to his patrician approach to development and refugee assistance. He also won over figures from the Ford Foundation and the Arabian American Oil Company (Aramco), the private entities that provided most of his support. In addition to McGhee, he impressed British diplomat Sir Geoffrey Furlonge, who would write al-'Alami's authorized biography, *Palestine Is My Country*. Former American University of Beirut (AUB) president Bayard Dodge and Aramco vice president James Terry Duce, whose company lent the ADS equipment and experts and would purchase much of what the ADS farm produced, met with al-'Alami during his 1951 visit to the United States.[23] Another key American supporter was economist Norman Burns, who held posts in the State Department and with the UN Relief and Works Agency (UNRWA) before himself becoming AUB president. In 1950, Burns had visited the 'Ayn Hilweh refugee camp in Lebanon and his description of it incorporated similar images of disrupted domestic life to those al-'Alami used. "All of the

---

[21] Alami, "The Lesson of Palestine," 380, 387, 394, 399.

[22] Musa al-'Alami, *'Ibrat Filastin* (Beirut: Dar al-Kashshaf lil-nashr wa al-tiba'a wa al-tawzi', 1949), 37.

[23] See Boardman to Burns, June 12, 1951, folder: Arab Development Society (Project of Musa Bey Alami), box 9, Office of Near Eastern Affairs Subject File Relating to Economic Affairs, 1947–1951, Lot 55 D643, RG 59, NARA.

children," Burns wrote, "looked ragged" but "appeared healthy," while "the adults appeared as healthy as the average peasant," although their "clothes were more ragged and their faces looked unhappy." In the valley, "speckled with khaki-colored conical tents for a distance of a half mile square," women and girls were forced to carry "huge earthen pots on their heads" from a distant water source, while other girls were put to work "sewing cotton cloth for baby clothes." Most tents "were practically empty of everything except children and adults sitting about in dejected fashion trying to keep out of the sun." One UNRWA official explained that in the camp "village and family heads try to keep their villagers and family members around them to maintain their importance." Burns nonetheless concluded that "Ain Helwi refugees are literally on the margin of existence."[24] By contrast, al-'Alami's ADS appealed to Burns as a modern and productive community in which vulnerable members of Palestinian society were cared for. Within the State Department, Burns rejected a pessimistic assessment of the ADS written by Herbert Stewart, a British consultant to the UN economic mission to the Middle East led by Gordon Clapp.[25] Burns criticized Stewart for neglecting to mention that "Musa Bey intends" vacant houses at the ADS site "for refugee orphans as soon as their means of subsistence can be arranged." Stewart also "fails to note that the project is giving employment to 100 to 200 additional refugee families from the Jericho refugee camp."[26] Burns reinforced al-'Alami's narrative, which pitted obstructionism on the part of the United Nations and other bureaucracies against the ADS patron's own practical knowledge and intimacy with his refugee wards.

Al-'Alami told State Department officials that "everyone had been against the project at the beginning." Opposed to any refugee resettlement, the "Grand Mufti [Hajj Amin al-Husayni] and the Arab League opposed it for political reasons," he told McGhee, while the "UNRWA and British experts opposed it for technical reasons." Nevertheless, "the scheme had finally become a going concern" in spite of "long opposition from several quarters."[27] The experts "said the land could not be reclaimed," he told U.S. officials, "but we've grown cotton, bananas, grapes and vegetables

[24] Burns to Gardiner, November 6, 1950, folder: Letters Norman Burns, box 8, Office of Near Eastern Affairs Subject File Relating to Economic Affairs, 1947–1951, Lot 55 D643, RG 59, NARA.

[25] See Gardiner to Berry, June 20, 1951, folder: NE – Jordan, box 6, Office of Near Eastern Affairs, Subject Files Related to Economic Affairs, 1947–1951, Lot 55 D643, RG 59, NARA; and memo by Stewart, December 22, 1949, FO 371/82253, BNA.

[26] Burns to Gardiner, July 3, 1951, folder: 1. Agriculture – Jordan 1. Land Reform, box 2, Office of Near Eastern Affairs, Subject Files Related to Economic Affairs, 1947–1951, Lot 55 D643, RG 59, NARA.

[27] Memoranda [2] of conversations by Boardman, May 18, 1951, folder: 1. Agriculture – Jordan 1. Land Reform, box 2, Office of Near Eastern Affairs, Subject Files Related to Economic Affairs, 1947–1951, Lot 55 D643, RG 59, NARA. See also *The Arab Development Society, Jericho, the Hashemite Kingdom of Jordan* (Jerusalem: The Commercial Press, 1953), 12.

successfully, and we've settled refugees near their homeland."[28] Among al-'Alami's opponents initially had been the Jordanian government, which had attempted to seize ADS accounts in Amman to help the kingdom cope with the refugee crisis. But al-'Alami spirited the funds to Beirut in his car and then prevailed on King 'Abdullah to grant the ADS 5,000 acres of barren land in the West Bank near the Allenby Bridge some five miles north of the Dead Sea, where "nothing grew except occasional patches of camel-thorn and a few scraggly bushes."[29] In contrast to the Western powers, which he believed sympathized with Israel, al-'Alami wanted to settle refugees in the Jordan Valley near their former homes. "Thinking over what he had been told by those international experts whose duty it was to deal with the problem of the refugees," Furlonge wrote, al-'Alami "found himself unable to accept" that Palestinians must move "to some unspecified haven in Syria, Iraq, or beyond." What convinced him, despite the naysayers, that it was possible to farm this part of the valley using groundwater was his own local knowledge: "He had spent part of every winter since boyhood in Jericho and had there watched as much rain as falls in England during a year pouring down in three months . . .; surely, he argued, all this rain must be somewhere in the subsoil and ought to be recoverable from it."[30] The story of how Musa al-'Alami found the water to sustain his ADS model farm served to legitimize the role he scripted for himself as the founding father of a post-1948 Palestinian community.

In a chapter that Furlonge titled "The Finding of the Water," al-'Alami described leading a drilling expedition consisting of "the members of my household and garden staff, eleven in all, with only one educated man among them." He found "a young man" from a nearby refugee camp who improvised "a rig made of pipes welded together into a tripod, with a pulley on it carrying a sort of thin cylinder for boring and another object intended to bale out the displaced earth." Since this Palestinian Arab version of the Ugly American "seemed to know what he was doing," al-'Alami took the "entirely illogical decision" to build "nineteen houses even before finding water." The gamble paid off when water was discovered in January 1950. Al-'Alami had been recuperating from an illness in Jerusalem, but returned to the ADS site to rejoin the youth whose ingenuity had made it all possible:

I said foolishly, "Have you found water?" and he said simply, "Drink." So I drank, and it was sweet; and I put down the pitcher, and I felt as if I were choking, and I looked round at the others and I saw tears running down all their faces, as well as mine.

[28] Boardman to Burns, May 18, 1951, folder: Jordan, box 16, Records of Near East Affairs Bureau, Office Files of Asst. Sec'y George C. McGhee, 1945–1953, Lot 53 D468, RG 59, NARA.

[29] Furlonge, *Palestine Is My Country*, 170; see also Simpson to Falle, August 13, 1955, FO 371/115712, BNA.

[30] Furlonge, *Palestine Is My Country*, 167, 168.

With similar practicality, al-'Alami and his refugee band planted a variety of crops in the newly reclaimed desert: "We had no idea what to try; but it was early in the year and things would grow, so we tried whatever anybody suggested." Wheat, barley, vegetables, beets, and turnips all flourished. For "three or four years none of the experts who came out could tell us the reason; all they could say was that according to the text-books there should be nothing there."[31] By growing crops in what was considered a barren desert, al-'Alami also defied the Ottoman land classification of the area as "dead [*mawat*]."[32] Al-'Alami related the finding of the water on numerous occasions to potential benefactors.[33] "The Society has so far dug eleven wells and found water where it had always been supposed none existed," he boasted to McGhee; "it has reclaimed and irrigated five hundred acres of land officially registered as dead and waste."[34] As one British diplomat said of al-'Alami, "ninety percent of his success was due to being on the spot day and night, and learning the vagaries of the Jordan Valley."[35] His story portrayed the ADS farm as exemplary for being deeply rooted in the land. It emphasized how exploiting local and practical knowledge could restore Palestinian self-respect while celebrating al-'Alami's personal role as both patriarch and modernizer.

The ADS reflected al-'Alami's vision of a modern Palestinian national community. "Its duty now was to create the very conditions of an ordered and settled life," an official Jordanian pamphlet about the ADS explained, "and to re-organize uprooted and fragmented human groups."[36] For him, "ordered and settled" meant prescribing strict gender roles. The ADS grew into a working commercial farm and included a Vocational Training Centre for refugee orphans but became an almost exclusively male community where masculinity was defined by practical ability and physical rigor. The same source explained that the Society's aim was "not to produce white collared young men seeking office jobs and lazing about in the towns," but "to make of them men with an all-round knowledge who can use their hands and their brains to the best advantage."[37] The boys were subjected to a "course of physical training and drill every day apart from the usual sports," and "taught to swim and have a dip year round in the swimming

31 Ibid., 171–73, 175–76.
32 Hourani, "Experimental Village in the Jordan Valley," 497. See also "The Arab Development Society, Jericho, Jordan," n.d., FO 957/220, BNA.
33 See minute by Duff, June 22, 1954, and Castle to Lloyd, June 24, 1954, FO 371/110950, BNA.
34 Al-'Alami to McGhee, June 12, 1951, folder: NE – Jordan, box 6, Office of Near Eastern Affairs, Subject Files Related to Economic Affairs, 1947-1951, Lot 55 D643, RG 59, NARA.
35 Simpson to Falle, August 13, 1955, cited earlier.
36 *The Arab Development Society*, 12.
37 Ibid., 25.

pool of the school."[38] Furlonge writes that in selecting orphans al-'Alami decided

not to take any who were seriously ill or mentally defective, for he had no means of treating them; nor girls, nor boys so young as to need the care of women, for he had no women helpers; nor those who were old enough to be set in their ways.[39]

As illustrated by his account of the dwellings in which he temporarily housed refugee families before taking on the orphans, domesticity was an essential component of al-'Alami's modernizing vision. The ADS "has constructed fifty houses of modern type, with running water, showers, lavatories, and kitchens," he wrote McGhee, "and it has given employment to between one and two hundred heads of families, twenty-five of which are now settled in the houses."[40] Furlonge, describing his first visit to the ADS in 1953, evokes a sort of patriarchal utopia. Arriving at the ADS compound, Furlonge observed how "[s]mall boys in a simple uniform of khaki shirts and shorts, busy and healthy, scurried to and fro." Al-'Alami, who was called "'Uncle'" by boys who would otherwise "still have been destitute and homeless," held court "in a tiny bare whitewashed room," where despite his poor health, "his brain was working overtime" on "ambitious plans for extension or development, on the smallest details of husbandry or of the boys' welfare." It seemed to Furlonge that al-'Alami "was creating something akin to the patriarchal society of his youth, that he was once more presiding over a clan wholly dependent on him."[41] If the refugee crisis forced the ADS to reconfigure its original strategy of rural modernization, then al-'Alami made Palestinian masculinity central to that mission.

Al-'Alami repeatedly stated his intention to build a training center for refugee girls whose role would complement that of Palestinian boys. Girls would receive an elementary education and "be trained in domestic skills, sewing and handicraft, dairy and poultry farming." Because "if we are to train and produce better farmers and artisans," the ADS pamphlet explained, and "build up better families and a solid family life," then this goal "can only be attained if their wives and mothers of their children are educated and trained."[42] According to *New York Times* reporter Kennett Love, al-'Alami believed that a "new generation of farmers ... must have wives of equal caliber if they are to hold to their standards and set the course for others."[43] Al-'Alami told British members of Parliament that he envisioned being able to train 500 orphans at a time, 250 boys and an equal number

[38] Ibid., 36.
[39] Furlonge, *Palestine Is My Country*, 179.
[40] al-'Alami to McGhee, June 12, 1951, cited earlier.
[41] Furlonge, *Palestine Is My Country*, 182–83.
[42] *The Arab Development Society*, 26.
[43] Kennett Love, "Arab 'Moses' Teaches Orphans to Make Jordan Desert Bloom," *NYT*, May 7, 1955, p. 3.

of girls.[44] But concerns about housing and supervising girls, and the higher priority he accorded to boys, led him to defer doing so indefinitely.[45] As an alternative, he took over a $500,000 Ford Foundation grant for supporting Palestinian villages along the ceasefire frontier, where Furlonge described girls' traditional role carrying water as putting them in danger from the Israelis.[46] The funds permitted al-'Alami to extend his vision beyond the ADS site into villages where "it was possible for girls to be taught while living at home." In addition to an education program supervised by inspectors based in Jerusalem, al-'Alami instituted handicraft training in embroidery, a skill that would complement the weaving taught to boys, "so that the girls could embroider what they wove."[47] In these frontier villages, the ADS could conceivably become more than just a reclamation experiment undertaken in one place using the local knowledge al-'Alami and Palestinian refugees possessed. It could demonstrate the "tremendous potentialities of self-help projects," as McGhee had put it, "in pointing the way toward a general improvement of village life in the Near East."

But al-'Alami's modernizing vision struggled to gain legitimacy given the revolutionary mood of West Bank refugees. He had developed the plan for an orphanage only when the original refugee families brought to the ADS site left, because they feared that resettlement would foreclose the possibility of ever returning to their former homes. The fact that the ADS survived on the basis of Western support also made it a target of mob violence that threatened its very survival. In December 1955, at a time when Jordan was shaken by riots opposing the kingdom's proposed membership in the Anglo-American Baghdad Pact, thousands of refugees from around Jericho descended on the ADS. Al-'Alami was away, and the young boys and staff who were present were unable to prevent "the mob from setting fire to all the buildings, destroying everything in sight, and looting all the livestock."[48] According to news reports, the rioters chanted anti-American slogans and "had wrecking tools and carried cans of gasoline." They concluded their apparently premeditated attack by carrying "all books, accounts, and documents from Mr. el Alami's office out to a waiting taxicab."[49]

The costs of rebuilding the ADS compound after the 1955 attack led to al-'Alami's even greater dependence on private American sources of support and, for the first time, to official U.S. government assistance. In addition to subsidizing al-'Alami's initiatives for girls and other inhabitants

[44] Simpson to Falle, August 13 1955, cited earlier.

[45] Furlonge, *Palestine Is My Country*, 206.

[46] Ibid., 194. See also unsigned memo of conversation between al-'Alami and Hart, June 2, 1959, folder: Jordan Economic Development General 1959 6, box 13, Near East Affairs, Subject Files Relating to Iraq and Jordan, 1956–1959, Lot 61 D20 [3 of 3], RG 59, NARA.

[47] Furlonge, *Palestine Is My Country*, 197.

[48] Ibid., 179, 190.

[49] Kennett Love, "School in Jordan Rising from Ruin," *NYT*, June 23, 1956, p. 4.

of the Palestinian frontier villages, the Ford Foundation had granted the ADS $149,000 over three years for the boys' Vocational Training Centre. Following the riots, Ford contributed another $30,000 immediately to the costs of reconstruction. Meanwhile, since 1953 Aramco had been purchasing fresh fruits and vegetables grown by the ADS, airlifting the produce directly from Amman to Dhahran on the Persian Gulf.[50] These sales helped to support the Vocational Training Centre, but after the riots, al-'Alami was forced to take out a commercial loan of £100,000 to meet his expenses. His difficulty repaying it prompted what a British diplomatic source called "a gentleman's agreement" in 1958 among the Ford Foundation, Aramco, and the State Department's International Cooperation Administration (ICA).[51] Ford made an additional grant of $200,000 for technical assistance and modern dairy facilities (Brigham Young University donated twenty-six cows), and Aramco indicated that it would continue buying agricultural produce.[52] The ICA agreed to subsidize 100 boys in an expanded Vocational Training Centre at an annual cost of $75,000 for three years, while pledging an additional $92,000 for dormitory and training facilities.[53] Al-'Alami's credo of masculine self-reliance gained him the admiration of Western benefactors, but accepting their assistance further eroded his standing as a Palestinian Arab nationalist.

In other ways, postwar Arab politics marginalized those of al-'Alami's social class. The rise of Egyptian leader Gamal 'Abd al-Nasser and Palestinian militant groups led al-'Alami to reconcile with Jordan's young King Husayn and to consolidate ADS aid requests to Washington with those made by Jordan. A shared paternalism in the cultivation of masculinity characterized the American, Hashemite, and ADS approaches to development. U.S. officials proposed linking the ADS to a program for training young men in Jordan modeled after the New Deal's Civilian Conservation Corps.[54] Norman Burns, al-'Alami's defender within the State Department, told a Jordanian general that the program would promote "good citizenship values, self-discipline, personal and national pride, and the development of leadership qualities." Husayn reportedly liked the idea.[55]

---

[50] Furlonge, *Palestine Is My Country*, 184, 185.

[51] "The Projects of the Arab Development Society," n.d., FO 957/220, BNA.

[52] See Furlonge, *Palestine Is My Country*, 201; and Strong to Talbot, June 8, 1961, folder: 1961 Chron Inter-office Memorandum [1 of 2], box 3, Bureau of Near Eastern and South Asian Affairs/Office of Near Eastern Affairs, Records of the Director, 1960–1963, RG 59, NARA.

[53] See Meyer to Jones, July 29, 1960 and Meyer to Hart, July 19, 1960, folder: 1960 Chron Inter-office Memos [2 of 2], box 1, Bureau of Near Eastern and South Asian Affairs/Office of Near Eastern Affairs, Records of the Director, 1960–1963, RG 59, NARA.

[54] Meyer to Hart, July 19, 1960, cited earlier.

[55] Keeley to State, foreign service dispatch 116, September 29, 1959, with attached memo of conversation, 785.5/9-2159, RG 59, NARA. See also Mills to State, September 5, 1959, *FRUS 1958–1960*, 11: 725.

But the image in which al-'Alami and Burns hoped to mold Palestinian males was rapidly being eclipsed by another, more radical model for manhood emerging from the refugee camps: that of the *fida'i*, or commando who raided Israeli-controlled territory. Scholar Dina Matar describes how the founding of Harakat al-Tahrir al-Filastini (Fatah) by Yasir 'Arafat and others in 1959 created a new role model for Palestinian youth:

Donning military fatigues and the Palestinian *kuffiyeh* – instead of a suit and a red tarbush – the leaders of Fatah radically changed the way Palestinians were represented, bringing to the fore a new generation and a new image. The new revolutionary leaders were drawn from diverse class, social, religious and regional backgrounds. Significantly, many of them had lower-middle-class, rural or refugee-camp origins.[56]

The *fida'iyin* commitment to armed struggle eclipsed the ADS boys' "lines of neat cottages," their "regular routine" of "the schoolroom, the workshops or fields, the refectory, and the sports field." As Fatah began scripting a new Palestinian masculinity, the ADS's most celebrated graduate, a once-sickly orphan named 'Ali, was adopted by "a rich American visitor" and eventually became a high school gym teacher in California.[57]

And while the ADS's "amateur" and "pioneer" character might have been endearing to al-'Alami's backers, these upstart qualities proved liabilities when it came to securing commercial markets and aid from international agencies. At the end of 1960, Aramco abruptly stopped buying ADS produce, shifting to cheaper sources from Eritrea and Saudi Arabia.[58] Al-'Alami subsequently struggled to find alternative customers, but he had been dependent on Aramco for transport, and the ICA denied a previous request for help purchasing refrigerated trucks and cargo planes. The Development Loan Fund (DLF) would advance monies only against anticipated revenues and insisted on calculating a "cost-benefit ratio" for further proposed reclamation to expand the ADS to some 40,000 acres.[59] Al-'Alami's applications to the World Bank were denied, despite warm personal relations with bank president Eugene Black, while the ADS was forced to rely on the Ford Foundation and King Husayn when the United States withdrew its assistance over a three-year period beginning in 1966. The ADS focused on producing "locally marketable" poultry and dairy products, forsaking the citrus and out-of-season produce al-'Alami had hoped to sell to Middle Eastern and European customers.[60] Even as the ADS limited its marketing to local customers, however, al-'Alami increasingly drew on global development

---

[56] Dina Matar, *What It Means to Be Palestinian: Stories of Palestinian Peoplehood* (New York: I.B. Tauris, 2011), 89.

[57] Furlonge, *Palestine Is My Country*, 202–03, 206n.

[58] See ibid., 200, 205; and Strong to Talbot, June 8, 1961, cited earlier.

[59] See unsigned memo of conversation between al-'Alami and Hart, June 2, 1959, cited earlier.

[60] See Furlonge, *Palestine Is My Country*, 206, 209–10; and "Arab 'Boys Town' Is Given $100,000," February 10, 1968, *NYT*, p. 3.

expertise to improve its operations. Al-'Alami traveled to the Imperial Valley in California to learn about irrigation and to Hawaii to consult with university experts on tropical agriculture.[61] In 1962, he stopped off in London to hire professional managers for his Vocational Training Centre after he found that two promising German candidates lacked sufficient command of English.[62] Al-'Alami had created the ADS enterprise by exploiting refugees' local knowledge, but could never make it into the basis for modernizing Palestinian communities beyond his model farm near Jericho. He also came to depend on just the sort of international experts whose skepticism he had first defied using his personal familiarity with the Jordan Valley.

When war broke out in 1967, al-'Alami was in Europe purchasing new equipment. Israeli troops occupied the ADS site on June 7 and confined the staff to their bungalows. Furlonge writes that the Israeli advance created a "scene of desolation reminiscent of 1955." Israeli "tanks had driven across the fields ... smashing water-conduits and putting all but two of the wells out of action." Alfalfa had withered, chickens and cows had died, "the transport had been taken and many of the houses looted." With Israel occupying the West Bank, al-'Alami shuttled between Amman and Beirut before eventually being permitted by Israeli authorities to settle in east Jerusalem. He again looked to the Ford Foundation for money with which to rebuild and drew support from charities established by friends in the United States and Britain. Having schooled Palestinian youth in manly self-reliance, al-'Alami found himself dependent on foreign benefactors and Israel. He failed to attain the role he had written for himself in 1949 as the father of a new Palestinian society that was both modern and firmly rooted in the land. In a concluding tribute, Furlonge nonetheless memorializes al-'Alami's vision combining rural modernization with masculinity: "what shall be said of one who, by his own labours and those he inspired in others, has made forty thousand acres of desert into gardens and a thousand waifs into men?"[63]

In contrast to al-'Alami, who dreamed of replicating the ADS farm at Jericho into the model for a gendered Palestinian modernity, Aramco's leadership faced the challenge of applying management techniques used in other global oil enclaves to the distinct setting of eastern Arabia. This was a political challenge in which community building played a central role, because the separate-and-unequal housing the company provided its American and Arab employees elicited protests from the Saudi government and helped to provoke violent strikes on the part of Arab workers. It reinforced impressions of Aramco as a neocolonial enterprise during a

---

[61] See unsigned memo of conversation between al-'Alami and Hart, June 2, 1959, cited earlier; and Meyer to Jones, July 29, 1960, cited earlier.

[62] See Archer to Johnston, March 31, 1962, FO 957/251, BNA.

[63] Furlonge, *Palestine Is My Country*, 214–16, 220.

time of revolutionary Arab nationalism. It was therefore incumbent upon managers to show how Aramco profits could be reconciled with practical local concerns regarding employment, wages, and housing. This imperative motivated the company to investigate local conditions intensively and to create a bureaucracy, the Arabian Affairs Division, to compile and organize that information.[64]

Scholars were not the first to understand modernization as the destruction of local diversity by an unsentimental rationality. The most influential literary critique of Aramco describes the obliteration of local communities before the onslaught of global capitalism. *Cities of Salt*, the series of novels written during the 1980s in Damascus by Saudi dissident 'Abd al-Rahman Munif (1933–2004), describes one character witnessing the destruction of his village's orchards by an American oil company:

[The] things that still break his heart in recalling those days are the tractors which attacked the orchards like ravenous wolves, tearing up the trees and throwing them to the earth one after another, and leveled all the orchards between the brook and the fields. After destroying the first grove of trees, the tractors turned to the next with the same bestial voracity and uprooted them. The trees shook violently and groaned before falling, cried for help, wailed, panicked, called out in helpless pain and then fell entreatingly to the ground, as if trying to snuggle into the earth to grow and spring forth alive again.[65]

Munif employs animal predators to evoke the relentless advance of capitalist enterprise, spinning a counter myth to Aramco's and utilizing what Vitalis characterizes as a "destruction of Eden" trope.[66] But even William A. Eddy, whose work for both Aramco and the CIA gave him an opposite perspective to Munif's, resorted to bestial images to capture Aramco's transformation of Saudi Arabia. In a letter to his family describing the company's construction of the Dammam–Riyadh railroad, Eddy wrote:

We landed at the Hofuf Airport and drove in cars another 30 miles out to the rail-head where the railway is a-building like a long snake lengthening itself toward the southwest.... Beyond that Saudis were spiking down the rails and laying rail at the rate of 4,000 feet a day. Ten miles beyond that the dinosaur-like steam shovels were building up the roadbed, dumping and packing down gravel and crushed stone, circling like dragons in the flying sand.[67]

---

[64] On the role of Aramco in Saudi Arabia's development, see Toby Craig Jones, *Desert Kingdom: How Oil and Water Forged Modern Saudi Arabia* (Cambridge, MA: Harvard University Press, 2010).

[65] Abdelrahman Munif, *Cities of Salt*, trans. Peter Theroux (New York: Vintage International, 1989), 106.

[66] Vitalis, *America's Kingdom*, 2. Journalist Thomas Lippman writes that Munif "dramatizes for effect." See Thomas Lippman, *Inside the Mirage: America's Fragile Partnership with Saudi Arabia* (Boulder, CO: Westview Press, 2004), 78.

[67] Eddy, "Dear Family," February 26, 1950, folder 4, box 6, WEP.

To contrasting effect, Munif and Eddy both emphasized the impact of global capitalism on eastern Arabian communities. Aramco's managers sought to compile local knowledge as part of their effort to dispel expectations of an inevitable conflict.

Aramco's harvesting of knowledge about Saudi Arabia served a political purpose inasmuch as it appeared to provide evidence of the company's concern for locals. "The oil company made it its business to know as much as possible about how the country functioned," writes journalist Thomas Lippman, "a prodigious task in the absence of statistics, reliable media, and competent government organizations." Arabist George Rentz (1912–1987), who headed the Arabian Affairs Division created after the war, even interviewed Bedouin "relators" who offered oral testimony about tribal relationships and geography.[68] Novelist Nora Johnson's husband worked in government relations studying "the minutiae of certain aspects of life in the Eastern Province," including "local history, place-names, and tribal customs" by interrogating what Johnson called "a phalanx of mangy, grizzled, half-asleep Aramco-hired Bedu."[69] In accumulating "a maximum possible knowledge of Arabia and the Arabs," Aramco management stressed that the information obtained "must be organized in a manner that makes it available to specific problems of the Company." Yet Rentz's staff extended its research broadly into areas of "history, geography, language, politics and culture," and Aramco maintained a "comprehensive research library" of Arabic materials.[70] In 1958, the company conducted a wide-ranging survey of its Arab employees, using IBM data cards to manage the information. It then used the survey as one basis, along with face-to-face interviews, for modifying its Home Ownership Loan Program for Arab employees.[71] "Having such a valid reason for asking questions and meeting people," observed one Aramco researcher, "provides an opportunity for gathering data on other subjects in which we are interested."[72]

Aramco's compiling of local knowledge served a similar political purpose to its denunciations of European colonialism and the contrasts drawn between formal empire and the company's role in Saudi Arabia. Just as the highly favorable 1949 article in *Life* had contrasted Aramco's benevolence against "the odium of old-style colonialism" (see Chapter 2), Rentz and his coauthors wrote in the 1960 *Aramco Handbook* that experts from the company's Arabian Affairs Division "assist in the solution of particular problems" and "contribute toward a better understanding of the people and the

---

[68] Lippman, *Inside the Mirage*, 49. On Rentz, see the biography in folder 57, box 1, WEM.
[69] Nora Johnson, *You Can Go Home Again: An Intimate Journey* (Garden City, NY: Doubleday & Company, 1982), 59.
[70] Barger to Henry, June 30, 1955 with attached paper, cited earlier.
[71] Quint to Mulligan, April 3, 1960, folder 64, box 2, WEM.
[72] Memo by Quint, April 11, 1960, folder 64, box 2, WEM.

country."[73] They presented Aramco as heir to the earlier "introduction of Western modernizing influences" in the Middle East by Britain and France, whose political rule under the mandate system had fomented "disillusionment and resentment among nationalist leaders."[74] European colonialism served as a useful foil against which to portray Aramco's modernizing mission as sensitive to local needs. Nora Johnson assessed Aramco's enterprise in contradictory terms as "a remarkably sensitive imposition of a Western culture on an older, Eastern one ... the transaction between us and Saudi Arabia was quite different than that of the British Empire."[75] Aramco engineer Larry Barnes, who was otherwise critical of the company in his self-published memoir, still concluded that "Saudi Arabia and its people would not be as well off if the oil had been exploited by a French or British company."[76] The presumed contrast between Aramco and the "British ... big stick" approach became typical even of internal State Department memoranda.[77] Aramco at least partially succeeded in brandishing local knowledge about Saudi Arabia to argue that its operations were the antithesis of a colonial imposition. Britain fulfilled the same legitimizing function in Aramco's modernizing narrative as UNRWA experts did in al-'Alami's.

The company's residential communities became crucial sites for displaying Aramco's commitment to modernization and its local knowledge. They were also places where gender politics functioned as a proxy for broader arguments about whether Aramco was modernizing or colonizing Saudi Arabia. Describing the "Little America," suburban quality of the company's Senior Staff Camp has become a set-piece in numerous accounts of the initially whites-only compound that Aramco built for its American employees at Dhahran on the Persian Gulf. Aramco clerk Michael Sheldon Cheney wrote of "neat blocks of houses set in lush gardens" with "jasmine hedges and clumps of oleander." For Lippman, the Americans' gated community was "*Pleasantville*."[78] Journalist Kai Bird, whose father served as U.S. consul in Dhahran, compared it to "a Dallas suburb," except for the siren that regulated workdays in this company town. Like any suburb, it boasted "an elementary and junior high school, a commissary [or market], swimming pools, a movie theatre, a bowling alley and a baseball field."[79] Mary Elizabeth Hartzell, who came from Seattle to manage Aramco's research library, wrote home to her mother about the consumer abundance available

---

73 Roy Lebkicher, George Rentz, Max Steineke et al., *Aramco Handbook* (Dhahran: Arabian American Oil Company, 1960), 208.

74 Ibid., 80.

75 Johnson, *You Can Go Home Again*, 57.

76 Larry Barnes, *Looking Back Over My Shoulder* (n.p., 1979), 31.

77 See Lippman, *Inside the Mirage*, 8–9; and Citino, *From Arab Nationalism to OPEC*, 54.

78 Quoted in Citino, *From Arab Nationalism to OPEC*, 57; Lippman, *Inside the Mirage*, 55–70.

79 Kai Bird, *Crossing the Mandelbaum Gate: Coming of Age Between the Arabs and Israelis, 1956–1978* (New York: Scribner, 2010), 90.

to the company's American employees. In the dining hall, she enjoyed "a big buffet with candles and a camel made of ice for a center piece ... salads & meat & fish, cheese, delicious cake with real butter icing, peaches & pears, roast turkey & dressing." Some of the fresh produce she bought in the commissary – "celery, lettuce, tomatoes, grapes, bananas, pears, apples, lemons, oranges, potatoes, onions, cabbage, limes, [and] avocadoes" – may well have come from al-'Alami's farm.[80]

Inside the fence surrounding what residents called "American Camp," criticism of the narrow roles permitted to women did not seriously jeopardize faith in Aramco's modernizing mission. One disgruntled male employee referred in his resignation letter to the hyper-masculine environment: "Though I am continually annoyed by the boarding school-army camp atmosphere of Dhahran I am full of admiration for many of the things which the Company has done."[81] As a "bachelorette," Hartzell lived in manufactured housing, "a portable with 4 rooms for 8 girls," rather than in a suburban ranch. Her hostess at a sewing party, Hartzell observed to her mother, "is a 'Mrs.,' " and so had a "lovely six room house." When she learned of a female acquaintance's engagement, Hartzell sighed: "They will have a brand new house."[82] The "Little America" in Dhahran replicated the postwar domesticity of home, even as the company relied on the labor of single women who worked as nurses, secretaries, and teachers. Though not members of the company's senior staff, these employees were still permitted to reside inside the "American Camp." Living in a compound that excluded Arabs, Hartzell nonetheless aligned herself with what she described as Aramco's progressive "foreign investment," contrasting it against British colonialism. The British "are not doing so well in the Arabian peninsula just now," she wrote her parents in 1957; "I think their local representatives must be living in the last century."[83] The wife of one executive juxtaposed women's boredom with men's participation in Aramco's mission. "You certainly had women there who were unhappy," she told Lippman, because "many of the men were in such exciting jobs." The development of Saudi oil "was the biggest thing that was going if you were a geologist or a petroleum engineer ... And here was the wife at home."[84] Johnson recalled that at social gatherings where men celebrated their professional achievements, husbands "tried to include their wives, and we all sat around and laughed politely," but "it made me sad that I would never have such adventures." Left at home during the day, wives

---

[80] Hartzell to mother, August 8, 1952, folder 8; and Hartzell to mother, November 16, 1953, folder 9, box 11, WEM.

[81] Peyton to Pendleton, September 1, 1957, folder 10, box 2, WEM.

[82] Hartzell to mother, August 8, 1952, folder 8; Hartzell to mother, January 28, 1953, folder 9; Hartzell to mother, August 14, 1953, folder 9, box 11, WEM. See also letter by Mulligan, September 19, 1959, folder 22, box 11, WEM.

[83] See Hartzell to "mother & daddy," n.d., [1957], folder 13, box 11, WEM.

[84] Lippman, *Inside the Mirage*, 64.

"not only cooked, but strained to outcook each other."[85] Deftly, however, Johnson used her experience with the "'[p]roblem that has no name'" in Aramco's "phony, plastic Levittown" to defend the company's role in Saudi Arabia: "it seems to me that Aramco was the ever patient and humoring wife, smilingly agreeing to everything, to the unreasonable, tyrannical husband that Saudi Arabia was. (Yes, dear. It's your country.)" Her defense of Aramco took the form of consciousness-raising. "Why should they respect us," she asked, "if we didn't respect ourselves?"[86]

Writing at about the same time as Johnson, Munif portrayed the arrival of American women and the invasion of foreign gender norms as the most compelling evidence for colonization. His fictionalized account of a huge American ship reaching shore offers one local perspective on gender politics from outside the fence:

There were dozens, hundreds of people, and with the men were a great many women. The women were perfumed, shining and laughing, like horses after a long race. Each was strong and clean, as if fresh from a hot bath, and each body was uncovered except for a small piece of colored cloth. Their legs were proud and bare, and stronger than rocks. Their faces, hands, breasts, bellies – everything, yes, everything glistened, danced, flew. Men and women embraced on the deck of the large ship and in the small boats, but no one could believe what was happening on the shore.[87]

In real life, when the future Saudi petroleum minister 'Abdullah al-Tariqi broke the color barrier and insisted on living inside the fence with his white American wife, residents harassed the interracial couple. According to *Time* magazine, "American matrons took his wife aside and reproved her for marrying an Arab." Tariqi's testimony concerning his domestic life reinforces the impression of Aramco as a colonial enterprise: "It was a perfect case of an Arab being a stranger in his own country."[88]

Aramco's housing policies for Arab employees evolved as the company's response to government demands and those made by workers in a series of postwar labor strikes. Following a 1945 strike, Aramco rejected Saudi officials' call for the merging of American and Arab residential communities and instead adopted a policy of loaning Arab employees funds with which to build their own homes in separate communities. Aramco borrowed its Home Ownership Loan Program from its corporate parent, Exxon, whose subsidiary Creole Petroleum utilized it in Venezuela.[89] In Venezuela, too, the oil company had built segregated communities for expatriate workers characterized by an idealized domesticity. "The enclosed camp dramatically constricted women's freedom of movement," writes historian Miguel Tinker

---

[85] Johnson, *You Can Go Home Again*, 45–46, 48.
[86] Ibid., 61, 62.
[87] Munif, *Cities of Salt*, 214.
[88] Quoted in Vitalis, *America's Kingdom*, 136.
[89] See Vitalis, *America's Kingdom*, 108.

Salas. "The persistence of racially and economically segregated oil camps throughout Venezuela," Salas further observes, describing the dilemma Aramco also faced, "increasingly clashed with the industries' broader social and cultural discourse."[90] Following a weeklong strike in the Saudi oil fields in 1953 during which demonstrators stoned a U.S. Air Force bus, Aramco made limited concessions in negotiations with Saudi government officials. The U.S. embassy reported, however, that Aramco was pleased that it was "able to oppose successfully" demands that it bear the cost of building workers' homes, rather than loaning them the funds to do so.[91] Aramco turned to a labor management technique utilized by the global oil industry to cope with its housing problem, but sustaining the argument about its modernizing role in Saudi Arabia depended on demonstrating that such a policy could be reconciled with local lifestyles.

It was on issues of gender that the Arabian Affairs Division staked much of the company's claim to respect local society. Following another strike in 1956, and internal deliberations in which Aramco adopted certain reforms but not the integration of housing, the company made a push to expand its Home Ownership Loan Program for Arab employees.[92] In 1960, the company noted a "sharp decline" in applications for loans to construct homes in Rahimah, one of two planned communities built for Arab employees. Rahimah and the newer town site of Madinat Abqaiq served as separate and less well-appointed versions of the American Camp. Researchers were charged with answering the question: "Why has Saudi Arab employee interest in the program declined and how may they be induced to participate in it?" The company was also interested in estimating the eventual size of these communities, which affected demand for "schools, playgrounds, medical facilities, etc.," and therefore in calculating fertility and child mortality rates among employee families. This information would come from "interviews with wives of employees" who, in the initial plan, would be the subject of "450 hours of interviewing." When this proved too ambitious, eighteen employee wives were interviewed in August and home visits made in September to speak with women living in Rahimah.[93]

The interviews were conducted by Phebe A. Marr, a Harvard PhD candidate in Middle East studies who, as a woman, could meet with Arab employee wives prohibited from contact with male nonrelatives. Marr's role in the Arabian Affairs Division and knowledge of Arabic enabled her to interact with Saudi women in a way that eluded other American women

[90] Miguel Tinker Salas, *The Enduring Legacy: Oil, Culture, and Society in Venezuela* (Durham, NC: Duke University Press, 2009), 149, 199.

[91] Jidda (Jones) to State, foreign service dispatch 277, January 23, 1954, 886A.062/1-2354, RG 59, NARA. On the strikers' demands, including housing reforms, see the correspondence in FO 371/104882, BNA.

[92] See Vitalis, *America's Kingdom*, 205–08.

[93] Quint to Mulligan, April 3, 1960, folder 64, box 2, WEM.

who lived inside the fence. Lippman describes the practice of having Saudi women visit American women's homes, though he also writes: "Aramco women could avoid Arabs entirely if they chose, and many of them did so."[94] In Dhahran, Johnson watched herself becoming like "those masked Arabian women" whom she regarded as "silent, protected, infantile creatures."[95] Hartzell described Arab women as "shapeless black figures," though, intriguingly, "one catches a glimpse of gay trousers just around the ankles."[96] Marr's contact with Arab women therefore gave her access to the sources of local knowledge that had been least available to Americans, but which the company regarded as most valuable.

Within her small sample, Marr made a point of speaking with both Sunni and Shi'a Muslim women and with those who lived in company town sites as well as in the "natural" communities of the nearby Qatif oasis. She concluded that female isolation was the overwhelming reason that families found the company communities undesirable. In fact, Marr uncovered "several cases of husbands moving out of Company houses in town sites and back to natural communities to please their wives." In a complaint echoed by American women, one twenty-three-year-old Shi'a Arab wife told Marr that "she missed her family and had no one to talk to all day." While the houses that the company constructed for both Americans and Arabs were built for nuclear families, Arab women's most important relationships were with other females from their extended families. "Cut off from family and friends of like religion and background," Marr wrote, "women are left without any means of contact with the world outside their houses." This problem was difficult to remedy within the town sites because it was "too expensive to build Company houses big enough to house the extended family." In Marr's view, amenities provided in the company homes did not suit Arab women either. Few used their kitchen ranges, "preferring to sit on the floor or on small, low, wooden platforms while preparing the food and cooking it" with a primus stove, which "provides a certain amount of mobility." Women "do not like to stand over a stove to cook, which they consider backbreaking work." They "are not ready to use modern facilities such as high sinks, bathtubs, and refrigerators," Marr reported. Overall, she concluded that the company should allow employees to build houses "in their home towns." Families "should not be urged to move into townsites where the traditional pattern of their lives is disturbed to a considerable degree." Such houses "should be modern in appearance, but preserve the best features of the traditional style, such as the open courtyard." This floorplan (which she sketched as part of her report)

94 Lippman, *Inside the Mirage*, 37–38, 56.
95 Johnson, *You Can Go Home Again*, 79.
96 Hartzell to mother, November 22, 1953, folder 9, box 11, WEM.

illustrates how Marr believed Aramco should accommodate its housing policy to local sensibilities.[97]

Marr's fellow researcher Malcolm Quint reached similar conclusions in a study titled "Home and Family in Qatif Oasis." Residential communities were organized around "the extended family group embracing three generations, since in Qatif communities, as in most of Saudi Arabia, the household unit is the extended family consisting of a father and mother, married sons and their wives and children, and unmarried daughters." Unlike in the company town sites, the layout of residences was meant to accommodate this larger group. "The building itself," Quint explained, "is more often than not a conglomeration of small rooms built helter-skelter around the inside of a compound wall." This arrangement facilitated extended family relations among women. Quint found that "visiting and gossiping among the women of the extended family takes place in the open courtyard area of the family dwelling, and much of the chatter so vital to the continued happiness of the women goes on while they perform their household tasks." Moreover, kinship networks bound together different extended family households in the residential quarters of the towns. "Just as the household is a family unit," Quint explained, "so also the village or quarter of the town is largely a kinship unit." For women living in such an environment, "the opportunity to meet people outside the family almost never exists." It was therefore "unrealistic to expect significant numbers of employees from the Oasis to obtain houses in the Company townsites," where women would be deprived of extended family contacts.[98]

Other Aramco research focused on domesticity and gender relations as the local knowledge most valuable to the company. The Arabian Affairs Division investigated whether significant numbers of Saudi Arab women could be hired by the company, but concluded that "the only socially sanctioned adult role for a woman ... is that of wife and mother, who is to be kept at home."[99] A report about family relations in the towns of Saihat and al-Mallahah explained that women "live under a rigidly defined system of sexual segregation," indicated by the "Arab word for woman (Hirmah – sing.; Harim – plural)," which "is derived from the root H-R-M" denoting "forbidden, prohibited, and unlawful." Even in the courtyard house meant to accommodate an extended family, "the woman must keep herself fully clothed." The Arabian Affairs Division thus went to great lengths to understand local domestic practices. Its work permitted researchers, so their reports implied, to penetrate beneath surface appearances and grasp

---

[97] Marr to Mulligan, "Home Ownership Program – Rahimah," December 22, 1960, folder 5, box 3, WEM.

[98] Jones to Weathers, January 25, 1961, with attached report by Quint, "Home and Family in Qatif Oasis," November 1960, folder 5 box 3, WEM.

[99] Vidal to Mulligan, "Employment of Saudi Arab Women," September 16, 1961, folder 9, box 3, WEM.

the reality of gender relations. "Despite the strictness of this ideal system," the report on Saihat and al-Mallahah revealed, "women are not quite as segregated as it would appear." It was virtually "impossible for a woman living in a large household" and "carrying out the ordinary household tasks" to "completely efface herself from the males of the household." Only the wealthiest women who could pay others to do such tasks are "really expected to observe this ideal system."[100]

Aramco adopted the recommendations made by Marr and Quint and permitted Arab employees to use the Home Ownership Loan Program to build houses in their home villages. According to company literature and favorable accounts of Aramco, the housing program was a successful example of the company ascertaining and then accommodating local needs. "Having gained sufficient experience as to Saudi Arab employees' desires," explained the *Aramco Handbook*, "the Company has placed increasing emphasis on the administration of the Home Ownership Program" to ensure quality control in the houses constructed.[101] Lippman writes that "the program proved generally popular and Aramco has always been proud of it." After the Saudi government bought out and nationalized the U.S. companies, Saudi Aramco continued the practice and more than 36,000 homes were eventually built or purchased.[102] But the *Handbook* made its claims about respecting workers' desires before Quint and Marr were charged with studying why most Arab employees declined to participate. The problems facing the program, moreover, were hardly unique to eastern Arabia. Salas writes of oil company communities in Venezuela:

[T]he design of the new living arrangements undermined traditional practices. By establishing a series of formal rules and regulations, the companies sought to "de-ruralize" their new laborers and recast their relationship with the land, producing modern laborers who depended on the company for their wages. Faced with small accommodation and no possibility of growth, camp life also recast the family and weakened the extended networks that pervaded Venezuelan society. Eroding the basis of the extended family and its multiple levels of authority emphasized the role of the male, and so did limiting women's ability to engage in independent productive activity.... Confronted by these conditions, some families opted to live in nearby villages instead of a camp.[103]

The company intensively studied local conditions, but did so in order to address a problem seen in other global oil enclaves.

---

[100] Unsigned memo to file, "Preliminary Notes Permitted Degrees of Relationship – Saihat and al-Mallahah," March 14, 1960, folder 64, box 2, WEM.

[101] Lebkicher, Rentz et al., *Aramco Handbook*, 215.

[102] Lippman, *Inside the Mirage*, 86; see also Thomas C. Barger, *Out in the Blue: Letters from Arabia, 1937–1940: A Young American Geologist Explores the Deserts of Early Saudi Arabia* (Vista, CA: Selwa Press, 2000), 264.

[103] Salas, *The Enduring Legacy*, 176.

Aramco did not succeed in mitigating housing as a focus of Arab protests. At the outbreak of war in June 1967, Arab mobs attacked American Camp. Despite her faith in Aramco's benevolence toward the Saudis, Johnson had feared just such a scenario during her time in the kingdom a dozen years earlier: "What would happen if there was revolution? War? Mass attack from mad armed Arabs, knives in teeth, eyes glittering?"[104] But demonstrators caused only limited property damage. Bird writes that "a mob invaded my childhood home in the American consulate compound, and one young man broke his leg while trying, successfully, to tear down the Stars and Stripes." Rioters "later moved on to Aramco's American Camp ... stoning cars and nearly ransacking the home of Tom Barger, Aramco's president."[105] Barnes, the Aramco engineer, was working in Abqaiq when the demonstrations broke out. Confronted with what he later called a "native uprising" similar to what the Belgians had faced in the Congo, he telephoned his wife, Marion, and told her to barricade herself in a bedroom closet with their daughter and his gun.[106] As Barnes' comparison suggests, domesticity had become entwined with anticolonialism in Saudi Arabia as elsewhere in the third world. Aramco leaders consequently recognized that gender was crucial to reconciling their enterprise with Arab nationalism. Far from an abstract knowledge that, in Scott's words, "ignores essential features of any real, functioning social order," Aramco's approach fetishized such details, particularly those regarding women and gender, to validate its role in the kingdom. The fact that Aramco maintained a bureaucratic office, the Arabian Affairs Division, to collect and manage local knowledge poses a challenge to the sharp dialectic underlying Scott's critique. Company literature, and an informal mythology accepted by many Americans, also positioned Aramco as the antithesis of British colonialism. That mythology is itself an artifact of postcolonial politics, which forced modernizers to legitimize development as fulfilling local desires.

In many respects, the villages constructed as part of the Egyptian government's Tahrir (Liberation) Province desert reclamation project appear to provide a textbook case of the "authoritarian high modernism" Scott criticized. A massive scheme initiated by the Free Officers' regime that seized power in July 1952, Tahrir Province initially envisioned reclaiming some 600,000 *feddans* of desert west of the Nile Delta on the way to eventually cultivating twice that area and increasing Egypt's total agricultural land by a staggering 5 to 10 percent. The first new village built in Tahrir Province, Umm Saber, consisted of public buildings plus 230 homes capable of

[104] Johnson, *You Can Go Home Again*, 79.
[105] Bird, *Crossing Mandelbaum Gate*, 209, 210.
[106] Barnes, *Looking Back Over My Shoulder*, 169.

housing 1,400 relocated peasants.[107] Eventually, planners hoped, the province would be organized into twelve districts, each containing eleven villages the size of Umm Saber.[108] Villages would be built of hollow mud bricks that could help manage extreme desert temperatures and whose local fabrication would contribute to the province's self-sufficiency. Those peasants carefully selected to live in the villages were subject to military-style training described as "complete human reconditioning" intended to create a new Egyptian citizen.[109] According to historian Jon B. Alterman, Tahrir reflected an "impatience bordering on urgency" among Free Officers eager to change Egypt's unfavorable land-to-population ratio. Alterman writes: "Tahrir was breathtakingly broad in scope ... it would provide the first breath for a model society that would revolutionize the countryside."[110] More than just reclamation, Tahrir appears to fit Scott's definition of "authoritarian high modernism" as an attempt at the "administrative ordering of nature and society" by the state.[111]

But a closer look reveals how Tahrir Province's legitimacy hinged on whether it was perceived as respecting peasants' way of life. Tahrir is therefore important because it highlights the political aspects of modernization Scott's critique neglected. Even as villages were being constructed and land reclaimed in the 1950s, a conflict was already under way over how the experiment would be remembered both within Egypt and abroad. Among the Egyptian elite, Tahrir served as a site for controversies over land reform policy. In addition, the province became entangled in Cold War politics and served as a useful foil for Americans who claimed that a rival, U.S.-sponsored project in Egypt fostered grass-roots democracy, in contrast to the top-down authoritarianism of Tahrir, which began receiving Soviet assistance in the 1960s. In both the domestic Egyptian and Cold War contexts, the value of the Tahrir scheme was debated in terms of its ability to deliver self-determination as well as modernity. In the political conflict over its value as a model, the legitimacy of Tahrir Province depended on its being perceived as an antiauthoritarian project.

No one defended Tahrir Province more tenaciously than its founder and early leader, Major Magdi Hasanayn. A Free Officer who was given wide latitude by Nasser in a bureaucratic fiefdom called the Tahrir Province

---

[107] Government of Egypt, *The Liberation "Tahreer" Province* (n.d.), 3, 5.

[108] See Doreen Warriner, *Land Reform and Development in the Middle East: A Study of Egypt, Syria, and Iraq*, 2nd ed. (London: Oxford University Press, 1962), 49.

[109] Quoted in El Shakry, *The Great Social Laboratory*, 197.

[110] Jon B. Alterman, *Egypt and American Foreign Assistance, 1952–1956: Hopes Dashed* (New York: Palgrave Macmillan, 2002), 79. See also Roel Meijer, *The Quest for Modernity: Secular Liberal and Left-Wing Political Thought in Egypt, 1945–1958* (New York: Routledge Curzon, 2002), 201.

[111] Scott, *Seeing Like a State*, 4.

Organization, Hasanayn managed the project until the National Assembly removed him in 1957 and placed Tahrir under the Ministry of Agrarian Reform.[112] From the earliest stages, Hasanayn combined an emphasis on Tahrir's impressive scale with a focus on its humanizing elements. He sought to deflect criticisms of Tahrir's Pharaonic ambitions by turning attention to the province's villages, which he portrayed as vibrant communities. He explained in contradictory terms to British journalist Harry Hopkins that it would be "the creation of a youthful, co-ordinated and coherent Egyptian society" that also possessed "peculiar individuality, aims, [and] ability, to serve as a model of what the Revolution intends for this noble nation." As one measure of the project's humane character, Hasanayn told Hopkins that peasants would be taught to play musical instruments because "a fellah who can appreciate music is more evolved."[113] He told British agriculturalist Doreen Warriner: "'Humanity is to be the keynote.'"[114] Hasanayn invoked the communitarian values and desert pilgrimage of America's Mormons: "*This is the place!* You know what they achieved. It will be so with us also.'"[115] His promotional materials even referred to Umm Saber as "the first new Egyptian 'neighbourhood.'"[116]

In his memoir, *Al-Sahara': al-Thawra wa al-Tharwa, qissat mudiriya al-Tahrir* [*The Desert: The Revolution and the Resources, the Story of Tahrir Province*] (1975), Hasanayn defended his project as creating autonomous communities where peasants would be free to live out the values of Egypt's revolution. This was a difficult task, because he presented this argument at the same time that he sought to defend the viability of collectivized agriculture in a running debate with opponents. Published following Nasser's death during the presidency of Anwar Sadat, *Al-Sahara'* reprinted historical materials from the time of Hasanayn's leadership and removal from office during 1950s, but also reinterpreted the meaning of Tahrir Province following two recent Arab–Israeli wars and amid Sadat's economic liberalization. Nevertheless, Hasanayn's attempt at reconciling his large development vision with small-scale communities situates him in the same historical moment with the ADS and Aramco's town sites, whose architects also sought to portray their new communities as places where modernization could coexist with humanity.

Hasanayn uses several strategies for infusing a sense of self-determination into an undertaking of such ambitious size. The first was evoking a radical egalitarianism among the technocratic elites who designed Tahrir Province,

[112] See Gabriel S. Saab, *The Egyptian Agrarian Reform, 1952–1962* (London: Oxford University Press, 1967), 64.

[113] Harry Hopkins, *Egypt, The Crucible: The Unfinished Revolution in the Arab World* (Boston, MA: Houghton Mifflin, 1969), 128, 130.

[114] Warriner, *Land Reform and Development in the Middle East*, 49.

[115] Hopkins, *Egypt, The Crucible*, 129.

[116] *The Liberation "Tahreer" Province*, 10.

the workers who built it, and the peasants who settled it. Tahrir overcame the colonial legacy that distinguished between ideas and labor, he insisted, and the absence of civilization in the desert imposed upon all people working there "one equal rank." The "democratic method [*al-uslub al-dimuqrati*]" utilized at Tahrir meant that any worker or peasant could make his voice heard at "the highest executive level" of the province.[117] Hasanayn similarly emphasized the camaraderie among engineers and workers, who rode side by side together on plows and bulldozers, lived in the same type of houses, ate in the same cafeteria, played on the same athletic teams, and shared nightly entertainments. He made much of the fact that while many of the 150 experts who worked on Tahrir were trained abroad (including some in the United States), they were all Egyptians, with no foreigners among them.[118]

Another strategy involved displaying empathy toward peasants and describing the brutal realities of life in rural Egypt that Tahrir promised to transform. *Al-Sahara'* presented a historical account of peasant oppression embellished with Hasanayn's borrowings from Marxism-Leninism. Like the slow turning of the water wheel, he explained, centuries of farming the Nile Valley had "changed the hand that held the whip, but the whip did not change." The Ottoman conquest had placed further burdens on peasants, while the rise of the colonial cotton trade partially integrated Egypt into global capitalism without creating any incentives for landowners to improve the primitive means of production based on peasant labor. Hasanayn's account both stereotypes the peasant and anticipates later critiques accusing reformers of appropriating him by trading on the "credit of his oppression [*sum'at zulmihi*]." Paradoxically, Tahrir Province must be ambitious in scale, Hasanayn insists, in order to break the oppressive cycle. Hasanayn's recounting of the bureaucratic and reactionary forces that persecuted him testify to Tahrir's humane approach. Portraying his political opponents as obstructing historical progress, he refers to those who ousted him from the leadership of Tahrir as "Ottoman chieftains." He castigates the functionaries who bungled agricultural reforms and the "knights of the routine" who sabotaged them.[119] Like other community builders, Hasanayn set up anti-democratic and bureaucratic rivals as straw men.

For Hasanayn, ground-level knowledge about Egyptian village life provided the basis for designing Tahrir's communities. Not unlike the study of Saudi towns undertaken by Aramco, Hasanayn's experts investigated the "objective conditions of the Egyptian village." They aimed to preserve "all the fundamental characteristics of the Egyptian peasant" while making "appropriate adjustments" to define a new type of Egyptian settlement.

[117] Hasanayn, *Al-Sahara'*, 86, 133–34.
[118] Ibid., 104; 106–07, 138.
[119] Ibid., 8, 26, 38, 62, 71.

Through this process, they arrived at the ideal size of 230 families and 1,400 people per community. Hasanayn claimed that these plans placed "the human being [*al-insan*]" at the center, and so villages were designed to a human scale in order to integrate family, work, and social life. Clusters of eight to ten houses were grouped around a courtyard of twenty-four square meters opening onto the main road, and each village was provided with a main square, market, school, mosque, and sports field.[120] As Hopkins described them:

[T]he villages were designed with amenity and a new pattern of life in view, not merely brute necessity. Council House, mosque and primary school were set around lawns and gardens. The houses themselves, each with its small front garden, were constructed in U-shaped blocks, front doors opening on a public square, back doors on a service road to the fields.

Houses came fully furnished for families, down to the pots and pans and standard-issue clothing for women and men. Hasanayn's deputies ushered Hopkins into one of the homes:

There was a chintz-covered sofa against a wall in the small living room and flowers in a vase on the table, which was covered with patterned oilcloth. One of the remaining two rooms had a double bed; the other, a double-decker iron bunk for the children. There was a bathroom with a flush toilet and shower. Cooking was by kerosene.[121]

The design of the houses and villages presupposed a community of nuclear families, and applicants for relocation to Tahrir Province had to be peasant heads of households who "possess[ed] only one wife, no dependants other than children, and no property; they must have been only once married and must have finished their military service."[122] Indeed, Hasanayn relied on the nuclear family structure of Tahrir's villages and a gendered division of labor as the means for integrating the household and community into his vision of Egypt's national development.

Hasanayn held up the integration of women into training programs and working life as evidence of the project's democratic character. Among the many "firsts" he claimed for the province was peasant women's training in cleanliness, weaving, and home management.[123] Warriner proclaimed women's participation in sports as "a revolution indeed."[124] During the first six months following their arrival, Hasanayn writes, peasants underwent

---

[120] Ibid., 124, 157, 158; see also 175.

[121] Hopkins, *Egypt, The Crucible*, 133, 134.

[122] Warriner, *Land Reform and Development in the Middle East*, 51. See also Hasanayn, *Al-Sahara'*, 164–65.

[123] Ibid., 322. On the "The Home Economics [*al-tadbir al-manzili*] of Nationhood" in Egypt, see Pollard, *Nurturing the Nation*, 132–65.

[124] Warriner, *Land Reform and Development in the Middle East*, 50.

training at the second village constructed, 'Umar Shahin, before being resettled permanently in their new homes. This training was conducted on the
level of each individual [*fardi*] man, woman, and child; on the level of the
family [*al-usra*] as the basic unit of the new society; and on the level of
the "local community [*lil-mujtama' al-mahalli*]." Women's training included
cleanliness, childcare, and "methods of modern management for the new
home [*turuq al-isti'mal al-haditha lil-manzil al-jadid*]," as well as "compulsory [*ijbari*]" literacy training. Consistent with a gendered division of labor,
female peasants were schooled in poultry science, milking, and rural handicrafts, as opposed to the agricultural and vocational training given to men.
Women learned to be consumers as well as producers, and their domestic
roles figured prominently in the way Hasanayn related the nuclear household to national development. Women learned what every modern home
needed: "a broom [*miqasha*]," "sackcloth [*khiyash*]," "feather-duster [*min-
fada*]," "bucket [*jardal*]," "phenol [*finik*]," "brush [*fursha*]," "soap [*sabun*],"
and so forth. In prioritizing the development of the countryside over urban
industries, Hasanayn emphasized the building up of peasants' "purchasing
power [*al-qudra al-shira'iya*]" to "broaden the internal market [*tawassu'
al-suq al-dakhiliya*]" for Egyptian manufactures.[125] For him, the efficiencies
large-scale collective farming provided would create the wealth with which
to grow peasant purchasing power and generate internal demand. In this
way, each peasant woman played a critical role in Egypt's national development through the modern management of her household.

In the battle over Tahrir Province, Hasanayn's opponents within Egypt
included civilian advocates of private landownership, such as Nasser's
agrarian reform chief, Sayid Marei, as well as military officers in the reclamation bureaucracy who became invested in state ownership of agricultural
land. Following a visit in 1964 by Khrushchev, Nasser accepted Soviet aid
to reclaim 10,000 additional *feddans* in northern Tahrir Province.[126] Given
that it became a Cold War symbol of Egyptian–Soviet cooperation second
only to the Aswan High Dam, Americans also had a stake in shaping perceptions of Tahrir Province. They attempted to do so negatively by contrasting its supposedly authoritarian nature with the grass-roots democracy
they associated with the Egyptian-American Rural Improvement Service
(EARIS). Modest only when compared to Tahrir, EARIS was a joint project
by the two countries to reclaim about 33,000 *feddans* in the marshlands
of Buhaira Province and the desert near the Fayyum oasis.[127] Like Tahrir,

---

[125] Hasanayn, *Al-Sahara'*, 76, 166–68; see also 80, 137.
[126] See Robert Springborg, "Patrimonialism and Policy Making in Egypt: Nasser and Sadat and
the Tenure Policy for Reclaimed Lands," *Middle Eastern Studies* 15 (January 1979): 56–58.
See also transcripts printed in Hasanayn, *Al-Sahara'*, 181ff.
[127] See Saab, *The Egyptian Agrarian Reform*, 212–18; and Alterman, *Egypt and American
Foreign Assistance*, 63–95.

EARIS envisioned resettling peasants in villages that would enhance traditional community ties through the construction of "wide streets, a mosque, piped water supply and community center (school, a meeting room, health clinic, community bath and training facilities)." Lebanese-born sociologist and U.S. Department of Agriculture expert Afif I. Tannous took control of community-planning efforts for EARIS in spring 1953 by calling for a grassroots approach that included the organization of "women to improve home life and increase their participation in community affairs." According to Tannous, "self-help is the basic method in the operation of the Program."[128] The architects of Tahrir and EARIS each cited their plans to mobilize women as evidence for the democratic approach taken by their respective projects.

Although U.S. officials identified problems with EARIS including the high cost of village amenities, they criticized Tahrir's alleged authoritarianism to portray EARIS as a success.[129] Political scientist Richard Hrair Dekmejian wrote a history of EARIS in 1981 for USAID that relied on government documents and interviews with former U.S. officials. Dekmejian's account of EARIS thus provides a counterpoint to Hasanayn's defense of Tahrir. Each author criticizes the rival project on the grounds of bureaucratic indifference toward its human subjects. Dekmejian writes:

In developmental terminology, Tahrir vs EARIS represented two distinct and divergent approaches – "modernization from the top" vs. "modernization from below." In the American perception, the Tahrir province represented a clear example of "modernization from the top," where the Egyptian government followed etatist-socialist principles by providing financing, organizational direction and technical cadres, and permitted only limited peasant participation. In sharp contrast, the American approach to EARIS emphasized voluntaristic, grass roots peasant participation in democratic village self-governance.[130]

Tannous himself recalled: "We were going to consult with the people and not just impose things on them." His later visits to EARIS villages confirmed that the project "was flourishing beautifully, in contrast with the Tahrir Province that the Egyptian government developed from top-down, without involving the people."[131] Yet Hasanayn similarly characterized Tahrir as an undertaking concerned with "civilization in its broad sense." The villages of Tahrir were not just places for housing workers or facilitating reclamation, Hasanayn insisted, as occurred in Abis, where EARIS built settlements. By contrast, Tahrir's superior planning respected the "objective, indigenous

---

[128] Richard Hrair Dekmejian, "An Analytical History and Evaluation of the Egyptian American Rural Improvement Service (EARIS), 1953–1965" (USAID, April 1981), 8, 9.

[129] See Alterman, *Egypt and American Foreign Assistance*, 87–95.

[130] Dekmejian, "An Analytical History and Evaluation of the Egyptian American Rural Improvement Service," 30.

[131] Interview with Afif I. Tannous, Foreign Affairs Oral History Collection, Library of Congress, http://www.loc.gov/item/mfdipbib001160/, accessed September 23, 2015.

characteristics" encompassing the "historical and contemporary circumstances" of both the land and those who worked it.[132]

Although Hasanayn and Tannous emphasized the "self-help" aspects of
their projects in retrospect, each also sought to legitimize his project through
respect for grass-roots community and peasant culture. Like other community architects, Hasanayn stressed the inclusion of women and an abundant
domestic lifestyle as proof of his project's antiauthoritarian nature. His prescription of standardized gender roles sought to reconcile the promise of
individual and community freedom with the vision of a mass society. One
female Egyptian social scientist employed by Tahrir Province believed that
its training programs would give peasants a new understanding of the state,
replacing the army's "spirit of domination [*ruh al-saytara*]" with a human
face.[133] Yet Warriner observed that in 'Umar Shahin, the "women, primly
tending the model house" under the supervision of female trainers, "seem
slightly dazed."[134] *Al-Sahara'* combined domestic with martial imagery, pro-
jecting Tahrir's two faces onto different gender roles. Hasanayn not only
focused on home and community, but also lauded Tahrir's sons for bearing
arms during the Suez War. In the wake of June 1967, he emphasized the
role of villages in holding Egyptian territory and described Tahrir as the
blueprint for the "total regulation [*taqnin shamil*]" of rural life.[135] Hasanayn
intended women to symbolize empowerment and to counter impressions of
state authority attempting to control the countryside.

Like Hasanayn in *Al-Sahara'* and al-'Alami in *Palestine Is My Country*,
Hassan Fathy engages in mythmaking and score-settling in his development memoir *Architecture for the Poor* (1973).[136] He blames "peasant
obscurantism and bureaucratic hostility" for the failure of New Gourna,
the model village he built during the late 1940s opposite Luxor in the
Nile Valley (Figure 3.1).[137] But Fathy's work also exemplifies how local
knowledge assumed political significance and shows that community
building was more than just the state's act of violence against the countryside. Among architects, debates have centered around whether Fathy's

[132] Hasanayn, *Al-Sahara'*, 135.

[133] Quoted in El Shakry, *The Great Social Laboratory*, 211.

[134] Warriner, *Land Reform and Development in the Middle East*, 52.

[135] Hasanayn, *Al-Sahara'*, 177. By 1971, Tahrir Province consisted of some 200,000 total
reclaimed acres and 40,000 households. See table 1, "Some Major Reclamation Projects
in the Arab World," in John Waterbury, "The Cairo Workshop on Land Reclamation and
Resettlement in the Arab World," *Fieldstaff Reports*: Africa: Northeast Africa, series 17
(December 1971): 7.

[136] Fathy, *Architecture for the Poor*. This chapter also draws on manuscripts from the Hassan
Fathy Archives [HFA], Rare Books and Special Collections Library, American University in
Cairo, Egypt. Fathy's first published account of New Gourna was *Gourna: A Tale of Two
Villages* (Cairo: Egyptian Ministry of Culture, 1969).

[137] Fathy, *Architecture for the Poor*, 149; see also 150–51.

FIGURE 3.1. Hassan Fathy at New Gourna. Copyright and Courtesy of Rare Books and Special Collections Library, the American University in Cairo.

vernacular architecture – mud brick structures with handcrafted, domed roofs – was local or cosmopolitan, modern or a protest against the postwar international style.[138] Mitchell portrays Fathy as caught between the state's

[138] See James Steele, *An Architecture for People: The Complete Works of Hassan Fathy* (New York: Whitney Library of Design, 1997); and Panayiota I. Pyla, "Ekistics, Architecture and Environmental Politics, 1945–1976: A Prehistory of Sustainable Development" (PhD diss., Massachusetts Institute of Technology, 2002).

determination to promote tourism in the Valley of the Kings and recalcitrant peasants living in the "Theban Necropolis" whom the Antiquities Department charged Fathy with relocating. For Mitchell, New Gourna built on previous state programs that had also dispossessed peasants. Fathy "insisted on the participation of villagers in the design" of New Gourna, Mitchell writes, but "never succeeded in persuading the Egyptian government that it had anything to learn from the peasant."[139]

New Gourna was more significant, however, for its method of aided self-help than for the architectural style Fathy developed there, a method he sought to replicate beyond Egypt. Nor was Fathy's role limited to that of a reluctant soldier in the Egyptian state's war against its people. As Joe Nasr and Mercedes Volait write:

The importance of urbanistic flows across the Middle East is derived from the extent to which Arab planners, architects, builders and so on have customarily worked in other countries in their region. These intraregional flows, carrying practices across national boundaries, are often not easy to capture and hence may be greatly underestimated.... Yet those who practice across a region represent only a partial enlargement of scale; at a higher scale of complexity is of course the global practitioner.[140]

Fathy became a global practitioner. His method emerged from Egypt but evolved in the course of his experiences working in Iraq, Saudi Arabia, West Africa, and the United States. His interpretation of "aided self-help" grew into a formula for housing the poor that simultaneously offered a strategy for legitimizing community projects through the incorporation of local knowledge.

Architecture for the Poor emphasized the active involvement of Gourna's residents and respect for their way of life in the design of the new model village. Fathy writes that the location for the new village was chosen by a committee consisting of himself, government officials, "the Mayor of Gourna and the sheikhs of the five hamlets" that composed the old village. The success of the project depended, Fathy argued, on understanding social and family relationships among Old Gourna's 7,000 residents:

All these people, related in a complex web of blood and marriage ties, with their habits and prejudices, their friendships and their feuds – a delicately balanced social organism intimately integrated with the topography, with the very bricks and timber of the village – this whole society had, as it were, to be dismantled and put together again in another setting.[141]

---

[139] Mitchell, *Rule of Experts*, 184, 186–87, 189.
[140] Joe Nasr and Mercedes Volait, "Introduction: Transporting Planning," in *Urbanism: Imported or Exported?*, ed. Joe Nasr and Mercedes Volait (Hoboken, NJ: Wiley-Academy, 2003), xxvi.
[141] Fathy, *Architecture for the Poor*, 17.

Fathy aimed "to uncover the everyday life of the Gournis and reveal it, perhaps even more minutely than they themselves knew it," a task that ideally would require researchers to "watch the village life for many months," both to "observe and invite suggestions."[142] Like Hasanayn, Fathy described a manner of community planning that supposedly closed the power gap between experts and residents, in the case of New Gourna by restoring the "unhurried, appreciative discussions" between craftsman and homeowner that used to characterize village construction. If "each family must be designed for separately," then the architect is no longer an imperious professional, let alone a government bureaucrat who "designs one house and adds six zeroes to it."[143]

Similarly, Fathy's use of mud brick and handcrafted domes of the sort he observed in upper Egypt represented the strategic composition of an "indigenous" style that could set New Gourna apart from what he portrayed as attempts to impose foreign or dehumanizing housing models on peasants. Criticisms of Fathy's claim to have found a "pure" Egyptian style or arguments that his was a cosmopolitan amalgam of different "local" practices therefore neglected its political purpose. Fathy proposed to restore peasant individuality in an explicitly Cold War context:

Inexorably and largely unchallenged, the promoters of sameness have prevailed and have eliminated from modern life the tradition of individuality. Mass communications, mass production, mass education are the marks of our modern societies, which, whether communist or capitalist, are in these respects indistinguishable.[144]

Mud brick, fabricated onsite using precise data about the composition of soils, as well as the courtyard house and wind-catch as architectural features to regulate the extreme local climate, held down construction costs. At the same time, the domes fashioned by craftsmen from upper Egypt freed him from a reliance on purchased building materials and foreign expertise. As al-'Alami did, Fathy made a statement about self-determination by portraying his community as arising from an intimate connection with the land itself. Dwellings, he wrote, "should look as much at home in the fields as the date-palm."[145] Among his complaints about the American EARIS villages was that "they employed materials and techniques applicable to town building but foreign to the countryside," including "industrially fabricated building materials."[146] Likewise, his use of the courtyard house was portrayed as preserving both Arab culture and the extended family networks on which Old Gourna was based. Along with the dome, he wrote, the courtyard house was

[142] Ibid., 50, 53.

[143] Ibid., 29, 31, 51.

[144] Ibid., 27.

[145] Ibid., 44.

[146] Hassan Fathy, "Agrarian Reform and Rural Housing in Iraq," November 3, 1958, binder II #30, HFA.

"part of a microcosm that parallels the order of the universe itself," while the clustering of houses inhabited by the same extended family around a common courtyard "will help to cement together the family group by a constant gentle emphasis on its oneness." The new village would be divided by curved streets into four quarters, each of which would house "one of the main tribal groups of Old Gourna." Fathy contrasted his respect for the Gournis' family relations against the inhumanity of bureaucratic plans symbolized by the grid pattern.[147] "This approach to habitation," he wrote of organizing New Gourna's layout by family, "is the antithesis of the anonymity of modern urban housing development commonly applied to villages."[148] Fathy's plan combined these residential quarters with public buildings meant to foster a rich community life, including a mosque and Coptic church, *khan* (or market) for displaying handicrafts, a public bath, theater, women's center, medical dispensary, and schools for boys and girls.[149]

Fathy claimed to be both preserving and enhancing the Gournis' way of life. It was through his observations about women's place in village life and prescriptions of their roles in New Gourna that Fathy proposed to reconcile these objectives. Fathy resorted to the same etymological strategy as Aramco's researchers for defining a traditional domesticity:

The Arabic name *sakan*, to denote the house, is related to the word *sakina*, peaceful and holy, while the word *harim*, which means "woman," is related to *haram*, "sacred," which denotes the family living quarters in the Arab house.

Fathy revered the courtyard house as a sacred space containing a "trembling liquid femininity." If the courtyard is not fully enclosed on four sides, then

this special atmosphere flows out and runs to waste in the desert sands. Such a fragile creation is this peace and holiness, this womanly inwardness, this atmosphere of a house for which "domesticity" is so inadequate a word, that the least little rupture in the frail walls that guard it destroys it.

The courtyard-and-square layout of New Gourna was therefore intended partly to regulate women's entry into the village's common areas and to provide for degrees of public exposure. Fathy's evocation of village women's role placed special emphasis on those occasions when they were permitted out in public. These included women's market day, "the one day in the week when they can leave the confinement of the house and enjoy the freedom of walking, dawdling, and gossiping as they please." In characterizing how female villagers fetch water, Fathy likewise conjures an image of traditional, local practices: "black-robed women, erect as queens, each with her water

---

[147] Fathy, *Architecture for the Poor*, 58, 70, 71–72.
[148] Hassan Fathy, "New Gourna: A Housing Experiment, March 26, 1955, binder I, #24, HFA.
[149] Fathy, *Architecture for the Poor*, 70. Mitchell notes that "there was also to be another kind of building not usually found in villages, a police station." See Mitchell, *Rule of Experts*, 187.

jar (*ballas*) carried nonchalantly on her head." His plans for New Gourna contained proposals for preserving what Fathy described as women's traditional practices at home and in public but that promised to modernize them according to his own vision of domestic and community life.[150]

In consulting with the Gournis about their new homes, Fathy was unable to speak with the women, who "were kept jealously out of the way," though he later had female intermediaries do so on his behalf, as Phebe Marr would for Aramco. Unlike al-'Alami and Hasanayn, Fathy did not directly assign women an economic role in New Gourna, though presumably they could participate in the production of the handicrafts that he envisioned as sustaining the village. Rather, the architect synthesized his conception of tradition with scientific expertise to legitimize prescribed roles for women in public and private. An example concerned the *hammam*, or public bath, which would offer women the opportunity "to escape from the restriction of the house" on the day set aside for them each week. There, women could gossip and "choose brides for their sons and brothers" from among village females whose charms would be on display. As individual homes were provided with internal faucets, the *hammam* would replace the village well as the site where women contracted marriages. Fathy sought to revive this "traditional" practice in a way that incorporated social and medical science. "When the prescriptive sociologist wishes to manipulate people into the patterns and activities he favors," he explained, "it is by means of institutions like the hammam that he will be most successful." The bath in New Gourna would fulfill a sociological role by giving women and men "a wide, varied, and strong collection of social contacts," as well as a hygienic one, by offering each villager "mental as well as physical refreshment" and "an opportunity to delouse himself." Fathy similarly invoked tradition and science when describing his design for cooking and washing facilities in the Gournis' new homes. "The peasant woman usually cooks over a fire built on the ground," he explains. The kitchen was designed "only after prolonged observation and careful analysis of a woman's movements while cooking," retaining "the squatting position for the cook, as this has been shown to be far more comfortable than a standing position."[151] The laundry pit that would be built into each home also permitted the woman to work while seated before a circular stand designed to hold a basin. "Scientific findings on the thermal metabolism of the body," he wrote, "show the wisdom of adopting such a posture in a warm climate." The "size, height and dimensions of the seat and the disk are designed to suite [*sic*] the bodily movements of the peasant woman while washing in the traditional way."[152] In

---

[150] Fathy, *Architecture for the Poor*, 57, 76, 100.

[151] Fathy, *Architecture for the Poor*, 40, 88, 89, 98.

[152] Hassan Fathy, "New Gourna Village: A Housing Experiment." See also Fathy to Marinos, "Quriyya al-Gourna al-Namudhijiya al-Jadida," n.d., pp. 16–17, binder I, #13, HFA.

Fathy's prescription of domestic roles for women, no distance separated the expert from the peasant, because scientific evidence confirmed the wisdom of traditional practices.

Fathy attempted to turn his project into an authentic expression of peasant self-determination. His memoir echoes Tayeb Salih's Arabic novel set in the upper Nile, *Season of Migration to the North* (1966). Salih's narrator praises the village craftsman who built the "vast and ancient door" to his grandfather's house from a single tree using the same self-taught expertise with which he fashioned water-wheels. Like New Gourna's buildings, the old house was built of mud brick created from the surrounding earth, "so that it is an extension of it."[153] Mud brick communicated an opposite message of local authenticity from the "abbreviated visual image of efficiency" that Scott regards as the high-modernist aesthetic.[154] Fathy's respect for local knowledge and tradition at New Gourna also enabled him to criticize other aided self-help projects. When governments, the United Nations, or "some other benevolent authority" provided equipment and materials for peasants to construct their own homes, wrote Fathy, "the 'self-help' lasts just as long as the 'aid' does." Villagers who acquired new skills to utilize the materials faced "that most frustrating of blind alleys" when the materials ran out and they could no longer practice their trade. This was precisely the problem Fathy sought to avoid by teaching Gournis how to fabricate mud bricks from "common local materials."[155] His approach made New Gourna replicable, "a true model village, whose buildings could be copied safely by any peasant with no technical help anywhere in Egypt."[156] In this way, Fathy set himself apart from people at "clean universities in nice, progressive countries" who were "offended by the existence of poverty and squalor among millions in the unfortunate countries." Aid bureaucracies might have provided assistance out of disdain for the poor ("'Give him sixpence to go away.' 'What a dreadful smell – give them some drains.'"), but Fathy presented himself as attuned to peasant lifeways.[157] Though the Gournis inconveniently revolted against relocation and sabotaged a dike, flooding Fathy's village, the architect had devised at New Gourna a method for legitimizing development programs by leveraging local knowledge.

In 1957, Fathy joined Doxiadis Associates, the Athens firm founded by the visionary architect and planner Constantinos Doxiadis.[158] A development

[153] Tayeb Salih, *Season of Migration to the North*, trans. Denys Johnson-Davies (New York: Michael Kesend Publishing, 1989), 70, 71. On the doors of village houses, see also Fathy, *Architecture for the Poor*, 35.

[154] Scott, *Seeing Like a State*, 224.

[155] Fathy, *Architecture for the Poor*, 117, 118.

[156] Ibid., 96.

[157] Ibid., 117.

[158] See Fathy to Doxiadis March 28, 1957, folder: DOXIADIS Associates, HFA. On Doxiadis' role in the urban planning of Riyadh, Saudi Arabia, see Pascal Menoret, *Joyriding in*

oracle and entrepreneur, Doxiadis originated the discipline he called "ekistics," or the science of human settlements. Social geographer Ray Bromley describes ekistics as "a unifying concept enabling scholars and policymakers to link micro-, meso- and macro-scale processes throughout history and far into the future."[159] Doxiadis used his experience working with Marshall Plan funds in his native Greece to land Ford Foundation support for the "City of the Future" (COF), a massive study that attempted to project the trends that would shape human settlements over the ensuing two centuries. For his part, Fathy's emphasis on local knowledge tempered Doxiadis' fixation on the global scale. Fathy contributed "evolving notions of 'tradition,' " scholar Panayiota I. Pyla writes, that complemented the future megacity of "ecumenopolis" prophesied by Doxiadis. During the time he worked on COF, Pyla explains, Fathy "assumed the role of a spokesman for the 'underdeveloped' parts of the world."[160]

While at Doxiadis, Fathy cultivated local knowledge about poor communities as a way of legitimizing his approach to aided self-help. His first major opportunity to do so came with his work on Greater Mussayib, a rural community of several thousand households constructed in Iraq's Babil Province. In "A Report on Housing for Greater Mussayib," Fathy wrote to Doxiadis that he had visited "archaeological sites as well as villages and towns" in the area "with the objective of getting acquainted with the national and local spirit" and "to spot out" the "methods of construction" that had "survived or could be rendered valid anew." Fathy believed that public facilities could logically be provided only "by grouping the people into villages of convenient size." As at New Gourna, however, Greater Mussayib would be planned around family relations. Doing so required

close investigation in the social field, with regard to the affinity between individuals in the family and tribe groups, their desires of proximity of their houses, of securing seclusion for the family groups and quarters, and the distribution of the family quarters in the village plan etc.

As he had done in the Nile Valley, Fathy sought to reconcile his concept of local tradition with the findings of modern science, particularly in the domestic amenities provided in peasants' homes. Such amenities would have to be "designed with respect of the customary ways of usage" yet also offer hygienic means for "washing of the body, the laundry, dishwashing, the disposal of waste water and the night-soil as well as the recommendation for

Riyadh: Oil, Urbanism, and Road Revolt (New York: Cambridge University Press, 2014), 67–101.

[159] Ray Bromley, "Towards Global Human Settlements: Constantinos Doxiadis as Entrepreneur, Coalition-Builder and Visionary," in *Urbanism: Imported or Exported?*, 316. See also Constantinos A. Doxiadis, *Ekistics: An Introduction to the Science of Human Settlements* (New York: Oxford University Press, 1968).

[160] Pyla, "Ekistics, Architecture, and Environmental Politics," 93, 106.

cooking, heating, baking and water storage, etc." Fathy juxtaposed arrangements for female domestic labor with his hope that Mussayib's male heads of
households would include retired police and military officers, who were given
special privileges under Iraq's land law. These men would "form an educated
class with a high level of living who will be setting new standards for the peasants."[161] A Doxiadis Associates bulletin published after the July 1958 Iraqi
revolution referred to a breakdown in the "patriarchal family system" that led
to the influx of the rural poor into *sarifa* shanties on Baghdad's periphery.[162]

For COF, in which researchers were assigned to study human settlements
in different regions of the world, Fathy barnstormed cities in West Africa
between December 1960 and February 1961 (see Chapter 1).[163] He portrayed his method of aided self-help as an antidote to the racist legacy of
colonialism evident in the region's towns. West African towns, Fathy wrote,
"are wholly European creations, serving foreign economic and political
interests, and the African shanty towns that have grown onto them are as
different in culture and life as they are in architecture from the smart modern buildings of the centre." Such cities are characterized by "separate areas
for different races," a "ghetto system" that foments "resentment and race-
hatred."[164] Colonial cities were artificial, in the sense that they did not emerge
naturally from their environment. When "a European town is planted in the
bush, the natural hierarchy of settlements is upset" because such a town
"does not have a genuine relationship with the countryside." This incon-
gruity is symbolized by the European preference for "impossibly expensive
air-conditioning" that few black Africans could afford. Blacks were also
excluded from city centers by "municipalities' laws preventing the building
of native-type dwellings in specified areas." Fathy argued that "Africans who
want houses should be encouraged to build for themselves" wherever possible. To make aided self-help work in the cities, and to make the resulting
dwellings suited to their inhabitants, the study of tribal relations and local
practices was essential. "There can be no question," Fathy wrote,

that one of the most vital pieces of research waiting to be done is on how to make
use of the existing habits of cooperation found in the tribal system, the village tradition of freely contributed labour for a common purpose, and to direct it into organized urban building projects.[165]

[161] Hassan Fathy, "A Report on Housing for Greater Mussayib," October 10, 1957, folder: Iraq
     Housing Project, box: Architectural Projects 1930s–1960s, HFA.
[162] Doxiadis Associates *Bulletin* no. 5 (September 1959), folder: S XI DOX A, box: Dox 11,
     HFA. On Doxiadis Associates' work on an urban housing program in Iraq, see Steele, *An
     Architecture for the People*, 111–16.
[163] See ibid., 117–23.
[164] Hassan Fathy, "Preliminary Sketch of the Report on Africa," March 22, 1961, folder: PP
     107 typescripts, COF, etc., box: 11 Dox, HFA.
[165] Hassan Fathy, "Future Insertion in the Report," June 14, 1961, folder: PP 107 typescripts,
     COF, etc., box: 11 Dox, HFA.

Fathy therefore insisted that his method could prove equally useful in urban and rural areas. Following his study of West African towns for COF, Fathy contributed to a UN rural housing project in Darʿiyya, Saudi Arabia, where he sought to mobilize local knowledge to help villagers build themselves dwellings near the Saudi ruling family's ancestral home.[166]

Fathy disparaged the United States as embodying a dehumanizing approach to human communities. For COF, Fathy had read a report on North American cities that criticized suburbanization and automobility, as well as class and racial segregation.[167] Reiterating Jacobs' critique of American city planning, Fathy linked the "problem of delinquency" to the "frame of the town plan" in the United States. "We have in the USA," Fathy wrote in a 1963 conference paper, "a unique chance to study the effects of an anonymous town plan on the individual."[168] In a larger sense, Fathy rejected modernization theorists' portrayal of America's present as the model for developing countries' future:

There is a tendency to take for granted that the type of civilization seen in the USA today ... represents the future for all societies that have not yet reached the USA level. Even those who look beyond the present scene in the USA tend to believe that it is at least a necessary stage in the evolution of societies, and that the countries that today are called underdeveloped must pass through a stage in which their society and urban scene will resemble that of the USA today. This view is surely far too simplistic.

In U.S. cities, "man has been subordinated to the machine, and the cities designed for cars." With respect to town planning, the United States was "the most backward country on earth."[169] Yet, as aided self-help gained support in official circles, and as Jacobs and others raised objections to city planning and urban renewal, Fathy found American allies. Though at times he had defined his community-building method in opposition to the United States, Fathy would attempt to bring it to Chicago.

Fathy's leading patron was William R. Polk, the Harvard Arabist who served at the State Department (see Chapter 6). Polk later headed the Adlai Stevenson Institute of International Affairs (ASIIA) at the University of Chicago. Polk admired Fathy, describing him as the "Third World's Walter Gropius" in a letter to the University of Chicago Press, which published

---

[166] See documentation in box: HF1 Series III/B Architectural Projects Sohar, Oman/Darʿiyya, KSA, HFA.

[167] G. Gutenschwager, "A Report on American and Canadian Cities," July 14, 1961, R-ERES 16(14), no folder, HFA. See also Gerald A. Gutenschwager, *Planning and Social Science: A Humanistic Approach* (Lanham, MD: University Press of America, 2004). Fathy makes similar criticisms in "The Dwelling within the Urban Settlement," August 18, 1961, binder II, #46, HFA.

[168] Hassan Fathy, "Dwelling in Developing Countries" [handwritten draft for 13th International Course in Criminology, June 22, 1963], no folder, box: Dox 11, HFA. See Jacobs, *Death and Life of Great American Cities*, 57, 74–88.

[169] "Dwelling in Developing Countries" [handwritten draft].

Architecture for the Poor on Polk's recommendation.[170] "He is certain[ly] the most humane, perceptive and socially sensitive architect in the Middle East," Polk wrote an ASIIA colleague, "and, I think, may be recognized as one of the great architectural thinkers of this period anywhere."[171] Polk brought Fathy to the ASIIA on a $10,000 fellowship in 1971–72. Fathy worked on development plans for Egypt and delivered talks including one titled "Architecture for the Billion Poor" at the Chicago Club.[172] In the summer of 1972, Polk met Fathy in Beirut and proposed that the architect assist Clyde Ross, a Mississippi-born neighborhood activist and later himself an ASIIA fellow, to design and build homes in the mostly African American area of Lawndale on Chicago's west side. Ross had appealed to the ASIIA for funds with which to rebuild the 3300 block of Flournoy Street into a "showcase for the west side," and Polk believed that Fathy should design it.[173] "It would demonstrate Hassan Fathy's technique [of] 'guided self-help', using cinder block construction," Polk wrote, "and would be an electrifying project."[174]

Ross's neighbors approximated the sort of community ties Fathy encouraged, although their determination to resist undesirable living conditions gave them something in common with the residents of Old Gourna. To protest unfair contract sales to African Americans by real estate speculators, Ross and others organized rent strikes and demanded the renegotiation of contracts. Their Contract Buyers' League filed a federal lawsuit, ultimately dismissed, alleging racial discrimination and redlining.[175] In the wake of late-1960s urban violence, Ross mobilized his neighbors to improve their homes through cooperative labor. They "tuckpointed, sandblasted and painted their houses, sodded their lawns and are building fences and installing lights to give additional security," declared an ASIIA press release.[176] Polk hoped to tap into this cooperative spirit to build dwellings using Fathy's method. The project would be designed on the basis of information, supplied by Polk, about the families living in Ross's Flournoy Street neighborhood along with their preferences for their new homes:

the most important room in the house in their estimation is the dining room. This can merge into a living room and should be made convenient to the kitchen by a bar or partial cutaway of the wall for serving. The kitchen can be fairly small. However,

[170] Polk to University of Chicago Press, November 29, 1971, folder 9, box 15, ASIIA.

[171] Polk to Diamandopoulos, July 30, 1970, folder 9, box 15, ASIIA.

[172] Polk to Fathy, May 3, 1971, folder: Adlai Stevenson Institute, 1970–73, HFA. See also the advertisement of Fathy's November 16, 1971 talk, ibid.

[173] Ross to Diamandopoulos, May 2, 1972, folder 1, box 19, ASIIA. On Ross's fellowship, see Polk to Ross, May 11, 1973, ibid.

[174] Polk to Diamandopoulos, June 22, 1972, folder 7, box 18, ASIIA.

[175] See Beryl Satter, *Family Properties: Race, Real Estate, and the Exploitation of Black Urban America* (New York: Metropolitan Books, 2009), 233–71.

[176] "Background," August 22, 1972, folder 1, box 19, ASIIA. See also "Victory Party," *Chicago Tribune*, August 31, 1972, sec W 4A, p. 10.

they do seem to want bedrooms larger than 9 ft. by 12 ft. (which seems to be the urban renewal standard).[177]

Fathy hoped to merge local knowledge with his own prescriptive vision. "There are several plans in my mind to ensure security within the quarter," he replied, "by correct implantation of the buildings ... gently forcing people to meet in the streets day and night."[178] ASIIA appeals to potential funders compared African Americans' displacement by urban renewal to the global problem of underdevelopment. "Solutions in Cairo, Calcutta and many other cities," one such letter explained, "may show us experiences applicable to Chicago."[179] The ASIIA had previously hosted a conference called "Making Black Power Work: Strategies and Proposals."[180] Just as Karen Ferguson has shown with respect to the Ford Foundation's support for Black Power activism, the ASIIA sought fresh approaches for "reforging a social consensus on race" and taming the revolutions that threatened liberalism at home and abroad.[181] Fathy claimed that his own technique for building model communities, though developed in the Middle East, could be implemented in West Africa and elsewhere. It appealed not only to experts such as Doxiadis and officials in developing countries, but also to Polk and dovetailed with the ASIIA's emphasis on liberal modernization.

In his foreword to *Architecture for the Poor*, Polk described Fathy's method as potentially helping to reverse the disintegration of the black family. "Mothers and children were often parted from one another" during slavery, Polk explained, while internal migration compounded "the rootlessness" of American blacks and urban renewal amounted to "yet a new uprooting of communities." Polk implied that self-help could restore the patriarchal family. Black families, "even when fatherless and plagued by instability," Polk wrote, "attempted to assert neighborhood." He praised New Gourna as the antithesis of public housing whose design was a "bureaucratic decision" that yielded slums "whether horizontal or vertical." Through guided self-help, the architect could "assist people in accomplishing their objectives by their own efforts better and more cheaply than they could" without him.[182]

The plan to build homes in Lawndale through aided self-help faced obstacles including city building codes and extreme winter weather. "Chicago is laced with building code restrictions," Polk wrote Fathy, "which will enormously complicate the realization of the project."[183] Chicago's bitter cold

---

[177] Polk to Fathy, June 27, 1972, folder 7, box 15, ASIIA.

[178] Fathy to Polk, August 27, 1972, folder 9, box 15, ASIIA.

[179] Elting to Cooke, October 24, 1972, folder 1, box 19, ASIIA.

[180] See file on William Ellis, folder 3, box 18, ASIIA.

[181] Karen Ferguson, *Top Down: The Ford Foundation, Black Power, and the Reinvention of Racial Liberalism* (Philadelphia: University of Pennsylvania Press, 2013), 5. See also Immerwahr, *Thinking Small*, 132–63.

[182] See Polk's foreword to Fathy, *Architecture for the Poor*, x, xi, xiii.

[183] See Polk to Fathy, June 27, 1972, cited earlier.

was the opposite temperature extreme from what Fathy had confronted in the Middle East, although Fathy had observed how "municipalities laws" similarly prevented self-help construction in West African cities. Ross did refurbish buildings in Lawndale with ASIIA support, but not on the basis of Fathy's designs.[184] Nevertheless, Polk's belief that the approach pioneered at New Gourna could work in urban Chicago testifies to Fathy's success in gaining legitimacy for his aided self-help method.

The examples from this chapter illustrate the oversimplification involved in trying to distinguish clearly between the knowledge of the state and that of local communities. Not only did planners incorporate local knowledge into their development schemes as a way of validating them, but they also played on the very distinction between bureaucratic and local knowledge that scholars later used to criticize modernization. Community-building expertise flowed within and across national borders, involving more actors than just the state. Fathy's method developed at New Gourna migrated to Iraq, Saudi Arabia, and West Africa before making an appearance in Chicago. Aramco applied a policy borrowed from Venezuela to the problem of housing employees in eastern Arabia. Al-'Alami received praise for using practical knowledge to make the ADS a going concern, but also turned to the international experts he had once repudiated. Fathy parlayed his knowledge of the Gournis into a job with Doxiadis and incorporated his Nile Valley experience into the global COF study. In Chicago, he became a fellow at one of those "clean universities" mentioned in *Architecture for the Poor*. Even Tahrir Province, a massive government project, was the subject of a debate within Egypt and abroad over whether it respected local knowledge.

Focusing on gender in community building bridges the gap between states and societies found in Scott's analysis, as well as the presumed cultural differences over modernity separating Arabs from Americans. Both Arab and American planners seized on gender practices as the ultimate marker of indigenous culture and self-determination. Their strategic references to how the poor "really" lived and alignment with ordinary people against dehumanizing bureaucracies were legitimizing devices. The English and Arabic sources cited for this chapter are replete with such mythmaking as those who designed communities went to great lengths to shape the historical meanings attached to their projects. Judging from the featured cases, they had more success convincing potential sponsors of these arguments than gaining acceptance from the poor themselves. But their claims to respect local knowledge reflected the imperatives of postcolonial politics and cannot be dismissed as mere pretense. Their projects embodied a contradiction between the drive for progress and the desire for liberation. Through their embrace of "self-help," community builders paradoxically argued that planning could deliver freedom.

---

[184] See Ross to Polk, March 22, 1973, folder 1, box 19, ASIIA.

4

Yeoman Farmers

"Land reform cannot be imposed on a country as an exotic by any outside agency. To be successful it must be suited to local needs, conform to local ideas and conditions and be established gradually by Government and people together."
– Sir Ernest Dowson, *Government of el 'Iraq, An Inquiry into Land Tenure and Related Questions: Proposals for the Initiation of Reform* (Letchworth, England: Garden City Press Ltd., 1931), 18; filed in folder: 1. Agriculture – Iraq 1. Land Reform, box 6, Office of Near Eastern Affairs, Subject File Relating to Economic Affairs, 1947–1951, Lot 55 D 643, RG 59, NARA.

"The creation of these small agricultural holdings is considered as the basis for building a sound democratic community. This social equity brings with it security for every individual, thus leaving no room for destructive ideologies.... In 1776 Thomas Jefferson postulated that the class of small landowners is the most valuable sector in the organization of a nation."
– Sayed Marei, *Agrarian Reform in Egypt* (Cairo: Ministry of Agriculture, 1957), 248.

"The Ambassador mentioned that our interest in the East Ghor project was based on our belief that it was in Jordan's interest to have the land irrigated by the project in the hands of yeoman farmers who we felt could help form the backbone of the country."
– Amman to State, foreign service dispatch 149, November 10, 1960, 785.00(W)/11–1060, RG 59, NARA.

Land reform, more than any other area of state policy, illustrates the neglected importance of regional histories for understanding Cold War–era economic development. Such a prescription runs counter to historians' recent globalism and focus on the transnational circulation of development expertise.[1]

---

[1] See Cullather, *The Hungry World*; Matthew Connelly, *Fatal Misconception: The Struggle to Control World Population* (Cambridge, MA: Belknap, 2008); Erez Manela, "A Pox on

Regionalism offers a needed complement to the worldwide comparative framework in which international experts themselves understood the struggle to improve peasant societies after World War II. By emphasizing common problems and universal solutions, their perspective grouped poor countries together in an undifferentiated state of "underdevelopment." In 1950, for example, the United States supported a Polish resolution in the UN General Assembly calling on the Food and Agriculture Organization and the Economic and Social Council to study how "unsatisfactory forms of agrarian structure and, in particular, systems of land tenure" work to "impede economic development and thus depress the standards of living."[2] As agriculture became a global Cold War issue, the U.S. State Department helped to organize a major conference on land tenure reform held at the University of Wisconsin in October 1951. Citing the need to take the issue away from "Soviet propagandists," Secretary of State Dean Acheson argued that "there is no more urgent problem than the impoverishment resulting from primitive methods of cultivation of the land under antiquated systems of landownership."[3] Dozens of agricultural specialists from around the world held sessions on the Middle East, Latin America, Asia, Africa, and Europe, but most panels featured general legal and technical approaches. In his introduction to the published proceedings, Wisconsin economist Kenneth H. Parsons portrayed the land tenure problem as a common, defining characteristic of underdeveloped countries and framed the conference "by identifying certain basic issues which cut across cultural and national boundaries."[4] Recent historiography on Cold War agricultural development has tended to follow Parsons' lead.

Historians of U.S. foreign relations have examined how American Cold War assistance sought to export New Deal agricultural policies. Their scholarship focuses on elites' faith that the American experience with agricultural reform held universal lessons for underdeveloped countries. David Ekbladh has studied the influence of Tennessee Valley Authority director David Lilienthal in promoting dam-building and hydropower projects overseas.[5]

Your Narrative: Writing Disease Control into Cold War History," *Diplomatic History* 34 (April 2010): 299–323; and Special Issue, "Toward a Global History of Modernization," *Diplomatic History* 33 (June 2009).

[2] UN General Assembly, 401 (V) 312th Plenary meeting, 5th sess., November 20, 1950. See also Warriner, *Land Reform and Development in the Middle East*, 4; UN Department of Economic Affairs, *Land Reform: Defects in Agrarian Structure as Obstacles to Economic Development* (New York: United Nations Publications, 1951); and Erich H. Jacoby, *Interrelationship Between Agrarian Reform and Agricultural Development: An FAO Land Tenure Study* (Rome: Food and Agriculture Organization, 1953).

[3] "Conference on World Land Tenure Problems," *State Department Bulletin* 25 (October 22, 1951): 660.

[4] *Land Tenure: Proceedings of the International Conference on Land Tenure and Related Problems in World Agriculture Held at Madison, Wisconsin, 1951*, ed. Kenneth H. Parsons, Raymond J. Penn, and Philip M. Raup (Madison: University of Wisconsin Press, 1956), 3.

[5] Ekbladh, *The Great American Mission*.

Nick Cullather has argued that reformers "projected an idealized New Deal onto other societies at a time when Americans were uncertain about the meaning of the New Deal experience." This domestic controversy resulted in the McCarthyist persecution of Wolf Ladejinsky, architect of Japan's postwar agricultural reforms who, by advocating family-sized farms as an economic and political strategy for development, "typecast peasants as sturdy yeomen in a frontier drama."[6] Sarah T. Phillips has identified rival policies that emerged from the New Deal and that competed to shape overseas agricultural development initiatives. The first sought "to help each and every farmer achieve a tolerable, though bounded, standard of living"; the second to "assist and sustain those farmers who embraced industrial practices and deployed the latest labor-saving and profit-maximizing technology." Phillips contends that "the industrial ideal would triumph" abroad because the policy of creating small-scale, yeoman farmers drew on a romanticized Jeffersonian past eclipsed by the rise of corporate agribusiness within the United States. It "represented the last expression of an already-discarded domestic strategy."[7] Like Cullather and other historians, Phillips is interested in how Americans battled over the New Deal legacy as they debated Cold War agricultural policy. They sought to mobilize that legacy in the struggle with the Soviet Union for influence in poor countries, where U.S. reformers presented America's history of agrarian liberalism as representing a more democratic path to development than the Soviet experience with collectivization. By analyzing attempts at replicating the American domestic experience across the third world, however, historians of agricultural development have framed the problem of land reform in much the same way as the American Cold War experts whom they study. Claims that the U.S. experience held universal lessons for agricultural development offered reformers a justification for modernizing peasant societies. Although historians today may approach such claims with skepticism, the American experience still serves as their point of departure.

In contrast to much of the recent historiography, this chapter takes a regional approach. It relates American Cold War policies to the history of land tenure in the Arab Middle East and portrays U.S. experts as successors to the Ottoman imperial and European colonial officials who had attempted previous reforms in the region. Framing U.S. agricultural policies regionally has several advantages. First, it measures American assumptions against conditions in a particular part of the developing world and reveals the pitfalls that beset attempts to translate Cold War development formulas into distinct local contexts. Second, it provides historical comparisons for American initiatives, in addition to the Cold War–era alternatives that competed with

---

[6] Cullather, *The Hungry World*, 76, 99.

[7] Sarah T. Phillips, *This Land, This Nation: Conservation, Rural America, and the New Deal* (New York: Cambridge University Press, 2007), 41, 283.

U.S. agricultural policies in the Arab world and beyond. As will be seen, U.S. agricultural reforms had goals similar to those the Ottomans and the Europeans had attempted earlier within the same Arab territories. Third, it illustrates how previous reforms prepared the ground for U.S. policies and played a role in determining their outcomes. American liberal ideals therefore took on varied meanings in different regions as they encountered other reform legacies. Finally, placing American power into regional historical contexts liberates scholars from the mental categories of the Cold War. It challenges an exceptionalist portrayal of the United States as the source of global reform and helps to unpack the diversity and complexity concealed by the term *third world*.

As in other aspects of Cold War development, those from the United States and developing countries waged their political battles within the bounds of similar assumptions about the nature of societal change. Both American and Arab experts seeking to reform peasant agriculture invoked the legacy of American liberalism. In his address "Land and Independence – America's Experience," Point Four administrator Henry G. Bennett lectured the Wisconsin delegates on the history of American agriculture from Jefferson and the Homestead Act to the reforms of the New Deal. Although the challenges America confronted in settling a continent were not identical to those developing countries faced, "there are certain general principles that can be adapted and applied to different situations," Bennett argued.[8] "We have promoted the family-size farm because it provides the incentive for individual initiative," wrote Isador Lubin, U.S. representative to the UN Economic and Social Council, in a *New York Times* article surveying the global land reform movement.

From the Homestead Laws down through our modern programs for encouraging soil conservation, crop insurance, reclamation and the purchase of farms by tenants, United States land policy has recognized the importance of the small farmer and his welfare.[9]

Arab elites, too, cited America's legacy of agrarian liberalism to advance their own agendas. Sayed Marei, who implemented the Egyptian Free Officers' land reform policy, defended the creation of small farmers in the Nile Valley by citing Jefferson and aligning himself with U.S. support for land reform. Marei's opponent Magdi Hasanayn (see Chapter 3) reached further back than the New Deal into America's Progressive era by citing the State of California's Durham Colony as a successful example of industrial-scale farming.[10] One Syrian official compared the tractor-based, commercial farming of his country's Jazira region to "the wild west of America in

---

[8] *Land Reform*, ed. Parsons et al., 37.
[9] Isador Lubin, "Hope of the Hungry Millions," *NYT*, February 10, 1952, p. 182.
[10] Hasanayn, *Al-Sahara'*, 177.

Gold Rush days," though his warning that over-cultivation would cause it to "revert to desert again" pointed to the need for modern farming techniques and implicitly to the lesson of the Dust Bowl.[11] Like their American counterparts, Arab elites agreed that new policies would not simply improve productivity and farming income, but that reforms could also help to achieve larger social and political goals. Sharing this basic assumption did not necessarily imply support for U.S. regional policies, however, as will be seen in the case of Jordan. King Husayn collaborated with the United States on a major irrigation and land reform program as part of a strategy to curb radicalism within the Hashemite kingdom. But even though he pursued such agricultural policies as a counterrevolutionary strategy, the king did not believe that they required him to abandon the struggle against Israel, as the United States insisted.

This chapter focuses first on the Americans who conceived and attempted to implement land reform policies in Arab countries. It juxtaposes their historical understandings of regional underdevelopment with the record of prior reforms. As this approach will demonstrate, while experts attributed a regressive rural social structure to the Arab states generally, a condition they blamed on the Ottoman imperial legacy, the implications of that legacy varied widely across the region. The Ottoman inheritance had also been mediated through the different agricultural policies of the European mandatory powers Britain and France. The contrast between American experts' sweeping interpretation of Middle Eastern agriculture and its uneven realities is especially apparent from the results of the East Ghor Canal, a U.S.-financed irrigation project in Jordan. This chapter concludes with an analysis of East Ghor, which serves on one level as an example of how different contemporary agendas could attach to the same development project. In historical perspective, East Ghor helps to illustrate the gap that could exist between policies conceived as part of a general Cold War strategy and local circumstances.

Americans seeking to improve agriculture in Arab countries used a sharply negative interpretation of the Ottoman legacy in land tenure to incorporate the Middle East into the Cold War strategy of agricultural development. This interpretation featured a critique of the empire's 1858 land reform law, which was portrayed as failing in its intended purpose of granting titles to individual cultivators and as unintentionally giving absentee landowners what amounted to private property rights instead. Oil company legal expert Herbert Liebesny told the Council on Foreign Relations that in theory the old Ottoman law sought "to establish title to the individual holdings of land by registering a claim under the name of the occupying owner." In reality,

---

[11] Quoted in Hanna Batatu, *Syria's Peasantry, the Descendants of Its Lesser Rural Notables, and Their Politics* (Princeton, NJ: Princeton University Press, 1999), 77.

however, "the villagers were deeply suspicious" that registration would lead to increased taxation and conscription, and so they "entered false returns and registered the land in the name of the tribal sheikh." As a result, the "registration had no relation whatsoever to reality and complete confusion resulted."[12] In land reform as in other aspects of Cold War strategy, a historical narrative about regional underdevelopment and earlier failed reforms helped to script a new role for the United States in the Middle East consistent with the global reach of its power.

The leading promoter of land reform as a U.S. political strategy in the Arab world was Lebanese sociologist Afif I. Tannous, whose role designing the EARIS villages has already been discussed (Chapter 3). In a larger sense, Tannous was pivotal to relating the Jeffersonian tradition of the "yeoman farmer" to the problem of land tenure in the Middle East, thereby incorporating the region into American Cold War strategy. Tannous' contribution centered around his identity as an Arab-American who could make plausible historical arguments about Arab countries that resonated with other U.S. officials lacking his background. Born in the Lebanese village of Bishmezzin, Tannous was educated at American missionary schools and the American University of Beirut (AUB) before earning a doctorate at Cornell in 1940. Part of his research examined Lebanese migrants from his home village who had settled in Jim Crow Mississippi, and while working for the U.S. Agriculture Department's Foreign Agricultural Service (FAS), Tannous capitalized on his cross-cultural upbringing to establish himself as its principal Middle East expert. As he later told an interviewer, he was "on-call to give what I knew to other government agencies, especially the State Department." At FAS, Tannous also fell under the influence of Ladejinsky and came to share his faith in land reform as a general development strategy: "Wolf was the leading light." Following a mission to the Middle East sponsored by the State Department during the first half of 1946, Tannous assumed the responsibility for explaining how the region could benefit from American assistance with land reform.[13]

Tannous combined the idealized image of American liberalism acquired from his missionary education abroad with a categorically negative historical assessment of nineteenth-century Ottoman land reform. He described himself as raised on tales of the American frontier: "I read about Daniel Boone, Squanto the Indian, [and] George Washington." Emigrants' reports also shaped his early impressions of the United States prior to the First World War. "I listened to the letters they sent home telling about America

---

[12] 2nd meeting of group on the Moslem world, 1948–49, January 24, 1949, folder 6, box 141, Series 3, CFR.

[13] Interview with Afif I. Tannous, Foreign Affairs Oral History Collection, Library of Congress, http://www.loc.gov/item/mfdipbib001160/, accessed September 23, 2015. See also memo by Malik to James Terry Duce, June 5, 1947, folder: Duce, James Terry, 1946–60, box 13, CHMP.

and its wonders," he recalled. One wrote that the "'rights of the individual are respected and guaranteed in America,'" which "contrasted strikingly with what we were used to under the alien Ottoman government." Grain rationing by Ottoman officials during the First World War and the famine blamed on those policies were formative experiences for Tannous, who contrasted abusive imperial authority with the "wholesome atmosphere of social interaction" and "clear consciousness of community identity" represented by his village.[14]

The ahistorical nature of Tannous' regionalism is apparent from a contrast between his perspective and a study on land tenure compiled during World War II by the Anglo-American Middle East Supply Centre (MESC).[15] The two accounts appear side by side in a file at the British National Archives. This file includes both a transcription of Tannous' 1943 article "Land Tenure in the Middle East," published in *Foreign Agriculture*, and a lengthy MESC report on the same topic. Tannous anchors his diagnosis of the region's problems in a description of six categories of land tenure without regard to time or place: the five categories recognized by the 1858 Ottoman Land Code, plus *musha'*, or commonly held land, which the Ottoman code had attempted to eliminate by issuing title deeds to individual cultivators. These categories, Tannous insists, comprise "the main background of the system that prevails today in the various countries of the Middle East." The longer MESC report, while criticizing the Ottomans' "stagnation" and "oppressive social system," nevertheless describes varied conditions of land tenure across the Arab successor states. Unlike Tannous' article, it insists that the 1858 land law cannot provide a blanket explanation for regional underdevelopment. Ottoman laws mandating land registration, for example, "were never enforced in the vilayets of Basra and Baghdad, which are now Southern Iraq." Also central to this more nuanced account was Britain's experience during the mandate period of attempting to administer existing Ottoman law by settling land titles. According to the report, this process had succeeded in Palestine and Transjordan as the result of reforms designed by Sir Ernest Dowson. In Transjordan, settlement "proceeded more rapidly and efficiently ... than it has in any other territory" to establish individual ownership rights. It "abolished the masha'a system," in which plots of common land were periodically redistributed among village families to ensure fairness with respect to the quality of land worked by each. The MESC even conceded, "at a time when it is unfashionable to praise anything French," that France's opposite approach in Syria and

---

[14] Afif I. Tannous, *Village Roots and Beyond: Memoirs of Afif I. Tannous* (Beirut: Dar Nelson, 2004), 83, 84, 104.

[15] See FO 922/258, BNA. For historical context on the Ottoman Land Code, see *An Economic and Social History of the Ottoman Empire, 1300–1914*, ed. Halil İnalcık with Donald Quataert (New York: Cambridge University Press, 1994), 856–75.

Lebanon of preserving common land tenure also held some benefits for peasants. In contrast to Tannous' article, the MESC document emphasized the uneven significance of the Ottoman inheritance in land tenure across the Arab successor states. While providing a generous assessment of British policies, it also acknowledged the different ways in which the mandatory powers had built upon the Ottoman legacy.[16]

It was Tannous' sweeping interpretation, however, that defined America's Cold War mission in regional terms. His perspective proved useful to U.S. officials because it portrayed the crisis in Middle East agriculture as a version of the global problem of "underdevelopment." In a 1951 *Middle East Journal* article, he explained the potential of the Point Four assistance program to change the region's rural social structure. "The Middle East (particularly the Arabic speaking portion of it)," he wrote, "constitutes a major and strategic field for this sort of democratic operation." While the United States and the United Nations offered technical agricultural assistance, such a policy "would amount only to half the job" and would neglect "the emancipation and welfare of the people." When the Ottomans, he explained, "attempted and largely failed to implement a comprehensive land reform (along the lines of their famous Land Code of 1858), abuse of the land and of the peasants was accentuated" and the region witnessed "the rise of a powerful class of absentee landlords." To "give substance to our general statement of the problem," Tannous surveyed agricultural conditions in various Arab countries. Absentee landlordism was pervasive, from the highly concentrated holdings in Egypt and Syria to the sparsely populated lands of Iraq controlled by tribal *shaykhs*, to the contrast apparent in Lebanon between the "small independent owner" in the mountains and the tenant farmer "in the Biqa valley of the interior." The implications for U.S. policy were clear: Point Four must address land tenure reform and not simply provide technical assistance to increase the production of existing holdings. It would be "ironical," observed Tannous, if Point Four – "a potent voice of Democracy in action on a global scale – should unwittingly serve as an instrument for the perpetuation of the present oppressive and undemocratic system of land tenure."[17]

Tannous' singular focus on addressing absentee landownership helped to form official U.S. perceptions of Middle Eastern agriculture. The sociologist formed a close relationship with Assistant Secretary of State George C. McGhee, which deepened, according to Tannous, "from mutual

---

[16] On the MESC's role in setting the stage for agricultural and other development policies in the postwar Middle East, see Robert Vitalis and Steven Heydemann, "Explaining State–Market Relations in the Postwar Middle East," in *War, Institutions, and Social Change in the Middle East*, ed. Steven Heydemann (Berkeley: University of California Press, 2000), pp. 100–45.

[17] Afif I. Tannous, "Land Reform: Key to the Development and Stability of the Arab World," *Middle East Journal* 5 (Winter 1951): 2, 3, 6, 9, 12, 20.

appreciation and effective involvement at the work level into friendship."
After becoming the assistant secretary of state, Tannous wrote, McGhee

> requested my office in USDA to have me attend his weekly staff meetings, wherein
> I always felt free to express my views (rooted in my village background, rural train-
> ing and experiences in the Middle East) on US policies for that area.[18]

The State Department selected Tannous to chair the Middle East session
at the Wisconsin land tenure conference, where he told delegates that the
Arab states and Iran shared "great similarities in their background of the
tenure system." The "whole system," Tannous stated in his introductory
remarks, "is characterized by absentee ownership of the land." Delegates
should therefore "think of the system as one for all," he urged, with only "a
few differences here and there."[19] Although Tannous successfully promoted
himself as a specialist on Middle Eastern agriculture, his expertise served
to portray the region as a "strategic field" awaiting transformation by the
United States and its tradition of agrarian liberalism. His reference to the
effects of nineteenth-century Ottoman land reform was a useful shorthand
for regional underdevelopment, an historical argument with which McGhee
sympathized given his own uses of the imperial past (see Chapter 2).

Another contrast to Tannous' unequivocal critique of the Ottoman
influence in the Arab countryside came from British agriculturalist Doreen
Warriner. After publishing *Land and Poverty in the Middle East* (1948),
Warriner received a grant from the Royal Institute of International Affairs
that enabled her to travel to Iraq, Syria, and Egypt in 1955–56. The resulting study, *Land Reform and Development in the Middle East*, offered a differentiated account of the challenges surrounding land reform in the three
countries. Warriner criticized the generic U.S. formula for agricultural development as "family farming by the Department of Agriculture out of the
New Deal." Such a policy corresponded most closely to conditions in Egypt,
with its "over-population, underemployment on the land," and the need for
public investment in irrigation that had made the Aswan High Dam a focus
of Cold War politics. By contrast, burgeoning grain production in Syria's
sparsely populated Jazira was the result of "Merchant-Tractorists," "pioneer
risk-taking capitalists investing in machinery and seed" who plowed huge
tracts of leased land in a region that was "a mixture of Macedonia and
Kansas."[20] The U.S. political equation – creating "yeoman farmers" would
prevent peasants from going communist – did not fully apply in Syria. The
most important rural leftist movement, Akram Hawrani's Arab Socialist
Party, which merged with the Syrian Ba'th Party, represented peasants mostly
from the more densely settled, western districts of Homs and Hama.[21] The

---

[18] Tannous, *Village Roots and Beyond*, 220.
[19] *Land Reform*, ed. Parsons et al., 84.
[20] Warriner, *Land Reform and Development in the Middle East*, 4, 10, 86, 89.
[21] Ibid., 108. See also Batatu, *Syria's Peasantry*, 124–30.

rise of the tractor, however, had fostered the kinds of commercial farming operations in Syria's northeast that characterized America's own Great Plains. Unlike Egypt, Syria did not lend itself to thinking "in terms of maximum farm sizes in accordance with the area which can be worked by the farm family with draught livestock."[22] Iraq, finally, presented the distinct combination of a depopulated countryside and rich oil revenues. Such circumstances gave rise to what Warriner called the "engineer's approach" of expensive flood control and irrigation works, such as the Wadi Tharthar scheme on the Tigris and the Habbaniya reservoir on the Euphrates. These projects served mostly to increase the value of property owned by landlords and tribal *shaykhs*: "Wealth accumulates and men decay."[23] Yet Warriner also recognized that Iraq's regressive rural structure was not simply a legacy of Ottoman land policies. In Iraq's southern irrigation zone, she notes, the Ottoman land code "was not applied even in theory."[24]

This point about Iraq is critical to understanding the flawed logic used to map the American experience with agricultural reform onto the Arab Middle East. In promoting Jefferson and the small-scale farmer as a development strategy, both Tannous and McGhee singled out Iraq's Dujayla land settlement, located below the Kut barrage on the Tigris 135 miles southeast of Baghdad, as a regional model. At Dujayla, the Iraqi government provided 62.5-acre parcels of irrigated, state-owned land to farming families rent-free "upon occupancy and cultivation for 10 years." Among the first U.S. officials to visit Dujayla in 1950 was Norman Burns, Musa al-'Alami's ally in the State Department (see Chapter 3). Burns compared the law establishing Dujayla to "our own Homestead Act of western pioneer days." In an official report and published article praising Dujayla, Burns applied Tannous' argument about the undemocratic character of the Arab countryside: "The root of that problem is that most of the land is controlled by a small minority of tribal sheiks and absentee urban landowners." Using terminology handed down from the Ottoman land code, Burns explained:

About 80% of the settled land in Iraq is state owned and leased either indefinitely (miri tapu) or temporarily (miri sirf), mostly to tribal sheiks and absentee city landlords, many of whom in the lower Tigris and Euphrates Valleys control 20,000 to 50,000 acres each.[25]

---

[22] Warriner, *Land Reform and Development in the Middle East*, 63.

[23] Ibid., 120, 126. See also Brad Fisk, "Development Projects in Iraq: II. The Wadi Tharthar Flood Control Project," *Middle East Journal* 5 (Summer 1951): 366–70; and J. H. G. Lebon, "The New Irrigation Era in Iraq," *Economic Geography* 31 (January 1955): 47–59.

[24] Warriner, *Land Reform and Development in the Middle East*, 69.

[25] Memo by Burns, "The Dujaila Settlement in Iraq," May 22, 1951, folder: 1. Agriculture – Iraq 1. Land Reform a. Dujaila Project, box 6, Lot File 55 D 643, Office of Near Eastern, South Asian, and African Affairs, Subject Files Related to Economic Affairs, 1947–1951, RG 59, NARA. See also Norman Burns, "Development Projects in Iraq: I. The Dujaylah Land Settlement," *Middle East Journal* 5 (Summer 1951): 362–66.

Beyond its promise of making yeoman farmers out of Iraqi peasants, however, Dujayla appealed to Tannous and Burns because it distributed state
lands and did not require the expropriation of landlords. Tannous cited
the Iraqi case to insist that Arab land reform "need not involve expropriation," and Burns insisted that the project had the support of "many far-
seeing landlords." As uncultivated state land was brought under irrigation,
he explained, "it could be made available to small individual holders." This
"class of small individual proprietors," he wrote to his State Department
superiors, "would alter in a fundamental way the social-economic structure of the Iraqi population" and "give Iraq the kind of progressive stability
needed in the Near East today."[26] In a meeting with McGhee, Iraq's envoy
to the United Nations, Fadl al-Jamali, also linked Dujayla to American anticommunism. When McGhee asked whether "the Iraqi people are afraid
of Communist aggression," al-Jamali replied that most "do not care" but
"could be made to care in ten years through such projects as the Dujaila."[27]

By attributing Arab rural underdevelopment to past Ottoman influences,
Tannous and other U.S. officials downplayed the political problems confronting their Cold War strategy in the present. As both Warriner and the
MESC report noted, the Ottoman land law was never applied in Iraq's
irrigation zone where Dujayla was located. Warriner explained that tribal
shaykhs had appropriated lands in Iraq's south only "in the last thirty
years." For her, merely distributing state lands, a "'line of least resistance'
policy," would be insufficient to help Iraq's peasants, because landlords
were the main beneficiaries of large irrigation works. "Without an expropriation of the very large landholdings," she wrote, "no legislation can
succeed," yet no law "which would infringe on the property rights of the
large landowners can secure parliamentary approval." She criticized Burns
explicitly for arguing that Dujayla could foster wider change in Iraqi agriculture.[28] Another problem with Tannous' historical approach was that the
meanings of the Ottoman legal terminology had shifted under the British
administration in Iraq after World War I, as had occurred in different ways
across other Arab mandates.[29] Dowson, who had authored British land

---

[26] See Tannous, "Land Reform," 16, 18; Burns, "The Dujaylah Land Settlement," 366; and
Burns, "The Dujaila Settlement in Iraq."

[27] Memo by Clark, December 19, 1950, folder: Iraq 1948 Memoranda, box 14, Records of
Near Eastern, South Asian, and African Affairs, Office Files of Assistant Secretary of State
George C. McGhee, 1945–1953, Lot 53 D 468, RG 59, NARA. For a British report critical
of Dujayla, see Crawford to Allen, April 11, 1951, and attachment, "The Dajeila Scheme,"
filed in folder: 1. Agriculture – Iraq 1. Land Reform a. Dujaila Project, box 6, Lot File 55
D 643, Office of Near Eastern, South Asian, and African Affairs, Subject Files Related to
Economic Affairs, 1947–1951, RG 59, NARA.

[28] Warriner, *Land Reform and Development in the Middle East*, 135, 157, 158n1. See also Lord
Salter, assisted by S. W. Payton, *The Development of Iraq: A Plan of Action* (London: Iraq
Development Board, 1955), 39–60.

[29] See Martin Bunton, *Colonial Land Policies in Palestine, 1917–1936* (New York: Oxford
University Press, 2007).

settlement policies in Palestine and Transjordan, noted a "curious but comprehensible reversal" in post-Ottoman Iraq by which *miri* came to refer only "to land retained in the legal possession of the State," as opposed to that "granted out on registered tenure" during the Ottoman period.[30] The scope for distributing lands to Iraqi farmers and creating a "class of small individual proprietors" was therefore narrower than Burns suggested. Tannous and Burns neglected the varied historical circumstances that had shaped agriculture in formerly Ottoman territories. But their static account of Arabs' rural underdevelopment and their portrayal of Jeffersonian ideals as the answer enabled them to define land reform as a nonrevolutionary, anticommunist strategy.

The State Department adopted an incremental policy reflected in officials' semantic preference for "agrarian" over "land" reform. They found the latter phrasing undesirable because it implied expropriation of property from social elements disposed to be anticommunist. As explained in one long memo addressed to McGhee: "Land redistribution necessarily requires that landlords be hurt economically." Smaller, family-owned plots, while fulfilling "political and sociological" aims, also did not necessarily advance the "productivity and output" needed for national economic development. As "bad as excessive landlordism is from the point of view of the peasant cultivators," the memo concluded, "it is, nevertheless, the landlord's share of the produce which is commercialized and converted into urban food supply." Rather than redistribution, the report emphasized better credit, farmers' cooperatives, and extension services, or what Warriner disparaged as the "all-inclusive catalogue" of the "American conception."[31] This definition received encouragement from Arab diplomats and technocrats, who told State Department officials that Arab governments should "start from the present rather than" attempt "retrocative [*sic*] redistribution of land." Those who made this argument included Syrian economic minister and AUB economist Husni Sawwaf, Lebanese delegate to the Wisconsin conference Najib Alamuddin, and George Hakim, a Lebanese diplomat who chaired the committee that authored the United Nations' *Measures for the Economic Development of Under-Developed Countries*.[32] Tannous himself used his connections as an AUB alumnus to secure support for U.S. assistance programs on the part of the Lebanese elite. On the eve of a key parliamentary

[30] Dowson, *Government of el 'Iraq, an Inquiry into Land Tenure and Related Questions*, 17.

[31] Loftus to McGhee, "Some Notes on Agrarian Reform," December 7, 1950, folder: "Loose Papers Not in Folder," box 2, Office of Near Eastern Affairs, Subject Files Relating to Economic Affairs, 1947–1951, Lot 55, D 643, RG 59, NARA; Warriner, *Land Reform and Development in the Middle East*, 5.

[32] See Boardman to Sands, October 15, 1951, Folder: Agricultural – General 2. Land Reform a. U.S. Policy, box 10, Office of Near Eastern Affairs, Subject Files Relating to Economic Affairs, 1947–1951, Lot 55 D 643, RG 59, NARA. In contrast to the cited document, Warriner cites Hakim as emphasizing landownership as the central question in agricultural reform. See Warriner, *Land Reform and Development in the Middle East*, 6 n2.

vote, Tannous described visiting "my old classmate," the speaker of parliament Adel Osseiran, who received him after midnight "because of the old ties." Osseiran assured him: "I will do my best tomorrow in the Parliament." Tannous interceded with other members of the AUB circle who served in Lebanon's parliament, including another of his classmates, public works minister Emile Bustani.[33]

Although Washington had backed the Free Officers' September 1952 land reform law in Egypt, promoting agrarian reform as a Cold War strategy in Arab countries presented the United States with a series of dilemmas.[34] The Egyptian law limited holdings to 200 *feddans* and compensated owners at ten times the estimated rental value of the land "plus the value of fixed and mobile installations and trees."[35] A disgruntled Egyptian landowner reportedly called it "Communism, engineered by the Americans," but one U.S. State Department analyst wrote of the Egyptian reform that "its achievements probably owe much to the modest nature of the program's goals and to the willingness of the Government to compromise with the landowners in program implementation."[36] Small family farms were not equally suited to agricultural conditions across the region, as Syria's Jazira illustrated, nor were they necessarily efficient enough to produce a surplus to fund development. At the same time, Tannous and Burns advocated creating "yeoman farmers" as the basis for Jeffersonian democracies, but held that such a policy did not require confronting landowners. Tannous made the contradictory argument that absentee landlordism was the pervasive legacy of the Ottoman past throughout the Arab world, yet land reform could be effective short of expropriation. His sweeping thesis served mainly to justify an American role in transforming the Middle East and to integrate the region into global U.S. strategy.

In rendering the Middle East susceptible to America's Cold War influence, Tannous was incapable of seeing himself as heir to the Ottoman and British officials who had previously tried to reform regional agriculture. Nor did he appreciate how U.S. policies could be constrained by those earlier initiatives and would be subject to the same regional patterns that had limited their success. Tannous and others who authored Cold War agricultural reforms attempted to translate general U.S. strategies for the third world into regional terms, rather than interpret the meaning of American power within distinct local contexts. Historians of the "global Cold War" can fall prey to the same fallacy. Focusing on Jordan's East Ghor Canal (Map 2)

---

[33] Interview with Afif I. Tannous, p. 12.

[34] See Joel Gordon, *Nasser's Blessed Movement: Egypt's Free Officers and the July Revolution* (New York: Oxford University Press, 1992), 166.

[35] Marei, *Agrarian Reform in Egypt*, 53.

[36] Warriner, *Land Reform and Development in the Middle East*, 31; Bovey to Palmer, "Land Reform in Egypt," August 8, 1958, folder: Egypt, Agriculture – General 1958, 6-B, box 11, General Subject Files Relating to the Middle East, 1955–1958, Lot 61 D12, RG 59, NARA.

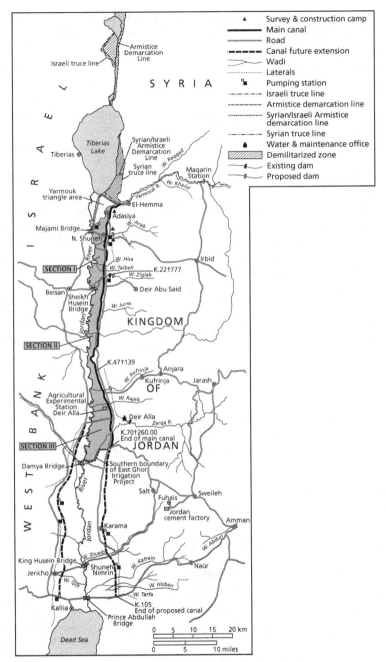

MAP 2. The East Ghor Canal Irrigation Project.

provides a valuable opportunity to escape this trap by interpreting Cold War development as one episode in the history of a particular place.

The Ghor (or *ghawr*, meaning "declivity") refers to the shelf running parallel to the River Jordan along its eastern bank beneath the uplands that look down into the valley. One report described it as a "terrace, 30 to 60 meters above" the Jordan and "ranging in width from 2 to 4 kilometers in the north" and broadening to "4 to 6 kilometers" further south.[37] Another characterized it as "a sharp barren cliff of salty marls and chalk deposits 50 to 60 metres high on the main Jordan Valley terrace, which slopes gently eastwards for 2 to 5 kilometres to the foot of the escarpment of the main Rift Valley."[38] Irrigating the Ghor's loamy soils had long been considered an essential strategy for increasing agricultural production in Transjordan. Doing so would require diverting the Yarmuk River, a tributary of the Jordan that rises in Syria, and taking advantage of the several *wadis*, or seasonal streams, that feed into the River Jordan when it rains. The Great Rift Valley of which the Jordan is a part includes the lowest elevations on earth, and planners envisioned the Ghor Canal as traversing all of its planned seventy-kilometer course below sea level, from a diversion tunnel at the Yarmuk at −203.6 meters down to its terminus south of the Zarqa River.[39] More than 80 percent of the East Ghor lands could be irrigated by the force of gravity without the use of electric pumps, raising hopes that the canal could be a cost-effective agricultural project. This hope was shared by British mandate officials as well as by the engineers who developed the postwar U.S. government scheme for irrigating the Ghor.[40]

During the Ottoman era, long before U.S.-financed development, the Ghor had been the site of both agriculture and pastoralism. Hilltop villages to the east generated wealth from cultivating the Ghor, while nomadic

---

[37] Jared E. Hezleton, *The Impact of the East Ghor Canal Project on Land Consolidation, Distribution, and Tenure* (Amman: Royal Scientific Society, Economic Research Department, 1974), 9.

[38] Middle East Secretariat to Chancery, August 18, 1949, FO 957/95, BNA.

[39] Joseph L. Dees, "Jordan's East Ghor Canal Project," *Middle East Journal* 13 (Autumn 1959): 358.

[40] See M. G. Ionides, "The Disputed Waters of Jordan," *Middle East Journal* 7 (Spring 1953): 153–64; M. G. Ionides, "Note on a Major Irrigation Project for the Jordan Valley in Transjordan," n.d., folder: Not labeled [Palestine][1], box 17, Records of the Office of Near Eastern Affairs, Office Files of Assistant Secretary of State George C. McGhee, 1945–1953, Lot 53 D468, RG 59, NARA; Baker, Davis to Jordan-US Technical Service for Range and Water Resources Development, July 15, 1955, filed in folder: POL Jordan Waters Incoming Feb.–Mar. 1964 POL 33/2 Waters, Boundaries, box 2, Bureau of the Office of the Country Director for Israel and Arab-Israel Affairs (NEA/IAI), Records Relating to Refugee Matters and Jordan Waters, 1957–1966, Lot 70 D66, RG 59, NARA; and Abdul Wahhab Jamil Awwad, *Agricultural Production and Income in the East Ghor Irrigation Project, Pre- and Post-Canal* (Amman: U.S. Agency for International Development, 1967), 8.

groups entered the valley by way of the *wadis* that intersected it.[41] The Ghor formed the western border, however, of 'Ajlun District, one of the most fertile regions east of the River Jordan. Extending east from the Jordan between the Yarmuk and Zarqa Rivers, 'Ajlun consists of hills to the north and southwest, while the "virtually uninterrupted nature" of its northeast plains, according to anthropologist Carol Palmer, "allows for almost continuous cultivation" of grains. It combines a Mediterranean climate with an average annual precipitation of 550 millimeters, which declines sharply to 221 millimeters to the district's east.[42] Fertile compared to the nearby desert, the area's highly variable rainfall nevertheless created the need for improved irrigation and for storage facilities that could capture winter rains. 'Ajlun's productive lands had been the focus of earlier attempts at agricultural reform by the Ottoman and British authorities who had previously governed Transjordan. By investing in the Ghor, U.S. policies would therefore try to develop 'Ajlun's underutilized periphery and contribute a new layer of reforms to a part of the Middle East that had already been shaped by prior agricultural initiatives. For this reason alone, East Ghor offers a useful case for analyzing U.S. agricultural policy for the region. At a total cost to the United States of more than $14 million, it was described in 1973 not only as "the largest and most important development project ever undertaken by Jordan," but also "one of the largest investments ever made by the United States in the development of the Arab Middle East."[43]

The Cold War–era Ghor project also represented the latest in a series of campaigns to incorporate the lands and peoples of the Jordan Valley into shifting geographies of political power. Although the town of Irbid served as the district capital of 'Ajlun during the Ottoman period, anthropologist Martha Mundy notes that the empire had governed some East Bank villages from Tiberias.[44] 'Ajlun, in turn, formed the southern part of the great plain of Hawran that stretched north of the Yarmuk and that the Ottomans had administered from Damascus. Even after the British created

[41] See Martha Mundy and Richard Saumarez Smith, *Governing Property, Making the Modern State: Law, Administration, and Production in Ottoman Syria* (New York: I. B. Tauris, 2007), 57, 64, 208, 220; and Martha Mundy and Richard Saumarez Smith, "'Al-Mahr Zaituna': Property and Family in the Hills Facing Palestine, 1880–1940," in *Family History in the Middle East: Household, Property, and Gender*, ed. Beshara Doumani (Albany: State University of New York Press, 2003), 126.

[42] Carol Palmer, "Whose Land Is It Anyway? An Historical Examination of Land Tenure and Agriculture in Northern Jordan," in *The Prehistory of Food: Appetites for Change*, ed. Chris Gosden and Jon Hather (New York: Routledge, 1999), 289.

[43] Claud R. Sutcliffe, "The East Ghor Canal Project: A Case Study of Refugee Resettlement, 1961–1966," *Middle East Journal* 27 (Autumn 1973): 471; see also Awwad, *Agricultural Production and Income in the East Ghor Irrigation Project*, 10.

[44] Martha Mundy, "Village Land and Individual Title: Musha' and Ottoman Land Registration in the 'Ajlun District," in *Village, Steppe, and State: The Social Origins of Modern Jordan*, ed. Eugene L. Rogan and Tariq Tell (London: British Academic Press, 1994), 67.

the mandate of Transjordan and attempted to police the border between 'Ajlun and the Syrian Hawran, colonial officials could not fully control the exchange of people and goods. In 1933, Britain's assistant resident in Amman, A. S. Kirkbride, reported that "consignments of hashish" were being smuggled from Syria into Palestine via 'Ajlun and that markers placed at the Syrian–Transjordanian border had been moved.[45] 'Ajlun also became a refuge for rebels fighting against French authority in Syria.[46] As historian Cyrus Schayegh writes, interwar boundary-making in the Middle East "did not create quick *faits accomplis*."[47] Americans would face similar concerns regarding the integrity of Jordan, which from 1950 encompassed both the east and west banks, particularly once its northern border with Syria became a fault line in the Cold War and a boundary between revolutionary and nonrevolutionary Arab regimes. Through the canal project, the Ghor would also come under the authority of the kingdom's 'Ajlun administrative district with its seat at Irbid.[48] U.S. officials hoped that increased agricultural produce resulting from the Ghor Canal would become a positive addition to the Hashemite kingdom's economy and that the social benefits of small-scale farming would contribute to the political viability of America's anticommunist ally, King Husayn.

As was the case with Iraq's Dujayla settlement, Tannous' thesis about the regressive legacy of Ottoman land reform in Arab agriculture did not apply to 'Ajlun District. "There is no evidence in the 'Ajlun registers," writes historian Eugene Rogan, "of peasants signing away their lands to urban notables or tribal *shaykhs* out of fear of registration," which has been one of the "assumed shortcomings of the Land Law."[49] Mundy has shown that the "timing of land registration" carried out by the Ottomans in 'Ajlun during the 1880s "coincided with a recession in the international price of grain."[50]

---

[45] Memo by Kirkbride, December 9, 1933, CO 831/28/11, BNA.

[46] See Khoury, *Syria and the French Mandate*, 110, 154, 277, 399. On the Hawran in the Great Syrian Revolt, see Michael Provence, *The Great Syrian Revolt and the Rise of Arab Nationalism* (Austin: University of Texas Press, 2005).

[47] Cyrus Schayegh, "The Many Worlds of 'Abud Yasin; or, What Narcotics Trafficking in the Interwar Middle East Can Tell Us about Territorialization," *American Historical Review* 116 (April 2011): 278.

[48] See D. Sourdel, "'Adjlun," in *Encyclopaedia of Islam*, ed. H. A. R. Gibb et al., vol. 1 (Leiden: Brill, 1960–), 208. According to Claud R. Sutcliffe, nearly all of the East Ghor Canal project area in 1961 corresponded to census areas 391, 392, 393, 394, and 313 of 'Ajlun District. Sutcliffe cites Department of Statistics, *Interim Report No. 9: Distribution and Characteristics of Population, 'Ajloun District* (Amman: Department of Statistics Press, 1963). See Claud R. Sutcliffe, "The East Ghor Canal Project: A Case Study of Refugee Resettlement, 1961–1966," *Middle East Journal* 27 (Autumn 1973): 472n6.

[49] Eugene L. Rogan, *Frontiers of State in the Late Ottoman Empire: Transjordan, 1850–1921* (New York: Cambridge University Press, 1999), 84.

[50] Martha Mundy, "The State of Property: Late Ottoman Southern Syria, the Kazâ of 'Ajlun (1875–1918)," in *Constituting Modernity: Private Property in the East and West*, ed. Huri

This collapse in world grain prices, which stoked agrarian radicalism and the rise of the People's Party in the United States, reduced the financial incentive for Damascus-based notables to invest in the southern Hawran. As a result, "large-scale alienation to urban capital" was "highly circumscribed."[51] More important, Mundy and her coauthor, Richard Saumarez Smith, note that 'Ajlun "was long ruled indirectly through local subregional and village leaders."[52] Village authorities in Ottoman 'Ajlun, who included *mukhtars* or headmen, had the capacity "to translate the plurality of local idioms for the description of land into uniform categories" as demanded by the state.[53] In practice, *mukhtars*' participation in Ottoman land registration helped to enable the survival of common landownership (*musha'*), because cultivators registered "their individually owned shares of agricultural land in a village as shares under the legal category of 'ownership by association.'"[54] East Ghor would be subject to the same pattern, in which village-level authorities influenced the meaning of state agricultural reforms through their roles in helping to implement them.

Land settlement during the British mandate period likewise involved a negotiation between state and society that shaped the outcome of reforms. Dowson's taxation and settlement policies for Transjordan, first implemented in 'Ajlun District, confronted locals' long-standing ability to reconcile the practice of *musha'* with the state's formal requirement of assigning individual title. Beginning in August 1933, settlement parties surveyed villages to establish ownership of agricultural land in what historian Michael Fischbach has called "the most significant and intrusive state policy ever carried out in Transjordan." For villages practicing *musha'*, officials "first recorded the number of shares each cultivator owned" and "posted the results to entertain objections." Iron markers were then sunk into the ground to permanently define the boundaries of plots assigned to individuals, whose names were recorded in loose-leaf binders. Initial attempts in 'Ajlun were "disasters in the eyes of land officials," according to Fischbach, because villagers distributed long, narrow, and noncontiguous plots to village families to ensure that each received lands of varying quality and to preserve the principle of *musha'*. Even after authorities took steps to combat this practice, however, the implementation of settlement brought about unexpected consequences. Anticipation of the new state policy raised the value of land, which after settlement could more easily be sold, divided, and mortgaged.

İslamoğlu (New York: I. B. Tauris, 2004), 223. See also Mundy and Smith, *Governing Property, Making the Modern State*, 96–99.

51 Martha Mundy, "Village Authority and the Legal Order of Property (the Southern Hawran, 1876–1922)," in *New Perspectives on Property and Land in the Middle East*, ed. Roger Owen (Cambridge, MA: Harvard University Press, 2000), 64.

52 Mundy and Smith, *Governing Property, Making the Modern State*, 66.

53 Mundy, "Village Land and Individual Title," 62.

54 Mundy, "The State of Property," 223. See also Palmer, "Whose Land Is It Anyway?," 293–94.

Indebtedness secured with land increased dramatically, with 'Ajlun bearing most of this debt by 1939. After the war, the state was forced to declare a moratorium on foreclosures and impose a ceiling on interest rates. By 1953, indebtedness on Jordan's east bank nevertheless reached a record £P 1.25 million.[55] "Fragmentation increased and joint holdings became common," wrote one analyst, while settlement also "facilitated the sale of land rights to merchants and other wealthy individuals who viewed land as a desirable form for holding wealth."[56] The concentration of landownership American officials attributed to the Ottoman land law actually resulted in northwest Transjordan when British reforms contributed to a market for land. This misinterpretation was part of the larger failure to place American policies within regional historical contexts. Invoking the Ottoman legacy did not provide a historically accurate critique of specific economic conditions so much as it served to identify the Middle East as an underdeveloped third world region in need of U.S.-administered reforms.

A major reason for the persistence of the "yeoman farmer" as a theme in U.S. Middle East policy, in contrast to the rise of agribusiness at home, was that it offered a strategy for resettling some of the 750,000 refugees driven from their homes in Palestine by the creation of Israel. According to this reckoning, investing in the East Ghor would help to relieve the United States of the political and financial costs associated with the Palestinian refugee crisis. McGhee's Bureau of Near Eastern, South Asian, and African Affairs (NEA) compiled a wide range of studies to consider options for refugee resettlement, with the east bank of the Jordan a particular focus of interest. Among those reports was a "Note on the Development of the Ghor by the Canalization of the River Jordan and River Yarmuk," authored in May 1949 by Transjordan Director of Lands and Surveys G. F. Walpole. It was Tannous' analysis, however, that explained how any resettlement policy would have to take the problem of land tenure into account. It "is no exaggeration to say," Tannous wrote, that the land tenure system in Arab countries "has been the most fundamental cause for the backward socio-economic state of the region as a whole." He identified absentee landownership, and the "great confusion" of rights resulting from "too many categories of land," as the main problems. Any resettlement policy had to provide "clear and free title to the land" for refugee families if it hoped to avoid perpetuating the "chaotic and initiative-killing system of land ownership." Otherwise, if refugees became "landless laborers," the "resulting chaos" would be "exploited by anti-American interests." While Egypt and Lebanon were too overpopulated to receive large numbers of refugees, Iraqi and Syrian land "was mostly in the vicious grip" of absentee landlords. Only a "combination of Arab

---

[55] Michael R. Fischbach, "British Land Policy in Transjordan," in *Village, Steppe, and State,* 93, 94, 99, 107.

[56] Hezleton, *The Impact of the East Ghor Canal Project,* 5–6.

Palestine and Transjordan," Tannous argued, offered the hope of land "for at least a substantial portion of the refugees." Doing so would require "technical and financial aid on a large scale sufficient for the development of the area." In these territories, he claimed, "much of the communal ownership has been liquidated" by land settlement policies carried out at the village level during the mandates, and land could be obtained from existing owners through nonrevolutionary means. "There is still the possibility of acquiring land from a number of enlightened large owners," Tannous insisted, "who would be willing to cooperate on the basis of sharing in the benefits of an over-all development project for the area where the refugees would be settled."[57]

The NEA Bureau adopted Tannous' arguments regarding land tenure, while Jordan became the focus of U.S. refugee resettlement efforts partly as the result of political conflicts with other Arab states. Appearing before the House Foreign Relations Committee, McGhee requested $50 million for refugee relief, citing refugees as "the most fertile ground" for communist infiltration of the Middle East. Although NEA identified the Syrian Jazira as a possible site for large-scale resettlement, congressmen pointed out that Syria had steadfastly refused to sign a Point Four aid agreement with the United States. McGhee entered an NEA memo into the congressional record that reflected Tannous' influence. "It would be hoped that the great majority of the refugees can be resettled on the land as freeholders," the memo explained, "so as not to perpetuate the feudal type of landholding so prevalent in the Near East." The document emphasized that the "availability of land and water is the key to resettlement" and offered the optimistic projection that up to 200,000 refugees "can be resettled in Jordan."[58]

Indeed, efforts during Dwight D. Eisenhower's administration to address regional conflicts over water envisioned resettling Palestinian families on irrigated farms in the East Ghor. In 1953, Eisenhower appointed Eric Johnston to facilitate Arab–Israeli cooperation in Jordan Valley

[57] G. F. Walpole, "Note on the Development of the Ghor by the Canalization of the River Jordan and River Yarmuk," August 1, 1949; and Afif Tannous, "The Problem of Land Tenure, Relative to the Settlement of Arab Refugees," May 18, 1949, folder: Not Labeled [Palestine][1], box 17, Records of Bureau of Near Eastern Affairs, Office Files of Assistant Secretary of State George C. McGhee, 1945–1953, Lot 53 D468, RG 59, NARA. On the impracticality of settling refugees in Arab countries, see Warriner, *Land Reform and Development in the Middle East*, 185.

[58] U.S. Congress, House, Committee on Foreign Relations, Hearings, *Mutual Security Program*, 82 Cong., 1 sess. (Washington, DC: Government Printing Office, 1951), 750, 757, 765. See also M. G. Ionides, "Note on a Major Irrigation Project for the Jordan Valley in Transjordan," n.d., folder: Not Labeled [Palestine][1], box 17, Records of Bureau of Near Eastern Affairs, Office Files of Assistant Secretary of State George C. McGhee, 1945–1953, Lot 53 D468, RG 59, NARA. On Syria, see also Fourth Meeting, Group on Political Implications of Economic Development, 1951–52, June 5, 1952, folder 2, box 149, CFR; and al-'Azm, *Mudhakkirat*, 2:433, 3:379.

development. Johnston negotiated what became known as the Unified Plan, which was devised by experts from the Tennessee Valley Authority but based on hydrological data compiled earlier by the British mandate authorities.[59] Johnston's diplomacy focused on negotiating water allotments among Israel and the riparian Arab states. Under Johnston's plan, as part of Jordan's total 720 million cubic meter (mcm) annual water allocation, the kingdom was to receive 377 mcm from the Yarmuk with which to irrigate lands on the eastern bank. While Arab technical experts recommended adoption of the plan, the Arab League Political Committee declined to endorse it.[60] The United States and Israel also failed to agree over how much water Israel had to deliver to Jordan from Lake Tiberias and the quantity of Yarmuk water needed to irrigate the fertile plot of Israeli-controlled land located between the Yarmuk, the Jordan, and Lake Tiberias known as the Adasiya Triangle.[61] Despite these setbacks, Johnston remained convinced that individual irrigation projects could still proceed within the overall framework of the water allocation limits. These included the East Ghor Canal, which he promoted as crucial for refugee resettlement in Jordan. Tapping the Yarmuk, he wrote in 1957, would "make sufficient water immediately available to irrigate about 330,000 dunums, or 80,000 acres, of land in the East Ghor in Jordan." Developing the Jordan-Yarmuk system, Johnston insisted, would aid in refugee resettlement and make Jordan's economy less dependent on external subsidies:

It would create the means of bolstering the basic economy of the country by creating an irrigated agriculture in the Jordan Valley, thereby offering the opportunity of permanent livelihood to some 175,000 persons, who, in large majority, would be Arab refugees.[62]

In focusing on the East Ghor, Johnston applied the Cold War strategy of creating yeoman farmers in underdeveloped countries to ameliorating the Arab-Israeli problem in U.S. foreign policy.

[59] See Memorandum of Agreement between UNRWAPRNE and Tennessee Valley Authority, n.d., folder: Eric Johnston Mission – 1. Framework of the Mission, box 1, Records Relating to the Eric Johnston Mission and Jordan River Waters, 1945–1959, Lot 70, D254, RG 59, NARA. See also Peter L. Hahn, *Caught in the Middle East: U.S. Policy toward the Arab–Israeli Conflict, 1945–1961* (Chapel Hill: University of North Carolina Press, 2004), 170–74.

[60] See CIA Special Report, "The Jordan Waters Issue," December 4, 1964, folder: Jordan vol. 1, memos, 11/63-2/65, box 146, NSF, LBJL.

[61] See memo of conversation by Wahl, November 20–21, 1959, folder: Political Affairs & Rel. 1961 and Previous POL 33 Waters. Boundaries. Jordan Waters Memoranda, box 7, NEA Bureau, Office of the Country Director for Israel and Arab-Israel Affairs (NEA/IAI) Lot 70 D229, RG 59, NARA.

[62] Eric Johnston, "Memorandum on the Middle East," June 10, 1957, folder: 1957–1958, box 2, NEA Bureau, Office of the Country Director for Israel and Arab-Israel Affairs (NEA/IAI), Records Relating to Refugee Matters and Jordan Waters, 1957–1966, Lot 70 D66, RG 59, NARA.

The East Ghor Canal subsequently became a symbol of the U.S. determination to maintain Jordan's tenuous pro-Western orientation. Days before the outbreak of the Suez War in 1956, Husayn was forced to appoint a cabinet led by Sulayman al-Nabulsi, who opposed a U.S.-aligned foreign policy. After forcing Nabulsi's resignation in April 1957, Husayn faced a showdown with mutinous troops in which the king managed to hold onto his throne by rallying pro-Hashemite forces and drawing on American support.[63] Later that year, Khalid al-'Azm concluded the agreement on behalf of Syria to accept aid from the Soviet Union, thereby dividing the region along Cold War lines (see Chapter 1).[64] The U.S. ambassador to Jordan, Lester Mallory, warned the State Department that "supporters of [the] King and [the] West [are] only [a] minor portion of [the] population." It was therefore essential, he argued, that a "much greater number [of] Jordanians be made [to] feel [that] they [are] benefitting economically from Jordan's pro-Western position."[65] Rather than a raft of modest initiatives, the State Department wanted to support high-profile projects that would provide "dramatic and clear-cut evidence" for the benefits of aligning with the United States.[66] Mallory believed that the East Ghor Canal fit the bill perfectly. It was "the most talked about project in Jordan" and had "prestige connotations beyond economic benefits." The only obstacle "is resolving land tenure and land distribution" issues.[67] "Nothing," Mallory wrote, "would do more [to] persuade [the] Jordanian people [that the] US was [a] friend of Jordan," than to finance East Ghor.[68] On February 21, 1958, just weeks following the union between Egypt and Syria in the United Arab Republic (UAR), Secretary of State John Foster Dulles transmitted a message to Husayn's government offering U.S. support for East Ghor.[69] Ground was broken in July 1958 when the Italian Imprese Venete Company began constructing the 1,097-meter inlet tunnel from the Yarmuk and digging the main canal, which was lined with concrete.[70] Jordanian prime minister Hazza' al-Majali, who helped to author legislation governing the project, told the head of the U.S. Operations Mission in Amman, Norman Burns, that he attached "major importance to the East Ghor Canal." Whereas "enemies of the West

---

[63] See Yaqub, *Containing Arab Nationalism*, 119–45.

[64] See al-'Azm, *Mudhakkirat*, 3: 9–22.

[65] Amman to State, telegram 621, September 30, 1957, 785.00/9-3057, RG 59, NARA.

[66] State/ICA to Amman, telegram 1050, November 1, 1957, 785.5-MSP/10-2357, RG 59, NARA.

[67] Amman to State, telegram 942, November 8, 1957, 785.5-MSP/11-757, RG 59, NARA.

[68] Amman to State, telegram 1140, December 5, 1957, 785.5-MSP/12-557, RG 59, NARA.

[69] State to Amman, telegram 1985, February 21, 1958, 785.5-MSP/2-2158, RG 59, NARA.

[70] "East Ghor Canal Agreement," May 28, 1960, folder: Jordan II. Economic Situation 1960 II.G.1 – East Ghor Canal, box 5, Records Relating to the Eric Johnston Mission and Jordan River Waters, 1945–1959, Lot 70 D254 RG 59, NARA. See also *al-Difa'*, May 29, 1960, p. 2.

had spread the talk" that the United States would not back major development projects in Jordan, al-Majali declared, the "East Ghor Canal provided a decisive answer to these people."[71]

But the American conception of East Ghor, as a public symbol of Jordan's pro-Western orientation and willingness to deescalate the conflict with Israel, was not shared by King Husayn. Facing political unrest and support for Nasser that was especially strong in the towns of the West Bank and among the Palestinian refugees who made up a third of Jordan's population, the king also pursued economic development as a counterrevolutionary political strategy. Jordan's foreign minister, Samir Rifa'i, explained this strategy when he told U.S. officials that the refugees who were concentrated in "large camps in the immediate vicinity of political centers like Amman and Zerka" and sympathetic to Nasser posed a direct political threat to the Hashemite regime. Rifa'i favored "breaking them down into smaller units which might facilitate integration of the refugees into the community life of scattered towns and villages." Relocating refugee populations from camps to farms, Rifa'i hoped, could simultaneously foster political stability and "benefit the Jordanian economy."[72]

In political terms, the king's approach sought to preempt Nasser by positioning the Hashemites as the historic torchbearers of Arab nationalism since the Great Arab Revolt against the Ottomans led by Husayn's great-grandfather during World War I. This strategy became particularly urgent after the July 1958 revolution in Iraq extinguished one of the Hashemite family's branches and abruptly ended negotiations to unite the two kingdoms.[73] As historian Betty S. Anderson explains: "The historical narrative of the Hashemite state would have to be accepted by the bulk of the population for the Hashemites to survive." Anderson continues:

To forestall a coup, the Hashemite state waged a multipronged campaign to win the hearts of the populace. From the creation of a comprehensive social safety net, to the writing of school textbooks, to the opening of museums of "national heritage," the state brought people under its wings, both physically and ideologically.[74]

This pro-Hashemite campaign was on full display during Husayn's June 1960 visit to 'Ajlun District, where he dedicated a new hospital. In a speech to the area's residents, the king described national economic development

---

[71] Amman (USOM/ICA) to State, June 4, 1959, airgram A-981, 785.5-MSP/6–459, RG 59, NARA.

[72] "Palestine Refugee Problem," November 21, 1957, folder: Refugees PCC 1950–1957 REF 1 General Policy & Plans, box 10, NEA Bureau Office of the Country Director for Israel and Arab-Israeli Affairs (NEA/IAI) Records Relating to Refugee Matters and Jordan Waters, 1957–1966, Lot 70 D 229, RG 59, NARA.

[73] See al-Suwaydi, *Mudhakkirati*, 580.

[74] Betty S. Anderson, *Nationalist Voices in Jordan: The Street and the State* (Austin: University Press of Texas, 2005), 193, 194.

as a continuation of the Great Arab Revolt. Nasser and his supporters were guilty of "distorting our nation's history [*tashwih ta'rikh ummatina*]" by falsely portraying the Hashemites as beholden to Israel and the Western powers.[75] East Ghor became part of Husayn's "counteroffensive" against Nasser, signifying both the Hashemites' modernity and resistance to Israel. In his memoir *Uneasy Lies the Head*, Husayn extolled "the great Yarmuk Project in the Jordan Valley" as a national irrigation and hydroelectric initiative, but concealed its earlier relationship to, and Husayn's own support for, the Johnston plan. Like Tannous and other Americans, Husayn wrapped East Ghor in a historical narrative about post-Ottoman development, but his strategy sought to contain Nasser and promote Jordan as Israel's leading Arab rival when it came to "'making the desert bloom.'"[76]

During the canal's planning and construction, American, Hashemite, and revolutionary agendas all competed for control over northwest Transjordan, where Cold War conflict intruded into a political geography shaped by earlier Ottoman and mandatory influences. In January 1956, 'Ajlun District had witnessed an attack on the American Friends Service Committee Village project at 'Ayn Dibbin, financed by the Ford Foundation. Reportedly incited by communists and the Muslim Brotherhood, some 2,000 people burned buildings to the ground in an incident that foreign service officer Richard B. Parker described as evidence of "rising communist strength."[77] The Jordanian government struggled to detach 'Ajlun from the Hawran and the orbit of Damascus, which had administered the region during Ottoman times. In reconceptualizing East Ghor as a national development initiative, Husayn set aside not only the Johnston plan but also an agreement with Syria to build a dam and hydroelectric works on the Yarmuk.[78] As had been the case for authorities during the British mandate, however, Jordanian officials were unable completely to secure the border with Syria. During a visit to 'Ajlun by a U.S. embassy official, a Jordanian colonel said that "his main worry had to do with smuggling across the long boundary separating 'Ajloun District from Syria," a trade he summed up as "sugar in return for explosives." The colonel denied that the district "had the reputation of tending to look toward Damascus rather than Amman," but he conceded that "there are some disaffected families that 'hate' the [Jordanian] government."[79] These Hashemite

---

[75] *al-Difaʻ*, June 29, 1960, p. 1.

[76] King Hussein, *Uneasy Lies the Head*, 216, 218.

[77] Amman to State, foreign service dispatch 229, January 12, 1956, 785.00/1-1256, RG 59, NARA. See also Shmuel Bar, *The Muslim Brotherhood in Jordan* (Tel Aviv: Moshe Dayan Center for Middle Eastern and African Studies, 2000), 25.

[78] Treaty between Jordan and Syria on Yarmuk Waters, July 15, 1953, folder: 65. The Jordan Valley Plan, Oliver L. Troxel, Jr., box 6, Records Relating to the Eric Johnston Mission and Jordan River Waters, 1945–1959, Lot 70 D254, RG 59, NARA. See also David Wishart, "The Breakdown of the Johnston Negotiations over the Jordan Waters," *Middle Eastern Studies* 26 (October 1990): 536–46.

[79] Amman to State, foreign service dispatch 277, February 2, 1961, 785.00/2-261, RG 59, NARA.

opponents included the Rushaydat family, who hailed from Irbid, a center of both Ba'thist and communist activism.[80] Shafiq Rushaydat had served in al-Nabulsi's cabinet and his cousin, Nabih, was a Syrian-trained doctor and communist who assisted the Soviets and Chinese in setting up Arabic broadcast services (see Chapter 1).[81] On August 29, 1960, Hazza' al-Majali and twelve others were killed in Amman when a bomb exploded at the prime minister's office. Nasser's Voice of the Arabs radio hailed the elimination of "an 'imperialist agent' " in a plot that appeared to have been launched from the Syrian region of the UAR.[82]

Among al-Majali's legacies was the land reform legislation that tried to reconcile the Americans' desire for "yeoman farmers" with Husayn's ambitions for East Ghor. The challenges stemmed from resistance on the part of existing landowners in the project area, who were not as "enlightened" as Tannous had predicted. As with previous Ottoman and British policies, the meaning of land reform was also determined partly at the village level, where the state depended on local authorities to help implement it. In 1959, Jordan enacted an East Ghor Canal land reform law establishing an initial maximum holding of 300 *dunums* (75 acres) in the project area and a sliding scale to determine how much of their land existing owners would be permitted to keep.[83] The following year, Law No. 13 charged an East Ghor Canal Authority (EGCA) with evaluating land values, settling claims, purchasing titles from existing owners, and selecting farmers to receive redistributed lands in the 42,000 *dunums* (10,500 acres) irrigated by the project's first stage.[84] A U.S. government planning report defined the new type of farm envisioned in the East Ghor: "Large enough to ensure a decent standard of living for a farm family averaging six persons."[85]

But Nicola Simansky, a Food and Agriculture Organization economist and the EGCA's managing director, pointed to the state's limited capacity to readjust land tenure in the Jordan Valley, even with help from the United

[80] See Anderson, *Nationalist Voices in Jordan*, 135, 136.

[81] See Rushaydat, *Awraq Laysat Shakhsiya*; and Jamal al-Sha'ir, *Siyasi Yatadhakkar: Tajribah fi al-'Amal al-Siyasi* (London: Riyad al Rayyis lil-Kutub, wa-al-Nashr, 1987), 162.

[82] King Hussein, *Uneasy Lies the Head*, 189. See memo of conversation by Killgore, March 27, 1963, folder: POL Political Affairs and Rel., Jordan, box 3959, 1963 Alpha Numeric File, RG 59, NARA; and Amman to State, foreign service dispatch 108, September 30, 1960, 785.00/9-3060, folder: 785.00/8-1060, box 2060, Central Decimal File, 1960–63, RG 59, NARA.

[83] Hezleton, *The Impact of the East Ghor Canal Project*, 16–17.

[84] Amman to State, foreign service dispatch 4, July 5, 1960, with attachment "Project Agreement between ICA and the Jordanian Development Board (JDB) an Agency of the Government of Jordan (GOJ)," folder: Jordan II. Economic Situation 1960 II.G.1 – East Ghor Canal, box 5, Records Relating to the Eric Johnston Mission and Jordan River Waters, 1945–1959, Lot 70 D254, RG 59, NARA.

[85] John N. Spencer, *Development Principles for East Ghor Canal Scheme* (Washington, DC: U.S. Department of Interior, Bureau of Reclamation, 1958), 25.

States and international agencies. In the "whole Kingdom of Jordan," he explained, "there are [fewer] than ten of the judges of the class which by Law 13 are suitable to be appointed as Chairmen of [the] Evaluation Committee." Moreover, by law the EGCA's schedules of evaluation had to be posted in "Village Administration Offices controlled by Mukhtars (or Heads of the Villages)" who participated in the settlement process. Given the need to respect existing owners' interests and the painstaking method for settling claims and land values, Simansky did not believe that East Ghor could facilitate a large-scale resettlement of farmers in the short term:

This small project is strictly speaking a remodeling of the existing irrigation with the addition of a fraction of the Yarmouk water. The traditional cultivators who existed for several decades are living in villages in the project area and there cannot be any appreciable influx of new people in the first few years until the entire Ghor is developed and storage facilities provided for.[86]

Indeed, the International Cooperation Agency (ICA) predicted that "there will be fewer land owners in the project area when the project is completed than live there now." ICA officials also noted the "high valuation of $360 per acre" at which the EGCA had offered to compensate existing landowners and the fact that the maximum holding in the area had to be raised to 600 *dunums* (150 acres) "as the political price which had to be paid by the Jordan Government in order not to arouse the undying hostility of the most important landowners in the valley."[87] Delays in assigning land titles to farmers in the East Ghor provoked the U.S. embassy's admonition to Husayn about the need to have land "in the hands of yeoman farmers" and a threat to withhold support for building the canal's second stage. Husayn promised to motivate the EGCA and, after opening the canal's floodgates on October 16, 1961, in a ceremony attended by Burns and other officials, the king distributed titles to some of the newly selected farmers.[88]

Even as the East Ghor Canal reenacted the experience of previous land reform programs in the Jordan Valley, it became the focus of rival contemporary political agendas. Husayn's campaign to preempt Nasser by envisioning a non-revolutionary path to development culminated in the appointment of Wasfi al-Tall as prime minister on January 27, 1962. Born in Irbid and educated at AUB, al-Tall had rejected Nasser's neutralism and

[86] N. Simansky, "Answers to Comments of the International Cooperation Administration," November 11, 1960, folder: PS – Protective Services, box 9, NEA Bureau Office of the Country Director for Israel and Arab-Israel Affairs (NEA/IAI) Records Relating to Refugee Matters and Jordan Waters, 1957–1966 Lot 70 D229, RG 59, NARA.

[87] Thacher to Jones, November 18, 1960, folder: 1960 Chron, Inter-office Memos (folder 1 of 2), box 1, Bureau of Near Eastern and South Asian Affairs, Office of Near Eastern Affairs, Records of the Director, 1960–1963, RG 59, NARA.

[88] Amman to State foreign service dispatch 128, October 18, 1961, 885.00/10–1861, State Department central file, RG 59, NARA. See also Sutcliffe, "The East Ghor Canal Project."

supported the Baghdad Pact.[89] Husayn instructed al-Tall "to realize the 'model' citizen through whom it can transform Jordan as a whole," a policy the U.S. embassy interpreted as a "mandate ... for reform, a 'new deal.' "[90] The king's ambassador announced to President John F. Kennedy that "The New Frontier has reached Jordan."[91] As part of his strategy, Husayn also appointed Kamal Sha'ir as vice president of Jordan's Development Board. Another AUB graduate from northwest Transjordan, Sha'ir had close ties to the Ba'th Party, whose suppression in Syria under the UAR had stoked resentment against Nasser. Sha'ir brought the East Ghor project under the direct authority of his Development Board.[92] He also negotiated a £4 million loan from the Kuwait Fund for Arab Economic and Social Development to facilitate "telescoping" a twenty-year plan for building the East Ghor Canal and irrigating the West Bank as well, completing it as part of the kingdom's seven-year development plan.[93] Sha'ir believed that irrigated agriculture would help to reduce the burden food imports imposed on Jordan's balance of payments, and he supported the Board's development of select industries for the same reason. But because "Arab economic union was inevitable," Sha'ir told British officials, Jordan could not rely on "industries which depended for survival on customs barriers."[94] He also shared with U.S. officials the belief that small farms could be a basis for Jordan's development. Al-Handasah, Sha'ir's Beirut-based engineering firm, partnered with the Dutch company Nedeco in carrying out "a full socio-economic study of the impact of the irrigation scheme on the West and East Banks." Jordan planned to settle Palestinian refugees on irrigated land, and the study was designed "to discover the size of the plot of land a family would need to sustain itself."[95] But Sha'ir withdrew his support for Husayn and resigned

[89] See Asher Susser, *On Both Banks of the Jordan: A Political Biography of Wasfi al-Tall* (Portland, OR: Frank Cass, 1994), 25–27.

[90] Amman to State, foreign service dispatch 347, May 9, 1962, 785.00/5–962, folder: 785.00/1–361, box 2060, Central Decimal File, 1960–63, RG 59, NARA.

[91] Memo of conversation by Strong, March 7, 1962, folder: Jordan, General, 1/61–3/62, box 125, NSF, JFKL.

[92] See Morris to Figg, February 1, 1963, FO 371/170331, BNA.

[93] Strong to Macomber, April 20, 1962, folder: Political Affairs & Rel. 1962 & Previous POL 33 Waters. Boundaries. Jordan Waters Outgoing, box 9, Near East Affairs Bureau Office of the Country Director for Israel and Arab-Israel Affairs (NEA/IAI), Records Relating to Refugee Matters and Jordan Waters, 1957–1966, Lot 70 D229, RG 59, NARA. See also memo by Crawford, April 25, 1962, folder: Political Affairs & Rel. 1962 POL 33 Waters. Boundaries. Jordan Waters Memoranda, box 9, Near East Affairs Bureau Office of the Country Director for Israel and Arab-Israel Affairs (NEA/IAI), Records Relating to Refugee Matters and Jordan Waters, 1957–1966, Lot 70 D229, RG 59, NARA. See also Kamal A. Shair, *Out of the Middle East: The Emergence of a Global Arab Business* (London: I.B. Tauris, 2006), 127–28.

[94] Coltman to Morris, September 17, 1962, FO 957/253, BNA.

[95] Shair, *Out of the Middle East*, 135. See also Hezleton, *The Impact of the East Ghor Canal Project*, 7n1.

abruptly after the king sent warplanes to defend the Yemeni imam against a revolution that erupted in September 1962 with Nasser's support. Sha'ir vehemently denied allegations that he had resigned at the instigation of the Ba'th, but he condemned Husayn's Yemen policy, telling a USAID official that the imam belonged to the "twelfth century."[96] A shared commitment to small-scale farming as a development strategy did not preclude political conflicts, whether between Husayn and the United States or between the Hashemite king and the Ba'thist Sha'ir.

Within months, Husayn had shifted his foreign policy and recast the East Ghor Canal as an anti-Israel measure. Following Ba'thist coups in Iraq and Syria, Husayn opted for a reconciliation with Nasser. Riots flared across the West Bank in April 1963 demanding that Jordan adhere to a new Arab union being negotiated among Egypt, Syria, and Iraq. Taking sides in ongoing conflicts between Nasser and the Ba'th, Husayn pursued secret talks in Kuwait with Egypt's security chief and cracked down on Jordanian Ba'thists.[97] Husayn also established relations with the Soviet Union, a move U.S. officials interpreted as the price that Nasser had placed on reconciliation.[98] At a January 1964 Arab summit in Cairo, Arab states endorsed plans for diverting the Jordan's waters to reduce their availability to Israel. Jordan offered the East Ghor Canal as its contribution.[99] According to the Arab League Technical Committee charged with drawing up the diversion plan, East Ghor would be expanded "to divert the waters of the Yarmuk and cut them off from existing Israel pumping stations in the Adasiya triangle and on the West Bank."[100] In Jordanian policy, diverting the Jordan's waters took precedence over irrigating new farms on the East Bank. Husayn conceded to U.S. ambassador Robert Barnes that going along with diversion would jeopardize his access to waters stored in Lake Tiberias and that the "Arab diversion scheme probably meant less water for Jordan" than had

[96] Morris to Figg, November 2, 1962, FO 957/253, BNA.

[97] See Amman to State, airgram A-575, April 30, 1963, folder: POL Political Affairs and Rel., Jordan, box 3959, 1963 Alpha Numeric File, RG 59, NARA; and Amman to State, airgram A-341, January 21, 1964, folder: Jordan, Vol. 1, Cables [2 of 2] 11/63-2/65, box 146, NSF, LBJL. See also Amman to State, telegram 104, August 25, 1963; and Amman to State, telegram 123, September 5, 1963 folder: POL – Political Affairs and Rel. Jor-A, box 3961, 1963 Alpha Numeric File, RG 59, NARA.

[98] On relations with USSR, see Amman to State, telegram 104, August 25, 1963; and Amman to State, telegram 123, September 5, 1963; and Jerusalem to State, airgram A-14, October 15, 1963. All documents filed in folder: POL – Political Affairs and Rel. Jor-A, box 3961, 1963 Alpha Numeric File, RG 59, NARA.

[99] See Read to Bundy, February 12, 1964, folder: Arab Summits 1964-1965-1966, box 12, NSF, Files of Robert W. Komer, LBJL.

[100] "Arab League Consideration of Israel's Planned Diversion of Jordan Waters," April 31, 1961, folder: PS – Protective Services, box 9, NEA Bureau, Office of the Country Director for Israel and Arab-Israel Affairs (NEA/IAI), Records Relating to Refugee Matters and Jordan Waters, 1957–1966, Lot 70 D229, RG 59, NARA.

been promised under the Johnston plan. But this "was the price he had to pay for he could not alone stand up and oppose what all Arabs thought they wanted." Husayn told Barnes that "one thing he could not afford to do and maintain his domestic position was to oppose [the] present trend toward Arab unity." [101]

Husayn's commitment to diversion further weakened prospects for settling large numbers of farmers along the East Ghor. Irrigating the East Ghor fully required water storage on the Yarmuk. But the Arab scheme compelled Jordan to undertake diversion prior to constructing a promised Yarmuk storage dam at Mukhaiba. The United States had conditioned its agreement to sponsor East Ghor in 1958 on Jordan's willingness to abide by the Johnston allocations, including Israel's access to the Yarmuk. In July 1964, Barnes had to remind Jordanian officials that depriving Israel of its 25 mcm share of Yarmuk waters would violate the terms of the East Ghor Canal agreement, and it was clear to Barnes that the government "had completely forgotten [the] 1958 agreement and is embarrassed by it." [102] Husayn's policy jeopardized the U.S. assistance that the king requested for building a separate storage dam at Maqarin. [103] Husayn nevertheless portrayed diversion as compatible with the Johnston plan water allocations. He told the U.S. ambassador to the United Nations, Adlai Stevenson, that Jordan hoped to "develop resources within the limits" negotiated by Johnston. [104] The kingdom hired Energo Projects, a company from neutral Yugoslavia, to study expanding the canal's capacity as part of the diversion plan from 10 to 20 cubic meters per second, which the U.S. embassy judged to be "not in conflict with" Johnston's limits. [105] To provide adequate Yarmuk water to the Adasiya triangle without publicity, the Jordanians also "quietly reduced intake" into the East Ghor Canal in summer 1964. [106]

So long as Husayn respected Israel's share of Jordan waters, the United States acquiesced in the king's East Ghor policy. Referring to Arab states' support for diversion at the Cairo conference, the Department instructed the embassy in Amman "to channel this energy into useful patterns (i.e. those that benefit Jordan and conform generally with [the] Unified Plan), even if

[101] Amman to State, telegram 84, August 11, 1964, folder: Jordan, Vol. I Cables [1 of 2] 11/ 63–2/65, box 146, NSF, LBJL.

[102] Amman to State, telegram 47, July 19, 1964, folder: Jordan, Vol. I Cables [2 of 2] 11/63–2/ 65, box 146, NSF, LBJL.

[103] State circular telegram 1950, April 18, 1964, folder: Jordan 4/14–15/64 Visit of King Hussein [1 of 3], box 148, NSF, LBJL.

[104] USUN to State, telegram 3811, April 21, 1964, folder: Jordan vol. I, Cables [2 of 2], 11/ 63–2/65, box 146, NSF, LBJL.

[105] Amman to State, airgram A-72, August 12, 1964, folder: E – Economic Affairs (GEN) Jor E- 2–3 Economic Summary, box 733, Central Foreign Policy Files, 1964–66, RG 59, NARA.

[106] Amman to State, telegram 54, July 28, 1964, folder: Jordan, Vol. I, cables [2 of 2] 11/63–2/ 65, box 146, NSF, LBJL.

called by another name" and "portrayed as anti-Israel in intent."[107] Officials nevertheless continued to regard the East Ghor Canal as central to containing radicalism in Jordan through the provision of irrigated farms to refugee and non-refugee families. In response to the 1963 disturbances, USAID undertook a "Survey of the Civil Police Forces of the Hashemite Kingdom of Jordan" recommending enhancements to Jordan's domestic security apparatus, and the embassy formulated an "Internal Defense Plan for Jordan." The plan noted that some "75 percent of Jordan's population is dependent on agriculture for its subsistence," yet "droughts and lack of arable land" impeded Jordan's agricultural self-sufficiency. USAID was therefore "assisting Jordan in a program to extend the area of cultivation." Its "major project in Jordan was the East Ghor Canal which is not only irrigating 30,000 acres of hitherto unfarmed land but includes a program of land classification and redistribution as well." Land reform, the basis of the East Ghor policy but an issue complicated by historical precedents and contemporary politics, barely received any mention. The embassy addressed it parenthetically, as an aside in the section of the "Internal Defense Plan" that reported on the canal: "(Land reform, however, is not a major problem in Jordan.)."[108]

It became a problem for the United States when Husayn decided to pursue his seven-year plan for developing the Jordan Valley outside of American assistance and the requirements imposed by its land reform principles. A shortage of water flowing into the canal and rising soil salinity made the construction of storage facilities urgent. USAID therefore reluctantly backed a British-financed irrigation project not governed by the East Ghor land laws.[109] As early as October 1964, USAID raised alarms about "pressures to extend irrigation to lands immediately south of the Zerka [River], where large land holdings exist, many of them owned by the Royal family, and where resistance to the land redistribution policies of the East Ghor Canal Law would be immediately encountered."[110] In early 1965, Husayn told the U.S. embassy in Amman that he would have to suspend American assistance in response to what the State Department called "Arab sensitivity to US activity in East Ghor." The State Department expressed "shock and

[107] State to Amman, telegram 346, February 12, 1964, folder: Jordan, Vol. 1, cables [2 of 2] 11/63-2/65, box 146, NSF, LBJL.

[108] Amman to State, airgram A-172, October 9, 1963, folder: POL 26 Rebellion. Coups. Box 3961, 1963 Alpha Numeric File, RG 59, NARA. See also "Survey of the Civil Police Forces of the Hashemite Kingdom of Jordan," August 1963, folder: Jordan IPS-1-7, box 63, Records of the U.S. Agency for International Development, RG 286, NARA.

[109] See Amman to State, airgram A-1026, June 16, 1964, folder: AID(US) Jordan 1/1/64, box 566, Central Foreign Policy Files, 1964–66, RG 59, NARA; and Amman to State, airgram A-647, February 22, 1965, folder: Jordan (Economic) 1964–1965-March 1966, box 35, NSF Files of Robert W. Komer, LBJL.

[110] U.S. Agency for International Development, "Long Range Assistance Strategy Review," October 1964, folder: Jordan, Vol. 1 Memos, 11/63-2/65, box 146, NSF, LBJL.

discouragement" that Husayn "should in effect reject [the] US presence and participation in East Ghor," which was "most symbolic of our support for Jordan's water development." The nearly 400-kilometer lateral distribution system linked to the main canal was not completed until 1966, when construction began on the Yarmuk storage dam at Mukhaiba. A dam at Wadi Ziglab, a side *wadi* of the River Jordan, was completed under British auspices but with U.S. financial support in May 1967.[111]

In that same month, the deputy director of Jordan's Natural Resources Authority and former EGCA official Sweilem Haddad was scheduled to present a paper about the East Ghor Canal at a Washington, DC, meeting titled the "Water for Peace Conference." The paper described his government's hopes that the canal would make it possible to take advantage of the "natural greenhouse" of the Ghor to produce crops for export and reduce Jordan's "existing balance of payments deficit." Providing irrigation facilities was indispensable to achieving this goal, but the principal obstacle was the existing "[p]attern of landownership," which was characterized both by small, fragmented holdings and by large concentrated ones. While fragmented holdings of less than 20 *dunums* characterized 10 percent of the lands to be irrigated, the 1 percent of original landowners owning more than 500 *dunums* accounted for more than a quarter of the project area. The EGCA's most difficult work therefore involved readjusting land tenure as provided by the authorizing legislation: "Cancelling all previous ownerships and pooling them under a land ownership reform program" and "Expropriation and evaluation of lands, water, and improvements, etc. with provisions for just compensation."[112] Haddad portrayed East Ghor as a successful example of the state administering the relationship between land and people, one that he envisioned could be replicated on the west bank of the Jordan.

In terms of raising agricultural productivity and contributing to Jordan's economy, the East Ghor Canal achieved some successes (Figure 4.1). Jordan's agricultural production reportedly doubled during the years 1959–65 and its agricultural exports increased by nearly 170 percent.[113] The United States helped to design an Agricultural Credit Corporation to provide low-interest loans to farmers and launched an East Ghor Rural Development Program that included financial incentives for land improvements, extension and

---

[111] State to Amman, telegram 407, January 29, 1965, folder: Jordan Waters December 1963–March 1966 [2 of 2], box 35, NSF, Files of Robert W. Komer, LBJL. See also Abdul Wahhab Jamil Awwad, *Agricultural Production and Income in the East Ghor Irrigation Project, Pre and Post-Canal* (Amman: U.S. Agency for International Development, 1967), 9–10; and Amman to State, airgram A-41, August 1, 1966, folder: E – Economic Affairs (GEN) Jor E-2–3 Economic Summary, box 733, Central Foreign Policy Files, 1964–66, RG 59, NARA.

[112] Amman to State, airgram A-207, December 13, 1966, folder: E – Economic Affairs (GEN) Jor E- 2–3 Economic Summary, box 733, Central Foreign Policy Files, 1964–66, RG 59, NARA.

[113] See Awwad, *Agricultural Production and Income in the East Ghor Irrigation Project*, 2–3.

FIGURE 4.1. The East Ghor Canal, 1965. © David Lees/Corbis.

health programs, and "construction of farm to market roads." By 1964, the U.S. embassy reported "bumper harvests."[114] In the East Ghor project area, one study reported, "the yields for wheat, tomatoes, cucumber, squash, marrow, and water melons appear to have more than doubled."[115] These trends corresponded to a 12 percent increase in domestic revenues annually so that they too doubled between 1959 and 1965 and could cover as much as two-thirds of state expenditures.[116] As national security advisor Walt Rostow wrote to President Lyndon B. Johnson, "an 8% annual growth rate raises hopes that Jordan is moving toward [an] ability to pay its own way."[117] At the same time, however, U.S. financial support to Jordan included large grants of farm products under Public Law 480.[118] Only one-time cash infusions in the form of a payment from the Trans-Arabian Pipeline and a loan

[114] Amman to State, November 4, 1964, airgram A-216, folder: E-Economic Affairs (Gen) Jordan 1/1/64, box 733, Central Foreign Policy Files, 1964–66, RG 59, NARA.

[115] Hezleton, *The Impact of the East Ghor Canal Project*, 44.

[116] USAID (Bell) to Johnson, May 14, 1966, folder: Jordan Vol. II Memos 3/65-11/66, box 146, NSF, LBJL.

[117] Rostow to Johnson, June 16, 1966, folder: Jordan Vol. II Memos 3/65-11/66, box 146, NSF, LBJL.

[118] On P.L. 480, see *al-Difaʿ*, July 4, July 27, August 24, 1960; Amman to State foreign service dispatch 338, March 22, 1961, folder: 885.00/1–760, box 2806, Central Decimal File, 1960–63, RG 59, NARA; and Rostow to Johnson, January 10, 1968, folder: Jordan Vol. IV Memos & Misc., 5/67-2/68, box 147, NSF, LBJL.

from Kuwait enabled Jordan temporarily to balance its books.[119] Increasing agricultural productivity could not meet the rising costs associated with the escalating Arab–Israeli conflict. Husayn sought substantial U.S. military aid to meet Jordan's commitments to the new United Arab Command (UAC), portrayed by Arab states as necessary to defend their water diversion works from Israeli attacks. Ambassador Barnes warned Husayn that if "he went ahead with the full UAC recommended build-up he completely destroyed his economic integrity."[120] In 1966, Johnson approved an additional $21.4 million loan to support Jordan's budget.[121] The United States increased its subsidy to ensure that the kingdom purchased military aircraft from the West rather than from the Soviet Bloc.[122]

Israel's seizure of Jordanian territory during the June 1967 war ended Jordan's plans for developing the West Bank. Despite ongoing Arab–Israeli clashes that threatened the canal itself, the Ghor and 'Ajlun remained the most fertile part of Transjordan. The CIA reported that in the years prior to the war, Jordan had achieved a 12 percent growth rate partly through the development of agricultural and irrigation projects, "the most important of which was the East Ghor Canal." In the months following the war:

agriculture on the East Bank, especially in the important East Ghor area, has been disrupted seriously by postwar military activity. Israeli artillery fire has damaged the East Ghor Canal and continues to hit the canal intermittently. Even more serious, however, is the loss of life by farmers from Israeli machinegun fire and mines. Most farmers have withdrawn from the East Ghor area because of fear, causing an immediate sharp reduction in output in this important area.

Although a new wave of refugees affected the demography of 'Ajlun District and the kingdom's northwest region, the CIA report nevertheless described it as "the 'garden spot' of Jordan" responsible for "about 45 percent of total East Bank agricultural production."[123]

With regard to land tenure reform, studies of East Ghor completed in the years following the 1967 war found that it did not succeed to the degree

---

[119] USAID (Bell) to Johnson, May 14, 1966, cited earlier.

[120] Amman to State, telegram 84, August 11, 1964, folder: Jordan Vol. I Cables [1 of 2], 11/63-2/65, box 146, NSF, LBJL.

[121] Rostow to Johnson, June 21, 1966, folder: Jordan Vol. II Memos 3/65-11/66, box 146, NSF, LBJL.

[122] See documentation in folder: Jordan vol. II Memos 3/65-11/66, box 146, NSF, LBJL. See also Arlene Lazarowitz, "Different Approaches to a Regional Search for Balance: The Johnson Administration, the State Department, and the Middle East, 1964–1967," *Diplomatic History* 32 (January 2008): 25–54; and Clea Lutz Bunch, "Strike at Samu: Jordan, Israel, the United States, and the Origins of the Six-Day War," *Diplomatic History* 32 (January 2008): 55–76.

[123] CIA Intelligence Memorandum, "Economic Outlook for the East Bank of Jordan," August 1968, folder: Jordan Vol. V Memos [2 of 2] 3/68-1/69, box 148, NSF, LBJL. See also Hezleton, *The Impact of the East Ghor Canal Project*, 44.

Haddad claimed in addressing either the fragmentation or concentration of landownership in the project area. A significant factor in the fragmentation of holdings in the Jordan Valley was the persistence of joint ownerships, despite the long history of successive efforts at legally assigning title to individual cultivators. By 1971, according to a Jordanian government study, as many as one-third of the parcels in the East Ghor project area were jointly owned, with some having as many as twenty-one separate owners. Ford Foundation researcher Jared E. Hezleton blamed the persistence of joint ownerships on the EGCA: "This resulted mainly from the failure of the Authority to settle rights among the parties, particularly where the old landowner and tenant were given joint rights." Hezleton also noted that "anticipation of the land reform aspects" of the East Ghor project "led large land holders to redistribute their holdings among members of their family to reduce their vulnerability to expropriation." The EGCA's "selection of holders in accordance with the system of priorities" established by the East Ghor land laws "was not always rigorous." As a result, "the percentage of share-croppers has actually increased."[124] On the basis of a separate survey, political scientist Claud R. Sutcliffe determined that "70 per cent of the project farmers were still sharecroppers," a result he also blamed on the EGCA for having given "first priority" in assigning lands to previous holders "regardless of whether or not they themselves actually exploited, *i.e.* operated, their land."[125]

Failure to create "yeoman farmers" along the East Ghor can be adequately explained only by understanding how the project replicated previous experiences with land tenure reform in the Jordan Valley. The EGCA operated in a different political context and as part of a massive new irrigation program, but faced similar challenges to those encountered by the Ottoman and mandatory officials who had previously attempted to administer land tenure in the fertile corner of Transjordan. Policies that attempted to change rural society were circumscribed by the self-interest of existing landowners and depended on local village leaders for their implementation. As Mundy and Smith explained with respect to Ottoman registration in 'Ajlun, the state was not separate from the society on which it imposed a new land regime but had to work through rural elites in what amounted to a reconciliation between formal legal requirements and prevailing practices. A report by the UN Relief and Works Agency had similarly noted the inability of land settlement policies initiated during the mandate to eliminate joint ownership, which remained prevalent throughout the valley and constituted "one of the remnants of the old Musha'a tenure."[126] Like the Ottomans and British, the

[124] Ibid., 30, 36, 37.
[125] Sutcliffe, "The East Ghor Canal Project," 476.
[126] UN Relief & Works Agency for Palestine Refugees, Bulletin of Economic Development, Number 14, Special Reports on Jordan, July 1956, p. 16, 885.16/8-1356, RG 59, NARA.

Americans confronted the limits of their ability to change relations between land and people on the East Bank. The U.S. policy of building the East Ghor Canal and distributing irrigated parcels of land therefore became part of this regional pattern, despite the growth of commercial agriculture fostered by investment in irrigation.

Placing East Ghor in this context serves as a broader critique of U.S. agricultural policy for the Arab Middle East and of recent scholarship on development. Tannous seized on Ottoman land reform as a useful foil for America's agrarian liberalism, without considering that the United States might become the latest power to discover the limits of agricultural development as a political strategy in the Jordan Valley. In exaggerating the earlier success of British mandatory authorities in settling titles, he overestimated the ability of the state to administer land tenure in Jordan. American officials also believed that a shared commitment to fostering small-scale farms would translate into acceptance of American priorities. This assumption proved true neither with respect to what Husayn called his "evolutionary" approach to fostering a Hashemite modernity nor with regard to Sha'ir's Ba'thist-inspired pan-Arab development agenda.[127]

Following Cold War–era policies, recent scholarship on the international circulation of development expertise subordinates regional histories to a homogenizing globalism. Tannous parlayed his Arab background into a policy-making role, but only because he tailored his regional knowledge to the needs of Cold War strategy. Analysis of agricultural reforms and other aspects of development pitched at the global level similarly sweeps different kinds of postcolonial societies into a flattened third world. Framing agricultural development globally conceals distinctions between and within regions, while such an approach portrays the developing world as a single field awaiting transformation by experts. It prevents scholars from describing how U.S. policies confronted the disparate legacies of earlier reforms. Regional cases are crucial complements to postwar histories based on the universal diffusion of development expertise. Such cases historicize American power within particular contexts and offset the tendency of an inherited globalism to legitimize that power.

---

[127] See the account of Husayn's conversation with former U.S. ambassador to the United Arab Republic John S. Badeau in Amman to State, airgram A-192, December 5, 1966, folder: POL 15-1 Jordan 1/1/66, box 2388, Central Foreign Policy Files, 1964–66, RG 59, NARA.

5

The People's Court

"Colonel al-Mahdawi is extremely aggressive, is anti-Western to the point of hatred and although it is not known whether he is a card carrying Communist he has taken a position which has given important support for the success of Communism and Soviet policy in Iraq. He has taken a position, more recently, of extreme animosity toward Egypt, and has been a major source of the Iraqi brand of the vitriolic propaganda verbiage emanating from Baghdad and from Cairo."

— State Department memo, March 1959.[1]

"[The Special National Intelligence Estimate on Iraq] also deals with the possibility of a gradual communist takeover, which worries [the] CIA as much as anything else ... it would be hard to tell when the litmus paper turns red."

— Memo by Halla of a meeting of the special committee on Iraq, January 4, 1960.[2]

"[The Iraqi Revolution] prescribed the establishment of a People's Republic (a democratic republic) and the Iraqi republic is neither an 'eastern province' nor a federal union, nor any sort of confederated dependency.... Communism is not, as with chickens' eggs, able to turn their white color to red in the blink of an eye."

— Col. Fadl 'Abbas al-Mahdawi, *Sawt al-Ahrar*, September 17, 1961.[3]

Modernization in Jordan took on practical meaning from the ways in which American development policies met the legacy of previous reforms. In revolutionary Iraq, the pursuit of social and economic progress could not be

---

[1] State Department memo, Division of Biographic Intelligence, March 1959, CK3100702306, DDRS.
[2] Memo by Halla of a meeting of the special committee on Iraq, January 4, 1960, folder: CP Iraq [1], box 4, Special Staff File Series, White House Office, NSC Staff: Papers, 1948–61, DDEL.
[3] Col. Fadl 'Abbas al- Mahdawi, *Sawt al-Ahrar*, September 17, 1961, reprinted in *M MAUK*, 17: ba'.

separated from an existing dispute over how to define the nation itself. Any scheme for modernizing Iraq through the development of its oil resources confronted perennial questions of national identity heightened by regional conflicts and the Cold War. American officials and rival Iraqi leaders advanced competing modernizing visions while also seeking to define Iraq's future negatively, in terms of either anticommunism or anticolonialism. In this formative encounter, the United States interceded to secure access to oil and as part of its global strategy of containment. The resulting violence undermined the possibilities for a pluralist society in Iraq.

Following July 14, 1958, when officers led by Brigadier 'Abd al-Karim Qasim seized power in Baghdad, rival Iraqis struggled to control the revolution within the context of an historical controversy over the meaning of Iraqi nationalism. The competing forms of Iraqi nationalism transcended conventional Cold War categories of East and West, "third way," or "neutralist" in a manner that fostered misunderstanding in Washington, prompted the first U.S. involvement in Iraqi domestic politics, and set the stage for the much more sustained interventions of recent years. Since the partition of the Ottoman Empire after World War I, politicians and intellectuals had debated whether to associate Iraq with pan-Arab nationalism (*qawmiya*) and to see its borders as creations of the colonial powers intended to divide and weaken Arabs; or whether to subordinate Arabism to an Iraqi state patriotism (*wataniya*) that appealed to non-Arab minorities such as Kurds and Turkmen, as well as to majority Shi'a, who would otherwise be marginalized in a Sunni-dominated, pan-Arab union.[4] The Iraqi Communist Party, which counted significant numbers of non-Arab minorities as members, extolled Arabism and even accepted an Arab federation in theory, but defended Iraq's independence and opposed immediate incorporation into the United Arab Republic (UAR) led by Gamal 'Abd al-Nasser. His suppression of Syrian communists following the UAR's establishment in February 1958 offered a cautionary tale for Iraq's communists and prompted them to refurbish Iraqi *wataniya* as a blueprint for independence, revolution, and modernization. Communists and their allies became the leading critics of adherence to the UAR and Nasserism within Iraq. Their propaganda and political organizing aided the regime's fight for nationalist legitimacy by praising global revolutionary movements other than Nasser's and by citing the economic achievements of socialist countries to justify similar reforms undertaken by the new government. The Cold War sharpened the controversy over Iraqi nationalism, but in the new global contexts of superpower rivalry and anticolonial revolution.

The situation in Iraq, where communists defended state patriotism against pan-Arab demands for unity, confounded analysts in Washington, who were

---

[4] See Jonathan Franzén, *Red Star over Iraq: Iraqi Communism before Saddam* (New York: Columbia University Press, 2011), 3; and Orit Bashkin, *The Other Iraq: Pluralism and Culture in Hashemite Iraq* (Stanford, CA: Stanford University Press, 2009).

used to describing communism and nationalism as mutually exclusive ideologies. As the authors of the key intelligence estimate about Iraq during this period explained: "We use the term 'nationalist' to describe a varied array of Iraqi elements whose chief common quality is that they are not Communist or pro-Communist."[5] Although these analysts acknowledged a distinction between "Iraqi as against Pan-Arab nationalism," their definitions could not accommodate, let alone explain, the role Iraqi communists played in promoting *wataniya*. Rather than understanding praise for non-Arab anticolonial movements and socialism as part of a competition with Arab nationalists for revolutionary legitimacy, they interpreted such sentiments as evidence of a creeping Soviet takeover. Struggling to comprehend Iraq's place in the Cold War, officials reached for comparisons that did not logically apply to the Iraqi case. A National Security Council (NSC) staff member disputed one State Department official's suggestion that Iraq, as a "'national Communist' state," could be "another Yugoslavia" while worrying that Iraq might instead be lost to communism and that "we may wake up some day with another China situation on our hands."[6] Iraq was not the only country in which communists and their allies claimed legitimacy as anticolonial nationalists. Ho Chi Minh's Viet Minh stands as perhaps the best-known example of an anticolonial communist movement that confronted the United States during the same period. Marxist class struggle was emphasized in many other countries as a way of attempting to overcome ethnic and sectarian differences. This was true of the Soviet Union itself, which made it appealing as a model to some Iraqis, as will be seen. But Iraq was distinct because of the communists' role in the clash between competing definitions of the nation, which predated the Cold War. During the Qasim era, communists served to counter the powerful influence Nasser exerted as the leading Arab nationalist figure from outside of Iraq's territory. Lost in Americans' narrow focus on whether Iraq had reached the point of no return and had "gone communist" was the conflict over Iraqi nationalism, which Iraqis waged rhetorically by situating their country in alternative regional and global settings.

Just as circumstances in Iraq did not conform to American officials' categories, the Iraqi case raises questions about historical analysis that subordinates postcolonial politics to the global Cold War. Although historians may offer nuanced and critical assessments of U.S. policies in the third world, they tend to portray developing countries primarily as objects of the superpower competition and as sharing underlying similarities based on their economic

---

[5] "Short-Term Prospects for Iraq," December 15, 1959, *FRUS, 1958–1960*, 12: 496 n1. See also Central Intelligence Agency Staff Memorandum No. 60-60 "The Outlook for Iraq," September 22, 1960, folder: CP Iraq[1], box 4, Special Staff File Series, White House Office: NSC Staff Papers, 1948–61, DDEL.

[6] Halla to Gleason, March 27, 1959, folder: CP Iraq[5], box 4, Special Staff File Series, White House Office: NSC Staff Papers, 1948–61, DDEL.

backwardness and relationship to Cold War politics. The significance of
the Cold War differed across particular countries to an extent that deprives
the term of an entirely coherent meaning. On the global level, Iraq offers a
case study in which the United States and the U.S.S.R. each sought influence
through appeals to assist Iraqis in developing their country's rich oil resources.
But explaining that conflict requires complementary analysis on the regional
level. As the Iraqi experience demonstrates, the distinctive features of a country's postcolonial politics could be the most crucial in shaping its relations
with the United States. Understanding those relations during the Qasim period
requires differentiating Iraq from other third world countries. Instead of simply looking to see whether the litmus paper turned red, as U.S. officials did,
a better understanding of revolutionary Iraq emerges from examining how a
changing global context affected existing patterns of national and regional
conflict. U.S. officials may have conceived of Iraq's modernization strictly in
terms of anticommunism, but, for Iraqis, development politics raised persistent questions about identity and nationhood. Rather than a universal process
as American global strategists imagined it, modernization in Iraq depended on
competing national and sectarian definitions of the state.

This chapter analyzes Iraq's struggles over political and economic development in light of the historic rivalry between pan-Arab and nation-state
conceptions of nationalism. It also examines American perceptions of those
struggles based on U.S. Cold War foreign policy and American visions for
Iraq's development. It does so by focusing attention on the Special High
Military Court [al-Mahkamah al-'Askariya al-'Ulya al-Khassa] established
by Qasim and the other officers who seized power and overthrew the
Hashemite monarchy. Set up initially to try old-regime figures, the "People's
Court," as it came to be known, was chaired by Colonel Fadl 'Abbas
al-Mahdawi, a cousin of Qasim's. Although not himself a member, Mahdawi
was close to the Iraqi Communist Party, and American officials used his
prominence at any given moment as a barometer of communist influence on
Qasim. Historians of Iraq have used the court's twenty-two-volume Arabic
transcript as an important source on Iraqi politics, but they have tended to
be dismissive of Mahdawi himself. Bombastic and theatrical, a butcher's son
lacking formal legal training, Mahdawi presided over quintessential show
trials in which he baited and abused witnesses in between giving speeches
from the chair.[7] One historian, following the sharply critical accounts British
and American diplomats filed, described Mahdawi as "of limited intelligence
and unlimited vanity," and even as unintentionally "funny."[8] In this interpretation, the court served simply as a platform for Mahdawi's megalomania.

---

[7] See Eric Davis, *Memories of State: Politics, History, and Collective Identity in Modern
Iraq* (Berkeley: University of California Press, 2005), 127; and Uriel Dann, *Iraq under
Qassem: A Political History, 1958–1963* (New York: Praeger, 1969), 46. See also the DDRS
document cited in the epigraph.

[8] Dann, *Iraq under Qassem*, 135.

Yet Mahdawi was not merely "anti-Western to the point of hatred," as the State Department claimed. Rather, he used the People's Court as a "pulpit [*minbar*]" for defining and communicating to Iraqi audiences a modern, socialist vision of *wataniya* nationalism. In this vision, Iraq would be an independent, multiethnic republic friendly toward but not subservient to the Soviet Union. As in the *Sawt al-Ahrar* interview quoted earlier, Mahdawi insisted that it was possible for the Iraqi Communist Party to play an important role in Iraq's economic development without making the country "communist" or compromising its neutrality, a claim the United States completely rejected. In a socialist Iraq, the government would "deliver justice to the worker and the peasant" and liberate those classes from the historical legacy of exploitation under the Hashemite monarchy, the British mandate, and Ottoman rule.[9] Iraq would assume its place among anti-imperialist nations, including not only neutral India, but also Fidel Castro's Cuba, and would take the development path blazed by the U.S.S.R. and successfully followed by other socialist countries. While American policy makers believed that revenues generated in partnership with the Iraq Petroleum Company would advance the country's development, Mahdawi promoted the autonomous use of the country's resources and called on Iraqis to resist the depredations of what he described as Western oil "monopolies [*ihtikarat*]." Most of all, from early in 1959, Mahdawi became a harsh critic of Nasser's UAR and its pan-Arabist allies inside Iraq, whom he depicted as agents of the imperialists. The Iraqi colonel deployed socialism as a weapon against Nasserists within Iraq and as the basis for an independent nation-state in which Arabs, Kurds, Turkmen, and other minorities would supposedly enjoy economic and political equality. The People's Court embodied both the expressions of pluralism that historian Orit Bashkin associates with the preceding Hashemite era and the violence that grew during the revolutionary period as the result of domestic political struggles and outside intervention.[10] Mahdawi's court therefore sat at a crossroads of modern Iraqi history and shows that Iraq's descent into sectarian and ethnic conflict was by no means predetermined.

Mahdawi fleshed out his agenda through the various interviews, news stories, letters, cartoons, and poetry printed as front matter in each volume of the court's transcripts. He himself had literary pretensions, though he once declared with false modesty that he was "neither poet nor litterateur."[11] His court transcript, whose political content he carefully controlled as compiler and contributor, became an important piece of propaganda through which Mahdawi related Iraq to the wider world.[12] Here were tributes to women guerillas fighting alongside Castro in Cuba, celebrations of Soviet

[9] *MMAUK*, 1:3.
[10] See Bashkin, *The Other Iraq*.
[11] *MMAUK*, 20: kha' ج
[12] Dann dismisses Mahdawi's work on the transcript as insignificant. See Dann, *Iraq under Qassem*, 259.

cosmonaut Yuri Gagarin's spaceflights, letters from Arab students involved in the communist-led peace movement, and a blistering parody of Nasser, thinly disguised as a mock defendant brought before the People's Court. Politically inexperienced as he was, Mahdawi nevertheless tried to maximize his usefulness by positioning himself between Qasim's government and the Iraqi Communist Party and its front organizations. He cultivated himself as an intermediary between the regime, which followed an ostensibly neutralist foreign policy, and the party that offered the best chance for countering the Nasserists and legitimizing Iraqi independence. Doing so required that Mahdawi use the People's Court to associate Iraq with revolutionary and economic reform movements outside the Arab world. His campaign began to emphasize the themes of modernization, revolution, and the competition among different development models just as these same issues increasingly became the focus of global politics and the superpower rivalry. By deploying socialist internationalism in the service of *wataniya*, however, Mahdawi sought to legitimize his own revolutionary credentials and undermine Nasserists' claims that they alone represented Arab anticolonialism and modernity. For a brief but important few years, Mahdawi was at the center of the conflict over whether Iraqis should develop their country as an independent nation-state or as part of a pan-Arab union. Studying his largely forgotten political career therefore reveals not just how Iraq's politics became subordinated to the Cold War, but also how Mahdawi and other Iraqis selectively invoked their global context in order to win political battles inside Iraq.

Not surprisingly, the U.S. mission in Baghdad and officials in Washington closely followed Mahdawi's activities, which they interpreted as evidence of communist influence. As in other areas of U.S.–Arab relations, this conflict over Iraq's future was conducted using a shared language of development. Whereas Mahdawi envisioned a pluralist, socialist Iraq that he sought to defend primarily against the regional threat posed by Nasser, American officials defined Iraq's modernization in terms of preserving Iraqi sovereignty from Soviet advances while securing Western oil investments. It was just as Mahdawi was turning the court into his *minbar* that the U.S. government began for the first time secretly discussing the overthrow of Qasim. Mahdawi's intended constituency were ordinary Iraqis who had been mobilized by the revolution whom he tried to win away from Nasser and the pan-Arabists with glowing accounts of Soviet industries and salutes to non-Arab revolutionaries. But his most consequential audience may have been U.S. officials. Mahdawi's promotion of an independent, socialist Iraq played an important role in shaping American perceptions of Iraqi politics. His use of the People's Court as a propaganda instrument updating Iraqi *wataniya* for the Cold War era strengthened the hand of those Americans who wished to change Iraq's government. Although the extent of U.S. responsibility cannot be fully established on the basis of available documents, Washington backed the movement by military officers linked to the pan-Arab Ba'th Party that overthrew Qasim in a coup on February 8, 1963. The next day, the Ba'th summarily executed Qasim and top aides including Mahdawi. A brutal anticommunist purge followed, which some U.S. officials justified as part of a modernization process and as helping to secure Iraq's oil resources from the communist threat. The Ba'thists' campaign against the communists and their supporters left thousands dead and set a precedent for political violence from which Iraqis are still trying to escape. American officials supported the purge because they regarded Iraq strictly through the lens of the global Cold War.

The People's Court helped the revolutionary government to establish its legitimacy and balance competing political forces. The provisional constitution issued following the July 14 revolution granted authority to a three-man sovereignty council, but real power rested with Qasim as prime minister and acting minister of defense and with Colonel 'Abd al-Salam 'Arif, another leading free officer who became deputy prime minister and acting minister of the interior.[13] Immediately after seizing power, the regime became embroiled in the controversy over whether to adhere to the UAR. Qasim struggled to maintain support both from pan-Arab nationalists and communists who opposed submitting Iraq to Nasser's rule and who underscored their opposition by hailing Qasim as the "Sole Leader." As historian Hanna Batatu explains, Qasim faced the "necessity of maneuvering between the nationalists and the Communists, counterpoising one against the other." Indeed, Qasim's "very survival depended upon his not allowing any of the two forces to become too strong or both to reach an accord."[14] In such an environment, the Iraqi Communist Party organized Popular Resistance militias as a force for defending the regime's independence, although Qasim insisted on bringing these under state authority. The regime also established a Ministry of Guidance that attempted to foster a unifying Iraqi culture above sect and ethnicity through the cultivation of folklore and an emphasis on Iraq's Mesopotamian heritage, a campaign symbolized by the adoption of the Akkadian sun for the national flag. According to political scientist Eric Davis, the regime used mass media as an important basis for reaching ordinary Iraqis. Television became "a medium upon which the revolutionary regime relied heavily in its attempts to mobilize support," and "Iraqi State Television's most important activity was to broadcast the trials of members of the monarchical regime" and other enemies.[15]

[13] See Dann, *Iraq under Qassem*, 40.
[14] Hanna Batatu, *The Old Social Classes and the Revolutionary Movements of Iraq*, New ed. (London: Saqi Books, 2004), 847.
[15] Davis, *Memories of State*, 125, 127.

Law Number Seven issued by the revolutionary government in early August established the Special High Military Court for trying old-regime figures. Mahdawi, who lacked a legal background, became president, although the chief prosecutor, Lt. Colonel Majid Muhammad Amin, had studied law while serving with the army's engineering corps.[16] An important function of the court initially was to justify the regime's repudiation of the monarchy's pro-Western foreign policy. Nuri al-Sa'id, the prime minister whom many Iraqis detested for joining the Anglo-American Baghdad Pact, had been brutally murdered by a mob during the revolution, his corpse then disinterred and desecrated. Those brought before the court included Fadl al-Jamali, the former prime minister who had discussed the Dujayla agricultural settlement with Assistant Secretary of State McGhee (see Chapter 4). The law governing the court retroactively defined as treasonable political interference in other Arab countries, which observers interpreted as aiming to criminalize former Iraqi officials' failed schemes for bringing Syria into the Baghdad Pact. Mahdawi himself endorsed this interpretation, while invoking the "principle of positive neutralism [*mabda' al-hiyad al-ijabi*]" and condemning "imperialist alliances" in general.[17] The Cairo newspaper *al-Masa'* quipped that the first defendants actually to appear before the court would be U.S. Secretary of State John Foster Dulles and British Foreign Secretary Selwyn Lloyd.[18] A British diplomat complained that "the guilty men were found first and the law was then tailored to meet their cases."[19] On behalf of the man in the street, the People's Court "can give vent to his hatred of Western imperialism," while offering him "emotional releases" in the form of the trials, "which are regularly televised in Baghdad." According to this diplomat, the court's proceedings served mainly to "keep hatred of the previous regime and, to a lesser extent, that of the Western Powers alive in the clientele of the coffee shops."[20]

Mahdawi attempted to carry out the court's political mission while insisting that its proceedings were fair and legitimate. The dedication of the bound transcript hailed the democratic Iraqi republic and great Iraqi people first before invoking the Arab nation [*umma*]. The court's coordinating committee praised the July revolution as a "new dawn of freedom" for Iraq and as bringing about the "unity of two nations," which it clarified as that between Arabs and Kurds within Iraq, rather than Iraqi adherence to the UAR. It defined the court's mission as removing obstacles to the revolution and urged those who opposed it to "join the freedom caravan [*al-rakb al-hurr*] leading to light and strength" under Qasim's leadership.[21] Printed immediately

---

[16] Dann, *Iraq under Qassem*, 46.

[17] *MMAUK*, 1:3.

[18] *MMAUK*, 2: kaf.

[19] Crawford to Lloyd, August 26, 1958, FO 481/12, BNA.

[20] Crawford to Lloyd, September 9, 1958, FO 481/12, BNA.

[21] *MMAUK*, 1:1–2.

following Mahdawi's declaration about delivering justice to workers and peasants was a description of the court's stately chamber. It provided places for defense counsel as well as for judges and the accused, and its microphones broadcast the proceedings to prove to the world that justice was being meted out, all beneath a banner that proclaimed "In the Name of the People" in red script (Figure 5.1).[22] Although subsequent volumes reprinted press articles testifying to the court's transparent fairness in trying figures from the monarchy, Mahdawi's tribunal soon turned its attention to the regime's current enemies. A dangerous rift opened within the Free Officers' government over the nature of Iraqi nationalism in general and about the question of joining the UAR in particular. Qasim uncovered an anti-regime plot backed by the UAR and led by venerable Iraqi nationalist Rashid 'Ali al-Kaylani, who was subjected to two secret (non-public) trials in Mahdawi's court in December.[23] In the coming months, Qasim would be forced to rely on communists to counter subsequent Nasserist plots, while Mahdawi would use the People's Court to formulate a credible *wataniya* conception of Iraq's revolution.

These developments raised American concerns about a communist takeover of Iraq. While the Eisenhower administration had recognized the new government, it was left to Assistant Secretary of State William Rountree to establish relations with Qasim following a regional crisis that had encompassed not only the end of the Hashemites in Iraq, but also British intervention to keep King Husayn on his throne in Jordan and the landing of U.S. marines in Lebanon.[24] Rountree visited Lebanon, Jordan, and Egypt before arriving in Baghdad at the worst possible moment. The U.S. embassy had been approached by anti-regime figures, and when the Rashid 'Ali plot was exposed, the Iraqi press accused the Americans of being behind it. At the airport, Rountree was greeted by an angry crowd and even about 100 hostile employees inside the airport fence. Demonstrators threw mud, rocks, eggs, and garbage at his limousine before pasting stickers on the car reading "Rountree go home."[25] When he met with Qasim on December 16, the prime minister apologized, but also accused the United States of inciting Iraqi Kurds against his regime. At this point, the CIA gave "non-Communist Arab nationalists (with Nasser's support) only an even chance of breaking the Communist drive to take over in Iraq."[26] Back in Washington, Rountree joked about his "'warm' reception" in Baghdad and told the NSC Planning

[22] *MMAUK*, 1:6–7.

[23] See Dann, *Iraq under Qassem*, 127–35.

[24] See Yaqub, *Containing Arab Nationalism*, 205–36.

[25] Telegram from the Embassy in Iraq to the Department of State, December 16, 1958, *FRUS, 1958–1960*, 12: 361n3. On contacts with anti-Qasim plotters, see Telegram from the Department of State to the Embassy in Iraq, December 4, 1958, *FRUS, 1958–1960*, 12: 355–56.

[26] CIA Office of National Estimates, Staff Memorandum No. 51–58, "Likelihood of a Communist Takeover in Iraq," December 17, 1958, folder: CP Iraq[6], box 4, Special Staff File Series, White House Office: NSC Staff Papers, 1948–61, DDEL.

FIGURE 5.1. The People's Court. *MMAUK*, vol. 2.

Board that the "demonstrations on his arrival were highly organized by Commies." The Soviets would never have resorted to such a crude demonstration, Rountree believed, which was instead the work of "'free wheeling' by local Communists." Although the CIA analysts saw Nasser as playing an anticommunist role, like them Rountree described communism and nationalism as ideologically opposed. He "reiterated the view that it is in our interest to have a nationalist government in Iraq, not dominated by [the] UAR or Commies." The idea that political circumstances and the struggle against Nasserists had made Iraq's communists into leading defenders of Iraqi nationalism was not part of U.S. policy making. Rather, Rountree wondered whether Qasim had "passed the point of no return" in relying on communist support.[27] This question would define U.S. policy toward Iraq until the end of Qasim's regime.

The role played by Mahdawi and his court grew as the political crisis worsened with the arrest of Col. 'Abd al-Salam 'Arif. After the revolution, Qasim and 'Arif cultivated different constituencies within Iraq and divided

---

[27] Memorandum by Halla, January 6, 1959, folder: CP Iraq[6], box 4, Special Staff File Series, White House Office: NSC Staff Papers, 1948–61, DDEL.

over joining the UAR. While Qasim relied on the communists and the social-ist National Democratic Party, 'Arif adopted the pan-Arabist slogan of "Unity Now." He traveled to Damascus to meet Nasser in the days after the revo-lution and maintained close ties to Iraqi Ba'thist leader Fu'ad al-Rikabi.[28] Qasim responded by removing 'Arif and other nationalists from the govern-ment. He sacked 'Arif as commander-in-chief of the armed forces and exiled him overseas as ambassador to West Germany. During a heated argument prior to his departure, 'Arif pulled a gun, with which he claimed, later, he had planned to commit suicide. When 'Arif returned to Baghdad on November 4, however, Qasim had him arrested and charged with attempting to over-throw the government and to assassinate the prime minister.[29] Mahdawi convened 'Arif's trial on December 27, and although it was conducted in a closed session, the proceedings served to vindicate a *wataniya* vision of Iraq. The prosecutor charged 'Arif with jeopardizing Iraq's "democratic republi-can system [*al-nizam al-jumhuri al-dimuqrati*]" and internal unity among "its Arabs and Kurds."[30] Mahdawi sparred with 'Abd al-Rahman al-Bazzaz, the legal scholar and diplomat who used the United States as an exam-ple of how a federation could evolve into a strong, centralized state (see Chapter 1). Called as a witness, al-Bazzaz told Mahdawi that he supported "the gradual unification [*al-ittihad al-tadriji*]" of Arab countries, though the court's printed transcript captioned a photo of al-Bazzaz with the comment that 'Arif's call for unity had been "hasty [*mutasar'a*]."[31] 'Arif was convicted on the assassination charge, but Mahdawi made a recommendation for clemency, probably at Qasim's request.[32] Although Qasim tried to sustain a balance between political forces in Iraq, he increasingly had to rely on com-munists to hold the Nasserist threat at bay. The People's Court proved useful in this regard, and it was during the 'Arif trial that Mahdawi first caught the attention of U.S. officials. Communists "closely advise both the chief judge and the prosecutor of the Military Court," explained a State Department intelligence report, "which is staging a series of show-trials of members of the old regime."[33]

Worse disorder was yet to come. Nationalist officers backed by the UAR and led by Brigadier Nazim al-Tabaqchali and Colonel 'Abd al-Wahhab

---

[28] See Elie Podeh, *The Decline of Arab Unity: The Rise and Fall of the United Arabic Republic* (Portland, OR: Sussex Academic Press, 1999), 61; and Charles Tripp, *A History of Iraq*, 2nd ed. (New York: Cambridge University Press, 2000), 152.

[29] See Dann, *Iraq under Qassem*, 62–88.

[30] MMAUK, 5:224.

[31] MMAUK, 5:315, 319. See also al-Bazzaz, *al-dawlah al-muwahhada wa-al-dawlah al-ittihadiya*, 17, 138–41.

[32] See Dann, *Iraq under Qassem*, 88.

[33] State Department Bureau of Intelligence and Research, "Iraq: The Crisis in Leadership and the Communist Advance," January 16, 1959, folder: CP Iraq[6], box 4, Special Staff File Series, White House Office: NSC Staff Papers, 1948–61, DDEL.

al-Shawwaf planned to launch an uprising in the northern city of Mosul in early March, during which army intelligence chief Colonel Rif'at al-Hajj Sirri would arrest Qasim in Baghdad. From Syria, Nasser's intelligence provided a radio transmitter and helped to arm Shammar tribal elements inside Iraq whose leaders opposed Qasim's recent land reform law.[34] The coup failed, however, when the communist-front Peace Partisans poured into Mosul in the hundreds of thousands and staged a show of force in a "monster gathering." The communists' Popular Resistance forces battled the nationalists, who failed to receive support from rank-and-file soldiers. Although nationalist aircraft were able to bomb the regime's radio transmitter in Baghdad, pro-Qasim forces quickly relieved Mosul, with Colonel Hasan 'Abbud, a procommunist former staffer of Mahdawi's, among the first to arrive with loyal troops.[35] Shawwaf was killed in the fighting, while Tabaqchali, Sirri, and other plotters were arrested. The first death sentences, for the pilots who bombed Baghdad, were handed down by the People's Court and carried out before the end of the month.[36]

The Mosul uprising was followed by an escalation in the propaganda war pitting Nasser and pan-Arabists against Qasim and supporters of his regime. Pro-Nasserists attacked Qasim as "the divider" of Iraq (the literal Arabic meaning of his name). The Egyptian press singled out Mahdawi as a communist dupe who ran a "circus." According to historian Uriel Dann's summary of Egyptian propaganda, Qasim's dimwitted cousin "was not only a clown, a boor and a sadist," but he was also a "felon who had stolen five hundred bags of coal under the old regime" and had cowered in his house during the July revolution.[37] Nasserists revived the insult of *shu'ubiyun*, which they applied to communists and to Qasim's non-Arab and Shi'a supporters. The term referred to those who had spread Persian influences during the Umayyad and 'Abbasid caliphates and so implied foreignness and disloyalty to Arabism. Nasser had used the epithet in a victory day speech on December 23, just prior to cracking down on communists within the UAR, and it became a mainstay of anti-Qasim propaganda.[38] "If the Shu'ubiyun in Iraq under the 'Abbasids sought to impose Persian culture on the Arabs," Davis explains, then Qasim's Arabist opponents believed that "communists sought to place Iraq politically and culturally in the Soviet orbit."[39] Mahdawi returned fire, using the court to attack Nasser as a fascist,

---

[34] See the account of Nasser's role in 'Abd al-Latif al-Baghdadi, *Mudhakkirat 'Abd al-Latif al-Baghdadi*, 2 vols. (Cairo: Al-Maktab al-Misri al-Hadith, 1977), 2:80–99.

[35] Dann, *Iraq under Qassem*, 169, 174.

[36] See Dann, *Iraq under Qassem*, 180; and Batatu, *The Old Social Classes and the Revolutionary Movements of Iraq*, 866–89.

[37] Dann, *Iraq under Qassem*, 161.

[38] Podeh, *The Decline of Arab Unity*, 66.

[39] Davis, *Memories of State*, 130. See also Franzén, *Red Star over Iraq*, 99; Bashkin, *The Other Iraq*, 170–71; and Dann, *Iraq under Qassem*, 162.

a "Pharaoh pretender," and a "little Hitler." In the months after the Mosul plot he published a series of letters and received visits from "free Arabs" denouncing Nasser's dictatorial rule over the UAR. One visitor described Egypt as a "big prison."[40] To combat the *shu'ubiyun* charge, Mahdawi spread the rumor that Nasser's wife was Persian.[41]

Although Mahdawi had since the early days of his court cultivated the Arab press, following Mosul his public statements increasingly sought to legitimize an independent, socialist Iraq in a non-Arab context. In a March 1959 interview, for the first time he compared Iraq to Castro's Cuba, whose government was similarly prosecuting members of a former regime in a "sister [*zamila*]" revolutionary court.[42] Mahdawi also decided to air his perspective on Mosul in a lengthy interview with the leading Indian journalist R. K. Karanjia, a former editor of the *Times of India* and founder of *Blitz*, an investigative weekly. Karanjia had interviewed Nasser weeks earlier and published a lengthy conversation with Nehru in which the Indian prime minister set out his economic and social vision.[43] The journalist claimed that he wanted to meet Mahdawi in person rather than simply accept the propaganda written about him. Although the interview was presented as impromptu, Mahdawi had obviously calculated how to turn an encounter with Karanjia to his advantage. Mahdawi compared Iraq to Karanjia's Indian homeland on the basis of the two countries' ancient civilizations. He listed the various dictators whom the Iraqi people had defeated, from the Mongol Hulagu and Tamerlane, to the Hashemite princes and Nuri al-Sa'id, and he traced the lineage of Iraqi nationalism to the Sumerians, Akkadians, and Babylonians. Using an Arabic word play, Mahdawi described India and Iraq as each being deeply rooted ['*ariq*] and possessing an ancient heritage ['*araqa*]. Having established independent Iraq's age-old pedigree, he depicted Mosul as the latest plot by the Americans, British, and French, who had also been behind those led by Rashid 'Ali and 'Arif. Nasser concealed this conspiracy behind the "mask of phony unity [*bi-qina' al-wahda al-za'ifa*]" and allied himself not only with the imperialists, but also with feudal elements such as the Shammar who opposed Qasim's reforms. Expressing admiration for Gandhi and Nehru, Mahdawi juxtaposed India's anti-imperial struggle with the July 14 revolution, which destroyed the supposedly impregnable fortress that imperialism had erected to guard Iraq's oil fields and material riches. Mahdawi thus used India as a foil that could help him to legitimize Iraqi independence from the UAR. Like U.S. officials he compared Iraq to other countries, but in Mahdawi's case it was in the interest of winning Iraq's internal political conflict and his feud with Nasserists. At the same

[40] *MMAUK*, 5:jim, ح waw ز
[41] *MMAUK*, 8: dal د
[42] *MMAUK*, 4:kha' خ
[43] Podeh, *The Decline of Arab Unity*, 224n113. See R. K. Karanjia, *The Mind of Mr. Nehru: An Interview* (London: George Allen & Unwin Ltd., 1960).

time, the People's Court president took the opportunity to burnish his own Arab nationalist credentials by asking Karanjia to join him in a moment of silence to recognize Palestinian suffering. His main audience was a domestic one. The text of Karanjia's interview was published in the court's transcript and in the Iraqi Arabic leftist daily *al-Bilad*. At the end of the interview, Karanjia was presented with a bound copy of volume 3 of the transcript, a clear indication of the propaganda value Mahdawi gave to it.[44]

The communist show of strength in Mosul set off alarms in Washington, where a more aggressive policy toward Iraq was being considered even before the fighting was over. The renewed concern, as explained by an NSC memo, "arises from reports that Col. Fadhil Mahwadi [*sic*], pro-Communist president of the Iraqi military court which has been carrying out the Baghdad 'treason' trials, is to be appointed minister of the interior." If he were, then it "would be the strongest indication to date that Qasim" is "subject to Communist influence."[45] From Baghdad, U.S. ambassador John Jernegan warned that "Mahdawis' [*sic*] excesses remain unchecked" and that it was "becoming increasingly clear" that he was either a Communist Party member "or its willing tool." His statements, which followed the "Communist line almost 100 percent," were receiving "wide coverage by Baghdad press, radio and TV."[46] Trying to force Iraq into Cold War categories, officials tried to imagine how Iraqi nationalism could be mobilized against the communist threat. After a briefing by CIA director Allen Dulles, President Eisenhower "still did not understand why Nasser could not make common cause with Qasim against Communism."[47] Vice President Richard Nixon wondered whether there were any "genuine Iraqi Nationalists" who could oppose both the communists and Nasser.[48] NSC staff member Philip Halla suggested establishing a "Special Ad Hoc Interdepartmental Committee on Iraq" that would be "somewhat similar to the 1957 Special Committee on Indonesia," which had attempted to overthrow that country's government. Halla proposed that the interagency group could consider "possible actions" the United States could take "in the event of imminent or actual Communist control of Iraq."[49] President Eisenhower approved establishment of a special committee but, in contrast to Halla's narrower concept, authorized it to

---

[44] *MMAUK*, 5:ha' ح -nun -ن

[45] Halla to Gleason, March 5, 1959, folder: CP Iraq[5], box 4, Special Staff File Series, White House Office: NSC Staff Papers, 1948–61, DDEL.

[46] Telegram from the Embassy in Baghdad to the Department of State, March 26, 1959, *FRUS, 1958–1960*, 12: 396.

[47] Ibid., 404.

[48] Ibid., 430.

[49] Briefing note by Halla, March 11 1959, folder: CP Iraq[5], box 4, Special Staff File Series, White House Office: NSC Staff Papers, 1948–61, DDEL. On the Eisenhower administration and Indonesia, see Bradley R. Simpson, *Economists with Guns: Authoritarian Development and U.S.–Indonesian Relations, 1960–1968* (Stanford, CA: Stanford University Press, 208), 33.

take preemptive action. The new group was instructed to consider what the United States "either alone or in concert with others, can do through overt or covert means, or a combination of both, to avoid a Communist take-over in Iraq."[50]

The publication of an Iraqi–Soviet economic aid agreement at the end of March piqued American concerns that Iraq's modernization would follow the communist blueprint. Under the agreement, Moscow would finance twenty-five projects through a seven-year loan of 550 million rubles offered at 2.5 percent interest. These included industrial projects such as steel, glassware, textile, and fertilizer plants. A second category of projects supervised by eighty Soviet experts would focus on agriculture and could, according to British ambassador Humphrey Trevelyan, assist the Iraqi Communist Party in its ongoing attempts to organize peasants. Negotiated by Economic Minister Ibrahim Kubba, the agreement corresponded to Mahdawi's vision of an independent, socialist Iraq. Like Mahdawi, Kubba appeared to believe that Iraq could accept the U.S.S.R.'s assistance in modernizing without succumbing to Soviet domination. Trevelyan wrote that the agreement's industrial emphasis drew on the "example and precept of the Soviet bloc countries," while Kubba assumed that Iraq could "with disinterested Soviet aid develop from a backward into a modern economy."[51] Ambassador Jerengan warned the State Department about Qasim's post-Mosul purge of nationalist ministers and Kubba's campaign to "tie Iraq economically as closely as possible to [the] Soviet Bloc."[52] The agreement also seemed to portend the abolition of the Iraq Development Board, which had exercised authority over the oil revenues derived from the Iraq Petroleum Company during the monarchy and enjoyed institutional independence from Iraq's ministries. Prior to the revolution, the Board had included a British and an American member, but was dominated by Nuri al-Sa'id.[53] Removing the Board's Anglo-American influence would enable Qasim to use oil royalties to obtain civilian and military equipment from the Soviets and deepen Iraq's economic relations with communist countries. The British feared this possibility, especially given the fact that Kubba had contracted a loan with the Soviets, rather than use his country's ample £140 million foreign exchange surplus to finance development. In May, Qasim eliminated the Development

[50] Memorandum of Discussion at the 402nd Meeting of the National Security Council, April 17, 1959, *FRUS, 1958–1960*, 12:437. The text excised from the document in *FRUS* was included in an uncensored version the author obtained under the Freedom of Information Act.

[51] Trevelyan to Lloyd, April 29, 1959, FO 481/13, BNA.

[52] Telegram from the Embassy in Iraq to the Department of State, March 26, 1959, *FRUS, 1958–1960*, 12: 396.

[53] See Pierce to Conrad, May 5, 1958, folder: Arab Union – General, box 11, General Subject Files Relating to the Middle East, 1955–1958, Lot 61 D12, RG 59, NARA.

Board, created a replacement board chaired by himself, and merged its functions with those of a new Planning Ministry.[54]

From the beginning, the Eisenhower administration's special committee on Iraq was sharply divided over how to respond to the threat of a communist takeover in Baghdad. Assistant Secretary of State Rountree, who chaired the committee, opposed undermining Qasim and was backed up by Ambassador Jernegan. The Defense Department, represented by Assistant Secretary F. Haydn Williams, and the CIA, represented by Norman Paul, pushed for greater contingency planning against Qasim's government. In response to proposals for an "approach to Nasser" and military intervention, Jerengan was "horrified" and said that he would "deeply deplore military intervention in Iraq" unless it was "in support of" Qasim.[55] The question of whether support for Qasim could help him remain independent of the communists, or whether he had already passed "the point of no return," was muddied by Qasim's domestic political strategy. As one analyst explained, Qasim "has not given the real tip off of his intentions, which might come ... if he cracks down on Col. Mahdawi of the military tribunal."[56] Qasim demoted Kubba in a cabinet reorganization, yet at the same time granted a portfolio to Dr. Naziha al-Dulaymi, head of the communist-front League for the Defense of Women's Rights. Riots between Kurds and Turkmen in Kirkuk during July were widely blamed on the Iraqi Communist Party's political overreaching and even resulted in rare public self-criticism by the party. Although Qasim condemned the perpetrators of the violence and halted training of the Popular Resistance forces, he stopped short of explicitly breaking with the communists.[57] By early September, a State Department official was telling Halla, the special committee's secretary, that "the need for the group no longer existed," while Haydn Williams of Defense informed Halla that he "objects strongly to State's unilateral attempt to terminate the group."[58]

Far from cracking down on the court, Qasim endorsed it and Mahdawi in a speech given on August 13 at a military officers' graduation ceremony. The People's Court had just convened its sixth and final trial related to the Mosul revolt, with Tabaqchali, Sirri, and other prominent defendants saved

---

[54] See "Kassem Heads Board for Iraqi Planning," May 7, 1959, *NYT*, p. 2; and Abbas Alnasrawi, *The Economy of Iraq: Oil, Wars, Destruction of Development and Prospects, 1950–2010* (Westport, CT: Greenwood Press, 1994), 37.

[55] Memos by Halla of Meetings of Special Committee on Iraq, May 8 and 20, 1959, folder: CP Iraq[3], box 4, Special Staff File Series, White House Office: NSC Staff Papers, 1948–61, DDEL.

[56] Memo by Halla of Meeting of Special Committee on Iraq, June 1, 1959, *FRUS, 1958–1960*, 12: 462.

[57] See Dann, *Iraq under Qassem*, 220–21, 224–28; and Batatu, *The Old Social Classes and the Revolutionary Movements of Iraq*, 926–30.

[58] Halla to Boggs, September 10, 1959, folder: CP Iraq[3], box 4, Special Staff File Series, White House Office: NSC Staff Papers, 1948–61, DDEL.

for last. During the trial, it came out that torture had been used to extract testimony from certain witnesses.[59] Qasim nevertheless portrayed the army in general, and the court in particular, as guardians of the revolution against those who conspired against the people and "the nation [*al-watan*]."[60] He then upheld Mahdawi's death sentences against Tabaqchali, Sirri, and others, which, to the surprise of many, were carried out on September 20. Trevelyan reported to the Foreign Office that it was widely expected that Qasim would break with "the hated President and Prosecutor of the Court, Mahdawi and Majid Amin" and commute the sentences as a way of distancing himself from the communists. The executions therefore came as a "great shock."[61] Iraq's military attaché in Washington, Major Mustafa Hasan al-Naqib, was "extremely upset" over the executions, according to William Lakeland, officer in charge of Iraqi-Jordanian affairs at the State Department. Naqib had left Baghdad only after being assured that they would not be carried out, and he spoke with some "two hundred Iraqi Nationalist officers" who had suffered "arrest and in some cases torture at the hands of the Communists." A Free Officer colleague of Qasim's, Naqib had warned the prime minister about the communist threat, but now predicted "wide-spread disorders and trouble in Iraq between pro-Communist and anti-Communist elements." Naqib himself joined the Ba'th Party.[62] On September 21, the CIA noted Qasim's unwillingness to move against the communists after Kirkuk, his "public approval of pro-Communist Col. Mahdawi's antinationalist activities in the notorious People's Court," and the executions of the Mosul defendants.[63] Under these circumstances, the State Department dropped its objections to the circulation of a CIA planning memo. When the special committee met on September 24, Lakeland broke with previous State Department reservations and argued that Qasim "is a weak reed on which to base our policy." Lakeland's perspective, shaped by his contact with Naqib and eventually the policy adopted by the United States, emerges from Halla's notes of the meeting: "We should look ahead; chances for stable Iraq diminishing under Kassem. Ought to be looking for alternatives."[64]

[59] Dann, *Iraq under Qassem*, 248–49.

[60] *MMAUK*, 6:ha'ʾ

[61] Trevelyan to Lloyd, October 8, 1959, FO 481/13, BNA.

[62] Memo by Lakeland, September 21, 1959, folder: Iraq – Iraqi Embassy Washington DC, 1959 I., box 13, Subject Files Relating to Iraq and Jordan, 1956–59, Lot 61 D20, RG 59, NARA. On Naqib's Ba'th party membership, see Batatu, *The Old Social Classes and the Revolutionary Movements of Iraq*, 790–91.

[63] Memo by Kent for the Director of Central Intelligence, September 21, 1959, folder: CP Iraq[3], box 4, Special Staff File Series, White House Office: NSC Staff Papers, 1948–61, DDEL. See also Central Intelligence Bulletin, September 17, 1959, CIA FOIA Reading Room.

[64] Memo by Halla of Meeting of Special Committee on Iraq, September 24, 1959, folder: CP Iraq[2], box 4, Special Staff File Series, White House Office: NSC Staff Papers, 1948–61, DDEL.

Immediately after the controversial executions, Mahdawi and chief prosecutor Amin left Baghdad on a previously scheduled trip to the People's Republic of China to attend celebrations marking the tenth anniversary of the Chinese revolution. Mahdawi headed the official Iraqi delegation. It was in Beijing that he received word about an assassination attempt against Qasim carried out by Ba'thist gunmen on October 7. There are two accounts in Arabic about how Mahdawi received the news. The first is from the memoir of Jordanian communist Nabih Rushaydat, who was also in Beijing and claimed to be the one who informed Mahdawi by telephone about the attack on Qasim. According to Rushaydat, Mahdawi was stunned on the phone but did not ask about the prime minister's condition. Later, when Rushaydat visited him in his hotel, Mahdawi was so annoyed with Qasim for disregarding the plots against him that the People's Court judge was oblivious to Rushaydat's words.[65] The other version is Mahdawi's own account, offered in an interview published in the newspaper *Al-Ra'i al-'Amm* on October 15 and reprinted in volume 7 of the court transcript. According to Mahdawi, he was rushing to put on his military uniform prior to meeting with Mao Zedong and Zhou Enlai. He received the news by phone and then assembled in the lobby of the Hotel Beijing with other delegates, whose facial expressions showed that they too had heard. The Iraqis were called to the front [*"ala ra's"*] of all the national delegations, from East and West, where Mao offered his personal condolences to Mahdawi, telling him that the act was a warning about the dangers of imperialist plots. Zhou placed his hand on Mahdawi's shoulder, reiterating the Great Helmsman's words and in a rhetorical flourish associating Moscow and Beijing with Baghdad.[66] The two versions together indicate the significance of the assassination attempt for Mahdawi. Rushaydat emphasizes Mahdawi's primary concern for the power struggle in Baghdad, while Mahdawi's carefully drawn account features Iraq's prominence in the global revolutionary movement. His experience in Beijing demonstrated to Mahdawi the usefulness of the international context for bolstering his own stature within an independent, socialist Iraq.

Mahdawi returned home from China with "alacrity" to join the power struggle following the attempt on Qasim, who was wounded but survived. Mahdawi began what U.S. officials called a "rabble rousing offensive" against General Ahmad Salih al-'Abdi, the figure favored by Arab nationalists.[67] The

---

[65] Rushaydat, *Awraq Laysat Shakhsiya*, 154–55.

[66] *MMAUK*, 7:waw و -za' ز

[67] Meyer to Jones, October 15, 1959, with attachments, folder: Inter-agency Group on Iraq, box 3, Bureau of Near Eastern and South Asian Affairs, Office of Near Eastern Affairs, Records of the Director, 1960–1963, RG 59, NARA. Even before the Tabaqchali and Sirri executions, Lakeland had inquired about the likelihood of an anti-Qasim coup by 'Abdi. See Glidden to Meyer, via Lakeland, September 14, 1959, folder: Baghdad [2 of 2], box 14,

army chief of staff had apparently been approached by the Ba'thist plotters after the shooting but remained loyal to Qasim.[68] Meanwhile, the attempt on Qasim heightened conflicts within the Eisenhower administration's special committee. Norman Paul pressed Assistant Secretary of State G. Lewis Jones to permit CIA consultations with Nasser and proposed what another official described as the "prepositioning of certain materials should they be necessary for later utilization in Iraq."[69] Paul told Halla that he had met with Lakeland but found Lakeland's boss, Jones, "basically opposed to covert activities."[70] To break the deadlock, the CIA called for a Special National Intelligence Estimate, which concluded that "the reliance of Qassim and the Communists on one another for support appears to be increasing."[71] Paul left for London to consult with the British and then traveled to the Middle East. When Qasim returned to work at the Ministry of Defense in early December, the Iraqi Communist Party took control of events welcoming him back and staged a massive parade.[72] The British ambassador reported that some in the crowd "were shouting for Mahdawi."[73] Mahdawi hastened to open the trials of those implicated in the plot, but the U.S. army attaché in Baghdad reported that 'Abdi wanted Mahdawi "to be assassinated" before they could begin.[74] The People's Court nevertheless reconvened on December 26.[75]

Mahdawi was determined to use the trials to educate ordinary Iraqis about how the British and Americans had made Nasser and the Ba'th into instruments for carrying out plots against Iraqi sovereignty. More than seventy defendants were accused, including many nationalists who had fled to the UAR. Those tried *in absentia* included Ba'thist leader Fu'ad al-Rikabi and future dictator Saddam Husayn al-Tikriti, one of the gunmen

Bureau of Near Eastern Affairs, Office Files Relating to Middle Eastern Affairs, 1958–1959, Lot 61 D43, RG 59, NARA.

[68] See Dann, *Iraq under Qassem*, 255n3.

[69] CIA memo to Jones, October 13, 1959, folder: CP Iraq[2], box 4, Special Staff File Series, White House Office: NSC Staff Papers, 1948–61, DDEL; Meyer to Jones, January 11, 1960, folder: Inter-agency Group on Iraq, box 3, Bureau of Near Eastern and South Asian Affairs, Office of Near Eastern Affairs, Records of the Director, 1960–1963, RG 59, NARA.

[70] Halla to Boggs, November 23, 1959, folder: CP Iraq[2], box 4, Special Staff File Series, White House Office: NSC Staff Papers, 1948–61, DDEL.

[71] Special National Intelligence Estimate, "Short-Term Prospects for Iraq," December 15, 1959, *FRUS, 1958–1960*, 12: 497.

[72] Jones to Acting Secretary, January 13, 1960, folder: Inter-agency Group on Iraq, box 3, Bureau of Near Eastern and South Asian Affairs, Office of Near Eastern Affairs, Records of the Director, 1960–1963, RG 59, NARA.

[73] Trevelyan to Lloyd, December 19, 1959, FO 481/13, BNA.

[74] USARMA to Washington, December 22, 1959, folder: Inter-agency Group on Iraq, box 3, Bureau of Near Eastern and South Asian Affairs, Office of Near Eastern Affairs, Records of the Director, 1960–1963, RG 59, NARA.

[75] Embassy in Baghdad to Department of State, foreign service dispatch 612, January 16, 1960, 787.00/1-1660, RG 59, NARA.

who had fired on Qasim's car.[76] The U.S. embassy described the proceedings as "one of the most gross perversions of justice yet witnessed" and a "forum for Mahdawi's demagoguery." Iraqis watched the televised trials with "disgusted fascination," it reported. Baghdad's commercial streets were "splattered here and there with knots of people watching the show through the window of shops," while in "many Iraqi homes the entire family gathers around the TV to spend the evening." Mahdawi denounced Cairo's "fascist rulers," charged "the British with complicity in virtually every plot against Qasim," and "missed few opportunities to link 'American' with anything reprehensible."[77] Mahdawi accused one witness, Jamaican Leslie Marsh, of being a "British spy" and claimed that Rikabi had received 400,000 Iraqi dinars from the U.S. embassy in Cairo.[78] Jernegan arranged a meeting with Qasim, who disavowed Mahdawi's accusations against the United States, but defended the People's Court president. According to Jernegan, Qasim said that Mahdawi was a "loyal man working very hard, dealing with criminals, sometimes tired, and we must make allowances for him."[79]

While Qasim continued to regard the People's Court as politically useful, Mahdawi sought to carve out a new role for himself in the aftermath of the assassination attempt. At the beginning of 1960, Qasim announced that a new law would be enacted permitting the licensing of political parties. According to a CIA report, the "pro-Communist People's Court President Col. Mahdawi has declared his intention of forming a 'People's' party with Qasim's blessing."[80] Mahdawi may have been encouraged in his bid to use the court as a springboard to party leadership by Qasim's decision to license a communist splinter group led by Christian attorney Daud al-Sayigh, rather than legitimize the main Iraqi Communist Party.[81] This decision opened up a political space for Mahdawi to court communist-front organizations while ostensibly hewing to Iraq's official neutralism. Khrushchev had subordinated Iraqi–Soviet relations to his attempts at reconciliation with Nasser following the anticommunist crackdown in the UAR. Sent to attend a ceremony initiating construction of the Aswan High Dam, the Soviet minister of

[76] See Dann, *Iraq under Qassem*, 257, and Trevelyan to Lloyd, March 15, 1960, FO 481/14, BNA. Saddam Husayn is among the defendants listed as "in absentia" opposite p. 1, *MMAUK*, vol. 20.

[77] Embassy in Baghdad to Department of State, Foreign service dispatch 612, January 16, 1960, 787.00/1-1660, RG 59, NARA.

[78] See Embassy in Baghdad to Department of State, telegram 1684, January 25, 1960, 787.00/1-2560, RG 59, NARA; Trevelyan to Lloyd, March 15, 1960, cited earlier; and Embassy in Baghdad to Department of State, foreign service dispatch 654, January 30, 1960, 787.00/1-3060, RG 59, NARA.

[79] Embassy in Baghdad to the Department of State, January 29, 1960, 787.00/1-2960, RG 59, NARA. See also Central Intelligence Bulletin, February 1, 1960, CIA FOIA Reading Room.

[80] See Central Intelligence Bulletin, January 19, 1960, CIA FOIA Reading Room; and Dann, *Iraq under Qassem*, 278–79.

[81] Ibid., 270; Batatu, *The Old Social Classes and the Revolutionary Movements of Iraq*, 937.

electric power carried Khrushchev's personal letter to Nasser.[82] Qasim was reportedly "extremely angered" to hear that the U.S.S.R. had also agreed to build the dam's second stage.[83] For State Department officials who were reluctant to intervene in Iraq, Qasim's attempt to split the communists was "the most hopeful sign" since the revolution, even though Qasim remained under the influence of "Mahdawi and his farcical Court." In March, however, Paul told the special committee that he had met outside Iraq with opposition figures and heard that Qasim "was going and that it was only a matter of time." The CIA therefore felt that the State Department was "perhaps a little too optimistic."[84] Although Mahdawi never officially founded his own party, he sought to boost his political profile through overseas trips and receiving delegates from the socialist bloc. For pro-intervention U.S. officials, Mahdawi's campaign kept alive the specter of a communist takeover in Iraq.

Mahdawi deliberately revived the historic debate concerning Iraqi nationalism, but in a manner that simultaneously addressed contemporary struggles over development. He sought to challenge the argument, made most forcefully a generation earlier by Director General of Education Sati' al-Husri, that Iraq's potential could best be realized in a pan-Arab context. According to his biographer, al-Husri believed that peoples attained their rights when they "began to discover the unique character of the nation to which they belonged in contradistinction to the political state of which they were citizens."[85] Mahdawi attempted to make just the opposite case, that Iraqi citizens could secure rights irrespective of ethnicity only in a progressive state that embraced universal socialist values. A prime example is Mahdawi's use of the festivities commemorating ninth-century Islamic philosopher Abu Yusuf Ya'qub ibn Ishaq al-Sabbah al-Kindi, a great translator of Greek scientific works into Arabic who lived in Baghdad during the 'Abbasid caliphate. For the occasion, Mahdawi invited delegates from the Soviet Institute for Afro-Asian Studies and the Soviet Cultural Center, as well as members of Iraq's communist-front Council of National Peace and various international visitors. He cited Soviet economic and cultural achievements, and acknowledged Soviet aid to Iraq and the many Iraqi students studying in the U.S.S.R. and other socialist countries. He then mentioned al-Kindi's "examples [*amthal*]" demonstrating that progress results from intellectual cosmopolitanism, connecting al-Kindi to struggles by modern Iraqi anticolonialists who were "Arab and Kurd, from the North and

---

[82] al-Baghdadi, *Mudhakkirat*, 2:102.

[83] Cumming to Secretary, January 26, 1960, 787.00/1-2660, RG 59, NARA.

[84] Meyer to Jones, October 15, 1959, with attachments, cited earlier; and memo by Halla of Meeting of Special Committee on Iraq, March 25, 1960, folder: CP Iraq[1], box 4, Special Staff File Series, White House Office: NSC Staff Papers, 1948–61, DDEL.

[85] Cleveland, *The Making of an Arab Nationalist*, 97.

the South" and who had set their country free to pursue a better life. One Soviet Orientalist testified that al-Kindi had made Baghdad into the center of world learning at a time when Europe was in darkness and most of its inhabitants wore animal skins. In a similar way, the multinational guests assembled from Morocco, Afghanistan, Iran, and the U.S.S.R. thought of Iraq's capital as "our Baghdad." For good measure, this Soviet scholar singled out the People's Court president as "well-known" in the U.S.S.R. The occasion allowed Mahdawi to place a multiethnic Iraqi republic at the forefront of socialist development and in an international setting that transcended the Arab world. Lavish praise for Baghdad as a regional and world capital of learning and progress was intended to diminish Cairo. In an implicit (but hardly subtle) way, the celebration of al-Kindi also elevated Mahdawi himself to the same level as the great philosopher.[86]

Mahdawi increasingly featured himself and Iraq on the world stage as a way of getting the upper hand over Arab nationalists in the domestic arena. Capitalizing on a series of interviews and visits, he began defining Iraq's development in regional and global terms. Mahdawi equated development with economic autonomy and with defeating the relentless conspiracies launched against Iraq by Western imperialists through their Nasserist agents. He told a female Polish reporter that the Mosul and anti-Qasim plots had their origins in alliances between imperialists and feudal tribal elements within Iraq disguised as "counterfeit" Arab nationalism. Nasser's conspiracies were only the latest instances in which Egypt served as the base for colonial "conquests [*futuhat*]" in the Middle East, which previously included those by the Greeks, Romans, Ottomans, French, and British. Mahdawi reinforced the link between underdevelopment and imperialism by reprinting an article from the Lebanese paper *Al-Nida'* about a mock People's Court defendant named "Abu Hanafi" but clearly meant to be Nasser. Charged with conspiring on behalf of imperialists in Mosul and the attempt on Qasim, Abu Hanafi had left Egypt "drowning in debts [*ghariq fi al-duyun*]," just like the khedive Isma'il, whose ruinous attempts at Westernizing Egypt in the nineteenth century had led to the British occupation.[87] Rather than surrendering to the Western powers as Nasser had, Iraq would accept Soviet assistance to develop itself economically while retaining its independence. Instead of succumbing to the false promise of pan-Arabism, Iraq would remain a sovereign republic committed to cultivating the multiethnic society living between the Tigris and Euphrates.

Like other Arab elites, Mahdawi played the trump card of experience abroad to establish his authority in development debates at home. To a journalist and official from Sudan (who needed no warnings from Mahdawi about Egyptian influence), he repeated the familiar charges against Nasser

[86] *MMAUK*, 22:za' ز -lam ل
[87] *MMAUK*, 8: jimح -za' ز, dha ذ

and celebrated a diverse Iraqi society in which Arabs, Kurds, Turkmen, Armenians, Yazidis, Sabians, Jews, and other minorities enjoyed equality. He used the interview to argue that Iraq could remain neutral while accepting Soviet aid and pursuing socialist development. Rejecting American warnings and the *shu'ubiyun* charge that Qasim had submitted to Soviet imperialism, Mahdawi insisted that the existence of communist parties in England, Italy, France, and even the United States did not make those countries "communist." His experiences traveling in Poland, China, and the U.S.S.R. had shown that states with communist governments could respect pluralism, as evidenced by the freedom of religion he had witnessed. In Poland, where he had been accompanied by Sudanese and other delegates, he had seen with his own eyes worshippers coming out of a church. Authorities in China freely permitted a procession of "the clergy [*al-kahanut*]." These experiences refuted imperialists' claims that all citizens in socialist and communist countries were "unbelievers [*mulhidin*]."[88] Mahdawi used his fall 1960 tour of the German Democratic Republic, Czechoslovakia, Bulgaria, and the U.S.S.R. to situate Iraq among the leading socialist states. This cosmopolitan internationalism promoted Iraqis' diversity at the same time that it advocated socialist economic policies. In a speech about the trip republished in *al-Bilad* and the court transcript, he praised the July 14 revolution, which "fused [*saharat*] Iraqis in its melting pot of true national unity" among Arabs, Kurds, and other regional and sectarian groups. Mahdawi's interview with Radio Moscow was reprinted as well, in which he spoke of traveling across the U.S.S.R. by train, car, and airplane before taking a boat on the Caspian to visit a petroleum industry city "of which there is nothing like it in the world." From Moscow, where he was dazzled by the metro, to Leningrad and the capitals of the polyglot republics in the Caucuses – Georgia, Armenia, and Azerbaijan – Mahdawi sensed "great stunning progress [*taqqadum 'azim mudhish*]" in all areas of life, whether agricultural, industrial, or cultural. The Soviet Union offered an example of economic progress joined to ethnic pluralism. He described "new buildings housing thousands," as well as the high standard of living indicated by the people's clothes, food, and drink. Everywhere, he saw the "Soviet people reading" and cultivating "refined human nature [*al-khulq al-insani al-rafi'*]." This testimony, he explained for Iraqis' benefit, was based on his extensive visits to institutes, schools, and hospitals where he witnessed for himself the lives of peasants, workers, and intellectuals.[89] For Mahdawi, faith in socialism had become inseparable from a commitment to Iraqi *wataniya*.

In the global arena, Mahdawi fought to win revolutionary legitimacy for Iraqi, as opposed to pan-Arab, nationalism. He pursued this drive as he cultivated his personal popularity within Iraq and a political constituency

---

[88] *MMAUK*, 9: ba'ب—kafك
[89] *MMAUK*, 13:kafك-mimم; nunن-sinس

among professional associations and the communist-front women's and peace movements. In an interview with Mahdawi titled "A Man of the People" that appeared in the leftist *Sawt al-Ahrar*, he rattled off the revolution's achievements, including agrarian reform, a free press, new organizations for workers, peasants, and women, as well as the restoration of neutralism and relations with Moscow. Mahdawi denigrated the UAR for oppressing Syrians, while reciting his rhyming *wataniya* slogan: "*Wifaq! Wifaq! Ya ahl al-'Iraq!* [Harmony! Harmony! O people of Iraq!]."[90] Yet it was through his conspicuous support for anticolonial movements that Mahdawi engaged Nasser in revolutionary one-upmanship. If opposition to French authority in Algeria was the *sine qua non* of Arab anticolonialism, then Mahdawi made certain to advertise his support for the Front de Libération Nationale (FLN). In speeches, letters, and interviews published in the court transcript, Mahdawi condemned Gaullist fascism, contrasted socialist bloc support for the FLN with that "silly stupid imbecile [*al-ghabi al-ahmaq al-ma'fun*]" Eisenhower, and praised the alleged million Algerian martyrs who had died in the struggle.[91] In Baghdad, Mahdawi welcomed a representative from Algeria's provisional republican government, accompanied by diplomats from communist China and North Vietnam.[92] He published photo tributes to Djamila Bouhired and other women FLN fighters.[93] When the Algerian female guerilla Zalikha bin Qadur visited the People's Court, Mahdawi ceremoniously presented her with a copy of volume 19 of the court transcript as a gift.[94]

Mahdawi also paid homage to non-Arab revolutionaries. Although he made positive mention of Congolese leader Patrice Lumumba, no figure received more praise from Mahdawi than Fidel Castro.[95] In an open letter to the Latin American Youth League, meeting in Havana in July 1960, Mahdawi praised Castro as heading up the struggle against the United States, the "leader of world imperialism [*za'ima al-isti'mar al-'alami*]."[96] He later repeated this acclaim in an interview with the Soviet news agency Tass and said that Iraqis – Arabs and Kurds, men and women – had closely followed the course of Cuba's revolution.[97] In a meeting with a Cuban delegate visiting his court, Mahdawi discussed French philosopher Jean-Paul Sartre's *Sartre on Cuba* and called Castro a "hero [*batal*]." Cuba's revolution was especially remarkable, Mahdawi noted, given the island's "proximity to the

90 *MMAUK*, 11: ba'ب—lamل
91 *MMAUK*, 13: za'ز; *MMAUK*, 20:za'ظ
92 *MMAUK*, 17: qafقʾ
93 *MMAUK*, 14: 'aynﻉ; 18: wawﻭ, ha'ﺡ
94 *MMAUK*, 20: nun ن-fa'ﻑ
95 On Lumumba, see *MMAUK*, 21: kafﻙ
96 *MMAUK*, 12: jim ﺝ
97 *MMAUK*, 19: jim ﺝ

citadel of world imperialism."[98] The People's Court transcript also included photo tributes to Castro, the fighters, including women, who had helped him to overthrow the U.S.-backed Fulgencio Batista, as well as teachers and other Cuban professional groups that corresponded to the constituencies that Mahdawi was courting in Iraq.[99] Mahdawi's superlative praise of Castro for standing up to the United States contained an implicit rebuke of Nasser, whom Mahdawi portrayed incessantly as an American stooge. Soviet enthusiasm for Cuba during the Khrushchev era has been described as advertising Moscow's support for third world anticolonialism, but Mahdawi borrowed this Soviet propaganda theme for his feud with Nasser.[100] By associating himself with world revolutionary movements including Castro's, Mahdawi sought to boost his own domestic political stature while contrasting the legitimacy of Iraq's national revolution against the fake pan-Arabism of Nasser and his supporters.

Mahdawi's foray into international politics spanned the transition from Dwight Eisenhower's administration to John F. Kennedy's and coincided with the increasing emphasis in U.S. policy on the third world. On one level, the People's Court president confronted Washington on the world stage as a Cold War enemy. Mahdawi's support for revolutionary movements corresponded to the Kennedy-era concern with counterinsurgency. His insistence on the superiority of socialism as an economic model mirrored the determination of Walt Rostow and others among the best and brightest to help developing peoples find a noncommunist path to modernization. It could be said that both Mahdawi and Kennedy were fixated on Fidel Castro, as a role model and antagonist, respectively. Mahdawi's attacks on Washington and praise for the Soviet Union heightened U.S.–Iraqi tensions at a moment when the superpower rivalry and decolonization had caused world politics to coalesce around universal themes of progress and development. Yet Mahdawi mobilized these themes to serve his political ends in the post-Ottoman, postcolonial setting of revolutionary Iraq. He pursued his activism on the world stage in the interest of *wataniya* consciousness and to defeat pan-Arabists in the long-term internal conflict over Iraqi nationalism. Officials in Washington may have regarded this activism in terms of their global struggle against revolution and Soviet influence, but Mahdawi remained focused on the Iraqi arena and invoked world politics as a way of bludgeoning domestic opponents and ingratiating himself with potential constituents. This strategy was apparent in his insistence on Iraq's sovereignty over its oil and alignment with the international peace movement during the waning months of Qasim's regime. Mahdawi's failed drive for

[98] *MMAUK*, 20: ba' ب
[99] See *MMAUK*, 14: za' ظ 19: dhal ذ
[100] See Anne E. Gorsuch, "'Cuba, My Love': The Romance of Revolutionary Cuba in the Soviet Sixties," *American Historical Review* 120 (April 2015): 500–01.

political leadership was the product of Iraq's distinct internal and regional circumstances, even if American officials justified their policies toward Baghdad as a response to the worldwide communist threat.

Beginning in the summer of 1960, Mahdawi forcefully endorsed Qasim's tougher stance against the Iraq Petroleum Company. When the Western companies curtailed Iraqi oil production in response to a government-imposed fee to finance the improvement of the Basra port, Mahdawi published an open letter supporting Qasim.[101] In it, Mahdawi claimed that he and Qasim had some twenty-five years earlier studied how the oil industry exploited Iraq. The reactionary monarchy had signed agreements with "the monopolistic companies [al-sharikat al-ihtikariya]," allowing them to amass "obscene profits [al-arbah al-fahisha]," rather than using national wealth to help workers and peasants, the "majority dispossessed poor," who, Mahdawi made clear, included Kurds and other minorities. In a rhyming couplet, the would-be poet compared the resolute Qasim to a "lion [al-asad al-hasur]" who would not allow Iraq to be "double-crossed [mughdur]."[102] Further steps by Qasim increased tensions with the West over oil. He hosted the September 1960 meeting of oil-producing states that formed the Organization of Petroleum Exporting Countries. In June 1961, he rejected Kuwait's independence and claimed the oil-rich emirate as an Iraqi province. Six months later, Qasim voided most of the IPC concession and declared unexploited areas, including the potentially rich fields around Basra, government property.[103] U.S. officials regarded these moves as Soviet-inspired, particularly after Moscow blocked Kuwait's membership in the United Nations.[104] Mahdawi, however, was mainly concerned with denying Nasserist claims on Iraqi (and Kuwaiti) oil wealth. He bitterly criticized Nasser and the Arab League for sending a military force to occupy "Iraqi" Kuwait and even delivered a lengthy rebuttal refuting the League's legal justification for admitting Iraq's "stolen [salib]" province as a member state.[105] In an interview granted to the *Indian News* in October 1961, Mahdawi dismissed the League as a British invention. By contrast, he favorably compared Qasim's campaign to liberate Kuwait with Indian claims on the Portuguese colonial enclave of Goa.[106] Mahdawi may have justified Iraq's oil policies in the language of global revolution and anticolonialism, but he approached oil politics as part of the paramount conflict over Iraqi nationalism. He attacked pan-Arab, Nasserist designs on the Iraqi-Kuwaiti

---

[101] See CIA Staff Memo 60-60, "The Outlook for Iraq," September 22, 1960, folder: CP Iraq[1], box 4, Special Staff File Series, White House Office: NSC Staff Papers, 1948–61, DDEL.

[102] *MMAUK*, 12: alif ا -ba' ب

[103] See Brandon Wolfe-Hunnicutt, "The End of the Concessionary Regime: Oil and American Power in Iraq, 1958–1972" (PhD diss., Stanford University, 2011), 68–72.

[104] See Talbot to Ball, December 18, 1961, *FRUS, 1961–1963*, 17: 364–66.

[105] *MMAUK*, 16: ta'ت – dad ض

[106] *MMAUK*, 18: ba'ب – ha' ه

oilfields as an imperialist plot. Mahdawi also emphasized the importance of petroleum for developing the multiethnic Iraqi nation-state, which he defined in a published message to Qasim as extending from the town of Zakho in the Kurdish far north all the way south to Kuwait.[107]

The significance of the peace movement in Mahdawi's political calculations grew as the result of dramatic events in the fall of 1961. Following a coup in Damascus on September 28, Syria seceded from the UAR. The *infisal*, as it was known, allowed Mahdawi to claim victory for Iraqi nationalism over "phony [*za'ifa*]" Arab unity, which he claimed had been based on Nasser's campaign to find markets for the Egyptian bourgeoisie.[108] Yet growing Kurdish separatism within Iraq erupted into full-scale armed revolt that same month after Qasim's regime rejected proposals for Kurdish autonomy. Kurdish forces attacked government troops, and Baghdad retaliated by bombing the home village of Kurdish leader Mulla Mustafa Barzani.[109] Mahdawi's vision of harmony among Iraq's ethnic groups was shattered just when the *infisal* deprived him of a larger-than-life regional enemy in the person of Nasser against whom he could direct his propaganda. In response, Mahdawi drew closer to the communist-front peace movement and publicized Iraqis' participation in Soviet-sponsored peace activism. The communist-front Peace Partisans' Arab chairman, 'Aziz Sharif, had been involved in an earlier attempt at reconciliation between the Iraqi communists and the leading Kurdish political party.[110] Mahdawi apparently believed that the peace movement, not only by promoting civil peace at home, but also through its international struggles for development and disarmament, offered a basis for rebuilding Arab-Kurdish unity. Although Qasim's government had officially shut down the Partisans in May 1961 as part of an effort to curb communist influence, the group was permitted to meet openly.[111] Mahdawi identified himself with the Partisans and the Council of National Peace, another communist-front organization, and delivered numerous speeches to peace groups. He addressed Iraqi delegations to the communist-organized peace conferences, the Festival for Youth and Students held in Helsinki and the Moscow Conference for Disarmament and Peace. His brother and sons, Munadil and Nidal, had organized a sports club that participated in the delegation to a previous youth festival. On the eve of the Helsinki conference in 1962, Mahdawi recalled how on that earlier occasion Iraq had proudly been represented abroad by Arabs, Kurds,

---

[107] *MMAUK*, 16: jim ج

[108] *MMAUK* 17: 'ayn ع - qaf ق

[109] See Hilsman to Rusk, April 11, 1962, folder: Iraq, 1961–1962, box 117, NSF, JFKL; and Tripp, *A History of Iraq*, 162–63.

[110] See Trevelyan to Lloyd, May 8, 1959, FO 481/13, BNA; and Dann, *Iraq under Qassem*, 198.

[111] See Dann, *Iraq under Qassem*, 321; and Batatu, *The Old Social Classes and the Revolutionary Movements of Iraq*, 945–46.

and members of other sects and minorities.[112] In a speech to the Council of National Peace, he praised delegates to the Moscow conference and peace activists for "raising the name of Iraq high among the peoples and nations" who participated in the global movement.[113] In the final volumes of his court transcript, Mahdawi published his speeches to peace organizations, reprinted letters to and from Iraqis active in the movement, and featured the theme of peace in his political commentary. This propaganda wove together themes of revolution, anticolonialism, and anti-Americanism, with tributes to the Soviets' peaceful uses of technology and the superiority of their socialist development model. In an attempt to restore Iraqis' domestic unity, Mahdawi became more invested than ever before in the global superpower conflict.

Mahdawi contrasted Americans' threats to use nuclear weapons with the peaceful achievements of the Soviet space program. This propaganda strategy portrayed socialism as a superior economic system that benefited rather than exploited mankind. He called for the international control of nuclear weapons on behalf of Iraq's Arabs, Kurds, and other national groups. The Cuban Missile Crisis in October 1962 gave Mahdawi the opportunity to fully develop this argument, while unifying it with his other propaganda themes. In an unaddressed open letter, Mahdawi described how Soviet premier Nikita Khrushchev had saved the world from nuclear war by defusing the crisis. Mahdawi condemned John Kennedy as an "American Hitler" for blockading Cuba while hypocritically shipping arms, maintaining bases, and sowing military alliances all over the world. Like Iraq, Cuba had freely chosen socialism as its system of government following a revolution against attempts by American monopolies to "plunder [*nahaba*]" the resources of other countries. Mahdawi identified himself "as a peace partisan faithful in the triumph of peace over war."[114] Mahdawi struck an anti-American, pro-Soviet stance in the paramount Cold War crisis to advertise his support for the Iraqi peace movement. His activism and the increasing prominence of the communist-front peace organizations did not go unnoticed by American officials.

Other historians have attempted to establish the extent of U.S. involvement in the Ba'thist coup against Qasim in February 1963 and the violence that followed.[115] Among the allegations is that the CIA supplied the lists of Iraqi communists the Ba'thist National Guard militia used in its

---

[112] *MMAUK*, 20: sad ص
[113] *MMAUK*, 21: ba' ٬ب
[114] *MMAUK*, 22: za' ز - shin ش; lam ل -٬ba ب
[115] See Wolfe-Hunnicutt, "The End of the Concessionary Regime"; Weldon C. Matthews, "The Kennedy Administration, Counterinsurgency, and Iraq's First Ba'thist Regime," *International Journal of Middle East Studies* 43 (November 2011): 635–53; Eric Jacobsen, "A Coincidence of Interests: Kennedy, U.S. Assistance, and the 1963 Iraqi Ba'th Regime," *Diplomatic History* 37 (November 2013): 1029–59; and William J. Zeman, "U.S. Covert

post-coup campaign of mass arrests and killings.[116] According to a CIA cable, the Baʻth leadership in Iraq first approached ʻArif about a coup in April 1962. Although ʻArif authored the coup strategy that was eventually used and subsequently became president, the Baʻthist conspirators pursued their plans without the knowledge of ʻArif, whom they regarded as a "security hazard." Two earlier plots, in July and December 1962, miscarried prior to the successful February 8 coup.[117] Historian Brandon Wolfe-Hunnicutt notes that in December 1962, Roy Melbourne, the ranking U.S. diplomat in Baghdad and a veteran of the operation against Musaddiq in Iran, informed Washington that "Qasim would be overthrown by a Baathi coup within a week."[118] While complete evidence regarding American responsibility is unlikely ever to be divulged by the CIA and other government agencies, a focus on Mahdawi can contribute new perspectives on U.S. covert activities against Qasim's government, the end of his regime, and the ensuing anticommunist purge.

Circumstantial evidence suggests that the CIA may have attempted to sicken or kill Mahdawi. In the *Interim Report* published in 1975 by the select committee chaired by Senator Frank Church on *Alleged Assassination Plots Involving Foreign Leaders*, reference is made to a "'special operation' to 'incapacitate' an Iraqi Colonel believed to be 'promoting Soviet bloc political interests in Iraq.'" The operation was proposed by the agency's Near East Division in February 1960, which coincided with the climax of the trials against Qasim's assailants, when Mahdawi became the focus of U.S. concerns about communist influence in Iraq. The goal was "to prevent the target from pursuing his usual activities for a minimum of three months." According to the *Interim Report*, the plan was eventually approved in April 1962 "to mail a monogrammed handkerchief containing an incapacitating agent to the colonel from an Asian country."[119] Testimony indicates that the handkerchief was sent, though it is not known whether it was ever received. In early 1962, Mahdawi and several members of his family fell seriously ill with what he called "influenza." Mahdawi was absent from the court

---

Intervention in Iraq, 1958–1963: The Origins of U.S. Supported Regime Change in Modern Iraq" (MA thesis, California State Polytechnic University, Pomona, 2006).

[116] For this allegation, see Batatu, *The Old Social Classes and the Revolutionary Movements of Iraq*, 985–86.

[117] CIA telegram, [redacted] February 1963, Iraq: General, 1963: January–February, box 117, NSF, JFKL.

[118] Quoted in Brandon Wolfe-Hunnicutt, "Embracing Regime Change in Iraq: American Foreign Policy and the 1963 Coup d'etat in Baghdad," *Diplomatic History* 39 (January 2015): 116.

[119] Senate Select Committee to Study Governmental Operations with Respect to Intelligence Activities (Church Committee), *Interim Report: Alleged Assassination Plots Involving Foreign Leaders*, 94th Cong. 1st sess. (Washington, DC: Government Printing Office, 1975), 181 n1. Testimony by CIA personnel indicated that the colonel for whom the handkerchief was intended later "[s]uffered a terminal illness before a firing squad in Baghdad."

while he and his family members received medical care. The timing of the illness does not correspond exactly to that of the "incapacitating" operation as described in the cited testimony. On the basis of available sources, it is impossible to know whether the two events were related.[120] Although this operation was approved by the Directorate of Plans, another agent working separately on Iraq for U.S. intelligence employed monogrammed handkerchiefs as gifts. Louise Page Morris, an operative for anticommunist labor organizer Jay Lovestone and CIA counterintelligence chief James Jesus Angleton, made contacts with anti-Qasim figures in Iraq and abroad.[121] In one letter to Morris, Lovestone lists some of her contacts. These most likely included diplomat Muhammad Adib Sulayman, who defected while serving as *chargé d'affaires* at the Iraqi embassy in Cairo.[122] Prior to leaving for Iraq, Morris asked Angleton for a "generous expense account." She explained: "In the Arab world you must give presents. For the men, linen baiste handkerchiefs, monogrammed, so they can't give them to their superiors, or gold cigarette lighters."[123]

More importantly, the Iraqi peace movement that Mahdawi promoted both for ideological reasons and out of a desire for national reconciliation attracted the attention of the U.S. embassy in Baghdad. Whereas Mahdawi regarded the communist-front peace organizations and their overseas activities as forums for Arab–Kurd cooperation, American officials saw them as evidence of Soviet penetration into Iraqi society. William Lakeland, the State Department official who had served on Eisenhower's special Iraq committee and had advocated finding an alternative to Qasim, joined the political section of the Baghdad embassy in 1960.[124] He and his colleague James Akins used coverage of the July 1962 Moscow Conference for Disarmament and Peace in Iraq's leftist press to compile lists of Iraqi communists and their supporters. *Al-Bilad*, the paper that had served as one of Mahdawi's main platforms, published lists of delegates to the conference as well as the names of those who had signed petitions supporting it. In transmitting these names to the State Department, Lakeland wrote that "these lists provide a 'Who's Who' of communists and communist sympathizers active in Iraq today." He found it significant that "they are thus willing to stand up together and be counted." Partial lists sent by Lakeland and Akins can be found in the State Department Central Files. On March 27, Lakeland transmitted a list

[120] See *MMAUK*, 19: lam ل

[121] See Michael Holzman, *James Jesus Angleton, the CIA, and the Craft of Counterintelligence* (Amherst: University of Massachusetts Press, 2008), 146–47.

[122] See Lovestone to Morris, February 10, 1961, box 2, Louise Page Morris Papers, Hoover Institution, Stanford University, Stanford, CA. See Dann, *Iraq under Qassem*, 192.

[123] Quoted in Ted Morgan, *A Covert Life: Jay Lovestone, Communist, Anti-Communist, and Spymaster* (New York: Random House, 1999), 278.

[124] See U.S. Department of State, *Foreign Service List, 1962* (Washington, DC: Government Printing Office, 1962), 44.

of 127 names copied from *al-Bilad* together with each individual's profession. Those listed included merchants, students, members of professional societies, and journalists, although university professors constituted the largest single group. On April 11, Akins transmitted thirty-nine names that he described as the eighth list culled from *al-Bilad*, consisting of Moscow Conference supporters living in 'Amara and Diwaniya Provinces. Lakeland and Akins also collected names from the publications *al-Akhbar* and *July 14*. Parenthetically, Lakeland noted that the Kurdish former cabinet minister Fu'ad 'Arif, who sided with the revolt in the north, had published a statement in *al-Thawra* objecting to reports that he had joined the delegation. 'Arif disavowed membership in the Peace Partisans and denied that he would travel to the Moscow Conference.[125] During the February 8 coup, this prominent Kurdish politician would rally to the Ba'thists.[126]

The British ambassador had once written that Iraqi "children play at 'nationalists and Communists' in the streets instead of 'cops and robbers.'"[127] This statement was borne out in a sense by a conflict that began in late December at al-Sharqiyya Secondary school in Baghdad, where Mahdawi's son Munadil became embroiled in a fight with nationalist students after reportedly circulating communist propaganda. When Munadil summoned his father's security detail, a violent conflict erupted. The incident quickly spread beyond the capital into a student strike led by an illegal nationalist group, the National Federation of Iraqi Students. Kurdish students and teachers joined the strike, and there were several deaths in violent incidents across the country. Historians differ over whether the strike was the opening shot in the latest Ba'thist rising against Qasim, but the episode demonstrated how the Kurdish revolt and renewed nationalist agitation had seriously undermined Mahdawi's *wataniya* vision for Iraq weeks prior to the coup.[128]

After Ba'thist military officers launched the coup of 14 Ramadan, as it came to be known, Mahdawi was arrested with Qasim following a siege of the defense ministry in Baghdad. They and others were taken to the state Broadcasting House, hastily court-martialed, and shot.[129] Their bodies were then exhibited on state television in a gruesome, five-minute film called *The End of the Criminals* that aired immediately following prayers and a "Felix the Cat" cartoon.[130] The head of the U.S. Information Service in Baghdad

[125] U.S. Embassy in Baghdad (Lakeland) to Department of State, dispatch 659, April 11, 1962, 787.001/4-1162; and U.S. Embassy in Baghdad (Akins) to Department of State, dispatch 777, May 31, 1962, 787.001/5-3162, RG 59, NARA.

[126] On Fu'ad 'Arif, see Dann, *Iraq under Qassem*, 312, 368.

[127] Trevelyan to Lloyd, June 13, 1960, FO 481/14, BNA.

[128] Dann, *Iraq under Qassem*, 360–61; and Batatu, *The Old Social Classes and the Revolutionary Movements of Iraq*, 971–72.

[129] Dann, *Iraq under Qassem*, 371–72.

[130] USARMA Baghdad to Washington, DC, February 9, 1963, folder: POL – Political Affairs & Rel. Iraq POL 26 Rebellion. Coups. Insurgency, box 2, Bureau of Near Eastern and South

photographed a TV screen as the bodies were displayed, and some of his black-and-white prints remain in the British Foreign Office records. A British official observed that "Qasim is recognizable" in the photos, but could only guess that "the most unpleasant-looking one on the floor is Fadhil Abbas al-Mahdawi."[131]

Although the United States did not initiate the 14 Ramadan coup, at best it condoned and at worst it contributed to the violence that followed. By late March, some 14,000 Iraqis had been arrested, and thousands were killed in anticommunist violence during 1963.[132] Political scientist Tareq Y. Ismael cites credible reports about the torture of Iraqi Communist Party officials.[133] For its part, the Kennedy administration offered the new Ba'thist regime military aid including helicopters.[134] Whether or not the CIA or other government agencies provided the lists of communists used by the Ba'thist National Guard in the post-coup violence, the United States worked closely with it. Historian Weldon C. Matthews has meticulously established that National Guard leaders who participated in human rights abuses had been trained in the United States as part of a police program run by the International Cooperation Administration and Agency for International Development. Lakeland personally maintained contact following the coup with a National Guard interrogator.[135] A directory of officials found in State Department files offers a fascinating representation of the Iraqi government and armed forces before and after 14 Ramadan. First compiled in September 1962 from press reports and government publications, the directory was edited in handwritten pencil and ink, indicating with an "x" those officials who had been killed or otherwise removed. Handwritten notes on the blank, reverse pages list key Ba'thist military officers. These include Lakeland's contact Lt. Col. Hasan Mustafa al-Naqib, who had joined the Ba'th Party after the Tabaqchali and Sirri executions and subsequently became commander of the First Tank Regiment. The names of twenty-two National Guard leaders are likewise penciled in and listed for Baghdad, Najaf, Karbala, Ba'quba, and Mosul. Written in pencil at the bottom of the first page, with an "x" next to his name, is "Fadhil 'Abbas Mahdawi," whom a scrawled note describes as "executed w. Qasim."[136]

Asian Affairs (NEA) Office of the Country Director for Lebanon, Jordan, Syria and Iraq (NEA/ARN), Records Relating to Iraq, 1963–1964, Lot 66 D470, RG 59, NARA.

[131] Thomas to Goodchild with photos enclosed, February 22, 1963, FO 371/170510, BNA.

[132] On arrests, see Matthews, "The Kennedy Administration, Counterinsurgency, and Iraq's First Ba'thist Regime," 642. Batatu is skeptical of reports that only hundreds of communists died in the days following the coup and gives greater credence to reports of more than 1,000 dead (see Batatu, *The Old Social Classes and the Revolutionary Movements of Iraq*, 985). Tripp estimates that 3,000 were killed during 1963. See Tripp, *A History of Iraq*, 171.

[133] Ismael, *The Rise and Fall of the Communist Party of Iraq*, 107–09.

[134] See Saunders to Bundy, April 2, 1963, folder: Iraq, 3/63–5/63, box 117A, NSF, JFKL.

[135] Matthews, "The Kennedy Administration, Counterinsurgency, and Iraq's First Ba'thist Regime."

[136] Directory of Government Officials in Iraq, September 1962, folder: Political Affairs & Rel. POL 15-4 Iraq Administration of Government, box 1, Bureau of Near Eastern and South

Examining Mahdawi's career is useful for understanding how the super-power rivalry and pursuit of universal values such as sovereignty and modernization intersected with the historic problem of defining Iraq as a nation. Mahdawi used class-based politics to overcome ethnic and sectarian differences and to aid Qasim in resisting the regional power Nasser wielded under the guise of pan-Arabism. Competing with Nasser for revolutionary legitimacy, Mahdawi created propaganda that increasingly placed Iraq (and himself) on the world stage, by praising the FLN and Castro, and publicizing his travels to China, the eastern bloc, and the U.S.S.R. His alignment with the communist-front peace movement, undertaken partly to restore domestic Arab–Kurdish unity, led him to escalate his anti-American rhetoric and to argue for the superiority of socialism as a development model. Mahdawi supported the peace movement as a way to salvage his beleaguered *wataniya* ideal, even if the movement seemed to Lakeland and other Americans to indicate the dangerous extent of communist influence in Iraq.

If the question of development was inseparable from that of nationhood for Iraqis, then U.S. officials approached the modernization of Iraq solely from the perspective of anticommunism. Top U.S. officials welcomed the coup, which they assumed would help to keep Iraq and its oil in the Western camp. NSC staffer Robert Komer assured President Kennedy on February 8 that the coup was a "net gain for our side" because it was led by the Ba'th, "a moderate left but anti-communist group with good military ties." Komer predicted that the new regime would "seek to balance heavy Soviet investment by better relations with the US and UK" and "be more reasonable with the oil companies." To the extent that Komer considered the dimensions of Iraq itself, he conjured up a government of Washington's dreams, one that would "be pro-Nasser, but opposed to union," and that "would compromise with the Kurds and lay off Kuwait."[137] A regime insider told State Department Arabist William Polk that Iraqis would negotiate with the British and Kuwaitis to incorporate Kuwait into a federation with provisions for sharing oil revenues. John J. McCloy, presidential envoy, banker, and chairman of the Ford Foundation, visited Baghdad, where he "got to see the new government" and "sort of broke the ice."[138]

Two weeks after Komer's memo, despite persistent reports of ongoing violence and arrests "in the thousands, apparently from prepared lists," the State Department instructed the embassy in Baghdad to increase friendly

Asian Affairs (NEA) Office of the Country Director for Lebanon, Jordan, Syria and Iraq (NEA/ARN), Records Relating to Iraq, 1963–1964, Lot 66 D470, RG 59, NARA. On Naqib, see Batatu, *The Old Social Classes and the Revolutionary Movements of Iraq*, 1011.

[137] Komer to Kennedy, February 8, 1963, folder: Iraq, 1/63–2/63, box 117, NSF, JFKL. I wish to thank William Zeman for providing me with an uncensored version of this document.

[138] Meyer (Beirut) to State Department, March 4, 1963, folder: Iraq, 3/63–5/63, box 117A, NSF, JFKL; Memo of telephone conversation, John J. McCloy and George Ball, March 23, 1963, folder: Saudi Arabia, 3/63–6/63, box 7, George W. Ball Papers, JFKL.

contacts with the new regime.[139] The embassy was to base its approach on the fact that Iraq's revolution advanced "a modernization process which points toward improving freedoms and living standards." This process included "aspirations for economic development ... social reform and political democracy," as well as "individual ownership of land" and "improving [the] life of [the] laboring man." Above all, it involved "rejection of [the] communist blueprint for modernization." Washington was "naturally interested in [the] well-being of private US investment," including American participation in the Iraq Petroleum Company, and the State Department was "happy to note" that the new regime "seeks reasonable solutions to outstanding problems with IPC." Compromise between Baghdad and the Kurds was essential, moreover, to avoid "making Kurds pawns of [the] Soviets."[140] Determined to make Iraq's realities fit the needs of Cold War containment, the United States simultaneously supported the Ba'thists' purge, opposed pan-Arabism, and advocated Arab–Kurdish reconciliation. This definition may have been consistent with American grand strategy, but it ignored the historic conflicts over Iraqi nationalism while weakening possibilities for a pluralist future in Iraq. By April, the Iraqi government's commitment to a federal union with Egypt and Syria following another coup in Damascus had sunk any hopes for securing internal peace with the Kurds. In June, a ceasefire negotiated with Barzani after 14 Ramadan collapsed and fighting resumed in the Kurdish north.[141]

The most important question about Mahdawi was not, as U.S. officials asked at the time, whether he exerted a procommunist influence over Iraq's political and economic development. Without doubt he did, although he was not an Iraqi Communist Party member and harbored personal ambitions apart from the party organization. More significant is what Mahdawi reveals about the meaning of communism in Iraq during his short and, in the end, fatal political career. That meaning was inseparable from the struggle to define Iraqi nationalism that dated to the origins of the state. Following communists and others on the left, Mahdawi used socialism and class politics as the basis for a state patriotism that could appeal to Arab and Kurd, Sunni and Shi'a, as well as to other minorities. His vision piqued fears about Soviet influence on the part of Americans committed to Cold War containment and noncommunist development of the third world, particularly once Mahdawi sought to legitimize *wataniya* against the backdrop of global revolutions and struggles for modernization. The slippage between U.S. Cold War strategy and Iraq's historical circumstances was revealed when officials insisted on distinguishing nationalism from communism in the Iraqi context. It had

---

[139] Melbourne to Secretary, February 14, 1963, folder: Iraq, 1/63-2/63, box 117, NSF, JFKL.
[140] Department of State to the Embassy in Baghdad, February 21, 1963, ibid.
[141] See Phebe Marr, *The Modern History of Iraq*, 3rd ed. (Boulder, CO: Westview Press, 2012), 118–20; and Tripp, *A History of Iraq*, 170–75.

human consequences when the United States condoned the arrests and killings of those whom officials condemned as communists and "criminals," but who were also Iraqis.[142] Historians can analyze that slippage critically only by paying closer attention to regional and national differences. Iraq was during the Qasim era, and has again become, an indication of what consequences can result from applying a foreign policy doctrine across regions and nations without sufficient regard for their untidy pasts.

[142] In a report about the execution of eleven communists, ten of whom were military officers, the U.S. army attaché in Baghdad cabled Washington that the dead were "best described as criminals." See USARMA to Washington, May 28, 1963, folder: POL – Political Affairs & Rel. Iraq POL 23 Internal Security, box 1, Bureau of Near Eastern and South Asian Affairs (NEA) Office of the Country Director for Lebanon, Jordan, Syria and Iraq (NEA/ARN), Records Relating to Iraq, 1963–1964, Lot 66 D470, RG 59, NARA.

6

The "New Men"

"The Revolution of the Egyptian people awakened the possibilities of revolution in the entire Arab world.
"The Arab man shall determine by himself the destiny of his nation on the fertile fields, in the huge factories, from the top of the high dams and with the enormous energies of the driving power."
– United Arab Republic, *Draft of the Charter*.[1]

"In fact, for the Arab area extending from Morocco to Iraq the *UAR government personifies the revolutionary, modernizing, anti-imperialist 'new men'* who have come or are coming to power in most of the underdeveloped world."
– William R. Polk.[2]

"[Nasser] mentioned that the Egyptian newspaper *Ahram* had published, in Arabic, Walt Rostow's *Stages of Economic Growth* in daily supplements for a whole month.... Nasser was quite intrigued by this and said that he was so concerned about the industrial and other economic problems that he would very much like to have a chance to talk with Walt at considerable length."
– Polk to Battle, November 16, 1965.[3]

John F. Kennedy sought to rebuild relations with Egypt on the basis of a shared commitment to modernization. He promised economic aid to President Gamal 'Abd al-Nasser as an incentive to reduce tensions with Israel

[1] United Arab Republic, *Draft of the Charter*, May 21, 1962 (Cairo: Information Department, 1962), 10, 53.
[2] Undated Draft [1964] by William R. Polk, folder: Egypt, box 12, Policy Planning Council (1961–1969), Lot 70 D 199, 72 D 124, 73 D 363, RG 59, NARA. Emphasis original.
[3] Polk to Battle, November 16, 1965, folder: POL 7 Visits. Meetings. UAR 1965., box 2, NEA Bureau, Office of the Country Director for the United Arab Republic (NEA/ UAR) Records Relating to United Arab Republic Affairs, 1961–1966, RG 59, NARA.

and Egypt's dependence on the Soviet Union. This policy attempted to overcome the effects of the Suez crisis, in which Dwight D. Eisenhower's administration had withdrawn financing for the Aswan High Dam and Nasser responded by nationalizing the Suez Canal. As a result, the Soviet Union rather than the United States helped Egypt to construct its most important state development project.[4] Historians have identified various reasons why Kennedy's attempt at a post-Suez reconciliation with Egypt was ultimately unsuccessful. Douglas Little, Warren Bass, and Fawaz A. Gerges have argued that Nasser's military intervention in the Yemeni civil war and clash with non-revolutionary Arab regimes friendly to the United States frustrated Kennedy's initiative.[5] Egypt's regional policies strengthened the hand of those in Congress whose pro-Israel orientation led them to oppose aiding Nasser in the first place. Kennedy also failed to contain the escalating Arab–Israeli conflict, and his untimely death and succession by Lyndon B. Johnson all but closed the brief opening to Nasser. By emphasizing political factors, these accounts portray the Kennedy initiative as destined for failure. Yet Kennedy's appeal to Nasser formed only a part of wide-ranging debates in English and Arabic about the nature of revolutionary change, discussions that brought elites from the two countries into dialogue and fostered opportunities for cooperation. Incorporating these ideas into the analysis points to a more contingent understanding of U.S.–Egyptian relations during the 1960s and to the repercussions of missed opportunities in the Middle East.

At the same time, historians of Egypt have examined the course of Nasser's revolution, the rise and failures of Arab socialism, and Egypt's support for revolutionary movements in the Arab world and beyond. Historians such as Roel Mejier and Rami Ginat, as well as journalists Muhammad Hasanayn Haykal and Muhammad Yusuf al-Qu'ayd, have evaluated the sources of Nasser's ideology. They have considered his relations with Egyptian intellectuals and their role in providing theoretical justifications for his policies. Meijer wonders how Nasser's regime managed to impose its control over a country characterized by intellectual pluralism: "Why did Egypt take the authoritarian road to modernity?"[6] Historians have addressed this question

---

[4] See Alterman, *Egypt and American Foreign Assistance*; and Laron, *Origins of the Suez Crisis*.

[5] Douglas Little, "The New Frontier on the Nile: JFK, Nasser, and Arab Nationalism," *Journal of American History* 75 (September 1988): 501–27; Warren Bass, *Support Any Friend: Kennedy's Middle East and the Making of the U.S.–Israel Alliance* (New York: Oxford University Press, 2003); and Fawaz A. Gerges, "The Kennedy Administration and the Egyptian–Saudi Conflict in Yemen: Co-opting Arab Nationalism," *Middle East Journal* 49 (Spring 1995): 292–311.

[6] Roel Meijer, *The Quest for Modernity: Secular Liberal and Left-Wing Thought in Egypt, 1945–1958* (New York: RoutledgeCurzon, 2002), 2. See also Rami Ginat, *Egypt's Incomplete Revolution: Lutfi al-Khuli and Nasser's Socialism in the 1960s* (Portland, OR: Frank Cass, 1997); Yusuf al-Qu'ayd, *'Abd al-Nasir wa al-muthaqqafun wa al-thaqafa: Muhammad Hasanayn Haykal yatadhakkar* (Cairo: Dar al-Shuruq, 2003); and Mohamed Heikal, *The Sphinx and the Commissar: The Rise and Fall of Soviet Influence in the Middle East* (New York: Harper & Row, 1978).

by studying Egypt's intelligentsia in the postwar contexts of neutralism, pan-Arabism, and anticolonialism. Although the United States was a crucial element of this international context, scholars have devoted greater attention to assessing Marxist influences on Egypt's revolutionary politics.

This chapter combines discussion of the Kennedy overture with analysis of Nasser's revolution. It argues that U.S. foreign policy debates and the struggle for development in Egypt were linked by the similar ideas about modernization held by American officials on one hand, and by Nasser and members of his circle on the other. Although they differed over the ultimate ends of modernization, their rapport and shared assumptions opened up possibilities for cooperation that went unfulfilled. The separate literatures on U.S. foreign policy and Nasser's Egypt have addressed disputes over modernization and revolution, but scholars have so far ignored the extent to which these debates intersected. This reinterpretation of American–Egyptian relations uses modernization as a window onto political conflicts that connected the United States to Egypt. It portrays modernization as a shared, twentieth-century framework within which global elites disputed the purpose of social change, rather than as a set of American ideas imposed on the third world.

The narrative focuses on the leading postwar U.S. Arabist, William Roe Polk (1929–). Acknowledged by historians as an important Middle East expert, Polk's significance as the bridge between U.S. and Egyptian debates about modernization has nevertheless been neglected.[7] Reinterpreting Arab nationalism as a progressive rather than a potentially procommunist force, Polk took his ideas not only from American social science, but also from Arabic historiography and intellectual currents. These influences on Polk point to a new way of understanding Middle East expertise. Rather than originating from a closed network of American scholars and officials who influenced U.S. policy, ideas about modernizing the Middle East circulated among intellectuals who shared assumptions about development despite their national and political differences. Polk's contribution was to incorporate such ideas into a new rationale that related American power to regional history and that claimed to show how the United States could help like-minded Arabs to fulfill the modernization process in the Middle East. This perspective challenges interpretations of the 1960s as a time of growing U.S.–Arab conflict on the road to the June 1967 war.

Working under Walt Rostow at the State Department's Policy Planning Council, Polk bore responsibility for mediating between Rostow's global anticommunist strategy to modernize third world countries and the distinct experience of the Arab Middle East. Polk sought to do so by formulating his theory of the "new men," Western-trained cadres who combined technical

---

[7] See Roland Popp, "An Application of Modernization Theory During the Cold War? The Case of Pahlavi Iran," *International History Review* 30 (2008): 93–94; and Jacobs, *Imagining the Middle East*, 45–46.

skills with modern attitudes. Polk associated these "new men" with the Egyptian regime and Nasser, whose authoritarian approach he legitimized through a historical comparison with that of Muhammad 'Ali Pasha, the nineteenth-century military ruler of Ottoman Egypt. Polk provided the intellectual underpinnings for U.S. relations with Nasser and revived ideas about financing Arab regional development by using revenues from the oil-producing states. He proved useful to the administration because of his wide contacts with Arabs prominent in politics and academia and his experience participating in their modernization debates. As a student, he had spent time in Cairo, Baghdad, and Beirut before studying with H.A.R. Gibb at Oxford and Harvard. He assisted the Rockefeller Foundation, which supported his education, in organizing Arab intellectuals' discussions about modernization and the region's Ottoman legacy. As part of these activities, Polk came into contact with Egyptian historiography that associated the country's modern national development with Muhammad 'Ali's military. This emphasis on military modernizers undergirded Polk's "new men" theory and helped him to reconcile Middle Eastern history with Kennedy-era policies toward the third world.

During his time at the State Department, Polk cultivated close ties with members of the Egyptian regime including vice presidents Anwar Sadat and Zakariyya Muhyi al-Din, Nasser's intelligence chief Sami Sharaf, and Cairo governor Salah Dessouki. Polk developed his "new men" theory just as Egyptians such as Dessouki and *al-Ahram* newspaper editor Haykal were debating the meaning of changes brought about in Egypt by Nasser's policies and seeking to define the new social groups that supported the regime. Most importantly, Polk developed a close personal relationship with Nasser himself based on their shared understanding of the problems of modernization. In fact, this relationship grew closer even in the face of policy differences between the United States and Egypt. Although the two men disagreed about the wisdom of Nasser's socialist economic policies, they believed that the regime could modernize Egyptian society without exacerbating class conflict. Both men saw the main challenge as increasing the rate of economic growth and restraining that of population growth before a widening disparity between the two triggered a political crisis. Polk and Nasser placed their faith in the state's ability to promote modernity through large-scale development projects. They also associated the Muslim Brotherhood with tradition and rural ways of life that were destined to fade away as the consequence of historical progress. Furthermore, the pair shared a view of Yemen as the most backward Arab society, the antithesis of the modern one Nasser was building in Egypt. Polk opposed Egyptian military intervention in Yemen, however, as he did Nasser's acquisition of arms from the Soviet Union, because he believed that both of these policies stole resources away from development at home. Despite issuing repeated warnings about the dangers of a regional conflict, Polk failed to convince the Egyptian leader and U.S. officials to get behind an Arab–Israeli arms limitation agreement. In the aftermath of the June 1967 war, Polk and Nasser counted the costs to Egypt's development. Their relationship provides a vivid example of how Cold War elites pursued politically divergent development visions within the context of a shared commitment to top-down modernization.

Descended from James K. Polk, president when the United States annexed northern Mexico, and related to diplomat Frank L. Polk, who confronted the Mexican government following Pancho Villa's raid, William Roe Polk seemed destined for a career in inter-American affairs.[8] Born in Fort Worth, Texas, Polk attended a reserve officers' training program in New Mexico during World War II and then studied at the University of Mexico and the University of Chile.[9] In 1946, however, he traveled to Egypt and visited the Palestine mandate. His studies at Harvard, which began the following year, focused on the Middle East. A family tragedy then confronted Polk personally with the ramifications of U.S. policy in the region. His brother George, a decorated combat pilot and journalist recruited by Edward R. Murrow for CBS Radio News, was murdered after disappearing on May 8, 1948, while covering the Greek civil war. Relentless in uncovering corruption among members of the right-wing Greek government just as Truman Doctrine aid began flowing to Greece, George Polk was shot and his body dumped in Salonika Bay. The government swiftly convicted four Greek communists on the basis of circumstantial evidence and coerced confessions, but William Polk, who put his studies on hold to attend the trial, doubted its impartiality given Greece's violent polarization. William "Wild Bill" Donovan, head of the wartime Office of Strategic Services, led an investigation on behalf of an American journalists' group, but seemed determined to avoid implicating the anticommunist Greek government and its supporters. The case remains unsolved. Journalist I. F. Stone declared George Polk "the first casualty of the Cold War."[10]

For a project sponsored by the National Student Association, whose overseas programs were administered by the CIA, William Polk returned to the Arab Middle East.[11] While just a Harvard undergraduate, he established connections with such prominent Arabs as Syrian intellectual Constantine

---

[8] William R. Polk, *Polk's Folly: An American Family History* (New York: Doubleday, 2000), 360–62.

[9] See "William R. Polk," December 4, 1961, folder: Polk, W. R. Administrative File, box 28, Policy Planning Council (1961–1969), Lot 70 D199, 72 D 124, 73 D 363, RG 59, NARA; and Polk, William Roe, Drawer 2, Record Group 10.2 Fellowship Cards, RFC, RAC.

[10] Polk, *Polk's Folly*, xxix, 422. See also Edmund Keeley, *The Salonika Bay Murder: Cold War Politics and the Polk Affair* (Princeton, NJ: Princeton University Press, 1989); and Yiannis P. Roubatis and Elias Vlanton, "Who Killed George Polk?" *More* 7 (May 1977): 12–32.

[11] See Middle East, William R. Polk Report, 1950–51, folder: Projects File, 1946–1963, box 132, Register of the U.S. National Student Association, International Commission Records, 1946–1968, HIA. On Polk, see Karen M. Paget, *Patriotic Betrayal: The Inside Story of the*

K. Zurayk and Arab League Secretary General 'Azzam Pasha.[12] Polk gained entrée into the world of elite Arabs through formal and informal networks of U.S. power. His work attracted the attention of John Marshall, associate director of the Rockefeller Foundation's humanities division. It was with the support of Marshall and the Foundation, which awarded him the first of four fellowships in 1951, that Polk would seek to become America's premier Arabist. Under Marshall's stewardship after World War II, the Foundation also awarded grants to individual Arab scholars and institutions such as the American University of Beirut (AUB) to study modern history and the problem of modernization. Marshall wrote, for instance, that he "spent a most interesting hour" listening to a lecture by AUB professor Zeine N. Zeine "on Ottoman history of the nineteenth century" that was "based on work [that Zeine] has done under the current RF grant for Arabic Studies."[13] As early as 1950, Marshall declared that he had "a most favorable impression of Polk" and later encouraged his protégé to "think in terms of something like a ten-year goal" for his training in Arabic studies.[14] With the Foundation's resources, Marshall helped Polk to acquire an exceptional education while expanding his contacts among prominent Arabs. In Baghdad, wrote Marshall, Polk and his first wife, Joan, "adhered strictly to their determination to avoid the local cocktail set, and are seeing hardly anyone but Iraqi's."[15] Polk studied Arabic at Baghdad University under Mahmud Ghannawi and met intellectuals 'Abd al-'Aziz al-Duri, Selim Nuaimi, 'Abd al-Rahman al-Bazzaz, 'Adil al-Jader, Kamil Chadirchi, and Nazik al-Malaika, a female poet and Rockefeller grantee.[16] In Lebanon, Polk worked with AUB professor of Arab studies Nabih Faris and spent time in a mountain village as the guest of Druze leader Kamal Jumblatt. Marshall helped to arrange for Polk's study first at Oxford and then at Harvard with Gibb, who Marshall said was "impressed" with Polk and who regarded the young Arabist as a "first-rate investment."[17] Speaking with the president of Wesleyan University, Marshall described Polk as embodying a postwar secular elite that had inherited religious missionaries' task of modernizing the Middle East. Polk exemplified the "new group of really dedicated western personnel," Marshall proclaimed, who "constitute in the Near East the present equivalent of the old missionary group."[18]

CIA's Secret Campaign to Enroll American Students in the Crusade Against Communism (New Haven, CT: Yale University Press, 2015), 76, 116.

[12] JMD, December 7, 1950, 042, volume 7, RAC.
[13] JMD, March 23, 1953, 057, volume 8, RAC.
[14] Marshall to Polk, October 26, 1953, folder 307 box 47, Series 816, RG 2 – 1953, RFC, RAC.
[15] JMD, February 26, 1952, 051, volume 8, RAC.
[16] See Marshall diary excerpt, February 21, 1951, folder 3839, box 563, RG 2, Series 804R, RFC, RAC.
[17] JMD, February 23, 1953, 056, March 29, April 12, 1953, 057, volume 8, RAC.
[18] JMD, December 18, 1952, 055, volume 8, RAC.

The first important round of debates concerning Arab modernization in which Polk was involved came during conferences organized by the Rockefeller Foundation at the Lebanese mountain resort of Bhamdoun in 1952 and 1953. Those in attendance included Western scholars such as Gibb, as well as mostly Christian Arab intellectuals such as Zurayk and Egyptian social scientist Mirrit Butrus Ghali.[19] In hosting the conferences, the Foundation sought to develop not only "ways in which Arab tradition, thought and outlook can be better interpreted for the non-Arab world," but also "a better understanding by Arabs themselves of the position of the Arab in the modern world."[20] Polk assisted Marshall with local arrangements and sat in on conference sessions and after-hours socializing. At the 1953 meetings, Zurayk chaired the discussions, which were conducted mostly in Arabic. Polk's AUB mentor Nabih Faris spoke on "Religious Movements in Arab Lands" and Egyptian historian Hussein Mones on "Sources of Information in the Arab World," among other topics addressed. To comprehend the proceedings Marshall relied on Polk's notes, "Polk's Arabic having progressed to the point where he is missing little."[21] In the evening, participants engaged in an Arabic literary game of "capping verses," in which "one participant recites some lines of poetry, stating the letter of the alphabet with which the last word quoted ends," and then the next person "must find a passage beginning with this letter." Polk brought along a tape recorder to preserve the friendly competition for posterity, Marshall wrote, "until something got too hot for it and it began to smoke!"[22] The language ability Polk displayed at Bhamdoun placed him at the junction between Arab and Western debates about modernizing the Middle East.

The most important Arab figure at Bhamdoun and in other Rockefeller initiatives was Egyptian historian Muhammad Shafiq Ghurbal (1894–1961). Born to a Muslim family in Alexandria, Ghurbal earned his master's degree in London after World War I studying under Arnold Toynbee. Although he never completed a doctorate, Ghurbal was the leading figure in what historian Yoav Di-Capua calls "*tamsir al-ta'rikh*," the Egyptianization of history, defined as professionally training Egyptians to write national history in Arabic.[23] Supported by the prerevolutionary Egyptian monarchy and working out of the 'Abdin palace archives, Ghurbal trained a generation of historians in empiricist methodology and established a nationalist

[19] See Mirrit Butrus Ghali, *The Policy of Tomorrow*, trans. Isma'il R. el Faruqi (Washington, DC: American Council of Learned Societies, 1953). The Rockefeller Foundation subsidized the translation of this book.

[20] Fellowship sheet, January 19, 1951, folder 1, box 1, Series 804, RG 1.2, RFC, RAC.

[21] JMD, March 26, 1953, 057, volume 8, RAC.

[22] JMD, March 27, 1953, 057, volume 8, RAC.

[23] Yoav Di-Capua, "'Jabarti of the 20th Century': The National Epic of 'Abd al-Rahman al-Rafi'i and Other Egyptian Histories," *International Journal of Middle East Studies* 36 (August 2004): 435.

school that associated the modernization of Egypt with Muhammad 'Ali's rule. This contribution was bookended by Ghurbal's works *The Beginnings of the Egyptian Question and the Rise of Mehmet Ali* (1928) and *Muhammad 'Ali al-Kabir [Muhammad 'Ali the Great]* (1944).[24] Di-Capua writes that Ghurbal's historical school was characterized by a "'before and after' approach, marked by Muhammad 'Ali's accession to power" and "a significant transformation in the status of education, commerce, industry and agriculture."[25] Ghurbal's emphasis on military-led modernization in nineteenth-century Egypt corresponded to the "new men" theory that Polk developed to understand Nasser, whom Polk repeatedly compared to Muhammad 'Ali. Both Polk and Ghurbal recognized the importance of Western knowledge and Egyptian educational missions to Europe during Muhammad 'Ali's reign.[26] The Egyptians who studied in Europe a century earlier "shape[d] Egyptian destiny in the following generations," Polk wrote, in an argument that resonated with his work for the National Student Association.[27] Indeed, Ghurbal corresponded with Marshall about funding Egyptian study abroad programs, and Polk socialized with many Arabs who had studied in the West and advised Marshall on worthy candidates for Foundation support.[28]

At a time when Rockefeller was sponsoring the translation of Western political literature into Arabic and discussions about developing an Arabic social science lexicon, Ghurbal's interests coincided with the Foundation's.[29] At Ghurbal's home in Heliopolis, he and Marshall had planned what would become the first Bhamdoun meeting.[30] Marshall wrote that "Ghorbal's

---

[24] See Muhammad Shafiq Ghurbal, *The Beginnings of the Egyptian Question and the Rise of Mehmet Ali: A Study of the Napoleonic Era Based on Researches in the British and French Archives*, reprinted ed. (New York, AMS Press, 1977), and *Muhammad 'Ali al-Kabir* (Cairo: Dar al-Hilal, 1986).

[25] Yoav Di-Capua, *Gatekeepers of the Arab Past: Historians and History Writing in Twentieth-Century Egypt* (Berkeley: University of California Press, 2009), 191.

[26] See Ghurbal, *Muhammad 'Ali al-Kabir*, 82–117.

[27] William R. Polk et al., *Backdrop to Tragedy: The Struggle for Palestine* (Boston, MA: Beacon Press, 1957), 256.

[28] See Marshall to Ghurbal, February 10, 1956, and Ghurbal to Marshall, February 18, 1956, folder 29, box 3, series 485, RG 1.2, RFC, RAC. See also JMD, February 28, 1952, 051, volume 8, RAC; Omari to Marshall, August 12, 1952, folder 269, box 43, series 470, RG 2, RFC, RAC; Marshall to Polk, February 4, 1957; and Polk to Marshall, February 7, 1957, folder 411, box 61, series 470, RG 2 – 1957, RFC, RAC. Ghurbal's nephew, Ashraf, earned a PhD in government at Harvard. See JMD excerpt, February 26, 1953, John Marshall Near East Trip 1953, folder 305, box 46, series 804R, RG 2, RFC, RAC. Ghurbal also gave a renowned radio lecture on Ibn Khaldun, the subject of one of the first courses Polk taught at Harvard. See Di-Capua, *Gatekeepers of the Arab Past*, 215; and JMD, December 20, 1956, 070, volume 11, RAC.

[29] See documents in folder 16, box 1, series 833 Lebanon, RG 1.2, RF, RAC; and PEM interview with Charles Issawi, February 21, 1951, folder 3654, box 548, series 804, RG 2 – 1951, RFC, RAC.

[30] JMD excerpt, February 21, 1951, folder 3839, box 563, series 804R, RG 2, RFC, RAC.

participation in the Conference is absolutely essential," and Ghurbal later convened a follow-up meeting in Cairo to the two held at Bhamdoun.[31] As head of the Egyptian Historical Society, Ghurbal proposed to edit a book that would be published in English and Arabic examining the history of Arab modernization, a project to which the Foundation pledged $19,500.[32] The volume would begin with the "accession of Sultan Mahmoud II of Turkey and of Mohammad Ali Pasha of Egypt," Ghurbal wrote, "the two great architects of the movement of modernisation."[33] Gibb endorsed this undertaking, but described it as daunting, comparing its ambition to that of *Islamic Society and the West*, the study that Gibb was writing with Harold Bowen.[34] Partially under Rockefeller's auspices, then, older Orientalist and nationalist historians of the Middle East helped to birth a postwar modernization paradigm that emphasized military leaders' positive role. This transition was enacted in the event that kicked off the first Bhamdoun meeting – an informal lunch shared by Marshall, Gibb, the Ghurbals, and the Polks.[35]

Polk's career illustrates changes in how Americans justified their postwar foreign policy as fulfilling the historical process of modernization in the Middle East. His scholarly writings drew from but modified Gibb's portrayal of modernization as resulting from the "impact of the West." In his Harvard dissertation, published as *The Opening of South Lebanon, 1788– 1840: A Study of the Impact of the West on the Middle East*, Polk examined the breakdown of traditional social and economic patterns in Mount Lebanon. "Mehmed 'Ali Pasha of Egypt," Polk argued, using an alternative spelling of the leader's name, "was a prime mover in this dislocation" between 1832 and 1841, when Egyptian forces occupied Lebanon and other territories in what was then Ottoman Syria. Rather than a direct product of European influences on imperial reform, Arab modernization was mediated through Muhammad 'Ali's military regime. He developed Lebanon economically through state monopolies and, above all, established security by settling Bedouin and raising an army. Polk's view of Muhammad 'Ali in the dissertation came from Lebanese historian Asad Rustum (1897–1965), whose "pioneering works" Polk acknowledged.[36] Through this engagement with Arab scholarship, Polk refined his understanding of modernization as depending on indigenous military leaders. His intellectual development held implications for U.S. diplomacy and the historical arguments with which

---

[31] Memo by Marshall, November 29, 1951, folder 2, box 1, series 804, RG 1.2, RFC, RAC. See also JMD excerpt, April 1–3, 1954, folder 8, box 1, series 804, RG 1.2, RFC, RAC.

[32] See Rockefeller Foundation, *Annual Report*, 1955, p. 164.

[33] Ghurbal to Rusk, August 23, 1954, folder 29, box 3, series 485, RG 1.2, RFC, RAC.

[34] Gibb to Marshall, September 24, 1954, folder 29, box 3, series 485, RG 1.2, RFC, RAC.

[35] JMD, March 8, 1952, 051, volume 8, RAC.

[36] William R. Polk, *The Opening of South Lebanon, 1788–1840: A Study of the Impact of the West on the Middle East* (Cambridge, MA: Harvard University Press, 1963), xviii, ix. Polk disagrees, however, with some of Rustum's interpretations of documents from the 'Abdin palace archives. See p. 270, note 15.

officials promoted alternative policies for the Middle East. With its emphasis on Muhammad 'Ali as the "prime mover" in transforming Ottoman Egypt and Syria, Polk's perspective spoke in favor of cultivating Nasser. This perspective challenged the earlier strategy of partnering with Turkey and the historical rationalization promoted by U.S. oil interests that a Turco-centric policy would contain Arab nationalism while helping the United States to complete the unfinished work of Ottoman imperial and Kemalist reforms (see Chapter 2).

Not content with a purely academic career, the ambitious Polk desired a role in shaping U.S. policies toward the Arab world. He displayed this drive in his early works as a student, *What the Arabs Think*, published in 1952 by the Foreign Policy Association, and the *Atlantic Monthly* supplement "Perspective of the Arab World," the research for which the Ford Foundation had sponsored.[37] From Harvard, Polk criticized the Eisenhower administration's insensitivity to Arab nationalism and mindless pursuit of anti-Soviet "[t]reaties, pacts and aid agreements," which Polk and Middle East expert Richard H. Nolte described as fostering neutralism and becoming almost "ends in themselves, to be sought even to the point of damaging the relationships they were designed to support."[38] Polk's aversion to kneejerk anticommunism may well have been inspired by his brother's death, but his concern for Arab modernization also aligned him with officials who believed in working with nationalists such as Nasser. Democratic Party leader and undersecretary of state in the new Kennedy administration Chester Bowles read Polk's criticisms of Eisenhower. Bowles recommended Polk to George C. McGhee, chair of the State Department's Policy Planning Council and chief Turcophile among Washington officials. Indeed, McGhee would raise objections within the administration to Kennedy's opening to Nasser. "I wonder if you know William R. Polk of Harvard," Bowles wrote to McGhee, "who is one of the most imaginative and brilliant people I know on the Middle East." The former coordinator of Truman Doctrine aid to Turkey must have been well acquainted with the Polks' Greek tragedy. In case McGhee had any reservations about Polk joining the council, Bowles added that Kennedy's national security advisor and former Harvard dean McGeorge Bundy "has an equally high regard for him" and "feels he would like to come to Washington."[39]

---

[37] William R. Polk, "What the Arabs Think," Foreign Policy Association, *Headline Series* 96 (November–December 1952): 3–57; and William Roe Polk, "Perspective of the Arab World," a supplement of *Atlantic Monthly* 198 (October 1956): 124–92. See also "William R. Polk," December 4, 1961, cited earlier.

[38] Richard H. Nolte and William R. Polk, "Toward a Policy for the Middle East," *Foreign Affairs* 36 (July 1958): 646.

[39] Bowles to McGhee, February 14, 1961, folder 526, box 300, CBP. See also Polk to Thomson, February 23 and March 22, 1961, and Bowles to Polk, April 19, 1961, folder 530, box 300, CBP.

FIGURE 6.1. William R. Polk, early 1960s. National Archives.

When Polk joined the council in July 1961, he stepped into administration debates concerning overtures to Nasser (Figure 6.1). Historians have associated that policy with Kennedy's anticommunist strategy of engaging nonaligned leaders and preference for military-led modernization.[40] But they have neglected the importance of area experts in reconciling this strategy with diverse circumstances across the third world. This is precisely the service Polk offered to Rostow, particularly in the latter's confrontation with McGhee, whose reputation rested on his Middle East experience. As deputy national security advisor, Rostow had indicated to McGhee that the administration would seek to engage Middle Eastern nationalism. Returning an "overcautious" State Department memo regarding Nasser that "may lead to our missing some opportunities," Rostow invoked his "experience with India" to argue for a bolder appeal. "As you know," Rostow noted, pointing out what was patently obvious to McGhee, "I do not regard myself as

---

[40] See Little, "New Frontier on the Nile," 502–04; Robert B. Rakove, *Kennedy, Johnson, and the Nonaligned World* (New York: Cambridge University Press, 2013); and Muhammad Hasanayn Haykal, *Harb al-Thalathin Sana*, part 1, *Sanawat al-Ghalayan* (Cairo: Markaz al-Ahram lil-Tarjamah wa-al-Nashr, 1988), 519–20.

a Middle East expert."[41] In December, Rostow replaced McGhee as head of the planning council at State and continued to press the Nasser gambit in cooperation with White House national security officials Bundy and Robert W. Komer. Polk supplied Rostow with arguments in favor of aiding Nasser. The United States could "turn his energies inward," Polk insisted, and "assist in solving some of the horrifying domestic problems in Egypt." Polk recommended that an envoy "should secretly see Nasser for a *tour d'horizon*" in the new year, followed by a visit from a "first-class economic planner."[42] Polk commiserated with Komer about the administration's inability to reach Nasser through formal diplomatic channels and dismissed excuses offered by the "not-very-active" U.S. embassy in Cairo. In citing his own easy access to Egyptian officials, Polk implicitly questioned the effectiveness of ambassador and former American University in Cairo president John Badeau. Komer praised Polk to Rostow for taking initiative, an exception within the hidebound State Department, whose "dominant foreign policy philosophy is 'wait and see.' "[43] Indeed, Komer complained to Bundy that McGhee, from his new position as undersecretary of state for political affairs, had been "raising some squawks" and "had some strenuous objections" to a Nasser opening. In the first week of 1962, however, Komer smugly reported that "even the Terrible Turk has caved."[44]

Komer's slur referred to McGhee's long career in Turkey, but it can also serve as shorthand for McGhee's approach to the Middle East that other administration officials sought to challenge. On one hand, McGhee's approach came from his oil industry background, which made him wary of Arab nationalism and gave him a preference for the sanctity of contracts and political stability. On the other hand, his self-education in Ottoman history gave him a regional perspective from the center of the old empire onto the "backward" Arab periphery, an orientation inherited secondhand from imperial reformers and buttressed by his admiring, Cold War image of Atatürk. But rising Arab nationalism and Nasser's prestige had changed the circumstances in which Americans sought to justify their policies in

[41] Rostow to McGhee, June 6, 1961, *FRUS, 1961–1963*, vol. 17: 155–56. On Rostow's experience with India, see David C. Engerman, "West Meets East: The Center for International Studies and Indian Economic Development," in *Staging Growth*, 199–223; and Cullather, *The Hungry World*, 149–52.

[42] Polk to Rostow, December 18, 1961, folder: W.R. Polk – Chron. July–Dec. 1962, box 237, Policy Planning Council Subject Files, 1954–1962, RG 59, NARA. See also Polk to Rostow, December 19, 1961, folder: Egypt, box 136, Policy Planning Council Subject Files, 1954–1962, RG 59, NARA.

[43] Komer to Rostow, December 6, 1961, folder: Staff Memoranda Robert Komer, 11/61-12/61, box 322, NSF, Meetings & Memoranda, JFKL. See also Komer to Rostow, June 2, 1961, folder: United Arab Republic, General, 1/61–6/61, box 168, NSF, JFKL.

[44] Komer to Bundy, January 5, 1962, folder: United Arab Republic, General 1/62-2/62, box 168, NSF, JFKL. See also Komer to Bundy, January 10, 1962, folder: United Arab Republic, General 1/62-2/62, box 168, NSF, JFKL.

historical terms. McGhee told a group of oil executives that the Near East had "changed a great deal" since he first came to the region. "Some ten years ago," he recalled, "we did not have to contend with Soviet penetration, Nasserism, or Arab socialism."[45] Polk's perspective was based on a different historical precedent of military-led modernization, that of Muhammad 'Ali in nineteenth-century Egypt. It offered a positive interpretation of revolutionary Arab nationalism as progressive and anticommunist, while positioning Nasser at the forefront of the region's development. This perspective served the interests of the administration's action intellectuals Rostow, Bundy, and Komer, and made Polk useful to them.

Other factors made Polk into a successful member of the Policy Planning Council and enabled the Arab expert to develop a close, if unlikely, working partnership with the global strategist Rostow. One important reason was Polk's relatively dispassionate attitude toward the Arab–Israeli conflict, compared with what Marshall had called "the old missionary group." Unlike figures such as William A. Eddy, Polk had never protested Truman's support for Zionism or felt betrayed by the president's decisions in favor of partitioning Palestine and recognizing Israel. Despite expressing sympathy for Palestinian refugees, Polk dismissed their right of return as "impossible."[46] Polk regarded Israel as an established fact of regional politics. For him, the Arab–Israeli conflict posed an obstacle to anticommunist modernization because it diverted resources to arms purchases and threatened to give an opening to the Soviets. This attitude enabled Polk to serve an administration attuned to domestic political pressures on behalf of Israel. Though the two men disagreed over the desirability of closer relations with Egypt, Polk even sided with Myer "Mike" Feldman, the administration's liaison to the Jewish-American community, in arguing that any invitation to Nasser to visit the United States be delayed until after the 1962 midterm elections.[47]

Polk accepted Rostow's development strategy of promoting economic growth, but the two men shared an even more important tendency to define modernization as a historical process. Economist Rostow met Polk on the latter's disciplinary home turf. If Rostow theorized about boosting purchasing power in developing countries, then Polk could recognize a regional precedent. His dissertation had documented the influx of consumer goods into nineteenth-century Lebanon at the same time that Muhammad 'Ali sought

---

[45] Memo of conversation by Blackiston, January 11, 1963, *FRUS, 1961–63*, vols. 17, 18, 20, 21, *Near East, Africa Microfiche Supplement* (Washington, DC: Government Printing Office, 1996), fiche 4. See also McGhee to Clapp, October 20, 1961, folder: Egypt, box 136, Policy Planning Council Subject Files, 1954–1962, RG 59, NARA.

[46] Polk et al., *Backdrop to Tragedy*, 296.

[47] See Polk to Rostow, January 26, 1962, folder: W. R. Polk – Chron–Jan.–May 1962, box 237, Policy Planning Council Subject Files, 1954–1962, RG 59, NARA; and memo by Komer, December 20, 1961, folder: Staff Memoranda Robert Komer, 11/61-12/61, box 322 NSF, Meetings & Memoranda, JFKL.

to establish state monopolies over the production of raw materials such as silk and timber.[48] The pair cited nineteenth-century America's experience to argue that just as the Sears-Roebuck catalog had done in the United States, Egypt could similarly curb radical populism by providing cheap consumables to rural areas.[49] Polk respected the comparative historical approach of *The Stages of Economic Growth* and regarded his task as helping Rostow to comprehend and manage modernization as it unfolded in the Middle East. As in the previous century this challenge was necessarily one for elites, who had the responsibility for establishing the secure environment in which they could safely promote change. These assumptions – about the dangers of too much democracy and the belief that modernization was an essentially technical problem – transcended policy disagreements and even national and linguistic differences among modernizers. They were the basis for Polk's relationships not only with Rostow, but also with Nasser and his circle.

A focus on Polk's role in bridging U.S. and Egyptian development debates sheds new light on the February 1962 mission that Bowles undertook as JFK's envoy to Nasser. A coup in Damascus the previous September had resulted in Syria's secession (*infisal*) from the United Arab Republic and expelled Nasser's influence, just as a Euro-Ottoman force had ejected Muhammad 'Ali from Syria more than a century earlier. This defeat prompted President Kennedy to revive attempts at appealing to a now chastened Nasser. Komer did an end run around the State Department's Near East Affairs Bureau.[50] Polk endorsed Bowles, who asked Rostow to "borrow Bill Polk" to accompany him on Bowles' trip to Egypt and other Middle Eastern and south Asian countries. Polk told Komer that "Bowles would not have been my first choice for the job," presumably because Bowles lacked the intelligence background of previous envoys to Nasser such as Kim Roosevelt and would therefore fail to impress the Egyptian leader.[51] In signing on to the mission Polk sought to redress this deficiency, coordinating relations between American and Egyptian intelligence officials and attempting to forge a new relationship between the two countries on the basis of promoting modernization.

Historians have not previously recognized Polk's intermediary role in intelligence. Polk spent January 24 at CIA headquarters preparing for his trip

[48] See Polk, *The Opening of South Lebanon*, chapter 10.
[49] See unsigned memorandum of conversation, November 28, 1962, folder: Egypt (UAR), Policy Planning Council Subject Files, 1954–1962, RG 59, NARA; and Polk to Rostow March 3, 1963, folder: W. R. Polk, Chron. Jan.–June 1963, box 28, Policy Planning Council (1961–1969) Planning and Coordination Staff (1970–1973), Subject Files, 1963–1973 Lot70D199, 72D124, 73D363, RG 59, NARA.
[50] See handwritten note R[obert] C[.] S[trong] to A[rmin] H[.] M[eyer], October 19, 1961, folder: Cairo – 1961, box 4, Bureau of Near Eastern and South Asian Affairs/Office of Near Eastern Affairs, Records of the Director, 1960–1963, RG 59, NARA.
[51] Bowles to Rostow, January 16, 1962, folder 535, box 300, CBP; Polk to Komer, January 10, 1962, folder: W. R. Polk – Chron –Jan.–May 1962, box 237, Policy Planning Council Subject Files, 1954–1962, RG 59, NARA.

and then met the following afternoon with James Critchfield, the Agency's operations chief for the Middle East and South Asia. Accompanying Bowles to Egypt, Iran, India, Pakistan, and Afghanistan, Polk "met with the CIA station chiefs in each post," noting that the CIA "provides better staffing" and "better funding for its people" than State, a cause of "much bitterness in the Embassies." Polk had previously remarked on Nasser's sense that American diplomats lacked authority.[52]

In Egypt, Polk spent two hours on February 16 at the home of Nasser's vice president, Zakariyya Muhyi al-Din, who was, like Polk, friends with the CIA's previous liaison in Egypt Charles D. Cremeans. Polk's appeal to Muhyi al-Din combined a concern for security with a commitment to development. He argued that "we must find ways of freeing resources from military expenditures to devote to national buidling [*sic*] activities." According to Polk, Muhyi al-Din "agreed" and insisted that "nothing has a higher priority than this." Polk noted that Egypt devoted a tenth of its economy to its military and suggested that it would be a "wonderful thing" if this figure could be reduced to 9 percent. The vice president raised concerns about Egyptian security, however, and the pair concluded that shifting monies away from defense required "stopping the escalation" in the Arab–Israeli arms race. Inserting into his dispatch to Rostow an argument for his own continued value in coordinating relations with Nasser, Polk described Muhyi al-Din as disappointed that "the warm personal relationship that he had with Chuck Cremeans had not been duplicated," because "the Arabs put a very heavy reliance on personal relations." Polk reported that he had "similar long talks" with Cairo governor Salah Dessouki, Nasser's head of Palestine affairs, Hasan Sabri al-Khuli, and intelligence chief Sami Sharaf, another intimate of Cremeans. "All of them were extremely receptive," Polk wrote, "very frank, and most eager to talk turkey."[53] Bowles incorporated the contents of Polk's conversations with Muhyi al-Din and Sharaf into his positive report about the mission sent to President Kennedy.[54]

As Komer later recalled, the months following the Bowles mission corresponded to the "high point" in U.S.–Egyptian relations.[55] The administration sent Harvard economist Edward Mason to meet with Nasser in March and by June had concluded a three-year agreement to provide Cairo with

[52] Polk to Bowles, January 29, 1962, Polk to Lewis, January 25, 1962, Polk to Rostow, March 29, 1962, folder: W. R. Polk – Chron – Jan.–May 1962, box 237, Policy Planning Council Subject Files, 1954–1962, RG 59, NARA.

[53] Polk to Rostow, February 17, 1962, folder: Egypt (UAR), box 215, Policy Planning Council Subject Files, 1954–1962, RG 59, NARA. See also Polk to Cremeans, February 19, 1962, folder: W. R. Polk – Chron – Jan.–May 1962, box 237, Policy Planning Council Subject Files, 1954–1962, RG 59, NARA.

[54] See document 195, *FRUS, 1961–1963*, 17: 483.

[55] Quoted in Little, "The New Frontier on the Nile," 510.

food assistance under Public Law 480 worth $431.8 million.[56] Polk concentrated on convincing Egyptian officials to tone down propaganda attacks on oil-producing Arab states delivered via Nasser's "Voice of the Arabs" radio. Although Bowles told JFK that he hoped Nasser could be "led to forsake the microphone for the bulldozer," Polk linked attempts at muting Nasser's propaganda to a regional vision for Arab development. Given the "maldistribution of capital, population, and developable resources," Polk explained, Nasser's attacks prevented oil exporters from subsidizing poorer Arab countries. U.S. policy should "assist the capital deficient states in formulating their requests to the Gulf states in a non-violent and constructive form rather than the present threats and radio subversion."[57] Polk cited his "conversations with Zacharia Muhiyadin, Sami Sharif [*sic*] and others" to argue that Egyptian officials could be persuaded to turn their energies inward.[58] When Salah Nasr, the chief of Egypt's general intelligence service, visited Washington as the CIA's guest, Polk urged Rostow to prevail on Nasr to turn down the volume on "Voice of the Arabs."[59] Polk suggested working through Muhyi al-Din to improve Egypt's relations first with non-Arab Iran and then with Saudi Arabia because "an Arab Development Fund would be useful to Egypt and would assist in the achievement of American policy objectives in the Middle East."[60] Rostow adopted Polk's argument, which resurrected the idea of finding a way to use Gulf oil wealth to develop the Arab world.[61] As chair of a Council on Foreign Relations study group, Cremeans agreed: "There was little doubt that over the long run the development of the area's economy as a unit would be advantageous to the majority of its inhabitants."[62] Polk reintroduced this concept into U.S. policy debates for the first time since the Eisenhower administration quashed Dag Hammarskjöld's plan at the United Nations four years earlier (see Chapter 2).

[56] See William J. Burns, *Economic Aid and American Policy Toward Egypt, 1955–1981* (Albany: State University of New York Press, 1985), 132–34. See also Jesse Ferris, *Nasser's Gamble: How Intervention in Yemen Caused the Six-Day War and the Decline of Egyptian Power* (Princeton, NJ: Princeton University Press, 2013), 105.

[57] See memo by Polk, "The Persian Gulf in Middle Eastern Politics," June 25, 1962, folder: Near and Middle East, box 222, Policy Planning Council Subject Files, 1954–1962, RG 59, NARA.

[58] Polk to Talbot, "Radio Propaganda in the Near East," May 8, 1962, folder: Near and Middle East, box 222, Policy Planning Council Subject Files, 1954–1962, RG 59, NARA.

[59] Polk to Rostow, May 23, 1962, folder: W. R. Polk – Chron – Jan.–May 1962, box 237, Policy Planning Council Subject Files, 1954–1962, RG 59, NARA.

[60] Polk to Rostow, May 23, 1962, folder: Near and Middle East, box 232, Policy Planning Council Subject Files, 1954–1962, RG 59, NARA.

[61] See memo by Rostow, September 14, 1962, folder: Near and Middle East, box 222, Policy Planning Council Subject Files, 1954–1962, RG 59, NARA.

[62] Charles D. Cremeans, *The Arabs and the World: Nasser's Arab Nationalist Policy* (New York: Frederick A. Praeger, 1963), 225.

The honeymoon in U.S.–Egyptian relations resulted not only from decisions made in Washington, but also from political changes in the UAR (as
Nasser continued to call post-*infisal* Egypt). Nasser's rule over Syria divided
him from Syrian Ba'thists and split the Ba'th Party itself, with Ramallah
activist 'Abdullah al-Rimawi forming a pro-Nasser Ba'thist splinter group.[63]
As these political rivalries escalated, so did battles over the meaning of Arab
nationalism. A period of ideological soul-searching within Egypt preceded
Syria's secession and intensified after the *infisal*. It was resolved in favor of
an Arab socialist program that accepted limited cooperation with the United
States. This program stressed economic growth, population control, and the
modernization of different sectors of Egyptian society without recourse to
class warfare. Such a political orientation indicated Nasser's arms-length
ideological distance from the Soviet Union and embrace of neutralism in foreign policy, as well as his decision to side with noncommunist intellectuals
against Marxists and others within the Egyptian establishment who defined
modernization in terms of class interests. The focus on internal development
also reflected Nasser's expressed desire to keep the Arab–Israeli conflict
"in the icebox."[64] Proclaiming the new policy, Nasser's government cited
the historical precedent of Muhammad 'Ali as the father of modern Egypt.
Nasser's Arab socialist concept of modernizing Egypt therefore overlapped
significantly with the anticommunist strategy Polk was promoting within
the Kennedy administration.

Just as Polk began working at the State Department, *al-Ahram* editor
Muhammad Hasanayn Haykal initiated a debate about the role of intellectuals in Egypt's revolution. This debate coincided with the government's
July 1961 decrees that nationalized much of the UAR's economy.[65] Haykal
simultaneously criticized intellectuals for withholding support from the government and defended its achievements. He did so by setting up a dichotomy between "experienced men" – intellectuals and managers of Egyptian
society under the monarchy – and "reliable men," the military leaders and
ex-officers who had overthrown and replaced the corrupt old regime.
Although the "reliable men" may have lacked the expertise of the "experienced men," the former were attempting to develop society in a disinterested
manner that was consistent with revolutionary values. In other words, summarized a British diplomat, Haykal impugned the "educated classes" for

---

[63] See Podeh, *The Decline of Arab Unity*, 104; and John F. Devlin, *The Ba'th Party: A History
    from Its Origins to 1966* (Stanford, CA: Hoover Institution Press, 1976), 158–59. See also
    'Abdullah al-Rimawi, *Al-Mantiq al-thawri* (Cairo: Dar al-ma'arifa, 1961).
[64] See Badeau to Talbot, May 26, 1962, folder: Cairo – 1962, box 6, Bureau of Near Eastern
    and South Asian Affairs/Office of Near Eastern Affairs, Records of the Director, 1960–1963,
    RG 59, NARA.
[65] See Thacher to Meyer, August 3, 1961, folder: Cairo – 1961, box 4, Bureau of Near Eastern
    and South Asian Affairs/Office of Near Eastern Affairs, Records of the Director, 1960–1963,
    RG 59, NARA.

being "closely linked to the ruling class before the revolution."[66] As part of an attempt to cultivate pro-regime intellectuals, Haykal had convinced Nasser to accept his appointment of the independent Marxist journalist Lutfi al-Khuli to edit *al-Ahram*'s opinion page following al-Khuli's release from prison. Al-Khuli then published a series called "The Crisis of the Arab Intellectuals" in which he argued that "each intellectual devotes his talents to ideas which basically serve his class interests."[67]

This perspective was challenged in *al-Ahram* and *al-Akhbar* by Salah Dessouki, the Cairo governor and former Olympic fencer whom Polk had met while accompanying Bowles. Dessouki told a meeting of the National Union that "cooperation [*al-ta'awun*]" was the "spirit of our revolution [*ruh thawratina*]." The regime should avoid setting one group against another and rule instead "according to the widest popular base ['*ala awsa' qa'ida sha'biya*]."[68] Dessouki rejected Haykal's distinction between "experienced men" and "reliable men." He argued that the intelligentsia cut across class lines and that the important division within Egyptian society was between the educated minority and uneducated masses. The debate thus centered on whether the vanguard that would modernize Egypt in partnership with the regime should be defined strictly along lines of social class or more inclusively by education and the practical contributions that different groups could make to national development.

As historian Eugene Rogan explains, Syria's secession "forced Nasser to ask hard questions about his own political orientations and the direction the Egyptian revolution had taken."[69] Nasser's government sought to redefine the meaning of the revolution within a restructured political organization, the Arab Socialist Union (ASU). Then on May 21, 1962, it unveiled the Charter of National Action.[70] Presented as a ten-chapter draft, the Charter took the form of a historical discourse that first described Egyptians' long anticolonial struggle, beginning with "Mohamed Aly" who "laid the foundation of modern Egypt," and then their campaign to overcome the economic legacies of imperialism and feudalism. It simultaneously claimed that the Egyptian revolution held lessons as a developmental system for non-Arab societies. Egypt's "new pioneering experiment," proclaimed the Charter, has already had "far-reaching effects on the liberation movement in Africa, Asia and Latin America." More importantly, the document muted class conflict and emphasized technical development goals, marginalizing

[66] Chancery to Foreign Office, July 15, 1961, FO 371/158786, BNA.
[67] Ginat, *Egypt's Incomplete Revolution*, 55, 57 [quotation].
[68] "Salah Dessouki ya'alana," *al-Akhbar*, July 2, 1961, p. 3.
[69] Eugene Rogan, *The Arabs: A History* (New York: Basic Books, 2009), 320.
[70] See memo by Barrow, "Nasser's Internal Policy in Theory and Practice: New Departures in the Draft Charter," June 11, 1962, folder: 1962 – Memoranda to the White House, box 6, Bureau of Near Eastern and South Asian Affairs/Office of Near Eastern Affairs, Records of the Director, 1960–1963, RG 59, NARA.

Marxists and other leftists domestically while tacitly accepting that Egypt needed U.S. economic assistance. "Political democracy cannot exist under the domination of any one class," the Charter declared. It envisioned the "peaceful resolution of class struggle" by ensuring that "the power of reaction" is "deprived of all its weapons." This would be achieved by the state through "economic and social planning." The Charter called for a doubling of national income every decade at least in order to keep pace with population growth, which it warned "constitutes the most dangerous obstacle that faces the Egyptian people" in their drive toward increased production.[71] In seeking to mobilize Egyptians across class lines to achieve development goals, Nasser effectively sided with Dessouki's perspective in the latter's debate with Haykal.

Arab Socialism attempted to propel economic growth ahead of population increase through industrialization. It did so through the build-up of a large state sector, with about 40 percent of the budget – an estimated 17 percent of Gross National Product – directed toward development by 1965. These expenditures contributed to a growth rate of between 5 and 6 percent, according to one U.S. government report, with particular expansion in the "manufacturing, electric power, communications, and petroleum industries."[72] Nasser's policy sought "to build Egypt's productive base," explains historian Saleh Omar, "to use its skilled but cheap labor to make it the industrial center of the Arab world, and to develop its hydraulic agriculture."[73] Under Arab Socialism, Nasser pursued a corporatist labor policy in which workers were supposed to partner with the regime to accelerate modernization. Labor unions, declared *al-Ahram al-Iqtisadi*, "must become centers of revolutionary radiation and instruments for pushing forward the wheels of production."[74] Although many analysts point to the influence of Yugoslavia's example on Arab Socialism, the Charter's muting of class-struggle rhetoric and emphasis on growth also made it partially compatible with the Polk-Rostow development concept.[75] Despite giving rise to an outsized state sector and increasingly unsustainable debt, Nasser's policy nevertheless kept open the possibilities for closer U.S.–Egyptian cooperation.

[71] United Arab Republic, *Draft of the Charter*, 10, 18, 38, 39, 53–54.

[72] Memo by Jones and Bennsky, "The UAR Political-Economic Situation," April 30, 1965 [revised September 2, 1965], folder: Political Affairs and Relations U.A.R. POL – 1–2 Basic Policies. Guidelines, Directives. 1965, box 2, Near East Affairs Bureau, Office of the Country Director for the United Arab Republic (NEA/UAR), Records Relating to United Arab Republic Affairs, 1961–1966, RG 59, NARA.

[73] Saleh Omar, "Arab Nationalism: A Retrospective Evaluation," *Arab Studies Quarterly* 14 (Fall 1992): 31.

[74] Quoted in Marsha Pripstein Posusney, *Labor and the State in Egypt: Workers, Unions, and Economic Restructuring* (New York: Columbia University Press, 1997), 73.

[75] On Yugoslavia, see Research Department Memo "The UAR Version of Socialism," February 19, 1964, FO 370/2720, BNA; and Ginat, *Egypt's Incomplete Revolution*, 16–17, 26–27, 31n26, 39, 58.

Nasser calibrated the socialist, noncommunist development strategy of the Charter with a neutralist foreign policy. On July 9, he opened the Cairo Conference on Questions of Economic Development, a meeting of representatives from developing countries including allies of both superpowers as well as from the other leading neutral states of Indonesia, Yugoslavia, and India. Nasser's speech, described by one U.S. official as "remarkable not only for its restraint but also for its positive tone," characterized the struggle for development as a race between the growth of the national economy and that of the population. Nasser addressed the delegates as representatives of peoples who "were forced into backwardness" by "historical circumstances" but were now "firmly determined to compensate for the past and catch up with the future under circumstances of rapid progress." Many of these societies were facing overpopulation, "which is increasing at a more rapid speed than average economic development." He compared this "population explosion" to "nuclear bomb explosions" and argued that even greater efforts than those devoted to non-proliferation would be needed to head off "problems caused by the lower standards of living" that would occur when the world population outstripped the global food supply. Nasser insisted that meeting this challenge required "broad international cooperation" and peace that "extended across all boundaries." At this conference, he pointed out, "the word 'against' does not exist in its agenda."[76] Just as his government had appealed to Egyptians of different social classes with the Charter, Nasser invoked economic development as a universal theme that could transcend regional and Cold War struggles.

But Nasser found it impossible to withdraw from regional conflicts altogether. On September 26, military officers in Yemen seized power from Imam Muhammad al-Badr, who had succeeded his deceased father, Ahmad bin Yahya, only a week earlier. Nasser had not sponsored the coup but moved quickly to support the new military government in San'a', deploying an Egyptian force that would grow to some 70,000 troops by summer 1965.[77] Saudi Arabia's bid to restore the imamate by arming Zaydi tribal forces in the north and other opponents of the new regime would turn Yemen's civil conflict into a grinding proxy war between Egypt and the Saudi kingdom.

Given Polk's interest in improving Saudi–Egyptian relations, and the now widely accepted argument that Yemen helped to sink Nasser's rapprochement with the United States, it stands to reason that the intervention would have driven a wedge between Polk and top Egyptian officials. It did nothing of the sort. On the contrary, Polk's relationships with Egyptian leaders, including Nasser, grew closer. Polk criticized Nasser's interventionist policy, but fully accepted its premise that as Yemen was the most backward Arab society, its

[76] Brubeck to Bundy, with enclosed speech, July 11, 1962, folder: UAR General 7/62–8/62, box 168A, NSF, JFKL.

[77] See Ferris, *Nasser's Gamble*, 2–3, 29–31.

development could be accelerated through contact with Egypt, the most advanced Arab country. Polk could not help but oppose Egypt's cooperation with the Soviet military, which provided the "air bridge" that transported Egyptian men and equipment across the Red Sea.[78] Yet Nasser's defense of the intervention as modernization reinforced Polk's image of Nasser as a military modernizer. The conflict between republican forces supported by Egypt and Saudi-backed royalists seemed to encapsulate the basic struggle that Polk perceived within the Arab world between the future and the past.

On the basis of these assumptions, Polk authored a new study of Egypt in the Policy Planning Council and pursued an opening to Nasser through Haykal's debating opponent, Salah Dessouki. "Rather than getting sidetracked by the crisis from my arms control effort" with Egypt, Polk wrote Rostow less than a month after the coup in San'a', "I would like to push ahead vigorously with it." He followed up by noting: "I have excellent contacts there and would like to do the job."[79] In January 1963, Polk circulated a twenty-six-page paper on U.S. relations with the UAR. Distinguishing between Egypt's role in the Middle East and its domestic crisis, the paper called for the United States to reduce regional tensions and to provide long-term aid to Egypt. Polk's arguments bore a striking resemblance to the Charter of National Action. As the most advanced Arab country, Egypt was able to "steal a march on the rest of the Middle East" largely "because of the strong and far-sighted administration of Mehmet Ali Pasha," who had, like Nasser, sought to control Syria. Egypt's "population is literally exploding," Polk warned, linking overpopulation with communism, which in combination threatened to turn Egypt into "a Middle Eastern China." In any solution to Egypt's domestic crisis, he wrote, the "*key ingredient* will be an improvement in the ratio between production and population."[80]

At the end of January, Polk left for Cairo to discuss his paper with Badeau and other U.S. embassy officials. They persuaded him to approach Nasser not through Muhyi al-Din, whose authority had diminished following a recent government reorganization, nor through Sharaf, who was "not

---

[78] See Ferris, *Nasser's Gamble*, 70–101, and "Soviet Support for Egypt's Intervention in Yemen, 1962–63," *Journal of Cold War Studies* 10 (Fall 2008): 5–36.

[79] Polk to Rostow, "The Crisis and Nasser," October 25, 1962, and Polk to Rostow, November 9, 1962, folder: W. R. Polk – Chron. July–Dec. 1962, box 237, Policy Planning Council Subject Files, 1954–1962, RG 59, NARA. See also Polk to Rostow, "Shaking the Kaleidoscope in the Middle East," October 29, 1962, folder: Near and Middle East 1962, box 222, Policy Planning Council Subject Files, 1954–1962, RG 59, NARA.

[80] January 16, 1963, paper by Polk, "United States–United Arab Republic Relations," folder: Egypt, box 12, Policy Planning Council (1961–1969) Planning and Coordination Staff (1970–1973), Subject Files, 1963–1973 Lot 70D199, 72D124, 73D363, RG 59, NARA. Quotations on pp. 1, 2, 3. Emphasis original. Polk showed off his language ability by writing out in Arabic a verse from the famous poem *Lamiyyat al-'Arab* by al-Shanfara [p. 10].

sufficiently astute," but through Dessouki.[81] Dessouki had recently traveled to the United States on a Foreign Leader Grant and had unsuccessfully tried to arrange a meeting with JFK to present him with a key to the city of Cairo.[82] Dessouki had also served the Germans as a go-between with Nasser. Polk spent two hours with the Cairo governor on January 31 discussing ideas from his recent paper. He again raised the alarm that a "growing imbalance of population and resources could make Egypt into a Middle Eastern China." Just as the United States pursued arms control efforts with the Soviet Union, Polk argued, Egypt and other Arab states needed to curb the arms race with Israel in the interest of shoring up their domestic economies. He interpreted the recent U.S. decision to provide Israel with HAWK missiles to mean that Washington would "not allow a serious imbalance to develop." Dessouki agreed that the arms race was "a waste of the resources of both sides," but expressed concern about Egypt's security and worried that the details of any discussion with U.S. officials about limiting arms would quickly be shared with Israel. As for Yemen, Polk accepted Egypt's goals there, but objected to armed intervention. "We understand the genuine desire of the Arabs who have experienced 'the urban revolution' for modernization," Polk explained, insisting that the United States had "no basic policy goals directed specifically to the support of Kings or regimes which Egypt would regard as corrupt and anachronistic." The meeting concluded with Dessouki making two promises. Dessouki urged Polk to meet with Nasser personally and pledged to act as his intermediary. According to Polk, Dessouki made another offer: "Bill," he said, "'if you would like to fly to Yemen I will arrange it.'"[83]

True to his word, Dessouki accompanied Polk to Nasser's house on February 5 for a two-hour meeting with the Egyptian president.[84] Polk outlined the United States' "basic policy objective" as "assisting Egypt in its internal development." Nasser confirmed that Egypt spent about 12 million Egyptian pounds annually on defense, which Polk estimated to be about a tenth of its gross national product. Polk argued that such expenditures "did not give Egypt a clear superiority over Israel," but that investment in Soviet arms "did remove from the UAR government's control a large amount of its budgetary resources." He told Nasser that a wiser policy would be to

[81] Polk to Rostow, January 31, 1963, folder: Cairo – 1963, box 7, Bureau of Near Eastern and South Asian Affairs/Office of Near Eastern Affairs, Records of the Director, 1960–1963, RG 59, NARA.

[82] See Brubeck to Bundy, September 5, 1962, and unsigned reply, folder: UAR General 9/62-12/62, box 168A, NSF, JFKL.

[83] Polk to Rostow, January 31, 1963, cited earlier. See also undated draft by Polk, folder: W. R. Polk Chron. Jan.–June 1963, box 28, Policy Planning Council (1961–1969) Planning and Coordination Staff (1970–1973), Subject Files, 1963–1973 Lot70D199, 72D124, 73D363, RG 59, NARA.

[84] Telegram from Polk to Rostow, February 5, 1963, folder: UAR 1/63-11/63 [folder 4 of 4], box 446, NSF, JFKL.

"buy security more cheaply." Nasser criticized the United States for "supporting reactionary regimes," such as in Jordan and Saudi Arabia. The UAR had intervened in Yemen, he said, to defend "the right of the Arab countries to 'have their revolutions.'" Polk said the U.S. administration had a "tactical" difference in the sense that "we believed that reform can and should come by evolution." He compared Yemen to Vietnam, pointing out that Mao Zedong's doctrine made it difficult to defeat guerrillas with conventional forces. According to Polk, Nasser insisted that "We can do it in Yemen." Nasser also defended his radio broadcasts as responding to attacks by King Sa'ud's government. Polk argued that Nasser's propaganda fostered a negative "international climate" in which "Egypt might not able to get the resources from abroad that would enable it to bring about better balance between its population and its domestic production." Polk judged his meeting with Nasser to have been "as frank and friendly as any I could imagine." He urged Rostow to push ahead with a Middle East arms control initiative. "Even a respite" from the Middle East arms race, Polk wrote, "would be valuable." Nasser's attitude was sufficiently positive that Komer urged Bundy to share Polk's account with the president. "Bill Polk's fascinating talk with Nasser," Komer exclaimed, "makes this a *real* exercise rather than just a planner's dream."[85]

Near midnight on February 6, Polk left for Yemen. He boarded a United Arab Airways flight that took him over the Red Sea and "some incredibly rough country" that gave Yemen "the general appearance" of "a dry and broken land." The trip served to reinforce Polk's view of the Egyptian military intervention as a campaign to modernize Yemen. He told Rostow that Nasser's army "is the only organized force I saw in Yemen" and that the Egyptians were using the Soviet-made TU-16 bomber to "put the fear of hell in the tribesmen." Polk compared Egypt's tribal pacification policy to "what the [Royal Air Force] did in Iraq and the Jordanian Defense Forces under John Glubb did in Iraq and Trans-Jordan" (and, as Polk saw it, what Muhammad 'Ali had done to establish security in nineteenth-century Lebanon). As a guest of the Egyptian military, Polk flew at dawn on February 8 from San'a' north to Sadah near the Saudi border, where he met General Muhammad Qadri, who to Polk "looked and acted like Alec Guinness playing the part of a British officer in the Libyan desert."[86] Qadri drove Polk through pacified villages and outlined plans for an armor advance on Marib. Polk met subsequently with Anwar Sadat and Field Marshall 'Abd al-Hakim 'Amir, who predicted that "the war would be all over within a few weeks at the most." Although Polk was favorably impressed by Colonel 'Abdullah al-Sallal, head

---

[85] Komer to Bundy, February 9, 1963, folder: Palestine Refugees General 12/62-11/63, box 148A, NSF, JFKL. See also *FRUS*, 1961–1963, vol. 18: 345–46.

[86] The film *Lawrence of Arabia* had premiered in 1962. Alec Guinness portrayed the role of Arab Revolt leader and later Iraqi king Faysal bin Husayn.

of the Yemeni republican regime, the government's ministers appeared "to be young boys, rather giggly and embarrassed over their new jobs." On the whole, Polk declared, "Yemen is far more backward than Afghanistan or even, I believe, than the Congo." The assistance it would require to develop is "literally infinite," and this would make it difficult for Egypt to disengage. If it did so, then the Yemeni government "would turn to the Chinese or the Soviet Union for help."[87] In Polk's sympathetic account, Nasser's war in Yemen was the most recent historical case of military-led modernization in the Middle East.

The Yemeni civil war reopened conflicts within the Kennedy administration between officials who viewed Nasser favorably as a modernizer and those who regarded him as a threat to U.S. petroleum interests in Saudi Arabia. Gulf Oil consultant Kim Roosevelt met Komer to "express oil company concern over our Yemen and Nasser policies." Roosevelt said that John J. McCloy was "also worried."[88] On February 8, while Polk toured Yemen, former Arabian American Oil Company vice president James Terry Duce met in Jidda with Crown Prince Faysal. Duce had been encouraged to serve as emissary to the kingdom by McGhee, who underscored the danger of a "chain reaction effect" leading to the overthrow of the government in Saudi Arabia as had happened in San'a' and, on the same day as Duce's audience, in Baghdad (see Chapter 5).[89] Polk took his turn meeting with Faysal for several days beginning on February 11. The Crown Prince was incensed that his U.S. ally had not done more to deter Egyptian air attacks on the Saudi side of the border with Yemen. He dismissed Polk's understanding as "faulty" because his trip was far too brief: "You Americans are always rushing; you land but keep one foot in an airplane!"[90] U.S. food assistance, Faysal insisted, was indirectly helping to finance subversion and military operations by Nasser, who "is determined to crush us." Polk was "greatly mistaken," declared the prince, "to think that you can subtly or gently guide Nasir back to the path of reasonableness or wisdom."[91] At least

---

[87] Polk to Rostow, February 8, 1963 [mistyped 1962], folder: W. R. Polk, Chron. Jan.–June 1963, box 28, Policy Planning Council (1961–1969) Planning and Coordination Staff (1970–1973), Subject Files, 1963–1973 Lot 70D199, 72D124, 73D363, RG 59, NARA. For Polk's recent retrospective account, see https://consortiumnews.com/2015/04/01/yemen-as-vietnam-or-afghanistan/, accessed September 23, 2015.

[88] See memo by Komer, January 28, 1963, folder: Staff Memoranda Robert Komer 1/63-2/63, box 322, NSF, Meetings & Memoranda, JFKL.

[89] *FRUS, 1961–1963*, vol. 18, 350–51.

[90] Memorandum of conversations by Sabbagh, February 11–12, 1963, folder: W. R. Polk Chron. Jan.–June 1963, box 28, Policy Planning Council (1961–1969) Planning and Coordination Staff (1970–1973), Subject Files, 1963–1973 Lot70D199, 72D124, 73D363, RG 59, NARA.

[91] Memorandum of conversation by Sabbagh, February 13, 1963, folder: W. R. Polk Chron. Jan.–June 1963, box 28, Policy Planning Council (1961–1969) Planning and Coordination Staff (1970–1973), Subject Files, 1963–1973 Lot70D199, 72D124, 73D363, RG 59, NARA.

one American official in Saudi Arabia apparently agreed; somebody at the embassy leaked Polk's classified UAR paper to the press. A *Time-Life* correspondent told Polk that "someone – I can't say who – in the Embassy in Jidda is trying to stick a knife in your back" and that Polk had been "tagged as favoring a 'soft' policy toward Nasser."[92]

Polk supported helping Saudi Arabia with its air defenses and was skeptical that the ruling family could easily be overthrown.[93] More important, however, was the way in which "Yemen" came to stand for a set of ideas about modernization that certain American and Egyptian officials shared. Polk served as intermediary in this meeting of the minds, which was based on the belief in linear historical progress and a faith that more advanced countries could accelerate the development of "backward" societies. This argument echoed the one that Rostow and other policy makers used to defend U.S. intervention in Vietnam. "Reaction or backwardness," Polk wrote in his UAR paper, was "exemplified by the Imam of Yemen or King Saud."[94] He told Rostow: "Saudi Arabia has wasted its income."[95] The administration's Special National Intelligence Estimate explained that although it possessed "some trappings of modernity – airplanes, motor vehicles, the telegraph – Yemen is in reality a medieval society."[96] Komer exhibited similar thinking when he described Yemen as stuck "back in the 15th Century" and claimed that despite Aramco's influence, the "staying power of the Saudi monarchy declines with each passing day."[97] Komer agreed about the necessity for U.S. mediation of the Saudi–Egyptian conflict, but he also shared Polk's sympathy for Nasser as representing Arab progress.

Egyptian officials justified their intervention in Yemen as modernization using virtually identical assumptions. Pressing for U.S. recognition of the Yemeni republic, Nasser's government argued that the people of Yemen had thrown off "the shackles of under-development and reaction," but that the Saudis were intent on "dragging" them "back to the darkness of pre-Islamic days and the despotic rule of the Middle Ages."[98] The chief of Nasser's office, Hasan Sabri al-Khuli, told Polk that Egyptian forces

---

[92] Polk to Rostow, March 5, 1963, folder: Egypt, box 12, Policy Planning Council (1961–1969) Planning and Coordination Staff (1970–1973), Subject Files, 1963–1973 Lot 70D199, 72D124, 73D363, RG 59, NARA.

[93] See Polk to Rostow, February 15, 1963, W. R. Polk Chron. Jan.–June 1963, box 28, Policy Planning Council (1961–1969) Planning and Coordination Staff (1970–1973), Subject Files, 1963–1973 Lot 70D199, 72D124, 73D363, RG 59, NARA.

[94] "United States–United Arab Republic Relations," January 16, 1963, cited earlier, p. 9.

[95] "Shaking the Kaleidoscope in the Middle East," October 29, 1962, cited earlier, p. 5.

[96] SNIE, "The Situation and Prospects in Yemen" [p. 3], November 6, 1963, folder: Near and Middle East, box 21, Policy Planning Council (1961–1969) Planning and Coordination Staff (1970–1973), Subject Files, 1963–1973 Lot 70D199, 72D124, 73D363, RG 59, NARA.

[97] Komer to Bundy, June 7, 1962, folder: Saudi Arabia, General 6/6/62–6/30/62, box 156A, NSF, JFKL.

[98] Quoted in Ferris, *Nasser's Gamble*, 110–11, note 25.

would have difficulty withdrawing because "25 or even 50 years would be required to bring Yemen into the 20th century."[99] Nasser himself declared in a December 1962 speech that 5 million liberated Yemenis would represent an Arab victory over "reaction [*raj'iya*]" and a force in "our path to progress [*tariqna ila al-taqaddum*]."[100] Haykal cited the Egyptian army's introduction of "transistors" as evidence for its modernizing role and described Yemen prior to the intervention as secluded in the "darkness of the Middle Ages [*zalam al-qurun al-wusta*]."[101] Sharaf wrote that Yemen was "the most backward part of the Arab nation" and that Egypt had brought administrators, teachers, doctors, and other personnel in order to establish the basis for "modern Yemen [*al-Yaman al-haditha*]." Like Polk, Sharaf referred to Saudi and Jordanian sponsorship of the royalists to portray Yemen as a principal Arab battleground between the past and the future.[102]

Other administration officials followed Polk in traveling to Egypt. First was Komer, with Dessouki responsible for arranging his itinerary between April 12 and 14. Through Badeau, Dessouki offered to "cooperate in setting up appointments and making possible Komer's visit to significant Egyptian projects including [the Aswan] High Dam."[103] With Dessouki and Badeau present, Komer then met Nasser on April 15 to promote the Kennedy administration's initiative to negotiate an end to the Yemeni war through envoy Ellsworth Bunker. Komer placed particular emphasis, however, on slowing the "escalating arms race in the Middle East" in order to free up resources for development. He informed Nasser that Dessouki and other provincial governors had intimated that "they could use effectively far more resources than were presently available." Komer was "impressed by the extent of industrial and agricultural development which seemed to be taking place" and by the "atmosphere of vigor and growth which could not fail to impress even a casual observer." Nasser raised the threat posed by Israel's nuclear program and dismissed U.S. security assurances as unreliable "because of the well-known US role in support of Israel." Komer nonetheless appealed

99 Memorandum by Polk, February 21, 1963, folder: Egypt, box 12, Policy Planning Council (1961–1969) Planning and Coordination Staff (1970–1973), Subject Files, 1963–1973 Lot 70D199, 72D124, 73D363, RG 59, NARA.

100 Gamal Abdel Nasser, *Majmu'at khutab wa tasrihat wa bayanat al-Ra'is Gamal 'Abd al-Nasir* (Cairo: Maslahat al-Isti'lamat, n.d.), 4: 265.

101 Memorandum by Parker, October 5, 1965, folder: POL 15 Government UAR 1965, box 2, Near East Affairs Bureau, Office of the Country Director for the United Arab Republic (NEA/UAR), Records Relating to United Arab Republic Affairs, 1961–1966, RG 59, NARA; Haykal, *Sanawat al-Ghalayan*, 618.

102 Sami Sharaf, *Sanawat wa ayyam ma' Gamal 'Abd al-Nasir: Shahadat Sami Sharaf*, 2 vols. (Cairo: Dar al-Fursan li-l-Nashr, 2005, 2006), 2: 594, 628.

103 Badeau to Secretary, April 8, 1963, folder: UAR General 4/63–5/63, box 168A, NSF, JFKL. Komer also visited Nasser's Inschauss nuclear reactor. See Bass, *Support Any Friend*, 298 note 131.

to the Egyptian president using Polk's arguments and relationship with Dessouki.[104] Later that summer came McCloy, who had already registered his opposition to cooperating with Nasser. McCloy promoted an arms control agreement, but Nasser demurred on submitting to its terms before Israel did.[105]

Polk's burgeoning relationship with Nasser and his circle suggests the possibilities of a path not taken in regional arms control and a negotiated Arab–Israeli peace, even as that relationship developed on the basis of a shared authoritarian approach to modernization. This rapport presents a partial challenge to existing accounts describing a turn for the worse in U.S.–Egyptian relations at the end of Kennedy's administration. Those accounts cite Bunker's inability to broker a Saudi–Egyptian compromise in Yemen and congressional restrictions placed on aid to Nasser.[106] Despite political disagreements over Yemen, the Arab–Israeli arms race, and Nasser's support for Congo rebels, American and Egyptian officials continued to share a belief in modernization as a historical process of social change guided by elite authority. This belief formed the basis for Polk's "new men" theory, which associated Nasser's government with progressive, anticommunist modernization. The two men struck up a friendship based on their similar concern about overpopulation and enthusiasm for ambitious state projects that promised to transform Egypt's land and people. Nasser would accuse Western intelligence agencies of attempting to turn back the clock on his revolution through support for what he termed the "reactionary [*raj'i*]" Muslim Brotherhood. Polk agreed to the extent that he contrasted the "new men" with the Brotherhood, which he described as seeking to mobilize rural migrants holding traditional values. Political differences may have divided Washington from Cairo, but Polk's bond with Nasser revealed the shared assumptions about modernization underlying U.S.–Egyptian relations.

Polk's theory represented the culmination of his role bridging Western and Arab debates about modernizing the Middle East, as well as his career combining academia with policy making. In April 1963, Polk wrote to the State Department's Bureau of Intelligence and Research about "Nasser's emphasis on a 'core society'" that constituted a "vertical group" associated with the army and distinct from "traditional society."[107] By early 1964, the "core society" of Nasser's Western-trained "effectives" had

---

[104] Memorandum by Badeau, April 18, 1963, airgram A-767, folder: UAR General 4/63–5/63, box 168A, NSF, JFKL.

[105] See _FRUS, 1961–1963_, 18: 609–19.

[106] See Bass, _Support Any Friend_, 98–143; and Little, "The New Frontier on the Nile," 524.

[107] See Polk to Elwood and Glidden, April 18, 1963, folder: W. R. Polk Chron. Jan.–June 1963, box 28, Policy Planning Council (1961–1969) Planning and Coordination Staff (1970–1973), Subject Files, 1963–1973 Lot 70D199, 72D124, 73D363, RG 59, NARA.

evolved into the "new men."[108] This was the phrase that Polk used in memos written to Rostow, in a new UAR paper drafted for the Policy Planning Council following Kennedy's death, and in published scholarship. Polk formulated his theory in dialogue with U.S.-based scholars such as Manfred Halpern, whose study *The Politics of Change in the Middle East and North Africa* Polk described to Bowles as "one of the very best things that has come out on the Middle East." Polk reviewed it favorably for the *Middle East Journal.*[109] Rather than the "remarkably ephemeral, even sterile" political science literature, he told Robert Bowie of Harvard's Center for International Affairs, Polk aimed to provide officers at the CIA and State Department with a "usable conceptual scheme" for analyzing "social and political change."[110] At the same time, Polk's "new men" should be understood as his contribution to the Haykal–Dessouki debate over "experienced men" versus "reliable men." Like Dessouki, Polk argued that the educated elite fostered by Nasser's regime cut across class lines and was defined by useful skills, rather than class interests. Our "analytical experience," he wrote in the volume *The United States and the Middle East* published by Columbia University, "has shown that explanations based on the middle class as we understand it in the West are inadequate to explain developments in other areas." In non-Western societies, "social *groups* are often more useful than classes." Polk validated military modernization historically by drawing on Ghurbal and Rustum. He argued that "Muhammad Ali had created, albeit for his own limited purposes, the first successive groups of 'new men' who were to come forward in the Middle East or Arab society over the next century."[111]

In Polk's account, the state would reorder society through the skills citizens acquired in military training and through large-scale projects. He described the army as "a school to impart modern skills, a hospital to cure the ills of society and turn out healthier men, and a source of discipline." The 20,000 males inducted into the army annually would gradually transform rural Egyptians, while the military officer would translate his leadership role into that of "a factory manager or a senior bureaucrat." The "ex-Army

[108] See Polk to Rostow, February 7, 1964, folder: W. R. Polk – Chron Jan.–June 1964, box 28, Policy Planning Council (1961–1969) Planning and Coordination Staff (1970–1973), Subject Files, 1963–1973 Lot 70D199, 72D124, 73D363, RG 59, NARA.

[109] Polk to Bowles, November 6, 1963, folder: W. R. Polk Chron – June–Dec. 1963, box 28, Policy Planning Council (1961–1969) Planning and Coordination Staff (1970–1973), Subject Files, 1963–1973 Lot 70D199, 72D124, 73D363, RG 59, NARA. See review by Polk, *Middle East Journal* 17 (Autumn 1963): 454–56.

[110] Polk to Bowie, October 23, 1964, folder: W. R. Polk – Chron July–Dec. 1964, box 28, Policy Planning Council (1961–1969) Planning and Coordination Staff (1970–1973), Subject Files, 1963–1973 Lot 70D199, 72D124, 73D363, RG 59, NARA.

[111] William R. Polk, "Social Modernization: The New Men," in *The United States and the Middle East*, ed. Georgiana G. Stevens (Englewood Cliffs, NJ: Prentice-Hall, 1964), 30, 31, 40.

officer," wrote Polk, "is the 'doer' of the new order." Programs such as Egypt's Tahrir Province (see Chapter 3) sought to mobilize the countryside and create "new men" out of peasants. Tahrir was a "straw in the wind of changes which most Arab rulers expect to see."[112] For Polk, the next frontier in the state's campaign to remake the land and society was using nuclear power to desalinate sea water, a technology that could potentially facilitate desert reclamation on an enormous scale. Polk shared an interest in desalination with his former Harvard student the Aga Khan and with Rostow, to whom he proposed a feasibility study in April 1963 after meeting with scientists.[113] A year later, he recommended approaching Hasan Sabri al-Khuli about building a desalination plant in Gaza to make Palestinian refugees living there self-sufficient in agriculture and to permit the United States to curtail its subsidy to the UN Relief and Works Agency.[114]

Polk's favorable interpretation of the Egyptian regime did not convince top officials of the need to continue working closely with Nasser. In fact, Polk's official influence peaked in April 1964. Rostow forwarded a memo by Polk to the new president, Lyndon B. Johnson, calling it a "clear and sound statement" of the value of keeping Nasser in play. The memo was a précis of a new UAR paper in which Polk described Egypt's struggle to keep pace economically with its population growth and argued that "a mellowing process will accompany development."[115] Rostow, Bundy, and Komer then campaigned to have LBJ appoint Polk to replace Badeau, who was retiring as ambassador. Komer praised Polk's "gadfly" role at the State Department and boasted that "he knows all the key Gyppos." Polk's White House allies even lined up wealthy Texans to vouch for him. Komer credited Polk's arms control initiative, "a first class conception," and wrote that Arab leaders associated Polk with "the Kennedy policy of taking them seriously."[116] But LBJ repudiated his predecessor's policy and adopted a more openly pro-Israel stance. In February at the Weizmann Institute in New York, the

[112] Polk, "Social Modernization," 51, 52.
[113] See Polk to the Aga Khan, August 15, 1962, folder: W. R. Polk – Chron. July–Dec. 1962, box 237, Policy Planning Council Subject Files, 1954–1962, RG 59, NARA; and Polk to Rostow, "Desalination," April 19, 1963, folder: W. R. Polk Chron. Jan.–June 1963, box 28, Policy Planning Council (1961–1969) Planning and Coordination Staff (1970–1973), Subject Files, 1963–1973 Lot 70D199, 72D124, 73D363, RG 59, NARA.
[114] Polk to Talbot, June 29, 1964, folder: Arab Refugees 1964-1965-1966, box 12, NSF, Files of Robert W. Komer, LBJL.
[115] See Rostow to Johnson, April 14, 1964, folder: United Arab Republic, Vol. I, Memos [2 of 2] 11/63–5/64, box 158, NSF, LBJL; and Polk to Rostow, April 7, 1964, folder: Egypt, box 12, Policy Planning Council (1961–1969) Planning and Coordination Staff (1970–1973), Subject Files, 1963–1973 Lot 70D199, 72D124, 73D363, RG 59, NARA.
[116] Komer to Bundy, April 7, 1964 and Komer to Davies, April 9, 1964, folder: United Arab Republic Vol. I Memos [2 of 2] 11/63–5/64, box 158, NSF, LBJL. See also Komer to Bundy, April 7, 1964, folder: United Arab Republic, Vol. III, Memos 11/64–6/65 [1 of 2], box 159 [1 of 2], NSF, LBJL.

president had announced that his administration was pursuing talks with Israel about sharing nuclear desalination technology.[117] Johnson decided to appoint career diplomat Lucius Battle instead of Polk. Some officials in the Defense Department and at CIA objected to Polk's proposals to limit the arsenals of Israel and the Arab states while assisting Egypt economically.[118] In an "eyes only" memo sent to Rostow in May, Polk warned about the dangers of the Middle East arms race. "I am absolutely certain that unless we stop the UAR and Israel, we will face – perhaps during the President's next term," Polk predicted, "a situation at least as dangerous as Cuba with perhaps many of the implications of a Viet Nam."[119]

Excluded from the center of policy making in Washington, Polk cultivated his contacts with Dessouki and Nasser. Dessouki sent Polk condolences following Kennedy's assassination and later asked him about inviting Jacqueline Kennedy to visit Cairo.[120] As a non-leftist regime insider, Dessouki embodied Polk's hopes for evolutionary modernization guided by the military. The pair's friendship reflected the assumptions regarding both class and gender on which Polk based his theory. On one hand, he defined the "*new men*" as distinct from prerevolutionary class conflicts in the Marxist sense. "The 'new men' of various social and economic levels share goals and values," he explained, "whereas within the 'middle class' there is a sharp cleavage."[121] On the other hand, Polk made clear that these were "new *men*." He shared in the "ideology of masculinity" that historian Robert D. Dean associates with the Kennedy era.[122] In gestures of masculine camaraderie with his U.S. colleagues, Polk joked about the "utility of a Playboy Club in Jidda" and sent Rostow a "large bomb fragment" as his memento of a near miss along the Saudi–Yemeni border.[123] Male bonding extended to his

[117] See "Remarks in New York City at the Dinner of the Weizmann Institute of Science," February 6, 1964, http://www.presidency.ucsb.edu/ws/index.php?pid=26060, accessed November 2, 2015. On Arab reaction, see Komer to Johnson, February 26, 1964, *FRUS 1964–1967*, 18: 43–44. See also Zach Levey, "The United States, Israel, and Nuclear Desalination: 1964–1968," *Diplomatic History* 39 (November 2015): 904–25.

[118] See Badeau to Talbot, January 31, 1964, folder: POL 1 Gen. Policy. UAR-US 1/1/64; and Davies to Talbot, October 20, 1964, folder: POL 1 UAR-US 7/31/64, box 2768, Central Foreign Policy Files, 1964–1966, RG 59, NARA.

[119] Polk to Rostow, May 25, 1964, folder: Near and Middle East, box 42, Policy Planning Council (1961–1969) Planning and Coordination Staff (1970–1973), Subject Files, 1963–1973 Lot 70D199, 72D124, 73D363, RG 59, NARA.

[120] See Polk to Dessouki, December 26, 1963, folder: W. R. Polk Chron – June–Dec. 1963; and Polk to Dessouki, August 14, 1964, folder: W. R. Polk – Chron July–Dec. 1964, box 28, Policy Planning Council (1961–1969) Planning and Coordination Staff (1970–1973), Subject Files, 1963–1973 Lot 70D199, 72D124, 73D363, RG 59, NARA.

[121] Polk, "Social Modernization," 47.

[122] Robert D. Dean, *Imperial Brotherhood: Gender and the Making of Cold War Foreign Policy* (Amherst: University of Massachusetts Press, 2001).

[123] Polk to Murphy, November 30, 1964, folder: W. R. Polk – Chron July–Dec. 1964, box 28, Policy Planning Council (1961–1969) Planning and Coordination Staff (1970–1973),

relationship with Dessouki. Polk arranged for Dessouki to visit the U.S. Sixth Fleet and requested that he "be taken up in a jet fighter (as I was) for a ride." Polk confessed that he had gotten "(briefly and slightly) sea-sick" and exhorted Dessouki: "Please be a better sailor than I!"[124] This gendered style was meaningful for Polk, father of two girls and a son born just after he returned from Yemen.[125] His approach to modernization envisioned making "new men" out of army conscripts and curbing overpopulation by imposing state control over women's fertility.

Indeed, Polk's ideas germinated within the mix of intensifying personal and ideological conflicts over the direction of Egypt's development. Just as Polk was formulating his theory, Egypt held elections in which half of the legislative seats were reserved for workers and peasants. The National Assembly drew up a revised constitution, and Nasser's prime minister, 'Ali Sabri, enacted a "shift towards socialism" reflected in a new five-year economic plan. Nasser had created a leadership organization within the Arab Socialist Union led by Sabri, Haykal, and ex-communists and authorized independent Marxist Lutfi al-Khuli to publish a journal of "socialist scientific thought" titled *al-Tali'a* [*The Vanguard*]. In April 1964, just prior to hosting a visit from Khrushchev, Nasser released jailed communists who dissolved their party and joined the ASU.[126] Judging from the 250 million ruble loan he negotiated with Khrushchev, Nasser appeared to be tacking toward the Soviet Union.[127] After Congolese students burned a U.S. Information Service Library in Cairo, Egyptian forces shot down a private American plane, and Nasser delivered an anti-American speech, Dessouki suggested that Sabri was exploiting these crises to further divide Cairo from Washington.[128] He warned Battle: "[Y]ou must be careful whom you listen to."[129] Later, in a candid talk with Polk, Dessouki bitterly denounced

---

Subject Files, 1963–1973 Lot 70D199, 72D124, 73D363, RG 59, NARA; and Polk to Rostow, February 15, 1963, cited earlier.

[124] Polk to Dessouki, July 24, 1964, folder: W. R. Polk – Chron July–Dec. 1964, box 28, Policy Planning Council (1961–1969) Planning and Coordination Staff (1970–1973), Subject Files, 1963–1973 Lot 70D199, 72D124, 73D363, RG 59, NARA.

[125] See Polk to Badeau, June 12, 1963, folder: W. R. Polk Chron. Jan.–June 1963, box 28, Policy Planning Council (1961–1969) Planning and Coordination Staff (1970–1973), Subject Files, 1963–1973 Lot 70D199, 72D124, 73D363, RG 59, NARA.

[126] Ginat, *Egypt's Incomplete Complete Revolution*, 23–29. See also Bergus to Department of State, December 26, 1964, airgram A-436, folder: POL 2-1 UAR 7/1/64, box 2760, Central Foreign Policy Files, 1964–1966, RG 59, NARA; and Evans to Rusk, June 11, 1965, folder: United Arab Republic, Vol. III, Memos 11/64–6/65 [1 of 2], box 159, NSF, Middle East – United Arab Republic, LBJL.

[127] See Heikal, *The Sphinx and the Commissar*, 137.

[128] See Springer (Port Said) to Department of State, December 24, 1964, airgram A-56, folder: POL 15-1 UAR 7/18/64, box 2763, Central Foreign Policy Files, 1964–1966, RG 59, NARA. See also Burns, *Economic Aid and American Policy Toward Egypt*, 158–59.

[129] Battle to Department of State, December 1, 1964, folder: United Arab Republic, Vol. II, Cables 6/64-12/64 [2 of 2], box 159, NSF, LBJL.

Sabri as a "liar."[130] In the conflict between Sabri and Dessouki over whether Egypt's modernizing elite should be defined by social class or transcend it, the political had become personal.

The role of the Muslim Brotherhood further illustrates the narrow concept of top-down transformation that framed Egypt's ideological battles. If Polk and Dessouki envisioned a technical-military elite, and Sabri and Lutfi al-Khuli a movement on behalf of the revolutionary classes, then Nasser's Islamist opponents called for a spiritual leadership to remake Egyptian society. Just as Polk was defining the "new men," Islamist Sayyid Qutb published *Signposts along the Road*, which he dedicated to the spiritual "vanguard."[131] The term he used [*al-tali'a*] was also the title of the new "scientific socialist" journal approved by Nasser. Its editor, Lutfi al-Khuli, was himself nephew to al-Bahi al-Khuli, the Brotherhood propagandist who had attempted before Qutb to redefine the group's mission in Cold War terms[132] (see Chapter 1). In the struggle to determine Egypt's future, Polk was among the ideological contestants who relied on similar concepts and terminology.

Nasser's innuendo associating the United States with an anti-regime plot by the Muslim Brotherhood punctuated the decline in Egyptian–American relations during 1965. The Johnson administration suspended food aid to Egypt, refused to renew such aid on a multiyear basis, and deferred negotiating a one-year renewal.[133] Washington also provided a new arms package to Israel. By June, Battle wrote that the tension was so thick "you can almost cut it with a knife."[134] Top Egyptians alleged that the CIA was plotting to overthrow Nasser, and Egyptian police arrested leading journalist and former Nasser confidant Mustafa Amin on July 21 after he met with a CIA officer.[135] Washington's long-term reliance on the CIA to conduct relations

[130] Polk to Battle, November 16, 1965, cited earlier.
[131] See Barbara Zollner, "Prison Talk: The Muslim Brotherhood's Internal Struggle during Gamal Abdel Nasser's Persecution, 1954–1971," *International Journal of Middle East Studies* 39 (August 2007): 411–33.
[132] Ginat, *Egypt's Incomplete Revolution*, 49.
[133] See Burns, *Economic Aid and American Policy Toward Egypt*, 163.
[134] Cairo (Battle) to Department of State, June 26, 1965, folder: United Arab Republic, Vol. IV, Cables 6/65–6/66 [2 of 2], box 159 [2 of 2], NSF, LBJL.
[135] See memorandum of conversation by Davies, August 27, 1965, folder: Political Affairs & Rel. UAR 1965 UAR – United States July–Dec., box 1, Near East Affairs Bureau, Office of the Country Director for the United Arab Republic (NEA/UAR), Records Relating to United Arab Republic Affairs, 1961–1966, RG 59, NARA. See also Cairo (Battle) to Department of State, January 28, 1965, folder: POL 1 UAR-US 1/1/65; and memoranda of conversations by Davies, August 3 and 10, 1965, folder: POL UAR-US 7/22/1965, box 2768, Central Foreign Policy Files, 1964–1966, RG 59, NARA. See also Muhammad Hasanayn Haykal, *Nahnu … wa Amrika*, 2nd ed. (Cairo: Dar al-'Asr al-Hadith, 1967), 29. On Amin, see Cairo (Battle) to the Department of State, July 22, 1965, folder: United Arab Republic, Vol. IV, Cables 6/65–6/66 [1 of 2], box 159 [2 of 2], NSF, LBJL; and Carden to Higgins, July 24, 1965, FO 371/183966, BNA. See also Tim Wiener, *Legacy of Ashes: The History of the CIA* (New York:

with the regime fed paranoia among the Egyptian leadership, who dismissed as unreliable the assurances Battle and other diplomats offered that the United States was not pursuing regime change.

The facts of the Brotherhood plot are difficult to separate from Nasser's political uses of it. Members of the group were rounded up, including Qutb, who was eventually executed. Security forces raided the group's stronghold of Kardasa.[136] In August, while visiting the Soviet Union, Nasser divulged the Brotherhood plot during a speech delivered to Arab students studying in Moscow. He denounced the "pressures" that the United States was attempting to place on Egypt by withholding food aid. He then revealed that Sa'id Ramadan, exiled son-in-law of Brotherhood founder Hasan al-Banna, together with conspirators inside Egypt, had undertaken the plot with help from "colonialism and reaction [*isti'mar wa raj'iya*]."[137] Accounts published in *al-Ahram* of the plot's ambitious scope seem far-fetched, although journalist Ian Johnson has established the fact of Ramadan's earlier relationship with the CIA.[138] Among the accusations made in *Ahram* was that female Islamist Zaynab al-Ghazzali served as the "direct link [*al-sila al-mubashara*]" between the domestic plotters and their foreign sponsors.[139] Official accounts ridiculed Qutb for peddling "stupidity and nonsense [*al-humq wa al-sakf*]" while portraying the plot as directed against the modern features of Egyptian society. Nasser's imputation of U.S. connivance with the plotters appeared to be contradicted by subsequent claims that the American ambassador was among their intended victims. Brotherhood cells allegedly schemed to kill Western and Soviet diplomats, target radio and television, and even attack beloved Egyptian entertainment stars such as Umm Kulthum![140] According to the U.S. embassy, the Egyptian press portrayed the Brothers as "despicable reactionaries."[141] Indictments filed on December 12 accused the conspirators of stockpiling weapons and planning to assassinate Nasser using funds provided by the Central Treaty Organization (CENTO) and Western intelligence agencies. These charges purposefully linked Ramadan to CENTO, the Shah of Iran, and Saudi-financed Islamic institutions.[142] The plot enabled

Doubleday, 2007), 326–27; and Richard B. Parker, *Memoirs of a Foreign Service Arabist* (Washington, DC: New Academia Publishing, 2013), 150–51.

[136] See Gilles Kepel, *Muslim Extremism in Egypt: The Prophet and the Pharaoh* (Berkeley: University of California Press, 1993), 31–35.

[137] *Al-Ahram*, August 30, 1965, pp. 1, 8, 11.

[138] See Ian Johnson, *A Mosque in Munich: Nazis, the CIA, and the Rise of the Muslim Brotherhood in the West* (Boston, MA: Houghton Mifflin Harcourt, 2010).

[139] *al-Ahram*, September 7, 1965, p. 1.

[140] *al-Ahram*, September 8, 1965, p. 1. See also Ambassador Telegram to Foreign Office, September 8, 1965, FO 371/183966, BNA.

[141] Parker to Department of State, October 13, 1965, airgram A-317, folder: POL 2-1 UAR 7/1/65, box 2760, Central Foreign Policy Files, 1964–1966, RG 59, NARA.

[142] Bullen (Cairo) to Department of State, December 15, 1965, airgram A-317, folder POL 3 Organizations and Alignments Muslim Brotherhood (Ikhwan), box 1, Records of the

Nasser to corral reactionary enemies at home and abroad into a single conspiracy against his revolution.

In spring 1964, Polk had turned to completing his book *The United States and the Arab World*, which was supported by a Guggenheim fellowship.[143] The following year, he resigned from the State Department to join the history faculty and administer the Middle East studies program at the University of Chicago. Polk's closest acquaintance among Egyptian officials, Dessouki, also resigned as Cairo governor prior to the Brotherhood crackdown in 1965. According to Polk, Dessouki had quit "in anger," although Egyptian feminist 'Aziza Husayn reported that Dessouki was removed because of his clash with Sabri.[144] Nasser kept the door open to improved relations with Washington, however, by sacking Sabri as prime minister and forming a new government on October 1 headed by Zakariyya Muhyi al-Din. The U.S. embassy explained the change using what it called the "pendulum theory." Having "now pinned down about all the [Soviet] block aid he can expect for the new 5-year plan," Nasser returned to friendlier relations with the West.[145] As part of his swing back toward the United States, Nasser renewed his friendship with Polk. Just as Polk was concluding a trip to Egypt on November 15, he received a last-minute phone call inviting him to the president's home for a private conversation.

Polk summarized the discussion in a letter sent to Battle.[146] Nasser, dressed casually in a sport shirt, spoke with Polk for an hour, mostly in English, before asking: "Are you forgetting your Arabic?" When they switched to Arabic, Polk recalled, Nasser "teased me about my Syrian accent." After the pair reminisced about their 1963 arms control discussion, Polk recommended that Nasser establish American studies programs in Egypt similar to the Middle East studies program at the University of Chicago. Nasser offered to support a visiting professorship at Chicago, but economic development was the topic that dominated the conversation. Polk addressed the widening gap between economic and population growth. He quoted Nasser as saying: "I am haunted by the birth of nearly 800,000 new people each year." Nasser doubted that the Egyptian masses could easily relinquish cultural attitudes against contraception. As for the economy, Nasser favored curbing consumption to preserve Egypt's balance of payments, while Polk

Foreign Service Posts of the Department of State, American Embassy, Cairo, Egypt, Subject Files, RG 84, NARA.

[143] Ford to Jackson, June 9, 1964, folder: W. R. Polk Administrative File, box 28, Policy Planning Council (1961–1969) Planning and Coordination Staff (1970–1973), Subject Files, 1963–1973 Lot 70D199, 72D124, 73D363, RG 59, NARA.

[144] Polk to Battle, November 5, 1965, cited earlier. See also memorandum by Parker, October 5, 1965, cited earlier; and Walter to Higgins, July 28, 1965, FO 371/183884, BNA.

[145] Cairo (Parker) to Department of State, October 13, 1965, airgram A-312, folder: POL 2-1 UAR 7/1/65, box 2760, Central Foreign Policy Files, 1964–1966, RG 59, NARA.

[146] Polk to Battle, November 16, 1965, cited earlier.

referred to Rostow's strategy of cultivating a "national market" and cited the experience of Iran. Nasser recalled *al-Ahram*'s serialization of *The Stages of Economic Growth* and expressed a desire "to talk with Walt at considerable length." Polk concluded that his own theory had mostly been vindicated. Recent events, "except for the residues of the Muslim brotherhood attempt, were predictable within the scheme of analysis I developed for Egypt." The "new men," who "are aware of their capabilities and skills in all fields but the political, are restive under the autocracy of Nasser's regime." If their "desires for a greater voice in government can be temporized," he wrote, then the regime could "slowly evolve a greater degree of representative government." Optimistic that military-led modernization could one day culminate in democracy, Polk predicted that "this is in the cards for Egypt over the coming ten to twenty years."

The friendship between Polk and Nasser grew on the basis of shared assumptions about Egypt's modernization. One of the most important was an interpretation of the Brotherhood as the vestige of a traditional past. Nasser repeatedly described it as "reactionary [*raj'i*]," while Polk tellingly chose the word "residues" to characterize the group's alleged plot. According to Polk's scholarship, the Brotherhood's main political chance had come in the 1930s and '40s, prior to Nasser's revolution, when Egyptians were "really leaderless" and "unable to find a path to their future." The Brotherhood had attempted to "cater to the lower-class vote" among urban migrants, but "politically these people are still rural."[147] Both men justified military leadership as essential for heading off a political and social crisis. Their view that economic development preceded and constituted a necessary condition for democracy helps to explain their approach to modernization as a set of technical problems requiring elite management. Nasser shared Polk's interest in population control and desalination using nuclear power. His government established a Higher Council for Family Planning in 1966 and received assistance from the Ford Foundation and other sources for its contraception program.[148] The UAR also accepted a bid from General Electric to build a $50 million uranium desalination plant at Burj al-'Arab on the Mediterranean coast west of Alexandria.[149] In the years following Polk's

[147] William R. Polk, *The United States and the Arab World* (Cambridge, MA: Harvard University Press, 1965), 153; and William R. Polk, "The Nature of Modernization: The Middle East and North Africa," *Foreign Affairs* 44 (October 1965), 103, 105.

[148] See Battle to Hare, February 4, 1966, folder: United Arab Republic, box 3, Near East Affairs Bureau, Office of the Assistant Secretary for Near Eastern and South Asian Affairs, Subject Files, 1965–1966, RG 59, NARA; and Gad G. Bilbar and Onn Winckler, "Nasser's Family Planning Policy in Perspective," in *Rethinking Nasserism: Revolution and Historical Memory in Modern Egypt*, ed. Elie Podeh and Onn Winckler (Gainesville: University Press of Florida, 2004), 286.

[149] See memorandum of conversation by Bahti, April 12, 1965, folder: Atomic Energy (Gen.) AE6, box 2, Near East Affairs Bureau, Office of the Country Director for the United Arab

departure from the State Department, he and Nasser would collaborate on planning the new rural communities they envisioned as part of a massive state reclamation project in the desert.

Like Nasser, Polk hoped that the Arab–Israeli conflict could be left "in the icebox" while Egypt pursued economic development. Yet the two men interpreted this phrase differently. The Burj al-'Arab scheme depended on getting both Israel and Egypt to submit their nuclear programs to International Atomic Energy Agency (IAEA) supervision. Nasser said that he would accept IAEA controls, although he would not grant the United States unilateral inspections, nor would he submit to supervision unless the Johnson administration compelled Israel to do so.[150] He also proved unwilling to withdraw from Yemen and regarded rivals, such as the Ba'thist military officers who seized power in Damascus in February 1966, as threatening his leadership of the Arab world.[151] In the fateful decisions of May 1967, Nasser's government remilitarized the Sinai Peninsula, evicted UN peacekeeping forces, and closed the Straits of Tiran to Israeli shipping. Nasser refused to accept the distinction Polk made between Egypt's internal revolution and role in regional politics. For Nasser, the revolution at home could never fully be separated from Egypt's, and his own, place in the region. Polk erred in thinking that modernization could turn Nasser inward and in believing, given Nasser's determination to hold onto Arab leadership and Israel's pursuit of a nuclear weapons program, that such a distinction was even possible.

National security advisor Walt Rostow called on Polk, his former colleague on the Policy Planning Council, to offer advice concerning the crisis. In a reply written on June 3, Polk admitted that "the future appears bleak."[152] If war erupted, then "[s]erious work on Middle Eastern poverty" would likely "be a casualty," and in "U.S.–USSR relations, serious strains will develop" that will carry over into "other areas." Nevertheless, he thought that the crisis finally offered the opportunity to "'bake a cake' which will taste sufficiently good" to Arabs and Israelis "that they will swallow some salt with their sugar." The ingredients included getting

Republic (NEA/UAR), Records Related to United Arab Republic Affairs, 1961–1966, RG 59, NARA; and "Summary of US Desalting Cooperation with UAR, to June 1, 1965," folder: Nuclear – Desalinization of Water (Nuclear Powered) [3 of 3], box 31, NSF, Files of Charles E. Johnson, LBJL.

[150] See Cairo (Badeau) to Department of State, June 8, 1964, folder: United Arab Republic Vol. II, Memos 6/64-12/64 [2 of 2]; Cairo (Battle) to Department of State, April 18, 1965, folder: United Arab Republic Vol. III Cables 11/64–6/65 [1 of 2]; and memorandum for the record by Saunders, August 10, 1966, folder: United Arab Republic, Vol. IV, Memos [1 of 4] 6/65–6/66, box 159 [2 of 2], NSF, LBJL.

[151] See CIA Special Report, "Syria under the Bath," May 20, 1966; and CIA Weekly Review, "Syria: A Center of Instability," March 24, 1967, folder: Syria, Vol. 1, Cables and Memos [1 of 2] 4/64-10/68, box 156, NSF, LBJL.

[152] Polk to Rostow, June 3, 1967, folder: Arab-Israel 4/1/66-12/31/67 [3 of 3], box 7, NSF, Files of Harold H. Saunders, LBJL.

Nasser to reopen the Straits in exchange for a "no attack" pledge from Israel and long-term economic aid to Egypt from the United States, the International Monetary Fund, and the World Bank. To further assist the Egyptian economy, Polk proposed "encouragement of loans from oil companies (reactivating the 1958 proposal)." These measures, he believed, could help to revive stalled cooperation on Palestinian refugees and the Jordan waters. Polk reached back to his 1963 UAR paper in recognizing Nasser's "two principal roles" as author of Egypt's domestic revolution and as "an Arab leader." As in the past, Polk hoped that it would be possible to persuade Nasser to exchange a focus on the latter for an emphasis on the former. The crisis could help him "to get out of Yemen without loss of face" but only with "significant assistance to the accomplishment of his domestic role" and, "at least symbolically," with "enhancement of his pan-Arab role." Two days after Polk's memo, Israel launched a devastating war that destroyed Egypt's military and redrew the Middle East map. Although it is impossible to know what might have happened, Polk's recipe was never tried. His negative predictions about the war's consequences proved largely correct.

In November 1968, Nasser hosted Polk again in Cairo. On this trip Polk also met separately with Haykal and Hasan Sabri al-Khuli. During Polk's three-hour chat at Nasser's home, the pair discussed John Foster Dulles, the Cuban Missile Crisis, Zambia and Rhodesia, the American Negro, and Polk's book.[153] Nasser disavowed responsibility for the May 1967 crisis, blaming his military and intelligence services for miscalculating. Reformulating the distinction between the revolution at home and Nasser's role abroad, Polk differentiated the "apparent power" represented by "tools and toys of warfare" from the "development of an educated, coherent and dedicated population." Polk had recently become president of the Adlai Stevenson Institute of International Affairs at the University of Chicago. The Institute provided a setting where visiting fellows and conferees addressed social and economic problems at a time when governments were beginning to retreat from large-scale planning. The "desalting project for Alexandria" was among Polk's major initiatives. He remained committed to ambitiously transforming Egypt's land and people, despite Israeli occupation of the Sinai and the war's economic toll on Egypt.

Polk told Nasser that the desalination project had already passed its initial planning phase. In the second stage, 10 million gallons of water would be processed daily to irrigate some 3,000 acres. He envisioned a third stage that would irrigate 350,000 acres and a fourth that would multiply the irrigated area "tenfold" by the late 1980s. Polk emphasized the "sociological,

---

[153] Memo by Polk, November 20, 1968, folder 13, box 26, ASIIA. See also http://www
.eisenhower.archives.gov/research/online_documents/declassified/fy_2012/1968_11_
20.pdf, accessed October 28, 2015.

cultural, health, and 'political' aspects of the project," in which community planners would have a priceless opportunity to circumvent "the horrendous mistakes made during the Industrial Revolution in the cities." This exercise in historical re-engineering would "carry forward the creation of the 'new men' into the rural sector of his society." Nasser's main concern was for rural population control. Placing responsibility for contraception entirely on women, Nasser said: "'You know, here in the cities we have the cinema and television to occupy us in the evenings, but in the villages making love is the only way that a man can find any pleasure.'" The desalination scheme not only projected the pair's enthusiasm for gargantuan state planning far into the future but also sought to reactivate the personal ties that had linked American-Egyptian visions of development from earlier in the decade. Polk had invited Salah Dessouki to the Stevenson Institute, where Polk hoped that his old acquaintance might help to supervise the desalination project. When Polk asked about "my good friend," however, Nasser said that he was "very annoyed" with the former Olympic fencer for his "assumption of aristocratic ways." The president had sent Dessouki on an assignment to Finland to "put him on ice."[154]

Nuclear desalination never became the panacea Polk had imagined, but it embodied the faith in transformative state projects that he shared with Nasser and other Egyptians. Throughout his career, Polk served as a bridge between American and Arab debates about modernization. As his "new men" theory illustrates, ideas about modernizing the Middle East were not merely the preserve of Western experts. Polk also drew from the Arab historiographical influences of Ghurbal and Rustum and participated in debates within Egypt regarding how to define the modernizing sector of Egyptian society. Polk's background as a historian, and his interpretation of Nasser as the second coming of Muhammad 'Ali, gave him an important role justifying Kennedy's foreign policy in terms of Middle Eastern history. Polk also conceived of Egypt's development as a race between the growth of the economy and that of the population. Doing so placed him in the company of Nasser and those among his advisors, such as Dessouki, who defined Egypt's revolution in terms other than class struggle. What linked Polk to like-minded Americans and Arabs was their insistence that security and development precede democracy. Polk's criticism of the economic and political consequences of military-led modernization in Turkey challenged the Turco-centric regional strategy McGhee advocated. But Polk made arguments to Rostow about the Turkish military's disproportionate power and claim on its society's resources that should have applied in equal

---

[154] See Dessouki to Polk, July 30, 1968, and Polk to Dessouki, August 7, 1968, folder 5, box 3, ASIIA. In his handwritten note, Dessouki wrote to Polk: "I became a retired millionaire."

measure to the military regime in Egypt.[155] Although Polk operated within a widely shared postwar modernization paradigm, his willingness to postpone Egyptian democracy for the sake of anticommunist stability is indefensible given the pernicious legacy of that Faustian bargain in U.S.–Egyptian relations down to the present day.

Like many of his Arab and American contemporaries, Polk subscribed to a belief in modernization as a linear process guided by elite men. They applied this assumption to understanding social change within developing countries, as well as to instances, such as Nasser's intervention in Yemen, when a supposedly more advanced society accelerated the modernization of a "backward" one. But Polk presciently identified two negative influences that continue to afflict Middle Eastern societies and economies in the twenty-first century. The first is inequality between major oil-exporting states and poorer, more populous countries. This disparity was fostered by postwar Anglo-American diplomacy, and Polk sought to address it through a revival of the Hammarskjöld plan and other measures for investing oil wealth in regional development. The other is the Arab–Israeli military conflict. In May 1964, Polk predicted that a disastrous war would erupt within a few years unless the United States negotiated an arms limitation agreement and pursued a political settlement. He was right. Polk's repeated warnings about the opportunity costs of militarism have never ceased to be relevant. The most valuable lessons from his career are the hard truths that missed opportunities carry long-term consequences and that conflicts in the Middle East are neither culturally nor historically inevitable.

---

[155] See Polk to Rostow, July 19, 1963, folder: W. R. Polk Chron – June–Dec. 1963; and Polk to Rostow, May 28, 1964, folder: W. R. Polk – Chron Jan.–June 1964, box 28, Policy Planning Council (1961–1969) Planning and Coordination Staff (1970–1973), Subject Files, 1963–1973 Lot 70D199, 72D124, 73D363, RG 59, NARA.

7

Changing Course

"In the immediate aftermath [of the *infisal*, Nasser] felt, according to his description, that he found himself in the position of the captain of a ship that had split in two in the middle of the sea."
— Muhammad Hasanayn Haykal, *Sanawat al-Ghalayan*.[1]

"The wheel of time keeps turning and history marches on – there is nothing you can do about that. What you can do is be at the helm, take control, and try to make sure it moves in the right direction. This was what we did or, at least, what we tried our best to do."
— Anwar el-Sadat, *In Search of Identity: An Autobiography*.[2]

"Experts estimate that the time elapsing between a driver of a typical automobile recognizing danger emerging in front of him and the immediate reaction to avoid danger fluctuates between one-fifth and one-tenth of a second.... As for the pilot who flies jet planes, he must, much of the time, reduce this time segment between the recognition of danger and appropriate avoidance behavior to the limit of one-hundredth of a second."
— Sadik al-'Azm, *Self-Criticism After the Defeat*.[3]

"The pilot tried to calm me down. He thought I was angry, but I was actually overjoyed. He warned the crew not to be obstinate in dealing with their new captain."
— Leila Khaled, *My People Shall Live: The Autobiography of a Revolutionary*.[4]

[1] Muhammad Hasanayn Haykal, *Sanawat al-Ghalayan*, 591.
[2] Anwar el-Sadat, *In Search of Identity: An Autobiography* (New York: Harper & Row, 1977), 108.
[3] Sadik al-'Azm, *Self-Criticism After the Defeat*, trans. George Stergios (London: Saqi, [1968] 2011). 125–26.
[4] Leila Khaled, *My People Shall Live: The Autobiography of a Revolutionary*, ed. George Hajjar (London: Hodder and Stoughton, 1973), 136.

According to historians of U.S. foreign policy, the ordeals of the Vietnam era contributed to the unraveling of assumptions that had constituted Cold War–era modernization theory. The concept that development followed a universal path, and the belief that progress in poor countries could be accelerated through economic inputs and social reconditioning administered by experts and secured by authoritarian modernizers, fell victim to America's late 1960s "crisis of liberalism." As the liberal consensus fractured over issues including civil rights and the war in southeast Asia, the Kennedy-era concept of modernization came under attack from political critiques on both the right and left. The United States could no longer credibly claim to offer the third world a successful model to emulate. In the words of one historian, the strains created by Lyndon B. Johnson's escalation of the Vietnam War and simultaneous pursuit of the Great Society at home "left growth liberalism in disarray and the American Century in retreat." By the 1980s, writes historian Michael Latham, "the ideology of modernization was in a state of near collapse."⁵ Crises in the Arab world during the same period are similarly described as triggering a political rupture – the decline of the secular Arab nationalism associated with Gamal 'Abd al-Nasser. From the breakup of the United Arab Republic [*al-infisal*], to the economic disappointments of Arab Socialism, and, especially, the June 1967 War, the setbacks of the decade are believed to mark Nasserism's fall and the corresponding rise of political Islam. "The defeat of Nasser was a defeat for the force he represented, secularism," writes Said K. Aburish, "and with Nasser diminished, the Islamic movements moved to assume the political leadership of the masses of [the] Arab Middle East."⁶ Although historians have not sufficiently analyzed parallels between the American and Arab experiences of the 1960s, some acknowledge them by using the phrase "Nasser's Vietnam" to refer to the ruinous Egyptian involvement in Yemen.⁷ The hubris many officials shared that they could sustain both domestic economic reforms and military interventions to modernize "backward" societies was among the casualties of this turbulent era.

This concluding chapter examines changes in the politics of development in U.S.–Arab relations and argues that the late 1960s did indeed bring to a close the postwar era's optimistic pursuit of modernization. The most

---

⁵ Robert M. Collins, *More: The Politics of Economic Growth in Postwar America* (New York: Oxford University Press, 2000), 68; Latham, *The Right Kind of Revolution*, 182. See also Gilman, *Mandarins of the Future*, 203–40; and Allen J. Matusow, *The Unraveling of America: A History of Liberalism in the 1960s* (New York: Harper & Row, 1984).

⁶ Said K. Aburish, *A Brutal Friendship: The West and the Arab Elite* (New York: St. Martin's Press, 1998), 58. For a similar argument, see Ferris, *Nasser's Gamble*, 302. Yezid Sayigh argues that Nasser's defeat "breathed new life into Islam as a force for political opposition," although "this was not to become apparent until the second half of the 1970s." See Yezid Sayigh, *Armed Struggle and the Search for State: The Palestinian National Movement, 1949–1993* (New York: Clarendon Press, 1997), 143.

⁷ See Bass, *Support Any Friend*, 98–143; and Ferris, *Nasser's Gamble*, 211.

important change came in the form of challenges to American power and to Arab elites who had laid claim to authority on the basis of promising to improve society. This argument considers the American and Arab crises together and describes the shifts in Middle East regional politics that corresponded to the revolutionary Global Sixties.[8] It challenges accounts describing the "rise of Islamism" as immediately following the "decline of Nasserism." By portraying Islamism and Arab nationalism as successive rather than contemporary ideologies, such an interpretation ignores their earlier competition and neglects how 1960s crises challenged structural accounts of modernization more broadly. Just as postwar elites across a political spectrum had internalized similar assumptions about the integrated nature of societies and promoted developmental systems, their critics mobilized resistance against oppressive political and economic structures while defining new agendas for change in opposition to the modernizing state.

In the aftermath of the 1967 war, it was the secular Palestinian revolutionaries, the *fida'iyin*, whose guerrilla operations captured Arab and world attention. Beyond representing the grievances of stateless Palestinian refugees, the *fida'iyin* became popular because their victories, however dubious and ephemeral, appeared to expose the hollowness of Arab officials' claims that they could deliver economic progress and victory over Israel. The *fida'iyin* operations of the late 1960s and early 1970s, including air hijackings carried out by the Popular Front for the Liberation of Palestine (PFLP), represented a new phase not only in the Arab–Israeli conflict, but also in the postwar struggle over authority within Arab societies. While the *fida'iyin* waged what they regarded as the final struggle to decolonize the Middle East, their repudiation of Nasserism and the authority of modernizing states mirrored the contemporary American crisis. As evidence of economic and military failures accumulated during the late 1960s, marginalized populations such as Palestinian refugees and African Americans, who were denied the promised benefits of postwar modernization, revolted against state-led development strategies and discredited ideologies.

Reexamining the *fida'iyin* hijackings by placing them in this shared historical context offers new perspective on the crisis of modernization. This perspective contributes to recent scholarship that goes beyond characterizing the late 1960s upheavals in U.S. and Arab societies and seeks to understand what values and ideas emerged afterward. Princeton historian Daniel T. Rodgers explains how, in American life, "[s]trong metaphors of society were supplanted by weaker ones" in "a great age of fracture." Initiative shifted away from the New Deal state to the market and to "'little platoons of society.'" Public discourse was "less about society, history, and power

---

[8] See *1968: The World Transformed*, ed. Carole Fink, Philipp Gassert, and Detlef Junker (New York: Cambridge University Press, 1998); and Jeremi Suri, *The Global Revolutions of 1968: A Norton Casebook in History* (New York: W. W. Norton, 2007).

and more about individuals, contingency, and choice." As political language lost the Cold War "sense of historically clashing structures," neoliberal microeconomics and game theory replaced Keynesian macroeconomics and modernization theory as the basic approaches that many used to imagine the future. In place of widely held assumptions about linear progress, "the boundary between past and present virtually dissolved," writes Rodgers, so that in postmodern fashion reformers could search retrospectively for edifying symbols through what he calls "a wrinkle in time." No longer restricted by structural interpretations of historical change, nostalgia became a positive political value that replaced the earlier emphasis on movement out of backwardness. The past became "an unbroken line of reassurance up and down which the imagination could freely run."[9] Cultural philosopher Elizabeth Suzanne Kassab examines a contemporary turn in Arab thought away from closed ideologies. Kassab describes the post-1967 ferment as a second *Nahda*, comparing it to the late nineteenth and early twentieth-century Arab cultural awakening in which intellectuals had formulated responses to European colonialism and reimagined their place within Ottoman society. Rather than focus on the "rise of Islamism," Kassab features the resurgence of historical criticism, or what she calls "the self-reflective critical turn" in Arabic letters.[10] She compares Arab arguments over identity to those occurring simultaneously elsewhere, including debates about race and gender in North America. For Kassab, challenging inherited gender norms was an important aspect of the second *Nahda*. Like Rodgers, she explains how late 1960s crises posed challenges to various forms of historical determinism and structural conceptions of society. These were replaced by a new emphasis on contingency, personal choice, and self-definition by the individual.

This chapter similarly describes the decline of the basic assumptions with which elite Americans and Arabs had envisioned modernizing the postwar Middle East. These assumptions included their shared sense of development as following a linear historical path; the fundamental distinction between tradition and modernity; their concept of closed, rival modernizing systems; faith in large-scale, transformative state development projects; and insistence that elite authority was necessary to efficiently manage interdependent economic, social, and cultural changes. As previously, ideas about modernization reflected underlying economic factors without being determined by them. A growing concentration of oil wealth and retreat from state development programs designed to raise income levels among the poor led to greater

---

[9] Rodgers, *Age of Fracture*, 3, 5, 197, 222. Thomas Borstelmann has argued that challenges to hierarchies of race and gender coincided during the 1970s with the rise of neoliberalism and increased economic inequality. See Thomas Borstelmann, *The 1970s: A New Global History from Civil Rights to Economic Inequality* (Princeton, NJ: Princeton University Press, 2012).

[10] Elizabeth Suzanne Kassab, *Contemporary Arab Thought: Cultural Critique in Comparative Perspective* (New York: Columbia University Press, 2010), 12.

inequality both within and between different Arab states. The declining economic role of the state, a global trend affecting many developed and third world countries, held special implications in the Arab Middle East, where Nasser had promised to defeat Israel and raise living standards. The years following the 1967 war witnessed not only attacks on state authority by the revolutionary left, but also the dismantling of Arab Socialism and a regional economic realignment based on the influx of petrodollars to oil-exporting countries. Nasser's 1962 Charter had renounced class conflict and called for state-led development to propel economic growth ahead of population increase. In an indication of how the crisis degraded state authority, this agenda gave way to the PFLP's call for anti-Zionist and class struggle without borders on one hand, and emigration by millions of Egyptians and other Arabs who were forced to sell their labor in the Gulf on the other.

These shifts in development politics were accompanied by revolutionary challenges to the dominant postwar metaphor used to represent modernization. As Rodgers reminds his readers, "metaphors are not idle." They "'think for us'" by circumscribing possibilities and reducing complex realities to common-sense parables.[11] After World War II, the leading development metaphor was Walt Rostow's "takeoff," which used the cutting-edge technology of aerospace to represent the achievement of self-sustaining economic growth by developing countries. As explained in Chapter 1, this metaphor associated modernization with the thrust and lift of a jet aircraft. The image functioned as a self-evident argument for elite authority, because technical skill was essential to managing a complex system through a dangerous process of transition. Arab modernizers across a political spectrum similarly used mobility and the technology of speed not only as positive evocations of progress but also as a means for contesting who among the postcolonial elite had the right to guide it. As will be shown, aerospace took on symbolic value in Arab politics prior to 1967 both as the pinnacle achievement of the modernizing state and as representations of the systems that contended to define the Arab future. It was this symbolic value, as much as aircraft themselves, that *fida'iyin* sought to expropriate in the highly publicized hijackings that followed Israel's sweeping victory over the Arab states. The repeated association made between the piloting of aircraft and modernizers' authority over society gave meaning to hijackings as the usurpation of that authority. Even under the leftist prime minister 'Ali Sabri, Egypt's parliament had borrowed Rostow's metaphor in June 1965 by enacting a "Charter of Labor for the Take-Off Stage [*Mithaq al-'Amal fi Marhalat al-Intilaq*]."[12] Nasser had used this same terminology in his May Day Speech, and the General Workers' Union described itself at this "critically decisive stage of history" as forming "one line of soldiers in the struggle for production"

[11] Donald McCloskey quoted in Rodgers, *Age of Fracture*, 47.
[12] Posusney, *Labor and the State in Egypt*, 170.

behind Nasser's leadership.[13] The Egyptian government similarly publicized goals for heavy industry under its five-year plan using the imagery of "takeoff."[14] This association helps to explain the significance of air piracy as the 1960s political crime par excellence. Aerospace's cachet as a signifier of modernity and metaphor for social authority provides an answer to the question the PFLP posed in its own publication, *al-Hadaf*: "Why Were the Airplanes Seized?"[15] Tracking the cultural significance of the airplane across the twentieth century offers a useful way of understanding changes in the politics of modernization.

The loss of faith in the modernizing state many societies experienced correlated in the Arab Middle East with the crisis of Palestinian statelessness. *Fida'iyin* operations, and especially the dramatic hijackings the PFLP carried out, were products of this convergence. They embodied a reimagined concept of revolutionary change as decentralized and resulting from autonomous personal and group actions, rather than from the planning of the bureaucratic state. As the first part of this chapter shows, the meaning of aerospace shifted from a political symbol of integrated progress and the state's dominion over it to the site of an insurgency against illegitimate power. To illustrate this shift, the chapter sets up a contrast between the uses of aerospace as a symbol of state-led modernization prior to 1967 and those employed by the *fida'iyin* during what has been called the "golden age of hijacking." This stark difference reflects the changing course of ideas about modernization both regionally and globally from the late 1960s. It captures the collapse of the statist development strategies from the postwar years and the beginnings of an era characterized by a diminished economic role for governments, ideological fluidity, and devolution of state authority onto society. Although these operations targeted Israel and the United States, they were also radical acts in which individuals and militant cells rejected the authority of Arab governments and leaders, such as Nasser and King Husayn, who had staked their authority on the promise of development. The second part of this chapter then surveys the broader changes in Arab development politics following the crises of the late 1960s. As in previous chapters, the discussion approaches U.S.–Arab relations historically rather than on the basis of static cultural assumptions and interprets a global theme, in this case the decline of state-led modernization, within a Middle Eastern regional context.

The late 1960s *fida'iyin* hijackings took their meaning from the radical appropriation of the airplane as a familiar and conventional surrogate for

---

[13] Muhammad Khalid, '*Abd al-Nasir wa al-haraka al-niqabiya* (Cairo: Mu'assasat Dar al-Ta'awun lil-Tab' wa-al-Nashr, 1971), 74. See 'Izz al-Din Amin, *Ta'rikh al-Tabaqah al- 'Amila al-Misriya mundhu Nushu'iha hata sanat 1970* (Cairo: Dar al-Ghad al-'Arabi, 1987), 979.

[14] See the *al-Ahram* supplement on heavy industry, June 8, 1965, "*daqaqtu al-sa'a al-intilaq ila al-sina'at al-thaqilat*," p. 1.

[15] *Al-Hadaf*, September 12, 1970, vol. 2, no. 59, p. 7.

the idea of progress. As Di-Capua has argued, the airplane served as a powerful symbol not only of technological advancement, but also of social authority in the Arab Middle East from early in the twentieth century. "More than the train, the car, and the telephone," he writes, "the airplane represented a superior mastery of how nature works." It was "arguably the archetypal form of 'high technology.'"[16] Decades before these acts of air piracy, aerospace had assumed symbolic value in debates about modernization. The fact that it did demonstrates the participation of the Middle East in global trends linking technology and culture. Early in the century, Italian Futurists had first interpreted the speed of automobiles and airplanes as offering individuals avant-garde experiences of modernity, linking the "celebration of virility" with the "cult of the machine." Poet F. T. Marinetti, author of the 1909 Futurist manifesto, was born in Alexandria, Egypt, and published the novel *Mafarka le futuriste* about "an Arabian king with imperialist ambitions." As art historian Christine Poggi writes, "it is not coincidental that flight, a triumph of technology and a metaphor of freedom from a (feminine) earthbound condition," became a dominant Futurist motif.[17] Arabia was the place, Priya Satia argues, where the avant-garde experience of flight became institutionalized as the air control regime with which Britain policed its Iraq mandate. Colonial agents "perceived a basic congruence between the liberty of action of the aircraft and the desert warrior, both operating in empty, unmapped, magical spaces."[18] In other settings, flight became a metaphor combining heroic masculine achievement with societal advance. Scholar Katerina Clark associates flight with the "overall Soviet narrative of movement forward at a revolutionary pace." For this reason, "[p]rowess in aviation and long-distance motorcar races were features of Stalinist official culture."[19] In 1933, Italian dictator Benito Mussolini sent his aviation minister, General Italo Balbo, on a 6,100-mile, forty-eight-hour flight from Rome to the "Century of Progress" World's Fair in Chicago to celebrate a decade of fascist achievements.[20] Flight had assumed political value in the interwar clash of ideologies.

By the mid-twentieth century, aviation had transitioned from the domain of heroic individuals such as Charles Lindbergh to an era of public and private bureaucracies. Several of the officials who went on to direct U.S. policies developing the third world were products of the military bureaucracies that grew up around air power. These men included Rostow, fellow

[16] Di-Capua, "Common Skies, Divided Horizons," 917, 918.

[17] Christine Poggi, *Inventing Futurism: The Art and Politics of Artificial Optimism* (Princeton, NJ: Princeton University Press, 2009), x, 156, 159.

[18] Priya Satia, "The Defense of Inhumanity: Air Control and the British Idea of Arabia." *American Historical Review* 111 (February 2006): 29.

[19] Katerina Clark, *Moscow, The Fourth Rome: Stalinism, Cosmopolitanism, and the Evolution of Soviet Culture, 1931–1941* (Cambridge, MA: Harvard University Press, 2011), 258.

[20] Ira Katznelson, *Fear Itself: The New Deal and the Origins of Our Time* (New York: W. W. Norton, 2013), 58.

economist and U.S. ambassador to India John Kenneth Galbraith, and Defense Secretary Robert McNamara, the Vietnam war architect and later World Bank president. They had spent World War II selecting targets, "doing program analysis," and calculating the variables needed to efficiently manage and assess America's strategic bombing campaign.[21] In the superpower competition, the United States and the U.S.S.R. each presented achievements in aerospace technology as evidence for the superiority of its socioeconomic system.[22] Aerospace is conventionally associated with the American Century and the Cold War "prestige race" between the superpowers to develop jet engine and missile technologies, launch satellites, and send men into orbit and eventually land them on the moon.[23] John F. Kennedy's scientific advisor Jerome Wiesner said that the president embraced a lunar mission because he "became convinced that space was the symbol of the twentieth century."[24] Historian Jenifer Van Vleck argues that aviation mapped out "the entire world as the United States' appropriate sphere of influence" and notes "aviation's extraordinary cultural salience as a symbol and catalyst of both nationalism and globalism."[25] In civil aviation, Kennedy appointed Syrian-American Najeeb Halaby to direct the Federal Aviation Agency. Halaby had helped to test-pilot America's early jet aircraft and completed the first, continuous transcontinental jet flight. He later served as consultant to the government of Saudi Arabia on the establishment of Saudi Arabian Airlines.[26] Described as "a New Frontier glamour boy, quick-witted, photogenic and possessed of intriguing credentials," Halaby embodied the aerospace

[21] David Halberstam, *The Best and the Brightest* (New York: Random House, 1972), 227. See also Michael S. Sherry, *The Rise of American Air Power: The Creation of Armageddon* (New Haven, CT: Yale University Press, 1987).

[22] See Osgood, *Total Cold War*, 323–53; and Scott W. Palmer, *Dictatorship of the Air: Aviation Culture and the Fate of Modern Russia* (New York: Cambridge University Press, 2006), 279–80. On the association between aerospace technology and living standards in the superpowers' competition, see Elidor Mëhilli, "Technology and the Cold War," in *The Routledge Handbook of the Cold War*, ed. Artemy Kalinovsky and Craig Daigle (New York: Routledge, 2014), 292–304.

[23] Yanek Mieczkowski, *Eisenhower's Sputnik Moment: The Race for Space and World Prestige* (Ithaca, NY: Cornell University Press, 2013), 6. See also Walter A. McDougall, *The Heavens and the Earth: A Political History of the Space Age* (New York: Basic Books, 1985); John Krige et al., *NASA in the World: Fifty Years of International Collaboration in Space* (New York: Palgrave Macmillan, 2013); and David Meerman Scott and Richard Jurek, *Marketing the Moon: The Selling of the Apollo Lunar Program* (Cambridge: MIT Press, 2014).

[24] Quoted in Mieczkowski, *Eisenhower's Sputnik Moment*, 193.

[25] Jenifer Van Vleck, *Empire of the Air: Aviation and the American Ascendancy* (Cambridge, MA: Harvard University Press, 2013), 5–6.

[26] See U.S. Senate, Committee on Interstate and Foreign Commerce, Hearings, *Nominations – Federal Aviation Agency and Commerce Department*, 85th Cong., 1st Sess., February 21, 1961 (Washington, DC: Government Printing Office, 1961); and William Stadiem, *Jet Set: The People, the Planes, the Glamour, and the Romance in Aviation's Glory Years* (New York: Ballantine Books, 2014), 286.

mystique.[27] Aerospace demonstrated not only the state's technological mastery, but also the effectiveness of its formula for progress. In two senses – both as a technology embedded within managerial bureaucracies and as the product of modernizing ideologies – Cold War aerospace became associated with "systems." Rostow brilliantly combined these two senses when he used the mathematical coordination of flight to represent macroeconomic management and the anticommunist strategies that he argued would help poor countries to achieve "takeoff."

Elites in developing countries appropriated aerospace, like other aspects of the superpower competition, for their own political purposes. To promote Arab unity and economic decolonization, Arab League member states endorsed the creation of an Arab airline in 1961 that the State Department feared would practice "discrimination" against American and European carriers and contribute toward the "arabizing [of] foreign investments in existing Arab national carriers."[28] The League also approved an Arab Civil Aviation Council that governments would organize in the atmosphere of heightened Arab nationalism following the 1967 war.[29] Indeed, aviation became a potent symbol that third world leaders employed as an emblem of modernization. The Afienya Gliding School, established for Ghanaian president Kwame Nkrumah by German pilot Hanna Reitsch, writes historian Jean Allman, "became a public centerpiece of Nkrumah's modernization efforts, second only to the ongoing construction of the Akosombo Dam" on the Volta. In order to achieve what "other countries have taken three hundred years or more to achieve," Nkrumah insisted, development in former colonies must be "'jet propelled.'" Reitsch also founded a flying academy for Indian prime minister Jawaharlal Nehru.[30] In Tanzania, "[s]pace exploration was a frequent front-page news item," according to historian Laura Fair. President Julius Nyerere's National Development Corporation even featured the Apollo moon landing in publications promoting the African socialist regime's drive-in movie theater, just as Tanzanian youth performed "their own modernity" with "The Apollo," a popular dance celebrating astronaut Neil Armstrong's moonwalk.[31] As the leading twentieth-century

[27] Marilyn Bender and Selig Altschul, *The Chosen Instrument: Pan Am, Juan Trippe, The Rise and Fall of an American Entrepreneur* (New York: Simon and Schuster, 1982), 496.

[28] Strong to Jones, April 18, 1961, folder: 1961 Chron Inter-office Memorandum (folder 2 of 2), box 3, Bureau of Near Eastern and South Asian Affairs, Office of Near Eastern Affairs, Records of the Director, 1960–1963, RG 59, NARA.

[29] See Elashiq Saad Said, "The Arab Civil Aviation Council ACAC" (LL.M. thesis, McGill University, 1987).

[30] Jean Allman, "Phantoms of the Archive: Kwame Nkrumah, a Nazi Pilot Named Hanna, and the Contingencies of Post-colonial History Writing," *American Historical Review* 118 (February 2013): 111. Nkrumah quoted in Westad, *The Global Cold War*, 91.

[31] Laura Fair, "Drive-In Socialism: Debating Modernities and Development in Dar es Salaam, Tanzania," *American Historical Review* 118 (October 2013): 1087.

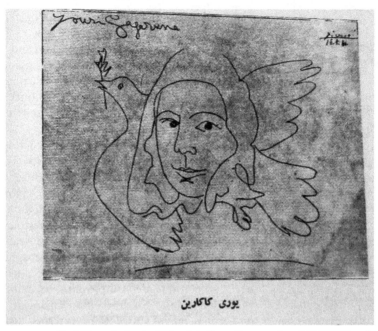

FIGURE 7.1. Yuri Gagarin in the "People's Court" transcript. *MMAUK*, vol. 16.

technology, aerospace carried metonymic value in the ubiquitous postwar debates over modernization and development.

Arab appropriation of the superpower aerospace race provided images and language for contesting the meaning of modernization with the United States. This was the case for conflicts covered in previous chapters of this book. For instance, aerospace appears as a symbol throughout the transcript of the Iraqi People's Court administered by Colonel Fadl 'Abbas al-Mahdawi (see Chapter 5). This appropriation is graphically illustrated by a pair of images that favorably contrasted what were portrayed as the Soviets' peaceful achievements in space against American capitalist militarism. The first is a sketch of cosmonaut Yuri Gagarin's face superimposed on a dove of peace (Figure 7.1). The sketch appears with an interview in which Mahdawi told Tass's Baghdad correspondent that Gagarin's spaceflight was evidence for the Soviets' "progressive system [*nizamihi al-taqaddumi*]" whose "singular genius" inspired those who were struggling against "the old, reactionary system [*al-nizam al-raj'i al-qadim*]."[32] The second is a cartoon of a U.S. bomber personified as a scowling, white military officer clutching a diminutive Asian soldier who is dropping bombs to create a firestorm (Figure 7.2). In

---

[32] *MMAUK* 16: lam ل

FIGURE 7.2. The American "system" in Asia. *MMAUK*, vol. 21.

an accompanying interview, Mahdawi hailed the cosmonauts' flights and advanced Soviet technology as illustrating "the superiority" of the socialist over the capitalist system. This peaceful use of technology he contrasted with the American crimes of killing hundreds of thousands of Japanese with atomic weapons at Hiroshima and Nagasaki.[33] In a letter to activists in the communist-front world disarmament movement, Mahdawi celebrated the Soviets' peaceful space program and condemned nuclear atmospheric testing by the Pentagon.[34] Like the United States and the U.S.S.R. each did in propaganda, the communist-aligned Mahdawi referenced advanced technologies to signify entire modernizing systems.

But it was not only proponents of the superpowers' mundane ideologies who invoked aerospace. The Egyptian Muslim Brotherhood also tapped into popular fascination with air and space travel both to emphasize the compatibility between Islam and technology and to define nonmaterialist standards for development. Opposed to secular regimes, the Brotherhood

---

[33] *MMAUK* 21: shin ش sad, ص
[34] *MMAUK* 22: ra' ر

دائل الصحف ان مخلوقـــا عجيب الشكل هبط بطبق طائر الى الأرض ..
فالأس - عندكم بترول .. عندكم مطاط .. عندكم مراكز استراتيجية كمان ؟؟ .. يبقى لازم نبجى نحرركم ؟؟

FIGURE 7.3. *Al-Da'wa*, September 21, 1954.

promoted Islam as a modernizing system and the idea of Islamic government. Rather than enhance the authority of any existing earthly power, it relied on extraterrestrials to explore the conjunction between speed and progress. A cartoon published in the September 21, 1954, issue of the Brotherhood's newspaper, *al-Da'wa*, provides a vivid example (Figure 7.3).[35] A little space-man with antennae protruding from his helmet confronts U.S. Secretary of State John Foster Dulles in an imposing government office with a large desk and gleaming floors. In the background, military officers plot American global strategy. The caption explains that a strange creature descended to earth in a "flying saucer." Dulles asks whether his world has petroleum, rubber, or valuable strategic positions. If so, then Americans might be obliged to "liberate" it. The spaceman's visit, like those of Sayyid Qutb and other Arab travelers, enables him to expose the falsity of American promises to democratize and develop the third world. In a Brotherhood tract titled *Risala min al-Mirrikh* [*Message from Mars*], extraterrestrials initiate contact by landing a "rocket ship" on earth, much like in H. G. Wells' *The War of the Worlds*. In this case, however, the spacecraft carries a "protest and a warning [*ihti-jaj wa indhar*]" that material achievements are worthless if a civilization pursues them at the expense of spiritual development.[36] Qutb himself made a point in *Ma'alim fi al-Tariq* of emphasizing that Islam did not preclude

---

[35] *Al-Da'wa*, September 21, 1954, p. 5.
[36] Ahmad Anas al-Hajaji, *Risala min al-Mirrikh* (Cairo: Al-Sharq al-Jadid lil-da'awa wa al-nashru wa al-tawzi', n.d.), 9.

the study of "chemistry, physics, astronomy," and other fields necessary for technological advance. But he argued that materialism alone leads to the disintegration of the family, reflected in the belief that woman's role was "merely to be attractive, sexy and flirtatious" and in her seeking a job such as a "stewardess" for an "air company." This sort of "civilization is 'backward' from the human point of view," Qutb proclaimed, "or 'jahili' in the Islamic terminology."[37]

Nasser associated aerospace with the Egyptian state's campaigns to modernize society and accelerate development of the Arab world as a whole. In an often-used phrase emphasizing the goal of industrialization at every level, Nasser insisted that Egypt needed "[t]o produce from the needle to the missile."[38] Rather than just weapons of war, Nasser told John J. McCloy, he regarded the acquisition of missiles and airplanes as attempts by Arabs to obtain modern scientific technology.[39] *Al-Ahram* editor Muhammad Hasanayn Haykal features tests of the missiles "al-Qahir" and "al-Zafir" alongside the Charter of National Action, the formulating of Arab Socialism, and construction of the Aswan High Dam as principal elements of Nasser's development agenda. Haykal even titled his book chapter about John Kennedy's administration "Heart of the Third World and the Surface of the Moon!"[40] Space technology became a symbol of Kennedy's attempt at reconciling with Egypt through a shared commitment to progress. Cairo governor Salah Dessouki wrote to William Polk to congratulate his friend on "the successful trip of Ranger VII," a "great contribution to man's knowledge of our universe."[41] Aerospace also held political value in Egypt's relations with the Soviet Union. Gagarin himself paid a visit to Egypt in February 1962, although Nasser also made sure to congratulate Kennedy on John Glenn's spaceflight.[42] That same year, a Russian journalist shared a joke with Nasser meant to poke fun at Khrushchev but also to contrast Soviet and American priorities for development. John Kennedy arrived in the first American rocket ship to reach the moon, it began. JFK told a moon man whom he met there that the lunar surface would make a great site for a "cosmic missile base." The moon man replied: "But sir, a rocket landed a few days ago and

37 Qutb, *Milestones*, 98, 112. In the original Arabic, Qutb uses the word "*mudifa* [hostess]." See Qutb, *Ma'alim fi al-Tariq*, 123.

38 M. Riad El-Ghonemy, "An Assessment of Egypt's Development Strategy, 1952–1970," in *Rethinking Nasserism*, 259.

39 Haykal, *Sanawat al-Ghalayan*, 715.

40 Ibid., 515, 601–02.

41 Dessouki to Polk, August 3, 1964, folder: W. R. Polk – Chron July–Dec. 1964, box 28, Policy Planning Council (1961–1969) Planning and Coordination Staff (1970–1973), Subject Files, 1963–1973, Lot 70 D 199, 72 D 124, 73 D 363, RG 59, NARA.

42 Hawley to Parents, February 6, 1962, HAW 12/1/5, DHP. See Nasser, *Majmu'at khutab wa tasrihat wa bayanat*, 4: 4.

a short, fat guy with a ruddy complexion and big bald head got out; he saw the surface and said, 'Plant it – all of it – with corn!' "[43]

On the eve of the June War, aerospace could still serve as the basis for envisioning human advancement. Brookings expert Wilfred Owen delivered the talk "Transportation, Communications, and the Future" for a centennial anniversary event held at the American University of Beirut (AUB) in May 1967. Owen began by imagining a "clairvoyant professor" from 1866 describing to his incredulous audience the wondrous world of a century later:

"In the next hundred years," the nineteenth century prophet would have begun, "I foresee south of AUB, along the shore of the Mediterranean, a jumble of concrete roadways called the Beirut International Airport, where every morning large numbers of men, women, and children, after breakfasting on scrambled eggs and sausages six miles above Iran, will swoop down over the Lebanese Range and come to a screaming halt just five hours after leaving Karachi." ... "By the mid-1960s," he would go on, "man will be able to fly around the Earth 18 times in one day and stroll in space en route at 300 miles a minute."

Owen's speech celebrated how the use of technology to conquer distance enabled man to achieve ever-higher levels of economic growth and civilization. His account spanned the "extension of jet services" to the Arab Middle East, road building in Thailand, railroads in India, and transport networks in South America. Owen acknowledged, however, that "despite all these wonders of transport and communications, two thirds of the world's people are bogged down right where they were 2,000 years ago." The "incredible thing about the modern world is that it turned out modern for a few," he admitted, "but is still the same old place for everyone else." He looked to developed countries such as the United States mainly for negative lessons about "correcting past mistakes," while simultaneously calling for a "global fund" to finance massive transportation and communication projects.[44] Ambivalently, Owen reasserted the optimistic association between spatial and temporal progress at the same time that he delivered the eulogy for Cold War modernization.

The events of June 5, 1967, eliminated any political value that aerospace may have held for Egypt and other Arab countries as a modern symbol of the state's authority. Beginning after 7:00 AM, Israel launched an air attack that destroyed more than half of Egypt's air force, more than 200 planes, in about half an hour. A second wave, lasting little more than an hour and a half, claimed more than 100 additional Egyptian aircraft, including dozens of Soviet-made MiG fighters and Topolev-16 and Ilyushin-28 bombers.

---

[43] Ibid., 4: 225.
[44] Wilfred Owen, "Transportation, Communications, and the Future," [Second Lecture on Transportation Held on May 4, 1967, in the West Hall Auditorium, American University of Beirut], *Centennial of the American University of Beirut Symposium Proceedings* (May 1967): 25–32.

Syria likewise lost two-thirds of its air force, which on April 7 had already suffered the downing of six MiG fighters by the Israelis, two of them in the skies above Damascus.[45] Israel's airstrikes set the stage for a sweeping military victory over the subsequent five days, in which the forfeiture of territories by Egypt, Jordan, and Syria compounded a loss of political legitimacy on the part of Arab governments.

The attack presented Nasser and other Arab leaders not only with a crushing military defeat, but also with a political crisis. One response to the debacle was the "Big Lie," the false reports broadcast over Radio Cairo and by other Arab news outlets that American and British pilots were participating in the attacks, and implying that it was the involvement of Western aviators that accounted for their devastating success. While these reports may initially have been part of an Egyptian bid to elicit Soviet intervention, they also served as an attempted rebuttal of the conclusion that Israel's air attack had been the victory of an advanced people over an underdeveloped society.[46] In contrast to the Kennedy era, the association between aerospace and modernity now divided Egypt from the United States, because Cairo had severed relations at the outbreak of war and Washington demanded a public retraction of the "Big Lie" as a condition for restoring them. In meetings held with State Department envoy Don Bergus and unofficial emissary James E. Birdsall, Nasser disclaimed responsibility for the "Big Lie" and blamed King Husayn as the source of the erroneous reports. Nasser repeated this explanation in a March 1968 interview published in *Look* magazine.[47] But privately Nasser admitted that Egyptians had been "soundly defeated" by Israel, Bergus reported, because they "did not know how to use Soviet weapons."[48] More than a military loss, the June War appeared to render a highly disparaging verdict about the success of Nasser's campaign to modernize Egypt and the Arab world.

---

[45] See Michael B. Oren, *Six Days of War: June 1967 and the Making of the Modern Middle East* (New York: Oxford University Press, 2002), 170–76, 195; and Moshe Gat, "On the Use of Air Power and Its Effect on the Outbreak of the Six Day War," *Journal of Military History* 68 (October 2004): 1209.

[46] Oren, *Six Days of War*, 217. See also Elie Podeh, "The 'Big Lie': Inventing the Myth of British-US Involvement in the 1967 War," *Review of International Affairs* 2 (Autumn 2002): 1–23; and Spencer Mawby, "The 'Big Lie' and the 'Great Betrayal': Explaining the British Collapse in Aden," in *The Cold War in the Middle East: Regional Conflict and the Superpowers, 1967–1973*, ed. Nigel J. Ashton (New York: Routledge, 2007), 167–68. While Podeh argues that Cairo's "Big Lie" became a myth that fulfilled psychological needs in Egypt and other Arab societies, Mawby interprets the branding of Egypt's false wartime reports as "the Big Lie" as part of a counterpropaganda campaign intended to discredit Nasser.

[47] "Nasser Talks," *Look* 32 no. 6 (March 19, 1968): 63.

[48] Cairo (Bergus) to State, December 10, 1967, folder: United Arab Republic, Vol. VI, Memos [2 of 2] 8/67–7/68, box 160, Country Files, NSF, LBJL. See also Cairo (Bergus) to State, January 6, 1968, ibid.

The defeat of the Arab states energized Palestinian militant activity in the Israeli-occupied territories and neighboring Arab countries. Historian Paul Thomas Chamberlin places the *fida'iyin* in a global context of revolutionary guerrilla movements, emphasizing the inspiration and support that Palestinians drew from North Vietnam and communist China, as well as their adoption of Mao Zedong's military doctrine.[49] But the *fida'iyin* style, including wearing of the *kufiyya* headscarf, hearkened back to the 1936–39 Arab Revolt, a previous instance when the struggle against Zionism had led elements of Palestinian society to challenge the existing Arab leadership.[50] According to historian Yezid Sayigh, Palestinian groups engaged in a "discursive contest" to define "revolution [*thawra*]" by reinterpreting the legacy of the Arab Revolt using references to other anticolonial struggles.[51] Global revolutionary movements were important to this discourse, even though the guerrilla tactics that were effective elsewhere stood little chance of success against Israel. Intellectuals such as Haykal and Sadik al-'Azm, who duly credited *fida'iyin* courage, nevertheless noted the impossibility of waging a "People's War" to liberate Arab territories. "The Arab struggle for the liberation of Palestine must develop its particular methods," al-'Azm wrote, "because the methods of the Vietnamese struggle are not applicable as a whole and in detail to our battle with the enemy."[52] A 1968 U.S. intelligence estimate agreed: "Fedayeen activity is unlikely to drive the Israelis from the occupied areas or endanger the existence of Israel itself."[53]

The *fida'iyin* movement represented a new stage in the regional struggle for authority within Arab societies, in which guerrilla groups sought prestige through *muzayada*, a competitive "bidding-up" of increasingly radical acts. As its opening strike against Israel in December 1967, the PFLP, a merger of Dr. George Habash's Arab Nationalists Movement with Ahmad Jibril's Palestinian Liberation Front, Abtal al-'Awda [Heroes of the Return] and others, attacked Lod Airport. Yasir 'Arafat's Fatah established its reputation by withstanding an Israeli attack on March 21, 1968, at the village of al-Karama on the east bank of the Jordan. For the PFLP, which had unhappily withdrawn its forces from al-Karama just prior to 'Arafat's "victory," airline hijackings carried out by the Special Apparatus organized by guerrilla

[49] Chamberlin, *The Global Offensive*. The influence of Chinese revolutionary doctrine may have been greater in the Dhufar revolution than among the Palestinian *fida'iyin*. See Abdel Razzaq Takriti, *Monsoon Revolution: Republicans, Sultans, and Empires in Oman, 1965–1976* (Oxford: Oxford University Press, 2013).

[50] See Weldon C. Matthews, *Confronting an Empire, Constructing a Nation: Arab Nationalists and Popular Politics in Mandate Palestine* (New York: Palgrave Macmillan, 2006), 233–63.

[51] See Sayigh, *Armed Struggle and the Search for State*, 195–96.

[52] Sadik al-'Azm, *Self-Criticism After the Defeat*, 113. See also the translations of Haykal's columns "Lessons for Arab Struggle … From Vietnam," n.d., FCO 39/247; and "Of Hope and Death," August 22, 1968, FCO 39/249, BNA.

[53] National Intelligence Estimate, "Terrorism and Internal Security in Israel and Jordan," April 18, 1968, folder: 30. Middle East, box 6, National Intelligence Estimates, NSF, LBJL.

leaders Wadi' Haddad and Hani al-Hindi served as a strategy for outbidding Fatah and Arab political leaders.[54] The perpetrators of these hijackings appropriated aviation as a modern symbol, as had occurred previously in regional politics. But rather than bolster state authority or validate a particular developmental system, they aimed to subvert that authority as well as the regional and global structures that the PFLP blamed for continued Palestinian dispossession.

The distinction between launching small-scale guerrilla actions and pursuing state development programs was apparent in the PFLP's conflicts not only with Nasser's regime, but also with established Arab communist parties. The PFLP helped to birth a "New Arab Left" with the promulgation of its August 1968 Basic Political Report. "National salvation rejects whatever is existing and pushes forward on a new course," proclaimed the Report, "the course of transforming the resistance movement into an organized mass movement." Its vanguard will be "equipped with political consciousness and the ideology of the proletariat, hostile to Israel and imperialism and its allies throughout the Arab land."[55] The Front sought to contrast its own interpretation of "Marxism as a revolutionary theoretical weapon" with the ways in which Arab communist parties "understood the theory in a rigid and fossilized manner." According to the PFLP manifesto *A Strategy for the Liberation of Palestine*, Arab communists proved unable "to deduce from [Marxism] a clear view of the battle and a sound strategy for its leadership."[56] Commitment to liberating Palestine became a divisive issue after 1967 within Arab communist party organizations whose leaders operated within national political contexts. When the venerable communist Khalid Bakdash presented economic and agricultural goals for building socialism within Syria to the Third Party Congress in 1969, he clashed with Politburo members demanding armed resistance against Israel.[57] The PFLP condemned Arab communists for hewing to the Soviet line of supporting

---

[54] See CIA, Directorate of Intelligence, Special Report Weekly Review, "The Arab Nationalists Movement," January 19, 1968, folder: United Arab Republic, Vol. VI, Memos [1 of 2] 8/67-7/68, box 160, NSF, LBJL; and CIA, Directorate of Intelligence, Special Report Weekly Review, "Anti-Israeli Arab Terrorist Organizations," [pp. 6–7] October 4, 1968, folder: United Arab Republic, Vol. VII, Memos 6/68-1/69, box 161, NSF, LBJL. The PFLP also included "a group of pro-Nasir exiles from Jordan led by former officer Ahmad Za'rur." See Sayigh, *Armed Struggle and the Search for State*, 165–67, 178, 213; and Riad El-Rayyes and Dunia Nahas, *Guerrillas for Palestine* (New York: St. Martin's Press, 1976), 36–37. On the evolution of the Arab Nationalists Movement, see Basil Raouf al-Kubaisi, "The Arab Nationalists Movement, 1951–1971: From Pressure Group to Socialist Party" (PhD Diss., American University, 1971). On al-Karama, see Chamberlin, *The Global Offensive*, 44–49.

[55] Tareq Y. Ismael, *The Arab Left* (Syracuse, NY: Syracuse University Press, 1976), 111, [appendix D] 177.

[56] Popular Front for the Liberation of Palestine, *A Strategy for the Liberation of Palestine* (Amman: PFLP Information Department, 1969), 93, 96.

[57] See Ismael and Ismael, *The Communist Movement in Syria and Lebanon*, 156–61.

peaceful resolution of the conflict between Israel and the Arab states on the basis of UN Security Council Resolution 242. Armed resistance divided those who regarded Marxism as a fighting doctrine that legitimized class warfare and the struggle for Palestine from those committed to it as a historical theory and developmental system. Palestinian communist Na'im Ashhab, a member of the generation that had organized the 1950s peace movement, recalls how in 1969–1970 "armed action and the party's participation in the Palestinian resistance" split the Jordanian Communist Party.[58]

Hijackings enabled the PFLP to distinguish itself most of all from Fatah. Sayigh contrasts Fatah's statist ambitions with the PFLP's initially pan-Arab and later class-based revolutionary ideology.[59] Assaults on planes and airports not only advanced the PFLP's revolutionary class-struggle, as opposed to state-building, agenda, but also echoed the actions that leftist Palestinian labor organizations had carried out against transport and other infrastructure during the 1936–39 revolt.[60] "Our action was a symbol," Habash declared in a defense of hijackings. He placed hijacking alongside PFLP attacks on the Trans-Arabian Pipeline and the Israeli-chartered oil tanker *Coral Sea* to illustrate his group's commitment to attacking Israeli interests "wherever they may be."[61] Female PFLP guerrilla Leila Khaled (Figure 7.4), who participated in the 1969 hijacking of a TWA flight out of Rome and the attempted seizure the following year of an El-Al aircraft just after it left Amsterdam, also refers explicitly to the "symbolic meaning" of hijackings. Khaled justifies revolutionary action against the West in an indictment that lists the aerospace and other advanced technologies transferred to Israel by the imperial powers. France "supplied Israel with Mystères, Super Mystères and Mirages," she writes, as well as with "the scientific know-how and material to manufacture the atomic bomb at Dimova [Dimona]." America "perpetuated Britain's crimes" by providing Israel "with Hawk missiles, Skyhawk and Phantom fighter-bombers." Khaled even critically cites candidate Richard Nixon's statement during the 1968 presidential campaign summing up his commitment to maintain Israel's military superiority over its Arab enemies: "'if it takes Phantom jets, then they shall have Phantom jets.'"[62]

---

[58] Na'im Ashhab, *Durub al-Alam, Durub al-Amal: Dirah Dhatiyah* (Ramallah: Dar al-Tanwir lil-Nashr wa-al-Tarjamah wa-al-Tawzi', 2009), 225.

[59] Sayigh, *Armed Struggle and the Search for State*, 217.

[60] See Zachary Lockman, *Comrades and Enemies: Arab and Jewish Workers in Palestine, 1906–1948* (Berkeley: University of California Press, 1996), 240–65.

[61] *Palestine Lives: Interviews with Leaders of the Resistance* (Beirut: Palestine Research Center and Kuwaiti Teachers Association, 1973), 79–80. On the PFLP's attack on Tapline, see Asher Kaufman, "Between Permeable and Sealed Borders: The Trans-Arabian Pipeline and the Arab-Israeli Conflict," *International Journal of Middle East Studies* 46 (February 2014): 105–06.

[62] Khaled, *My People Shall Live*, 127, 128, 130, 133. See also "Wara'a masrahiya al-fantum," *al-Hadaf*, March 28, 1970, vol. 1, no. 35, pp. 16–17.

FIGURE 7.4. Leila Khaled. © Bettmann/Corbis.

Khaled's memoir *My People Shall Live* offers the fullest available explanation of the significance attached to hijackings by one of the Palestinian guerrillas who carried them out. Her account reflects anti-Zionism as well as the commitment to class struggle throughout the Arab world that characterized the PFLP's late 1960s ideology. Born in Haifa, Khaled fled to Lebanon with her family when the Haganah attacked the city in April 1948. She joined Habash's Arab Nationalists Movement as a teenager, attended the American University of Beirut, and taught in Kuwait. Her radicalization into an operative of the PFLP's Special Apparatus combined anti-Zionism and class struggle with her determination to challenge gender norms. An admirer of 'Izz al-Din al-Qassam, "who organized the first working class and peasant revolution in the Arab homeland" during the 1930s, Khaled overcame sexual oppression by pursuing her education, challenging Kuwait's restrictions on women, and undergoing military training. Her account of the 1969 TWA hijacking emphasizes her technical knowledge of flight, which surprised the crew given that she was female. Sparring with the flight engineer about the aircraft's remaining fuel level, Khaled boasted: "I knew just as much as he did about the Boeing." Khaled portrays the hijacking as a reversal of gender roles when she recalls "the moment I entered the pilot's cabin and how he shivered before me." Her career as a hijacker even required the attractive Khaled to have her appearance surgically altered in what she called a "'face twisting'" to render her unrecognizable. Khaled interpreted her actions as an indictment of Arab Socialism. "Nasserism was becoming inward-looking, repressive, managerial," wrote Khaled. "Economically bourgeoi-sie, it became a spent force in historical terms," she declared. Nasser was "turning Egypt into a 'paradise' of colonels, managers, clerks." With Israel's attack, which took less than three hours to "pulverise the Egyptian air force on the ground," she argued, a "whole era ended; a social class had failed to safeguard Arab interests through stupidity; Arab soldiery lost its moral cred-ibility"; and "Nasserism, if not Nasser, was dead."[63] Only her own personal audacity, and not the failed policies of Arab leaders, enabled her to see Haifa again from the flight deck of the hijacked TWA plane.

Khaled's El-Al hijacking, along with four others that the PFLP carried out in early September 1970, set the stage for a bloody showdown between the *fida'iyin* operating in Jordan and King Husayn's government. Ghassan Kanafani, editor of the PFLP journal, *al-Hadaf*, called it a "'hijacking carni-val'" that was an attack on the "world nervous system."[64] The PFLP tried not only to assassinate Husayn, but also to discredit the Hashemite Arab moder-nity that the king had attempted to burnish using his own public image as a pilot. With the September hijackings, the PFLP signaled its decisive break with Nasser, who had accepted U.S. Secretary of State William Rogers' pro-posal for a ceasefire in the War of Attrition with Israel. With no provision for Palestinian liberation, Kanafani condemned Rogers' ceasefire as offering only "the terms of surrender."[65] Khaled's operation failed when Israeli agents killed her accomplice and she was arrested by the British. Associates who failed to board the same El Al flight hijacked a Pan Am plane to Cairo. PFLP commandos nevertheless landed a SwissAir and a TWA airliner at Dawson's Field near Zarqa, Jordan on September 6 and then hijacked a BOAC plane a few days later in order to bargain for Khaled's freedom. The PFLP destroyed the aircraft, but eventually released the passengers in exchange for Khaled and other Palestinians imprisoned in Europe.[66]

PFLP statements went beyond attempts at merely justifying the hijack-ings in what amounted to a full-scale attack on the U.S. role in the region. Rostow had described the universal stages of development in which

---

[63] Khaled, *My People Shall Live*, 22–23, 58, 74, 80, 90, 136, 147, 180.

[64] Quoted in Sayigh, *Armed Struggle and the Search for State*, 257.

[65] *Al-Hadaf*, August 8, 1970, vol. 2, no. 54, p. 4. See Daigle, *The Limits of Détente*, 120.

[66] See Sayigh, *Armed Struggle and the Search for State*, 257; Nigel Ashton, *King Hussein of Jordan: A Political Life* (New Haven, CT: Yale University Press, 2008), 144–57; Chamberlin, *The Global Offensive*, 108–41; and Bird, *Crossing Mandelbaum Gate*, chapter 7.

American aid to developing countries would culminate in their achievement of self-sustaining growth. He invoked the takeoff of a jet airplane to represent this process. In the article "Why Were the Airplanes Seized?" *al-Hadaf* portrayed the hijackings as the first in a series of defined stages in the Palestinian armed struggle, which it described as "propagating the revolutionary environment." The article also identified the "air transport system [*nizam al-naql al-jawwi*]" as a legitimate target because it was tied to "industrial, business, and security monopolies" and constituted "a capitalist economic instrument" for "stealing the people's resources and reaping the fruits of their toil." Most of all, by supplying Israel with material resources in the forms of money and destructive weapons, the United States had perpetuated the dispossession and impoverishment of thousands of Arab refugees. American policies had left Palestinians "abandoned [*qabi'a*]" in refugee camps for more than twenty-two years, living "in the shadow of hunger and sickness [*fi zill al-ju' wa al-marad*]." The hijackings were an antisystemic assault on the oppressive structures held in place by U.S. policy. In a scathing indictment of postwar American influence, and a reversal of Rostow's metaphor, the Front hijacked aircraft to draw world attention to deliberate U.S. underdevelopment of the Arab Middle East.[67]

On September 17, Husayn's forces attacked the *fida'iyin*, shelling the refugee camps in which they were based. Sayigh estimates that up to 5,000 were killed in the fighting, many of them Palestinian civilians.[68] The hijackings had provoked a violent confrontation in which state power was employed not to develop society but negatively for the purposes of eradicating the guerrillas and punishing the refugee communities that harbored them. According to the PFLP, the U.S. Agency for International Development had established a "direct link" with Jordanian security forces in June 1970 "for training and giving advice as a consultant." Rather than an example of nonrevolutionary Arab modernity, it argued, this relationship had made Jordan into the "police station for imperialism."[69] Black September is usually interpreted as securing Husayn's survival and eventually pushing the *fida'iyin* groups into Lebanon. But just as importantly it demonstrated that the era was over when Arab leaders could optimistically promote their policies as advancing a historical process of modernization. On September 27, King Husayn piloted a Royal Jordanian Airlines Caravelle to Cairo, where Nasser negotiated a ceasefire between Husayn and the *fida'iyin*.[70] Nasser died unexpectedly of

[67] *Al-Hadaf*, September 12, 1970, vol. 2, no. 59, pp. 4, 7.

[68] Sayigh, *Armed Struggle and the Search for State*, 267.

[69] Popular Front for the Liberation of Palestine, *Tasks of the New Stage*, ["Filmed by the University of Chicago Photoduplication Laboratory for the Middle East Microfilm Project at the Center for Research Libraries," 1994], pp. 15, 95.

[70] See Peter Snow and David Phillips, *The Arab Hijack War: The True Story of 25 Days in September 1970* (New York: Ballantine Books, 1971), 160.

a heart attack the next day at the age of fifty-two. The ceasefire he negotiated in Jordan's civil war was only temporary. The monarchy fought its
culminating battles against the *fida'iyin* in northwest Transjordan, where
the United States had previously invested in development projects including
the East Ghor Canal. Husayn's army reclaimed Irbid in March 1971 and
then won its final victory at the town of 'Ajlun in July. A few months later,
Palestinian militants assassinated Jordan's prime minister, Wasfi al-Tall, in
Cairo as revenge for Black September.[71] Al-Tall had embodied Husayn's
ambition to promote nonrevolutionary economic development in partnership with the United States as an alternative to Nasser. On the occasion of
al-Tall's earlier appointment as prime minister in 1962, Jordan's government had appealed to the Kennedy administration for help in developing
the Hashemite kingdom. But just as JFK's soaring rhetoric assumed ironic
overtones for Americans looking back from their bitter Vietnam experience,
Black September vitiated Husayn's dream of Hashemite-led development
once represented by al-Tall and condensed into the bold slogan: "the New
Frontier has reached Jordan."

The PFLP's hijackings were one regional manifestation of the disillusionment with state-led modernization that also affected the United States and
many other societies. Interpreting hijackings solely as the tactic of Middle
Eastern or Islamic terrorists is a fallacy based on the recent experience of
the 9/11 attacks. The phenomenon is better seen as originating in the historical circumstances of the 1960s, when marginalized peoples began revolting
against the ideas and leaders that had failed to deliver on postwar promises of freedom and prosperity. Indeed, the insurgency against Cold War
liberalism on the part of certain African American activists paralleled that
by Palestinian militants against Nasser's pan-Arab nationalism. In a peti-
tion presented in Cairo at the 1964 meeting of the Organization of African
Unity (OAU), Malcolm X cited Supreme Court Justice Arthur J. Goldberg's
recent call for the United Nations to address human rights abuses against
Soviet Jews to argue that the United Nations should investigate African
American oppression. The Black Muslim leader criticized U.S. support
for Israel and referred to Washington, DC, as an "Israeli capital." While
Malcolm X condemned President Johnson's Civil Rights Act as a "fraud,"
however, the Egyptian government declined to admit Malcolm X to the
meeting as an official observer and Nasser made a point of praising the Act
in his address to the OAU delegates.[72] Melani McAlister has noted not only

---

[71] See Sayigh, *Armed Struggle and the Search for State*, 278–81; and Bird, *Crossing Mandelbaum Gate*, 281.

[72] Cameron to Read, "Activities of Malcolm X in the UAR," August 10, 1964, and attachments, Folder: Political Affairs & Rel. UAR 1964 UAR – United States, box 3, NEA Bureau
Office of the Country Director for the United Arab Republic (NEA/UAR) Records Relating
to United Arab Republic Affairs, 1961–1966, RG 59, NARA.

the pro-Palestinian responses to the 1967 Arab–Israeli War on the part of the Student Non-violent Coordinating Committee, but also the importance of the Middle East conflict for "constructing transnational definitions of blackness." Relinquishing a historic biblical association with the Israelites, she explains, some African Americans came to identify with Palestinian nationalism as they rejected liberal civil rights policies.[73] As with Malcolm X, condemnation of LBJ's civil rights policy went hand in hand with criticism of his pro-Israel diplomacy. Judy Tzu-Chun Wu has described Black Panther Eldridge Cleaver's Anti-Imperialist Delegation, which consisted of radical critics of the Vietnam War and other American policies toward the third world. Although not a hijacking, Cleaver's 1970 tour arranged flights to destinations in countries that were Cold War enemies of the United States and were therefore officially off-limits to its citizens, including North Korea, North Vietnam, and communist China. Delegates condemned U.S. policy without necessarily challenging its underlying premise regarding linear progress engineered by elites according to a developmental system. Their accounts advanced the idea that "socialist Asia was ahead of Western development," Wu explains, and "developed a critique of imperialist worldviews by inverting assumptions regarding modernization and civilization."[74]

Rather than an expression of tendencies particular to the Middle East, hijacking belonged to that moment in global history when postwar optimism began its initial descent. One-hundred fifty-nine commercial flights were hijacked in U.S. air space between 1961 and 1972. As legal expert Nancy Douglas Joyner observes, "the United States was most heavily affected by the 'hijacking disease' of the 1960's."[75] In the early 1960s, most skyjackers wanted to fly to Cuba, but motivations diversified as the number of incidents surged at the end of the decade.[76] Ex-Black Panther William Lee Brent, who hijacked a flight to Havana in 1969 two months before Khaled seized TWA flight 840, decided that hijacking would be the easiest way to seek exile in Castro's Cuba. "Twenty-seven other people had pulled it off that year alone," Brent wrote later, "and it was only mid-June."[77] According to government statistics, 134 hijackings of U.S.-registered aircraft occurred between 1968 and 1972, during what journalist Brendan I. Koerner calls "the golden age of hijackings." Koerner focuses on African American Vietnam veteran Willie Roger Holder and his female accomplice, Catherine Kerkow, whose 1972 hijacking of Western Airlines Flight 701 was part of a plan to free pro–Black

73 McAlister, *Epic Encounters*, 110–15 [quotation on p. 115].

74 See Judy Tzu-Chun Wu, *Radicals on the Road: Internationalism, Orientalism, and Feminism during the Vietnam Era* (Ithaca, NY: Cornell University Press, 2013), 147.

75 Nancy Douglas Joyner, *Aerial Hijacking as an International Crime* (Dobbs Ferry, NY: Oceana Publications, 1974), 153.

76 See Teishan A. Latner, "Take Me to Havana! Airline Hijacking, U.S.–Cuba Relations, and Political Protest in Late Sixties' America," *Diplomatic History* 39 (January 2015): 16–44.

77 William Lee Brent, *Long Time Gone* (New York: Random House/Times Books, 1996), 132.

Panther activist Angela Davis from prison and then fly to North Vietnam. The pair eventually landed in Algiers, where they joined Cleaver and other exiled Panthers who were themselves guests of Algerian president Houari Boumédiène. Cleaver's deputy told a reporter that ransom money paid to the hijacking duo would be devoted "'to the Palestinian Liberation Forces ... the Afro-American struggle'" and "'to fight Zionism or American imperialism.'" The "epidemic" of skyjackings occurred "as the last vestiges of 1960s idealism were being extinguished," Koerner explains. Because flight "retained an aura of wonder and privilege" and aircraft were "themselves marvels of technological might," air piracy offered a "spectacular way for the marginalized to feel the rush of power."[78]

Given aviation's association with modernity and privilege, hijacking signaled a repudiation of postwar elites and the concept of modernization as an integrated process that required their authority to guide it. As historian David Steigerwald notes, Americans who criticized their society as "overly bureaucratic" and "dominated by technocrats" during the late 1960s "decried 'the system.'"[79] In *Soul on Ice* (1968), Cleaver himself wrote: "We live today in a system that is in the last stages of the protracted process of breaking up on a worldwide basis."[80] The meaning of hijackings can be fully appreciated only as part of the more comprehensive break with postwar structuralism that Rodgers describes as the "age of fracture" in the United States and that Kassab labels the second *Nahda* in Arab thought. In the Arab world, the shift held regional consequences based on the ways in which elites had pursued modernization between the end of World War II and the crises of the late 1960s. If hijacking was a revolt against power, then it signified a disruption in the prevailing intellectual, political, and economic assumptions that had helped to create the postcolonial Middle East. Truisms of third world development, such as the linear movement of history and the capacity of state development projects to remake society, were challenged from opposite ends of the spectrum not only by revolutionary, but also by neoliberal attacks. Leaders in Iraq, Syria, and Egypt responded by compromising their earlier ideological rigidity and seeking alliances with former political enemies. Changing course meant, most of all, an assault on Nasser's pan-Arab nationalism and other modernizing ideologies. These had been described as "systems" by intellectuals who imagined societies' development over time as movement through space.

---

[78] Brendan I. Koerner, *The Skies Belong to Us: Love and Terror in the Golden Age of Hijacking* (New York: Crown Publishers, 2013), 8–9, 175. For Federal Aviation Administration statistics on hijackings, see https://www.ncjrs.gov/pdffiles1/Digitization/28885NCJRS.pdf, accessed September 23, 2015.

[79] David Steigerwald, *The Sixties and the End of Modern America* (New York: St. Martin's Press, 1995), 164.

[80] Eldridge Cleaver, *Soul on Ice* (New York: Dell Publishing, 1968), 147.

The idea of modernizing ideologies as closed, antagonistic systems had emerged as Arab leaders transformed competing anticolonial movements from the interwar period using Cold War terminology. This totalizing concept of modernization had narrowed possibilities for political compromise and intensified battles over who would control postcolonial Arab states. In response to the late 1960s crises and just as the superpowers began pursuing détente, however, Arab elites exchanged their belief in fixed modernizing systems for experiments in political improvisation. In Iraq, where Ba'thists had arrested and killed thousands of communists, a limited reconciliation followed the seizure of power in July 1968 by a new Ba'thist regime led by Ahmad Hasan al-Bakr. As historian Brandon Wolfe-Hunnicutt writes, "the 'Bakr Ba'thists' were nothing if not ideologically flexible and pragmatic in their approach to power politics" compared to the Ba'th that had plotted the 1963 coup.[81] Ba'thists pursued a rapprochement with the communists based on a commitment to nationalizing the Iraq Petroleum Company and seeking Soviet help in developing and marketing Iraqi oil. Ba'thist figures were invited to join the communist-front peace movement, and two members of the Iraqi Communist Party-Central Committee received cabinet portfolios. In 1972, the Ba'thist Iraqi government and the Soviet Union signed a treaty of friendship, an agreement that would have been unimaginable a decade earlier.[82]

When air force officer Hafiz al-Asad seized power in Syria in 1970, he substituted economic pluralism for the socialist and centrally planned development policies of the preceding radical Ba'th regime in Damascus. Asad's corrective movement, writes historian Raymond A. Hinnebusch, involved a "détente with the Damascene bourgeoisie based on a limited liberalization of trade."[83] Journalist Patrick Seale explains that the 'Alawite Asad "knew he needed allies in the urban middle class," and "so, breaking with his political past, he tried to win over the shopkeepers, businessmen and artisans of the towns as well as the many citizens who had fled Syria since 1963, mainly Sunnis from the former leading families."[84] This compromise across lines of sect and class to foster a mixed economy was reflected in the term *ta'addudiyya* [pluralism]. Asad retreated from the ideological conflict that had previously driven Syrian Ba'thists to unite with Nasser against their communist rivals and to the formation of the United Arab Republic.

In Egypt, Nasser had followed up attempts at ideological rectification within the Arab Socialist Union with a crackdown on the Muslim

---

[81] Wolfe-Hunnicutt, "The End of the Concessionary Regime," 212.

[82] See Ismael, *The Rise and Fall of the Communist Party of Iraq*, 166–69.

[83] Raymond A. Hinnebusch, "The Political Economy of Economic Liberalization in Syria," *International Journal of Middle East Studies* 27 (August 1995): 306. See also Matthew Gray, "The Political Economy of Tourism in Syria: State, Society and Economic Liberalization," *Arab Studies Quarterly* 19 (Spring 1997): 57–73.

[84] Seale, *Asad of Syria*, 171.

Brotherhood and what were described as feudal elements in the country-side. After becoming president following Nasser's death, however, Anwar Sadat implemented a pause in Nasser's policies before reconciling with students and other Brotherhood elements. Sadat released Brotherhood members from prison over a four-year period, invited exiles to return from Saudi Arabia, and permitted publication of the group's previously banned newspaper, *al-Daʿwa*.[85] With his eventual policy of opening Egypt's economy to private investment [*al-infitah*], Sadat largely dismantled Nasser's Arab Socialism while at the same time presiding over the expansion of subsidies to the poor and other welfare policies. Labor historian Marsha Pripstein Posusney associates strikes and class conflict during this period with the remaking of class relations by market forces and a breakdown in the moral economy of "reciprocal rights and responsibilities" between workers and the state on which Nasser had attempted to base Arab Socialism. "The moral economy perspective can account for the defensive nature of collective action in the 1960s and early 1970s," she writes, because "workers came to accept what the state had given them as an entitlement, and were therefore angered when they began receiving less remuneration than before with no reduction in their responsibilities."[86] A new constitution enacted in 1971 under Sadat removed existing restrictions on emigrant labor and "was designed to encourage temporary and permanent migration."[87] Rather than finding employment in state-led national industries and irrigated agriculture as Nasser had envisioned under Arab Socialism, Egypt's surplus labor was exported to the Gulf.

Islamists did not suddenly displace secular nationalists in Arab politics so much as their ideas reflected broader conceptual changes in the Middle East and elsewhere. Sustained organizing within student groups and professional societies, tolerated and even encouraged by Sadat, gradually gave rise to what social scientist Carrie Rosefsky Wickham calls the influential "Middle Generation" of Western-educated Muslim Brothers in Egypt.[88] Radical heirs

[85] See Carrie Rosefsky Wickham, *The Muslim Brotherhood: Evolution of an Islamist Movement* (Princeton, NJ: Princeton University Press, 2013), 30.

[86] Posusney, *Labor and the State in Egypt: Workers, Unions, and Economic Restructuring*, 73, 136. See also Robert Bianchi, *Unruly Corporatism: Associational Life in Twentieth-Century Egypt* (New York: Oxford University Press, 1989), 45–55; and John Waterbury, *The Egypt of Nasser and Sadat: The Political Economy of Two Regimes* (Princeton, NJ: Princeton University Press, 1983), 207–31.

[87] Saad Eddin Ibrahim, *The New Arab Social Order: A Study of the Social Impact of Oil Wealth* (Boulder, CO: Westview Press, 1982), 68. See also Delwin A. Roy, "Egyptian Emigrant Labor: Domestic Consequences," *Middle Eastern Studies* 27 (October 1991): 554.

[88] Carrie Rosefsky Wickham, *Mobilizing Islam: Religion, Activism, and Political Change in Egypt* (New York: Columbia University Press, 2002), 189–94. For a parallel example of religious organizing on U.S. campuses, see John G. Turner, *Bill Bright and Campus Crusade for Christ: The Renewal of Evangelicalism in Postwar America* (Chapel Hill: University of North Carolina Press, 2008).

of Sayyid Qutb, meanwhile, carried on the struggle against supposedly apostate regimes, although not in terms of the journey that Qutb had depicted in *Ma'alim fi al-Tariq*. Qutb had defined Islam as a system and compared it to the superpowers' secular ideologies. He had also used the metaphor of a spiritual pilgrimage out of the pre-Islamic *jahiliya* in a conflation of temporal, spatial, and moral progress (see Chapter 1). In *Kitab Tawhid al-Khaliq [Book of the Unity of the Creator]*, Yemeni cleric 'Abd al-Majid 'Aziz al-Zindani referred to the "fabrication of planes, submarines, and battleships [*san'a al-ta'irat, wa al-ghawwasat, wa al-bawarij*]." Rather than representing unilinear motion, however, these conveyances illustrated that while Muslims were not opposed to technology, their principal duty was to combat "distortion in the meaning of progress" whenever a dissolute society permitted moral corruptions including drinking alcohol and fornication.[89] Egyptian Muhammad 'Abd al-Salam Farraj's tract *Al-Farida al-Gha'iba [The Neglected Duty]*, described as inspiring Sadat's 1981 assassination, provided justification for waging jihad against corrupt Muslim rulers. It did so through the strict Hanbali school of Sunni Islamic jurisprudence and the ideas of its medieval interpreter, Ibn Taymiyyah (d. 1328). In seeking religious authenticity and legitimacy for struggles against twentieth-century regimes, Farraj and other radical Islamists abandoned the forward movement Qutb had evoked with *Signposts along the Road*. Like the PFLP had done in the aftermath of the June 1967 war, they rejected the developmental claims of the postcolonial state, seeing it instead as an oppressive and dehumanizing structure. As Fawaz A. Gerges notes, Farraj emphasized struggle against the "near enemy," by which he meant Sadat's government.[90] Juhayman al-'Utaybi, whose forces seized the Great Mosque in Mecca, revived the teachings of eighteenth-century cleric Muhammad ibn 'Abd al-Wahhab to attack the religious legitimacy of the Saudi ruling family. According to al-'Utaybi, the Saudis regarded religion solely as a "means for pursuing their worldly interests" while they disdained Muslims and "consorted with Christians (America)."[91] In religious as well as in secular politics, the language of resistance supplanted talk of development, while a rhetoric of historical symbols replaced the imagery of spatial progress. The Islamist resurgence of the 1970s was not merely a reaction to Westernization, but part of a larger

[89] 'Abd al-Majid 'Aziz Zindani, *Kitab Tawhid al-Khaliq*, 3 vols. (Cairo: Dar al-Salam; Jiddah: Dar al-Mujtama', 1985), 3:67.

[90] See Johannes J. G. Jansen, *The Neglected Duty: The Creed of Sadat's Assassins and Islamic Resurgence in the Middle East* (New York: Macmillan, 1986); and Fawaz A. Gerges, *The Far Enemy: Why Jihad Went Global* (New York: Cambridge University Press, 2005), 9–11, 290n36.

[91] Rif'at Sayyid Ahmad, *Rasa'il Juhayman al-'Utaybi, qa'id al-muqtahimin lil-Masjid al-Haram bi-Makkah* (Cairo: Maktabat Madbuli, 1988), 14. See also Madawi al-Rasheed, *Contesting the Saudi State: Islamic Voices from a New Generation* (New York: Cambridge University Press, 2007), 106–07.

revolt against postwar modernization through self-conscious idealization of the past, or what historian Ibrahim M. Abu-Rabi' described as the "redis-covery of tradition."[92] Just as Khaled and other *fida'iyin* looked back to 'Izz al-Din al-Qassam and the 1930s Arab Revolt as their inspiration for revolu-tion against Nasser and U.S. imperialism, Farraj and al-'Utaybi waged anti-regime struggles by appropriating sources of Sunni theology through what Rodgers calls "a wrinkle in time."

Secular intellectuals also rediscovered the value of cultural heritage while distancing themselves from the optimistic concept of history as a linear journey susceptible to acceleration. In *al-Ahram*, Haykal reassessed Egypt's attempt to develop itself internally while leading the movement for Arab unity. He observed that "pushing history's motion more than one should leads to stum-bling." Haykal conceded that "the movement of history cannot be pushed on wheels although much can be done to help these elements in their nat-ural development."[93] At a 1971 conference on Authenticity and Renewal in Contemporary Arab Culture sponsored by the Arab League Educational, Cultural, and Scientific Organization, attendees spent the first plenary ses-sion debating the past's relationship to the future. Palestinian writer Mahmud Sayf al-Din al-Irani recognized a "degree of exaggeration" in the modern and emphasized the value of the Arab cultural "heritage [*turath*]." He advocated "caution" in pursuing what he described as the "convoy of development [*muwakaba al-tatawwur*]." Conference members shared his skepticism and in the text of the session's resolution voted to endorse "careful development." Although Kassab is surely correct to associate the conference with "the self-reflective critical turn," participants consulted the past as a repository of useful symbols rather than imagining it as a continuum of progress. They called for the reform of historical writing to reflect Arab unity and to rectify its distortion by "partisans." Delegates also accepted Islamic tradition, in terms of its general principles, as a legitimate basis of authentic modern identity.[94]

Economically, the years following the 1967 Arab–Israeli War witnessed diminishing prospects for heroic state projects in Egypt and poorer Arab states, while petrodollars concentrated development in major oil-exporting countries.[95] According to one U.S. intelligence report, Egypt's emergency

[92] See Ibrahim M. Abu-Rabi' *Contemporary Arab Thought: Studies in Post-1967 Arab Intellectual History* (London: Pluto Press, 2004), 12.

[93] See translation of Haykal's editorial column, "Landmarks," February 2, 1968, FCO 39/ 247, BNA.

[94] Arab League Educational, Cultural, and Scientific Organization, *Mu'tamar al-Asalah wa-al-Tajdid fi al-Thaqafah al-'Arabiyah al-Mu'asirah* (Cairo: Idarat al-Thaqafah, 1973), 24, 54. On Islam, see 'Iffat al-Sharqawi, "Mawqif al-Thaqafa al-'Arabiya al-Haditha fi Muwajaha al-'Asr (al-Janib al-Dini)," published in ibid., 136–42. See also Kassab, *Contemporary Arab Thought*, 117–20.

[95] On development in Saudi Arabia, see Jones, *Desert Kingdom*; and Sarah Yizraeli, *Politics and Society in Saudi Arabia: The Crucial Years of Development, 1960–1982* (New York: Columbia University Press, 2012).

budget for the fiscal year following the war included "measures to collect additional revenues of about $300 million and to slash nonmilitary expenditures by about $500 million." Most of these cuts were taken from the country's development budget.[96] The CIA concluded that the $66.7 million in quarterly subsidies that Saudi Arabia, Kuwait, and Libya pledged to Egypt at the summit meeting of Arab states held at Khartoum "were somewhat less than enough to compensate for Egypt's continuing hard currency losses."[97] In agriculture, Egypt's reclamation projects exceeded cost estimates but fell far short of anticipated productivity. Construction on a model mechanized farm provided by the Soviet Union was halted in 1970 immediately after its dedication, and two years later the agriculture ministry suspended its activities at the major reclamation sites of South Tahrir, Wadi Natrun, and the New Valley.[98]

Meanwhile, the campaign to raise incomes in the most populous Arab country through industrialization and irrigated agriculture came to a virtual halt by the late 1960s. Beginning just before the 1967 war, political scientist Robert Bianchi observes a slowdown in the industrial sector growth that had followed the 1952 revolution. Contrasting the economy under Sadat with Nasser's industrializing policies, Bianchi concludes that "the picture is one of nearly complete stagnation throughout the *infitah* period." He notes the "regressive impact of the *infitah* policies on income distribution" and rising inequality within Egypt at the same time that growing numbers of Egyptians sought work abroad. Besides earnings from tourism, petroleum, and Suez Canal tolls, the country's key source of foreign exchange has come "from remittances of the estimated 4 million Egyptians who have found employment out of the country."[99] In the immediate aftermath of the 1967 war, the Johnson administration had cited these opportunities as the rationale for curtailing support for irrigation projects in Jordan and other Arab states. Whereas the United States had invested in the East Ghor Canal in the late 1950s as part of an effort to resettle thousands of Palestinian refugees, after the war officials proposed that refugees seek work "*in the fields of tourism and overseas employment*" instead, particularly in the "rapidly growing economies of Kuwait, Saudi Arabia and Libya." Given that "remittances contributed the largest single block of foreign exchange earnings to the Jordanian balance of payments," one report concluded, a "substantial investment in vocational

96 Special National Intelligence Estimate, "The Situation and Prospects in Egypt," August 17, 1967, folder: 36.1 UAR, box 6, National Intelligence Estimates, NSF, LBJL.
97 CIA Directorate of Intelligence, "Consequences of the Arab Summit Meeting," September 13, 1967, folder: United Arab Republic, Vol. VI, Memos [2 of 2] 8/67-7/68, box 160, NSF, LBJL.
98 Waterbury, *The Egypt of Nasser and Sadat*, 299.
99 Bianchi, *Unruly Corporatism*, 42, 45, 46.

training might have a much greater impact on the backlog of refugees than equal investment in water development."[100]

Growing inequality during the 1970s reflected the costs of having missed earlier opportunities to invest in economic diversification and more balanced development across the Arab Middle East. Disparities between Arab states expanded with the earnings of oil exporters, especially after the 1973–74 embargo and price hike. The gap in per capita Gross Domestic Product between major oil-exporting and other Arab states rose from $460 before the embargo to $5,000 by 1980.[101] One economist estimates that for the period 1974–82, developing states received about 17 percent of oil-exporters' current account surpluses ($72 billion out of a total $421 billion), with the majority flowing to the developed world in the form of bank deposits, loans, and investments.[102] Significant as this percentage was, it could not stem growing regional imbalances in wealth and development across the Arab world. Infrastructure and construction projects in the oil states created a demand for migrant laborers. According to political scientist Hélène Thiollet, about one-quarter of Saudi Arabia's workforce in 1975 came from Yemen and 60 percent of the Jordanian labor force (including Palestinians with Jordanian passports) worked in the Gulf during the 1970s.[103] By 1979, remittances accounted for 13 percent of Egypt's Gross National Product and 46 percent of North Yemen's. Between 1973 and 1984, remittances grew as a share of Jordan's GNP from 7 to 27 percent.[104] Years earlier, UN secretary general Dag Hammarskjöld had sought to prevent such regional disparities with his proposal to direct a percentage of oil revenues toward developing poor Arab countries. Had Hammarskjöld's plan been implemented, there would have been a mechanism in place for distributing the post-embargo bonanza more equitably throughout the Arab world. But rather than circulating capital to develop industries and agriculture in various Arab states as

[100] Saunders to Rostow, December 12, 1967, folder: Middle East, Vol. I [2 of 3], 6/65-3/68, box 104 Middle East, NSF, LBJL. Emphasis original. See also Ward to Williams, "Measures for Absorbing Arab Refugees," July 7, 1967, folder: Middle East, vol. 1[3 of 3] 6/65-3/68, box 104, NSF, LBJL.

[101] R. Paul Shaw, "The Political Economy of Inequality in the Arab World," *Arab Studies Quarterly* 6 (Winter/Spring 1984): 126.

[102] Abbas Alnasrawi, "The Rise and Fall of Arab Oil Power," *Arab Studies Quarterly* 6 (Winter/Spring 1984): 3–4. See also Abbas Alnasrawi, *Arab Nationalism, Oil, and the Political Economy of Dependency* (Westport, CT: Greenwood Press, 1991), 103–04.

[103] Hélène Thiollet, "Migration as Diplomacy: Labor Migrants, Refugees, and Arab Regional Politics in the Oil-Rich Countries," *International Labor and Working-Class History* 79 (Spring 2011): 111. On Saudi demand for Yemeni labor, see Kiren Aziz Chaudhry, *The Price of Wealth: Economies and Institutions in the Middle East* (Ithaca, NY: Cornell University Press, 2007), 193–225.

[104] Alnasrawi, *Arab Nationalism, Oil, and the Political Economy of Dependency*, 161.

he had envisioned, petrodollars instead attracted Arab laborers from across the region to work in the oil-exporting countries.

William Polk, who had advocated revival of Hammarskjöld's idea and urged Nasser to reconcile with Gulf regimes, sought to keep the flame of development planning burning at the University of Chicago's Adlai Stevenson Institute of International Affairs (ASIIA). Polk invited architect Hassan Fathy to Chicago not only to work on a self-help housing project (see Chapter 3), but also to plan the villages Polk and Nasser had envisioned building on new agricultural land reclaimed from Egypt's desert using desalinated seawater. "Even if the project is totally successful in every other way," Polk warned Fathy, "it could simply create a large, new rural slum perpetuating many of the health and other problems of Egypt's traditional poverty."[105] Fathy's career corresponded to the rise and decline of large-scale state planning. During the 1940s, he had conceived of "The New Model Village of Gourna" as a prototype that could be replicated in thousands of self-help villages built with local materials throughout the Nile Valley.[106] It was this sort of ambitious scale that Polk sought to revive by inviting him to the ASIIA. Polk never realized his vision in which Fathy's designs could be scaled up to provide the basis for vast new agricultural settlements. Fathy had worked for Doxiadis Associates at a time when the international firm fulfilled contracts for state development projects around the world. By the early 1970s, however, Fathy was exhibiting his work for museums such as the Field Museum of Natural History in Chicago and designing standalone projects for wealthy sponsors.[107] His house at Sidi Karir on Egypt's Mediterranean coast was planned as part of a tourist village, which he bitingly described to Polk as a "touristic 'bidonville' for the millionaires where everybody would be in rags for a change."[108] Fathy even designed a vacation house for Polk in the ski resort of Aspen, Colorado (it was never built).[109] In the 1980s, the architect's Dar al-Islam center was constructed near Abiquiu, New Mexico with financial support from Saudi donors.[110]

Polk's career also tracked with the authority of the modernizing state. During May 1970 antiwar demonstrations, members of Students for a Democratic Society (SDS) and the Worker Student Alliance ransacked the ASIIA's University of Chicago headquarters, located in Frank Lloyd Wright's Robie House at 5757 South Woodlawn Avenue. The intruders rifled through

---

[105] Polk to Fathy, August 19, 1970, folder 12, box 15, ASIIA.

[106] See Fathy to Marinos and undated report, "*Qariyat al-Jurna al-Namudhajiyya al-Jadida*," binder I, #13, HFA.

[107] See Polk to Fathy, January 11, 1974, folder 7, box 15, ASIIA.

[108] Fathy to Polk, May 19, 1971, folder 7, box 15, ASIIA.

[109] See Fathy to Polk, February 12, 1972, folder 9, box 15, ASIIA. Polk email message to the author, November 21, 2002.

[110] See the documentation in folder: 81.01 Dar al-Islam, HFA.

files, searching for evidence of links with the CIA and affiliated private philanthropies, the very organizations that had subsidized Polk's education and activities. Polk told George Ball and other ASIIA board members that Robie House had sustained more than $35,000 in damages.[111] The attacks reflected challenges to the official and private networks that had dominated the postwar era of modernization in the United States. The raids also simulated the small-scale guerrilla actions organized by Palestinian militants targeting what were regarded as systems of oppression. An FBI report from June 1970 detailed political support given by the SDS and other "domestic subversive groups" to the Palestinian *fida'iyin*.[112] The radicalism and challenges to the authority of postwar elites on U.S. campuses had parallels in many societies worldwide, including Egypt, where Nasser had been forced to close five universities after student demonstrations against the regime resulted in several deaths and hundreds of arrests.[113]

The year after the sacking of Robie House, Polk undertook a "quixotic journey" that epitomizes how the technology of speed could symbolize changing ideas about modernization. He decided to make a pilgrimage across Arabia, from Riyadh to Amman. Polk aimed to "cross the great sand barrier of northern Arabia in a way that had been traditional for nearly three thousand years until the advent of the motorcar," following in the footsteps of previous Western travelers such as Charles Doughty, Wilfrid Blunt, and Harry St. John Philby. In contrast to his 1963 Arabian trip, when he had observed Egypt's campaign to pacify Yemen from the air in a visit lasting several days, Polk spent an entire month crossing the desert by camel. This nostalgic caravan reversed Polk's earlier perspective, in which the Yemeni civil war had encapsulated the Arab struggle to escape the past and embrace the future. Saudi Arabia's King Faysal, who as crown prince had complained angrily to Polk that the United States was not helping to defend his country against attacks by Nasser's air force, generously provided the expedition with animals, guides, and supplies. Polk's choice of the camel over the airplane indicated his retreat from the notion that modernization should follow a universal path. "Our aim," he explained, "was to taste the desert." If it were simply to reach the destination quickly, he wrote, then "we

---

[111] Polk to Ball, June 9, 1970, folder 7, box 7, ASIIA.

[112] Federal Bureau of Investigation, *The Fedayeen Impact – Middle East and United States* (Washington, DC: FBI Monograph, 1970), 44–46.

[113] See Martin Klimke, *The Other Alliance: Student Protest in West Germany and the United States in the Global Sixties* (Princeton, NJ: Princeton University Press, 2009). See Paul Chamberlin, "A World Restored: Religion, Counterrevolution, and the Search for Order in the Middle East," *Diplomatic History* 32 (June 2008): 445. On Egypt, see Ghada Hashem Talhami, *The Mobilization of Muslim Women in Egypt* (Gainesville: University Press of Florida, 1996), 53; Ahmed Abdalla, *The Student Movement and National Politics in Egypt, 1923–1973* (London: Al-Saqi Books, 1985), 226–28; and Wickham, *Mobilizing Islam*, 115–18.

could fly there by jet." Polk came to regret that the human race was "converging toward a single species of modern, urban, and industrial, rational man." Given "all of our riches, in all of our capacities," he declared, "we should somehow be able to find a way to make a world safe for diversity."[114]

The "age of speed" described in Chapter 1 came to an end, in the sense that descriptions of its technology could no longer be used to represent elite-managed change or tied convincingly to expectations of state-administered progress. Governments would still try to make these associations. Reports in *al-Ahram* of the Apollo 11 moon landing described it as the greatest event of the century and juxtaposed Armstrong's moonwalk with what it claimed were "huge victories [*intisarat dakhma*]" won against the Israelis by the Egyptian air force on the same day.[115] But some accounts published after the 1967 war used the dangers of speed to render negative verdicts about revolutionary and non-revolutionary development agendas. Rather than evoking rapid progress, certain portrayals used speed to criticize Nasserist pan-Arabism and to suggest its brutal consequences for those such as peasants and women whom Nasser had promised to modernize.[116] Journalist Yusuf al-Qu'ayd remembers people from the Delta village of Tawfiqiyya crowding the train station immediately after the revolution in 1952 to catch a glimpse of the Free Officers' figurehead Muhammad Neguib. The villagers expected Neguib's train to stop, but it was a "diesel express" from Cairo to Alexandria that did not even slow down. The high-speed train "sucked in" a great number from the crush of villagers along the tracks in what al-Qu'ayd describes as a "disaster [*karitha*]."[117] Zaynab al-Ghazzali, the female Egyptian Islamist who helped to circulate Qutb's *Ma'alim fi al-Tariq*, opens her memoir with a speeding car, presumably driven by one of Nasser's secret police, smashing into hers, causing it to flip over and leaving her "semi-conscious" and suffering "intense agony" once she awoke.[118] Citing poetry and other artifacts of street culture, Pascal Menoret portrays the high-speed drifting of cars by young Saudi men as a symptom of *tufush*, the feeling of "social impotence" or "loss of future," that Menoret links to the failure of the kingdom's economic development plans. Saudi youth from Bedouin backgrounds were driven to experiment dangerously with speed by "unemployment or low income, broken families, and poor housing." Riyadh's broad, rectilinear streets, designed as part of a city plan drawn up by Doxiadis Associates and

---

[114] William R. Polk and William J. Mares, *Passing Brave* (New York: Alfred A. Knopf, 1973), 3, 15, 40, 202.

[115] *Al-Ahram*, July 21, 1969, p. 1; see also *al-Ahram*, July 22, 1969, p. 5.

[116] On "accidents" as sites of conflict over modernity in late nineteenth- and early twentieth-century Egypt, see Barak, *On Time*.

[117] al-Qu'ayd, *'Abd al-Nasir wa al-muthaqqafun wa al-thaqafa*, 11.

[118] Zaynab al-Ghazzali, *Ayyam min Hayati* (Cairo: Dar al-Shuruq, 1978), 11.

financed by petrodollars, proved ideal for this practice.[119] Just as speed had served a range of elites as a way of evoking postwar optimism and their own capacity to steer society's historical evolution, the meaning of speed turned negative once expectations for development went unfulfilled and military and economic failures delegitimized Arab leaders.

This chapter has described the decline of modernization in U.S.–Arab relations by examining shifting uses of postwar aerospace technology as a metaphor for social change. Palestinian militants who carried out hijackings were fully conscious of the value of aircraft as modern symbols, which they appropriated as part of a political discourse that related the history of the anti-Zionist campaign in Palestine to class struggle throughout the Arab world and to other global revolutionary movements. More than just guerrilla tactics employed against Israel and the United States, *fida'iyin* hijackings repudiated Nasser, Husayn, and other Arab leaders who had based their authority on promises to develop society and defeat Zionism. *Fida'iyin* attacks against what they regarded as systems of oppression sustained by the U.S. and Arab leaders came at a time when the entire edifice of postwar thought regarding modernization was collapsing. In U.S. and Soviet, as well as in Islamist and Arab nationalist ideologies, aerospace had once symbolized forward progress, elite authority, state-administered technology, and the integrated mechanism of society. By the late 1960s, aerospace's declining fortunes corresponded to a loss in postwar optimism. Aerospace historian Matthew D. Tribbe describes how the "decline of the postwar big-vision liberalism that especially marked the 1960s" went hand in hand with Americans' post-Apollo ambivalence toward the space program and its "problematic urge toward mastering the universe."[120] As chief executive at Pan Am, Najeeb Halaby presided over losses of $26 million in 1969 and $48 million in 1970. In tribute to the optimism JFK had once shared with the New Frontier on the Jordan, however, Halaby's daughter Lisa would go on to wed King Husayn.[121] Aviation itself would point the way toward greater deregulation of the U.S. economy and neoliberal reform of the Cold War state.[122] From the revolutionary left, skyjackings signified revolt against

[119] Pascal Menoret, *Joyriding in Riyadh: Oil, Urbanism, and Road Revolt* (New York: Cambridge University Press, 2014), 58. See also Pascal Menoret, "Urban Unrest and Non-Religious Radicalization in Saudi Arabia," in *Dying for Faith: Religiously Motivated Violence in the Contemporary World*, ed. Madawi al-Rasheed and Marat Shterin (New York: Palgrave Macmillan, 2009), 131.

[120] Matthew D. Tribbe, *No Requiem for the Space Age: The Apollo Moon Landings and American Culture* (New York: Oxford University Press, 2014), 14, 221.

[121] See U.S. Senate, Committee on Commerce, Hearings, *Economic Condition of the Air Transportation Industry*, 92nd Cong., 1 sess. (Washington, DC: Government Printing Office, 1971), 573. See Ashton, *King Hussein of Jordan*, 208.

[122] See Thomas K. McCraw, *Prophets of Regulation: Charles Francis Adams, Louis D. Brandeis, James M. Landis, Alfred E. Kahn* (Cambridge, MA: Belknap Press, 1984), 259–99; and Borstelmann, *The 1970s*, 148–51.

state authority, a decentralized conception of how "little platoons" could catalyze social transformations, and even personal liberation from gender constraints. Just as the "golden age of hijacking" affected both American and Arab skies, U.S. and Arab societies experienced the decline of postwar modernization and the vision of it as an integrated process that elites had shared across barriers of language and politics. Placing hijacking into this political and intellectual context not only helps to remove the phenomenon from the shadow of 9/11. It also advances the more significant aim of reinterpreting U.S.–Arab relations historically rather than assuming the centrality of cultural difference.

Conclusion

A Better Future

"We are entering an age of supersonic and hypersonic speeds, a period in which the news of the whole world will be seen everywhere and every day on satellite television, a time when computer information systems will carry us still farther along the road to a single interconnected world community."
　　　　– Owen, "Transportation, Communications, and the Future."[1]

"We Are All Khaled Said."
　　　　– Wael Ghonim, Facebook, June 10, 2010.

"Tendencies to a better future continue and thrive."
　　　　– Vijay Prashad, *Arab Spring, Libyan Winter.*[2]

This book has observed how the leading postwar technology of aerospace helped to influence competing accounts of progress in U.S. relations with the Arab Middle East. The jet plane served as a useful symbol for such diametrically opposed visions as those of Walt Rostow, who argued that American aid would help developing countries to achieve "takeoff," and the PFLP, whose hijackings signified revolutionary resistance against Israel, Arab governments, and American imperialism. If, as historian Thomas Haskell argues, the post-Enlightenment world has witnessed successive campaigns to perfect and liberate society, then technological change was part of the evolving context in which such dreams were continuously reimagined.[3] This is the case in early accounts of the 2011 Arab Spring that feature young protestors' use of cell phones, social media, and the Internet. These accounts present a conception of society and social change that is as networked and decentralized as postwar modernizers' vision was integrated and elite-centered. For instance,

---

[1] Owen, "Transportation, Communications, and the Future," 31.
[2] Vijay Prashad, *Arab Spring, Libyan Winter* (Edinburgh: AK Press, 2012), 8.
[3] Thomas Haskell, "Modernization on Trial," *Modern Intellectual History* 2 (August 2005): 244–45.

historian Elizabeth F. Thompson focuses on Wael Ghonim, the Google "computer geek" whose Facebook page publicizing the death of Khaled Said at the hands of police helped to mobilize other young Egyptians against the regime of Hosni Mubarak. "The Arab Spring was most novel in that it produced no clear leaders," Thompson writes. "Not so much leader*less*," she explains, "it was leader*ful*. Many small groups coordinated the protests." Thompson uses Ghonim to illustrate how the 2011 protests in Cairo's Tahrir Square drew not only on global Internet culture, but also on the legacy of a century of struggles in the Middle East for democracy and justice.[4]

This book has similarly analyzed the intersection of global Cold War politics with the history of anticolonialism and reform in Arab societies. It has called for a renewed focus on regional histories to complement the globalism of Cold War studies and to expose the diverse third world circumstances for which no strategic doctrine could possibly account. Interpreting U.S. foreign relations with stereoscopic vision, in regional as well as global historical contexts, offers a critical approach to studying American power. Doing so can challenge American exceptionalism, as illustrated by the ways in which U.S. officials appropriated the Ottoman past and formulated similar land reform policies to those pursued earlier by Ottomans and Europeans. It demonstrates how anticommunism implicated the United States in older political conflicts, such as the clash between competing definitions of Iraqi nationalism, and led Washington to support antidemocratic policies. Synthesizing Cold War with Arab history around the theme of modernization yields a complex understanding of America's role in the Middle East region and in the world. Liberal development strategies pursued by the United States took on varied meanings and produced different outcomes as those strategies encountered diverse postcolonial societies and other people's reform legacies.

As a complementary way of framing modernization, regionalism provides for "the relativity of ways of seeing" that Osterhammel argues is essential for avoiding the "illusory neutrality of an omniscient narrator or a 'global' observation point." Without it, a global Cold War perspective draws third world conflicts and development politics into a single historical field, dissociating them from their colonial antecedents and validating

---

[4] Elizabeth F. Thompson, *Justice Interrupted: The Struggle for Constitutional Government in the Middle East* (Cambridge, MA: Harvard University Press, 2013), 310, 311. [Emphasis original.] See also Juan Cole, *The New Arabs: How the Millennial Generation Is Changing the Middle East* (New York: Simon & Schuster, 2014). Ali M. Ansari makes similar observations about non-Arab Iran: "The advent of the computer had affected [*sic*] a decentralisation of power giving individuals access not only to information, but a new and highly efficient means of dissemination.... This technological transformation was (and is) perhaps the single most dramatic revolution in state–society relations in recent memory, and by extension, the definition and articulation of nationalism and national identity." See Ali M. Ansari, *The Politics of Nationalism in Modern Iran* (New York: Cambridge University Press, 2012), 247.

the orthodox interpretation in which American power expanded onto every continent in order to contain a worldwide communist threat. Such a perspective corroborates accounts from the twentieth century, such as those by Rustow, Tannous, and Polk, who drew selectively on the past to integrate the Middle East into a Cold War framework. Portraying third world countries as squares on the chessboard of the U.S.–Soviet rivalry reproduces that perspective in which "questions of culture and history tended to disappear," as Latham wrote about modernization theory. Studying the Cold War as a universal experience "flattens history, elevating messy histories into a consistent project," to borrow the phrase historian Frederick Cooper applies to the concept of colonial modernity.[5] This book has demonstrated how the global contexts of the Cold War and decolonization are essential for understanding the shared concepts within which Arab and American modernizers contended to shape the future. But it has also based its analysis in regional historiography to reveal the distinct ways in which postwar conflicts over modernization intersected with the Ottoman legacy, the interwar competition among Arab anticolonial movements, the confrontation with Zionism, and struggles for social authority. Among the benefits of this approach is a better sense of how Islamists appropriated the language of postwar modernization and participated in postcolonial development debates. Greater attention to regional diversity can usefully complicate grand narratives and restore contingency to the study of international politics, in which phenomena such as the collapse of communism, ethno-religious conflict, and globalization too often seem to unfold with a sense of inevitability.

In *Culture and Imperialism*, Edward Said wrote that "the universalizing discourses of modern Europe and the United States assume the silence, willing or otherwise, of the non-European world."[6] This study has sought to fill that silence with the voices of Arabs from across a political spectrum who engaged in postwar conflicts over modernization. As they confronted ideological opponents at home and abroad, Arab modernizers such as Qutb, Mahdawi, and Nasser synthesized the regional competition among anticolonial movements with Cold War and third world politics. Examining this interaction offers a useful way to link the late twentieth century to earlier periods in Arab history. At the same time, incorporating Arabic sources demonstrates that American ideas about modernization and perceptions of the Middle East were not solely the products of domestic liberalism, popular culture, or a network of U.S. experts. Rather, they also emerged through encounters with other societies, from the intersections between conflicting,

---

[5] Michael Latham, "Introduction: Modernization, International History, and the Cold War," in *Staging Growth: Modernization, Development, and the Global Cold War*, ed. David C. Engerman, et al. (Amherst: University of Massachusetts Press, 2003), 13; Frederick Cooper, *Colonialism in Question: Theory, Knowledge, History* (Berkeley: University of California Press, 2005), 117.

[6] Edward Said, *Culture and Imperialism* (New York: Alfred A. Knopf, 1993), 50.

contemporary agendas that nevertheless shared underlying assumptions. It is therefore not sufficient to study American ideas and perceptions in isolation.

The study of modernization debates historically casts further doubt on the analytical value of an inherent "clash" between Islam and the West. Such a stark opposition obscures Islamists' incorporation into global political trends including the rise and decline of modernization, the faith shared with their secular counterparts that society was a system that could be developed over time, and the shift of some Islamists to antisystemic resistance once postwar hopes went unfulfilled and regimes pursued repressive policies. Considering Arab and American elites together makes it possible to criticize the authoritarian tendencies that dominated thinking about development globally during the Cold War era. If elites with different ideologies shared an antidemocratic concept of social change, then historians can hold individuals responsible for the human costs of pursuing such ideologies without falling back on easy explanations based on the supposedly essential traits of Arabs or any other people.

The theme of modernization also provides an important perspective on the conflict over Zionism in U.S.–Arab relations. Rather than transcending regional conflict, as many American officials hoped, a focus on development reformulated the U.S.–Arab clash over Israel on the basis of universal principles such as freedom, progress, and growth. Although Arab elites regarded Israel's existence and Palestinian statelessness as expressions of U.S. power, they also justified anti-Zionist policies in terms of the commitment to development that they shared with their American counterparts. As the East Ghor Canal shows, the same project could be imagined by the Americans as mitigating the Arab–Israeli problem in U.S. diplomacy and by Jordanians as a means for continuing the struggle against Israel and coping with the refugee crisis. The PFLP commandeered the language of Cold War modernization by attributing Palestinian dispossession and underdevelopment to U.S. support for Israel and Arab leaders' submission to imperialism. At the same time, however, modernization provides a basis for integrating the Middle East into the global history of development in areas such as community building, land reform, and population control. Doing so broadens the discussion of postwar Arab history beyond anti-Zionism and challenges the argument that unwarranted preoccupation with Israel has been a principal obstacle to Arab progress. Such a reinterpretation identifies multiple historical causes for regional problems while acknowledging the consequences of American power. In the Middle East, the United States supported antidemocratic regimes, condoned violence in the name of anticommunism, militarized the region by arming Israel and other countries, and defended a system of economic inequality linked to oil extraction. These policy aims were by design. But studying the Cold War's implications in the Middle East also reveals the contingent effects of U.S. policies, the unpredictable ways that grand strategies can intersect with the past and present in regions with complex histories. As Westad demonstrates, Cold War interventions helped to create many of today's conflicts. These remain essential lessons at a time of open-ended American military engagements.

Although this book began by criticizing Said's concept of Orientalism as a closed Western discourse, it concludes by reiterating his faith in the potential of humanistic study, a steady charge for confronting the dismal state of U.S.–Arab relations during the twenty-first century so far. By reading another people's history and language, it is possible to transcend inherited cultural images and to discover a common humanity.

Bibliography

Government Archives

United States
Dwight D. Eisenhower Library, Abilene, Kansas
  Dwight D. Eisenhower, Papers as President of the United States (Ann C. Whitman File)
    DDE Diary Series
    NSC Series
  National Security Council Staff Papers
    OCB Central File Series
    Special Staff File Series

Lyndon B. Johnson Library, Austin, Texas
  Lyndon B. Johnson, Papers as President of the United States
    National Security File

John F. Kennedy Library, Boston, Massachusetts
  George W. Ball Papers
  John F. Kennedy, Papers as President of the United States
    National Security File

National Archives and Records Administration, College Park, Maryland
  Record Group 59 General Records of the Department of State
  Record Group 84 Records of the Foreign Service Posts of the Department of State
  Record Group 286 Records of the Agency for International Development
  Record Group 434 Records of the Department of Energy

Harry S. Truman Library, Independence, Missouri
  Max Ball Papers
  Oscar Chapman Papers
  George McGhee Papers

United Kingdom
The National Archives, Kew, Richmond, Surrey

CO 831 Colonial Office: Transjordan Original Correspondence
FCO 39 Foreign Office, North and East African Department: Registered Files
FO 370 Foreign Office: Library and Research Department
FO 371 General Correspondence of the Foreign Office
FO 481 Foreign Office: Confidential Print Iraq
FO 922 Middle East Supply Centre: Registered Files
FO 957 Foreign Office, British Middle East Office, and Department of Technical
    Co-operation, Middle East Development Division: Registered Files

Manuscript Collections

American Heritage Center, University of Wyoming, Laramie, Wyoming
    Walter Levy Papers

Everette DeGolyer Library, Southern Methodist University, Dallas, Texas
    Everette DeGolyer Sr. Papers

Hoover Institution Archives, Stanford University, Stanford, California
    Louise Page Morris Papers
    Register of the United States National Student Association
        International Commission Records, 1946–1968

Jafet Library, Special Collections, American University of Beirut, Lebanon
    American University of Beirut, Minutes of the Board of Trustees

Lauinger Library, Special Collections, Georgetown University, Washington, DC
    William E. Mulligan Papers

Library of Congress, Manuscript Division, Washington, DC
    Charles Habib Malik Papers

Palace Green Library, Special Collections, Durham University, Durham, England
    Donald W. Hawley Papers

Rare Books and Special Collections Library, American University in Cairo, Egypt
    Hassan Fathy Archive

Regenstein Library, Special Collections Research Center, University of Chicago,
    Chicago, Illinois
    Papers of the Adlai Stevenson Institute of International Affairs

Rockefeller Archive Center, Sleepy Hollow, New York
    John Marshall Diary
    Rockefeller Foundation, Record Groups 1.2, 2, 10.2, 12

Seeley G. Mudd Library, Princeton University, Princeton, New Jersey
    Records of the Council on Foreign Relations
    Allen Welsh Dulles Papers
    William A. Eddy Papers

Sterling Memorial Library, Manuscripts and Archives, Yale University, New Haven,
    Connecticut
    Chester Bowles Papers

Periodicals

Arabic

al-Ahram
al-Akhbar
al-Da'wa
al-Difa'
al-Hadaf
Ruz al-Yusuf

English

Chicago Tribune
Foreign Affairs
Fortune
Life
Look
Middle East Journal
New York Times
Washington Post

Published Documents and Government Reports

Arabic

Abdel Nasser, Gamal. *Majmu'at khutab wa tasrihat wa bayanat al-Ra'is Gamal 'Abd al-Nasir*. 4 vols. Cairo: Maslahat al-Isti'lamat, n.d.
Iraq Ministry of Defense. *Muhakamat al-Mahkamah al-'Askariyah al-'Ulya al-Khassah*. 22 vols. Baghdad: Iraqi Defense Ministry, 1958–62.

English

Government of Egypt. *Gourna: A Tale of Two Villages*. Cairo: Egyptian Ministry of Culture, 1969.
———. *The Liberation "Tahreer" Province*. Cairo: Undated.
Hashemite Kingdom of Jordan. *The Arab Development Society, Jericho, the Hashemite Kingdom of Jordan*. Jerusalem: The Commercial Press, 1953.
Iraq Development Board. *The Development of Iraq: A Plan of Action*. By Lord Salter, assisted by S. W. Payton. London: Iraq Development Board, 1955.
Rockefeller Foundation. *Annual Report, 1955*.
Royal Scientific Society. Hashemite Kingdom of Jordan. *The Impact of the East Ghor Canal Project on Land Consolidation, Distribution, and Tenure*. By Jared E. Hezleton. Amman: Economic Research Department, 1974.
United Arab Republic. *Draft of the Charter*. Cairo: Information Department, 1962.

United Nations Department of Economic Affairs. *Land Reform: Defects in Agrarian Structure as Obstacles to Economic Development.* New York: United Nations Publications, 1951.

——. *Measures for the Economic Development of Under-developed Countries.* New York: UN Department of Economic Affairs, 1951.

United Nations Development Programme. Arab Fund for Social and Economic Development. *Arab Human Development Report 2002: Creating Opportunities for Future Generations.* New York: United Nations Publications, 2002.

United Nations Food and Agriculture Organization. *Inter-relationship Between Agrarian Reform and Agricultural Development: An FAO Land Tenure Study.* By Erich H. Jacoby. Rome: Food and Agriculture Organization, 1953.

U.S. Agency for International Development. *Agricultural Production and Income in the East Ghor Irrigation Project, Pre- and Post-Canal.* By Abdul Wahhab Jamil Awwad. Amman: USAID, 1967.

——. "An Analytical History and Evaluation of the Egyptian American Rural Improvement Service (EARIS), 1953–1965." By Richard Hrair Dekmejian. Washington, DC: USAID, 1981.

——. *Community Development: An Introduction to CD for Village Workers.* Washington, DC: USAID, 1962.

U.S. Congress. House Committee on Foreign Affairs. *Selected Executive Session Hearings of the Committee, 1951–56.* vol. 16: *The Middle East, Africa, and Inter-American Affairs.* Washington, DC: Government Printing Office, 1980.

——. Committee on Foreign Relations. Hearings. *Mutual Security Program.* 82nd Cong., 1st sess. Washington, DC: Government Printing Office, 1951.

U.S. Congress. Senate Committee on Commerce. Hearings. *Economic Condition of the Air Transportation Industry.* 92nd Cong., 1st sess. Washington, DC: Government Printing Office, 1971.

——. Committee on Interstate and Foreign Commerce. Hearings. *Nominations – Federal Aviation Agency and Commerce Department.* 85th Cong., 1st Sess. Washington, DC: Government Printing Office, 1961.

——. Select Committee to Study Governmental Operations with Respect to Intelligence Activities (Church Committee). *Interim Report: Alleged Assassination Plots Involving Foreign Leaders.* 94th Cong., 1st sess. Washington, DC: Government Printing Office, 1975.

——. Special Committee to Study the Foreign Aid Program. *The Objectives of United States Economic Assistance Programs* [Study Prepared by the Center for International Studies, Massachusetts Institute of Technology]. 85th Cong., 1st Sess. Washington, DC: Government Printing Office, 1957.

U.S. Department of the Interior. *Development Principles for the East Ghor Canal Scheme.* By John N. Spencer. Washington, DC: U.S. Department of Interior, Bureau of Reclamation, 1958.

U.S. Department of State. *Bulletin,* 1951.

——. *Foreign Relations of the United States, 1949.* vol. 6: *The Near East, South Asia, and Africa.* Washington, DC: Government Printing Office, 1977.

——. *Foreign Relations of the United States, 1950.* vol. 5: *The Near East, South Asia, and Africa.* Washington, DC: Government Printing Office, 1978.

——. *Foreign Relations of the United States, 1951.* vol. 5: *The Near East and Africa.* Washington, DC: Government Printing Office, 1982.

——. *Foreign Relations of the United States, 1952–1954*. vol. 1: *General: Economic and Political Matters*. Washington, DC: Government Printing Office, 1983.

——. *Foreign Relations of the United States, 1952–1954*. vol. 8: *Eastern Europe; Soviet Union; Eastern Mediterranean*. Washington, DC: Government Printing Office, 1988.

——. *Foreign Relations of the United States, 1952–1954*. vol. 9: *The Near and Middle East*. Washington, DC: Government Printing Office, 1986.

——. *Foreign Relations of the United States, 1952–1954*. vol. 10: *Iran*. Washington, DC: Government Printing Office, 1989.

——. *Foreign Relations of the United States, 1958–1960*, vol. 10: *Eastern Europe; Finland; Greece; Turkey*. Washington, DC: Government Printing Office, 1993.

——. *Foreign Relations of the United States, 1958–1960*. vol. 12: *Near East Region; Iraq; Iran; Arabian Peninsula*. Washington, DC: Government Printing Office, 1992.

——. *Foreign Relations of the United States, 1961–1963*. vol. 17: *Near East, 1961–1962*. Washington, DC: Government Printing Office, 1994.

——. *Foreign Relations of the United States, 1961–1963*. vol. 18: *The Near and Middle East, 1962–1963*. Washington, DC: Government Printing Office, 1995.

——. *Foreign Relations of the United States, 1964–1968*. vol. 3: *Vietnam, June–December 1965*. Washington, DC: Government Printing Office, 1996.

——. *Foreign Relations of the United States, 1964–1968*. vol. 16: *Cyprus; Greece; Turkey*. Washington, DC: Government Printing Office, 1999.

——. *Foreign Service List*. Washington, DC: Government Printing Office, 1962.

U.S. Federal Bureau of Investigation. *The Fedayeen Impact – Middle East and United States*. FBI Monograph. 1970.

Conference Proceedings

Arabic

Arab League. Educational, Cultural, and Scientific Organization. *Mu'tamar al-Asalah wa-al-Tajdid fi al-Thaqafah al-'Arabiyah al-Mu'asirah*. Cairo: Idarat al-Thaqafah, 1973.

English

Owen, Wilfred. "Transportation, Communications, and the Future." [Second Lecture on Transportation Held on May 4, 1967, in the West Hall Auditorium, American University of Beirut] *Centennial of the American University of Beirut Symposium Proceedings* (May 1967): 25–32.

Parsons, Kenneth H., et al. eds. *Land Tenure: Proceedings of the International Conference on Land Tenure and Related Problems in World Agriculture Held at Madison, Wisconsin, 1951*. Madison: University of Wisconsin Press, 1956.

Databases

Declassified Documents Reference System.

Oral Histories

Interview with Afif I. Tannous, Foreign Affairs Oral History Collection, Library of Congress.

Palestine Lives: Interviews with Leaders of the Resistance. Beirut: Palestine Research Center and Kuwaiti Teachers Association, 1973.

Naff, Thomas, ed. *Paths to the Middle East: Ten Scholars Look Back.* Albany: State University Press of New York, 1993.

Memoirs, Political Writings in Arabic

Ahmad, Rif'at Sayyid. *Rasa'il Juhayman al-'Utaybi, qa'id al-muqtahimin lil-Masjid al-Haram bi-Makkah.* Cairo: Maktabat Madbuli, 1988.

al-'Alami, Musa. *'Ibrat Filastin.* Beirut: Dar al-Kashshaf lil-nashr wa al-tiba'a wa al-tawzi', 1949.

Arsuzi, Zaki. *Mashakiluna al-Qawmiya.* Damascus: Mu'assasa al-Thaqafiya lil-nushr wa al-tawziy', 1958.

Ashhab, Na'im. *Durub al-Alam, Durub al-Amal: Dirah Dhatiyah.* Ramallah: Dar al-Tanwir lil-Nashr wa-al-Tarjamah wa-al-Tawzi', 2009.

al-'Azm, Khalid. *Mudhakkirat Khalid al-'Azm.* 3 vols. Beirut: Dar al-Muttahida li-l Nashr, 1973.

al-Baghdadi, 'Abd al-Latif. *Mudhakkirat 'Abd al-Latif al-Baghdadi.* 2 vols. Cairo: Al-Maktab al-Misri al-Hadith, 1977.

Bakdash, Khalid. *Al-'Arab wa al-harb al-ahliyya fi Isbaniya.* Damascus: n.p., 1937.

———. *Al-Hizb al-shuyu'i fi al-nidal li-ajli al-istiqlal wa-al-siyada al-wataniya.* Damascus: Dar al-Taqaddum, n.d.

al-Bazzaz, 'Abd al-Rahman. *Al-dawlah al-muwahhada wa-al-dawlah al-ittihadiya.* 2nd ed. Cairo: Dar al-Qalam, 1960.

al-Bitar, Salah al-Din. *Al-siyasa al-'Arabiya bayna al-mabda' wa al-tatbiq.* Beirut: Dar al-Tali'ah lil-Tiba'ah wa-al-Nashr, 1960.

Daklah, Salah Mahdi. *Min al-Dhakira (sira hiyat).* Nicosia, Cyprus: Al Mada, 2000.

al-Ghazzali, Zaynab. *Ayyam min Hayati.* Cairo: Dar al-Shuruq, 1978.

al-Hajaji, Ahmad Anas. *Risala min al-Mirrikh.* Cairo: Al-Sharq al-Jadid lil-da'awa wa al-nashru wa al-tawzi', n.d.

Hasanayn, Magdi. *Al-Sahara'... al-thawra wa al-tharwa: qissa mudiriya al-tahrir.* Cairo: Al-Hay'a al-Misriya al-'Ama lil-Kitab, 1975.

Haykal, Muhammad Hasanayn. *Harb al-Thalathin Sana.* Part 1. *Sanawat al-Ghalayan.* Cairo: Markaz al-Ahram lil-Tarjamah wa-al-Nashr, 1988.

———. *Nahnu ... wa Amrika.* 2nd ed. Cairo: Dar al-'Asr al-Hadith, 1967.

al-Husri, Abu Khaldun Sati'. *Al-'Aruba bayna du'atiha wa mu'aridiha.* Beirut: Dar al-'Ilm lil-malayin, 1961.

———. *Difa' 'an al-'uruba.* 2nd ed. Beirut: Dar al-'Ilm li-Malayin, [1956] 1961.

———. *Ma hiya al-qawmiyya? Abhath wa dirasat 'ala daw' al-ahdath wa al-nazariyyat.* Beirut: Markaz dirasat al-wahda al-'Arabiyya, [1959] 1985.

al-Khalidi, Salah 'Abd al-Fattah. *Amrika min al-dakhil bi-minzar Sayyid Qutb.* Jidda, Saudi Arabia: Dar al-Manarah, 1986.

al-Khuli, al-Bahi. *Al-Ishtirakiya fi al-mujtama' al-Islami: bayna al-nazariya wa al-tatbiq.* Cairo, Egypt: Maktabat Wahbah, 1964.

——. *Al-Islam: La shuyu'iya wa la ra'smaliya*. Kuwait: Maktaba al-Falah, [1948] 1981.
al-Qu'ayd, Yusuf. *'Abd al-Nasir wa al-muthaqqafun wa al-thaqafa: Muhammad Hasanayn Haykal yatadhakkar*. Cairo: Dar al-Shuruq, 2003.
Qutb, Sayyid. *Ma'alim fi al-Tariq*. Cairo: Dar al-Shuruq, 1982.
——. *Ma'rakat al-Islam wa al-ra'smaliyah*. 4th ed. Beirut: Dar al-Shuruq, 1975.
al-Rifa'i, 'Abd al-Munim. *Al-Amwaj: safahat min rihlat al-hayah*. Amman: Wizarat al-Thaqafa, 2001.
al-Rimawi, 'Abdullah. *Al-Mantiq al-thawri*. Cairo: Dar al-ma'arifa, 1961.
Rushaydat, Nabih. *Awraq Laysat Shakhsiya: Mudhakkirat*. Damascus: Dar al-Yanabi', 2001.
al-Sadr, Muhammad Baqir. *Falsafatuna*. Beirut: Dar al-Fakr, 1969.
Sharaf, Sami. *Sanawat wa ayyam ma' Gamal 'Abd al-Nasir: Shahadat Sami Sharaf*. 2 vols. Cairo: Dar al-Fursan li-l-Nashr, 2005, 2006.
al-Sha'ir, Jamal. *Siyasi Yatadhakkar: Tajribah fi al-'Amal al-Siyasi*. London: Riyad al Rayyis lil-Kutub, wa-al-Nashr, 1987.
Shawi, Niqula. *Tariqi ila al-hizb*. Beirut: Dar al-Farabi, 1984.
al-Suwaydi, Tawfiq. *Mudhakkirati: nisf qarn min ta'rikh al-Iraq wa-l qadiya al-'Arabiya*. Beirut: Dar al-Katib al-'Arabi, 1969.
al-Zindani, 'Abd al-Majid 'Aziz. *Kitab Tawhid al-Khaliq*. 3 vols. Cairo: Dar al-Salam; Jiddah: Dar al-Mujtama', 1985.

Sources in Translation

'Abd al-Nasser, Gamal. *The Philosophy of the Revolution*. Buffalo, NY: Economica Books, 1959.
Abdel-Malik, Kamal. *America in an Arab Mirror: Images of America in Arabic Travel Literature, an Anthology*. New York: St. Martin's Press, 2000.
Alami, Musa. "The Lesson of Palestine," *Middle East Journal* 3 (October 1949): 373–405.
al-'Azm, Sadik. *Self-Criticism after the Defeat*. Trans. George Stergios. London: Saqi, [1968] 2011.
Bakdash, Khalid. "For the Successful Struggle for Peace, National Independence, and Democracy, We Must Resolutely Turn toward the Workers and the Peasants." *Middle East Journal* 7 (Spring 1953): 206–21.
Butrus Ghali, Mirrit. *The Policy of Tomorrow*. Trans. Isma'il R. el Faruqi. Washington, DC: American Council of Learned Societies, 1953.
Husayn, Taha. *The Days*. trans. E. H. Paxton et al. Cairo: American University in Cairo Press, 1997.
Jansen, Johannes J. G. *The Neglected Duty: The Creed of Sadat's Assassins and Islamic Resurgence in the Middle East*. New York: Macmillan, 1986.
Popular Front for the Liberation of Palestine. *A Strategy for the Liberation of Palestine*. Amman: PFLP Information Department, 1969.
——. *Tasks of the New Stage*. [Filmed by the University of Chicago Photoduplication Laboratory for the Middle East Microfilm Project at the Center for Research Libraries] 1994.
Qutb, Sayyid. *Islam: The Religion of the Future*. Beirut: Dar al-Kalam Press, 1971.
——. *Milestones*. Damascus: Dar al-Ilm, 1990.

Sa'ade, Antoune. *The Genesis of Nations*. Beirut: Syrian Social Nationalist Party, 2004.

al-Sadr, Muhammad Baqir. *Our Philosophy*, trans. Shams C. Inati. New York: Muhammadi Trust, KPI, 1987.

Shepard, William, ed. *Sayyid Qutb and Islamic Activism: A Translation and Critical Analysis of Social Justice in Islam*. Leiden, Netherlands: E.J. Brill, 1996.

Memoirs, Political Writings in English

Barger, Tom C. *Out in the Blue: Letters from Arabia, 1937–1940: A Young American Geologist Explores the Deserts of Early Saudi Arabia*. Vista, CA: Selwa Press, 2000.

Barnes, Larry. *Looking Back Over My Shoulder*. n.p., 1979.

Brent, William Lee. *Long Time Gone*. New York: Random House/Times Books, 1996.

Cleaver, Eldridge. *Soul on Ice*. New York: Dell Publishing, 1968.

Cremeans, Charles D. *The Arabs and the World: Nasser's Arab Nationalist Policy*. New York: Frederick A. Praeger, 1963.

Furlonge, Geoffrey. *Palestine Is My Country: The Story of Musa Alami*. New York: Praeger, 1969.

Heikal, Mohamed Hassanein. *The Cairo Documents: The Inside Story of Nasser and His Relationship with World Leaders, Rebels, and Statesmen*. New York: Doubleday & Co., 1973.

H. M. King Hussein of Jordan. *Uneasy Lies the Head*. London: Heinemann, 1962.

Johnson, Nora. *You Can Go Home Again: An Intimate Journey*. Garden City, NY: Doubleday & Company, 1982.

Karanjia, R. K. *The Mind of Mr. Nehru: An Interview*. London: George Allen & Unwin Ltd., 1960.

Khaled, Leila. *My People Shall Live: The Autobiography of a Revolutionary*. Ed. George Hajjar. London: Hodder and Stoughton, 1973.

Marei, Sayed. *Agrarian Reform in Egypt*. Cairo: Ministry of Agriculture, 1957.

McGhee, George. *Envoy to the Middle World: Adventures in Diplomacy*. New York: Harper & Row Publishers, 1983.

McGhee, George and Cecilia McGhee. *Life in Alanya: Turkish Delight*. Benson, VT: Chalidze Publications, 1992.

Midhat Bey, Ali Haydar. *The Life of Midhat Pasha: A Record of His Services, Political Reforms, Banishment, and Judicial Murder*. London: John Murray, 1903.

Parker, Richard B. *Memoirs of a Foreign Service Arabist*. Washington, DC: New Academia Publishing, 2013.

Polk, William Roe. "Perspective of the Arab World." *Atlantic Monthly* 198 (October 1956): 124–92.

Polk, William R. *Polk's Folly: An American Family History*. New York: Doubleday, 2000.

Polk, William R. and W. Jack Butler. "What the Arabs Think." *Headline Series*. No. 96. New York: Foreign Policy Association, 1952.

Polk, William R. and William J. Mares. *Passing Brave*. New York: Alfred A. Knopf, 1973.

Polk, William R., et al. *Backdrop to Tragedy: The Struggle for Palestine.* Boston, MA: Beacon Press, 1957.

el-Sadat, Anwar. *In Search of Identity: An Autobiography.* New York: Harper & Row, 1977.

Shair, Kamal A. *Out of the Middle East: The Emergence of a Global Arab Business.* London: I. B. Tauris, 2006.

Tannous, Afif I. *Village Roots and Beyond: Memoirs of Afif I. Tannous.* Beirut: Dar Nelson, 2004.

Secondary Sources

Arabic

Amin, 'Izz al-Din. *Ta'rikh al-Tabaqah al- 'Amila al-Misriya mundhu Nushu'iha hata sanat 1970.* Cairo: Dar al-Ghad al-'Arabi, 1987.

al-'Azm, Yusuf. *Al-Shahid Sayyid Qutb: Hayatuhu wa madarasatuhu wa atharuh.* Damascus and Beirut: Dar al-Qalam, 1980.

Ghurbal, Muhammad Shafiq. *Muhammad 'Ali al-Kabir.* Cairo: Dar al-Hilal, 1986.

Khalid, Muhammad. *'Abd al-Nasir wa al-haraka al-niqabiya.* Cairo: Mu'assasat Dar al-Ta'awun lil-Tab' wa-al-Nashr, 1971.

Zaki, Muhammad Shawqi. *Al-Ikhwan al-Muslimun wa al-Mujtama' al-Misri.* Cairo, Egypt: Dar al-Ansar, 1980[1952].

English

Abdalla, Ahmed. *The Student Movement and National Politics in Egypt, 1923–1973.* London: Al-Saqi Books, 1985.

Abu-Lughod, Ibrahim. *The Arab Rediscovery of Europe: A Study in Cultural Encounters.* Rev. ed. London: Saqi Books, 2011.

Abu-Rabi', Ibrahim. *Contemporary Arab Thought: Studies in Post-1967 Arab Intellectual History.* London: Pluto Press, 2004.

Aburish, Said K. *A Brutal Friendship: The West and the Arab Elite.* New York: St. Martin's Press, 1998.

Adas, Michael. *Dominance by Design: Technological Imperatives and America's Civilizing Mission.* Cambridge, MA: Belknap/Harvard, 2006.

Allman, Jean. "Phantoms of the Archive: Kwame Nkrumah, a Nazi Pilot Named Hanna, and the Contingencies of Post-colonial History Writing." *American Historical Review* 118 (February 2013): 104–29.

Almond, Gabriel and James S. Coleman, eds. *The Politics of the Developing Areas.* Princeton, NJ: Princeton University Press, 1960.

Alnasrawi, Abbas. *Arab Nationalism, Oil, and the Political Economy of Dependency.* Westport, CT: Greenwood Press, 1991.

——. *The Economy of Iraq: Oil, Wars, Destruction of Development and Prospects, 1950–2010.* Westport, CT: Greenwood Press, 1994.

——. "The Rise and Fall of Arab Oil Power." *Arab Studies Quarterly* 6 (Winter/Spring 1984): 1–12.

Alterman, Jon B. *Egypt and American Foreign Assistance, 1952–1956: Hopes Dashed*. New York: Palgrave Macmillan, 2002.

Alvandi, Roham. *Nixon, Kissinger, and the Shah: The United States and Iran in the Cold War*. New York: Oxford University Press, 2014.

Anderson, Betty S. *Nationalist Voices in Jordan: The Street and the State*. Austin: University Press of Texas, 2005.

Anderson, Irvine. *Aramco, the United States, and Saudi Arabia: A Study of the Dynamics of Foreign Oil Policy, 1933–1950*. Princeton, NJ: Princeton University Press, 1981.

Ansari, Ali M. *The Politics of Nationalism in Modern Iran*. New York: Cambridge University Press, 2012.

Apter, David E. *The Politics of Modernization*. Chicago: University of Chicago Press, 1965.

Ashton, Nigel J. *King Hussein of Jordan: A Political Life*. New Haven, CT: Yale University Press, 2008.

Ashton, Nigel J., ed. *The Cold War in the Middle East: Regional Conflict and the Superpowers, 1967–1973*. New York: Routledge, 2007.

Aydin, Cemil. *The Politics of Anti-Westernism in Asia: Visions of World Order in Pan-Islamic and Pan-Asian Thought*. New York: Columbia University Press, 2007.

Babiracki, Patryk and Kenyon Zimmer, eds. *Cold War Crossings: International Travel and Exchange across the Soviet Bloc, 1940s–1960s*. College Station: Texas A & M University Press, 2014.

Badran, Margot. *Feminists, Islam, and Nation: Gender and the Making of Modern Egypt*. Princeton, NJ: Princeton University Press, 1996.

Baer, Marc David. "Muslim Encounters with Nazism and the Holocaust: The Ahmadi of Berlin and the Jewish Convert to Islam Hugo Marcus." *American Historical Review* 120 (February 2015): 140–71.

Bar, Shmuel. *The Muslim Brotherhood in Jordan*. Tel Aviv: Moshe Dayan Center for Middle Eastern and African Studies, 2000.

Barak, On. *On Time: Technology and Temporality in Modern Egypt*. Berkeley: University of California Press, 2013.

Bashkin, Orit. *The Other Iraq: Pluralism and Culture in Hashemite Iraq*. Stanford, CA: Stanford University Press, 2009.

Bass, Warren. *Support Any Friend: Kennedy's Middle East and the Making of the U.S.–Israel Alliance*. New York: Oxford University Press, 2003.

Batatu, Hanna. *The Old Social Classes and the Revolutionary Movements of Iraq*. New ed. London: Saqi Books, 2004.

——. *Syria's Peasantry, the Descendants of Its Lesser Rural Notables, and Their Politics*. Princeton, NJ: Princeton University Press, 1999.

Bayly, C. A. *The Birth of the Modern World: 1780–1914*. Malden, MA: Blackwell Publishing, 2004.

Beckert, Sven. *Empire of Cotton: A Global History*. New York: Alfred A. Knopf, 2014.

Beinin, Joel and Zachary Lockman, *Workers on the Nile: Nationalism, Communism, Islam, and the Egyptian Working Class, 1882–1954*. Cairo, Egypt: American University in Cairo Press, 1998.

Bender, Marilyn and Selig Altschul. *The Chosen Instrument: Pan Am, Juan Trippe, the Rise and Fall of an American Entrepreneur*. New York: Simon and Schuster, 1982.

Berger, Mark T. "Decolonisation, Modernisation and Nation-Building: Political Development Theory and the Appeal of Communism in Southeast Asia, 1945–1975." *Journal of Southeast Asian Studies* 34 (October 2003): 421–48.

Beshara, Adel, ed. *Antun Sa'adeh: The Man, His Thought, an Anthology*. Reading, England: Ithaca Press, 2007.

Bevis, Teresa Brawner and Christopher J. Lucas, *International Students in American Colleges and Universities: A History*. New York: Palgrave Macmillan, 2007.

Bianchi, Robert. *Unruly Corporatism: Associational Life in Twentieth-Century Egypt*. New York: Oxford University Press, 1989.

Biggs, David A. *Quagmire: Nation-Building and Nature in the Mekong Delta*. Seattle: University of Washington Press, 2010.

Bird, Kai. *The Chairman: John J. McCloy and the Making of the American Establishment*. New York: Simon & Schuster, 1992.

———. *Crossing Mandelbaum Gate: Coming of Age Between the Arabs and Israelis, 1956–1978*. New York: Scribner, 2010.

Black, Cyril E. *The Dynamics of Modernization: A Study in Comparative History*. New York: Harper & Row, 1966.

Borstelmann, Thomas. *The 1970s: A New Global History from Civil Rights to Economic Inequality*. Princeton, NJ: Princeton University Press, 2012.

Brazinsky, Gregg. *Nation Building in South Korea: Koreans, Americans, and the Making of a Democracy*. Chapel Hill: University of North Carolina Press, 2007.

Brown, L. Carl, ed. *Imperial Legacy: The Ottoman Imprint on the Balkans and the Middle East*. New York: Columbia University Press, 1996.

Bunch, Clea. "Strike at Samu: Jordan, Israel, the United States, and the Origins of the Six-Day War." *Diplomatic History* 32 (January 2008): 55–76.

Bunton, Martin. *Colonial Land Policies in Palestine, 1917–1936*. New York: Oxford University Press, 2007.

Burns, William J. *Economic Aid and American Policy Toward Egypt, 1955–1981*. Albany: State University of New York Press, 1985.

Calvert, John. *Sayyid Qutb and the Origins of Radical Islamism*. New York: Columbia University Press, 2010.

Campos, Michelle U. *Ottoman Brothers: Muslims, Christians, and Jews in Early Twentieth-Century Palestine*. Stanford, CA: Stanford University Press, 2011.

Chamberlin, Paul Thomas. *The Global Offensive: The United States, the Palestine Liberation Organization, and the Making of the Post–Cold War Order*. New York: Oxford University Press, 2012.

———. "A World Restored: Religion, Counterrevolution, and the Search for Order in the Middle East." *Diplomatic History* 32 (June 2008): 441–69.

Chapman, Jessica M. *Cauldron of Resistance: Ngo Dinh Diem, the United States, and 1950s Southern Vietnam*. Ithaca, NY: Cornell University Press, 2013.

Chaudhry, Kiren Aziz. *The Price of Wealth: Economies and Institutions in the Middle East*. Ithaca, NY: Cornell University Press, 2007.

Citino, Nathan J. "The 'Crush' of Ideologies: The United States, the Arab World, and Cold War Modernization." *Cold War History* 12 (January 2012): 89–110.

———. *From Arab Nationalism to OPEC: Eisenhower, King Sa'ud, and the Making of U.S.–Saudi Relations*. 2nd ed. Bloomington: Indiana University Press, 2010.

Clark, Katerina. *Moscow, the Fourth Rome: Stalinism, Cosmopolitanism, and the Evolution of Soviet Culture, 1931–1941*. Cambridge, MA: Harvard University Press, 2011.

Cleveland, William L. *The Making of an Arab Nationalist: Ottomanism and Arabism in the Life and Thought of Sati' al-Husri*. Princeton, NJ: Princeton University Press, 1971.

Cohen, Lizabeth. *A Consumers' Republic: The Politics of Mass Consumption in Postwar America*. New York: Alfred A. Knopf, 2003.

Cohn, Edwin J. *Turkish Economic, Social, and Political Change: The Development of a More Prosperous and Open Society*. New York: Praeger, 1970.

Cole, Juan. *The New Arabs: How the Millennial Generation Is Changing the Middle East*. New York: Simon & Schuster, 2014.

Collins, Robert M. *More: The Politics of Economic Growth in Postwar America*. New York: Oxford University Press, 2000.

Cooper, Frederick. *Colonialism in Question: Theory, Knowledge, History*. Berkeley: University of California Press, 2005.

Cullather, Nick. *The Hungry World: America's Cold War Battle Against Poverty in Asia*. Cambridge, MA: Harvard University Press, 2010.

Cumings, Bruce. *The Origins of the Korean War*. 2 vols. Princeton, NJ: Princeton University Press, 1981, 1990.

Daigle, Craig. *The Limits of Détente: The United States, the Soviet Union, and the Arab–Israeli Conflict, 1969–1973*. New Haven, CT: Yale University Press, 2012.

Danforth, Nick. "Multi-purpose Empire: Ottoman History in Republican Turkey." *Middle Eastern Studies* 50 (July 2014): 655–78.

Dann, Uriel. *Iraq under Qassem: A Political History, 1958–1963*. New York: Praeger, 1969.

Davis, Eric. *Memories of State: Politics, History, and Collective Identity in Modern Iraq*. Berkeley: University of California Press, 2005.

Dean, Robert D. *Imperial Brotherhood: Gender and the Making of Cold War Foreign Policy*. Amherst: University of Massachusetts Press, 2001.

Devlin, John F. *The Ba'th Party: A History from Its Origins to 1966*. Stanford, CA: Hoover Institution Press, 1976.

Di-Capua, Yoav. "Common Skies, Divided Horizons: Aviation, Class and Modernity in Early Twentieth Century Egypt." *Journal of Social History* 41 (Summer 2008): 917–42.

———. *Gatekeepers of the Arab Past: Historians and History Writing in Twentieth-Century Egypt*. Berkeley: University of California Press, 2009.

———. "'Jabarti of the 20th Century': The National Epic of 'Abd al-Rahman al-Rafi'i and Other Egyptian Histories." *International Journal of Middle East Studies* 36 (August 2004): 429–50.

Dosman, Edgar J. *The Life and Times of Raul Prebisch, 1901–1986*. Kingston, Ontario: McGill-Queen's University Press, 2008.

Doumani, Beshara, ed. *Family History in the Middle East: Household, Property, and Gender*. Albany: State University of New York Press, 2003.

Doxiadis, Constantinos A. *Ekistics: An Introduction to the Science of Human Settlements*. New York: Oxford University Press, 1968.

Duffy, Enda. *The Speed Handbook: Velocity, Pleasure, Modernism*. Durham, NC: Duke University Press, 2009.

Eisenstadt, Shmuel Noah. *The Political Systems of Empires*. New York: The Free Press of Glencoe, 1963.

Ekbladh, David. *The Great American Mission: Modernization and the Construction of an American World Order*. Princeton, NJ: Princeton University Press, 2010.

El Shakry, Omnia. *The Great Social Laboratory: Subjects of Knowledge in Colonial and Postcolonial Egypt*. Stanford, CA: Stanford University Press, 2007.

Elshakry, Marwa. *Reading Darwin in Arabic, 1860–1950*. Chicago: University of Chicago Press, 2013.

Endy, Christopher. *Cold War Holidays: American Tourism in France*. Chapel Hill: University of North Carolina Press, 2004.

Engerman, David. *Modernization from the Other Shore: American Intellectuals and the Romance of Russian Development*. Cambridge, MA: Harvard University Press, 2003.

Engerman, David, et al. eds. *Staging Growth: Modernization, Development, and the Global Cold War*. Amherst: University of Massachusetts Press, 2003.

Eppel, Michael. "Note about the Term *Effendiyya* in the History of the Middle East." *International Journal of Middle East Studies* 41 (August 2009): 535–39.

Euben, Roxanne L. *Enemy in the Mirror: Islamic Fundamentalism and the Limits of Modern Rationalism, a Work of Comparative Political Theory*. Princeton, NJ: Princeton University Press, 1999.

——. *Journeys to the Other Shore: Muslim and Western Travelers in Search of Knowledge*. Princeton, NJ: Princeton University Press, 2006.

Fabian, Johannes. *Time and the Other: How Anthropology Makes Its Object*. New York: Columbia University Press, 1983.

Fair, Laura. "Drive-In Socialism: Debating Modernities and Development in Dar es Salaam, Tanzania." *American Historical Review* 118 (October 2013): 1077–1104.

Fanon, Frantz. *The Wretched of the Earth*. New York: Grove Press, 1963.

Faroqhi, Suraiya. *Approaching Ottoman History: An Introduction to the Sources*. Cambridge, England: Cambridge University Press, 1999.

Fathy, Hassan. *Architecture for the Poor: An Experiment in Rural Egypt*. Chicago: University of Chicago Press, 1973.

Ferguson, Karen. *Top Down: The Ford Foundation, Black Power, and the Reinvention of Racial Liberalism*. Philadelphia: University of Pennsylvania Press, 2013.

Ferris, Jesse. *Nasser's Gamble: How Intervention in Yemen Caused the Six-Day War and the Decline of Egyptian Power*. Princeton, NJ: Princeton University Press, 2013.

——. "Soviet Support for Egypt's Intervention in Yemen, 1962–63." *Journal of Cold War Studies* 10 (Fall 2008): 5–36.

Field, Thomas C. Jr., "Ideology as Strategy: Military-Led Modernization and the Origins of the Alliance for Progress in Bolivia." *Diplomatic History* 36 (January 2012): 147–83.

Findley, Carter V. "Mouradgea D'Ohsson (1740–1807): Liminality and Cosmopolitanism in the Author of the *Tableau Général de L'empire Othman*." *Turkish Studies Association Bulletin* 22 (1998): 21–35.

——. *Ottoman Civil Officialdom: A Social History*. Princeton, NJ: Princeton University Press, 1989.

——. "An Ottoman Occidentalist in Europe: Ahmed Midhat Meets Madame Gülnar, 1889," *American Historical Review* 103 (February 1998): 15–49.

——. *Turkey, Islam, Nationalism, and Modernity*. New Haven, CT: Yale University Press, 2010.

Fink, Carole, Philipp Gassert, and Detlef Junker, eds. *1968: The World Transformed*. New York: Cambridge University Press, 1998.

Franzén, Jonathan. *Red Star over Iraq: Iraqi Communism Before Saddam*. New York: Columbia University Press, 2011.

Frey, Frederick W. *The Turkish Political Elite*. Cambridge, MA: MIT Press, 1965.

Frye, Richard N., ed. *The Near East and the Great Powers*. Port Washington, NY: Kennikat Press, 1951.

Fuccaro, Nelida. *Histories of City and State in the Persian Gulf: Manama since 1800*. New York: Cambridge University Press, 2009.

Gasiorowski, Mark J. *U.S. Foreign Policy and the Shah: Building a Client State in Iran*. Ithaca, NY: Cornell University Press, 1991.

Gat, Moshe. "On the Use of Air Power and Its Effect on the Outbreak of the Six Day War." *Journal of Military History* 68 (October 2004): 1187–1215.

Gelvin, James and Nile Green, eds. *Global Muslims in the Age of Steam and Print*. Berkeley: University of California Press, 2013.

Gendzier, Irene L. *Managing Political Change: Social Scientists and the Third World*. Boulder, CO: Westview Press, 1985.

Gerges, Fawaz A. *The Far Enemy: Why Jihad Went Global*. New York: Cambridge University Press, 2005.

——. "The Kennedy Administration and the Egyptian–Saudi Conflict in Yemen: Co-opting Arab Nationalism." *Middle East Journal* 49 (Spring 1995): 292–311.

Gershoni, Israel, et al. eds. *Middle East Historiographies: Narrating the Twentieth Century*. Seattle: University of Washington Press, 2006.

Gershoni, Israel and James Jankowski. *Confronting Fascism in Egypt: Dictatorship versus Democracy in the 1930s*. Stanford, CA: Stanford University Press, 2010.

Ghurbal, Muhammad Shafiq. *The Beginnings of the Egyptian Question and the Rise of Mehmet Ali: A Study of the Napoleonic Era Based on Researches in the British and French Archives*. Reprinted ed. New York, AMS Press, 1977.

Gibb, H. A. R. "The Heritage of Islam in the Modern World (I)." *International Journal of Middle East Studies* 1 (January 1970): 3–17.

——. "Luṭfi Paşa on the Ottoman Caliphate." *Oriens* 15 (December 1, 1962): 287–95.

Gibb, H.A.R. and Harold Bowen. *Islamic Society and the West: A Study of the Impact of Western Civilization on Moslem Culture in the Near East*. London: Oxford University Press, 1950, 1957.

Gilman, Nils. *Mandarins of the Future: Modernization Theory in Postwar America*. Baltimore, MD: Johns Hopkins University Press, 2003.

Ginat, Rami. *Egypt's Incomplete Revolution: Lutfi al-Khuli and Nasser's Socialism in the 1960s*. Portland, OR: Frank Cass, 1997.

Gleijeses, Piero. *Conflicting Missions: Havana, Washington, and Africa, 1959–1976*. Chapel Hill: University of North Carolina Press, 2002.

——. *Visions of Freedom: Havana, Washington, Pretoria and the Struggle for Southern Africa, 1976–1991*. Chapel Hill: University of North Carolina Press, 2013.

Goode, James F. *The United States and Iran: In the Shadow of Musaddiq*. New York: St. Martin's Press, 1997.

Gordon, Joel. *Nasser's Blessed Movement: Egypt's Free Officers and the July Revolution.* New York: Oxford University Press, 1992.

Gorsuch, Anne E. "'Cuba, My Love': The Romance of Revolutionary Cuba in the Soviet Sixties." *American Historical Review* 120 (April 2015): 497–526.

Gosden, Chris and Jon Hather, ed. *The Prehistory of Food: Appetites for Change.* New York: Routledge, 1999.

Grandin, Greg. *The Last Colonial Massacre: Latin America in the Cold War.* Chicago: University of Chicago Press, 2004.

Gray, Matthew. "The Political Economy of Tourism in Syria: State, Society and Economic Liberalization." *Arab Studies Quarterly* 19 (Spring 1997): 57–73.

Gutenschwager, Gerald A. *Planning and Social Science: A Humanistic Approach.* Lanham, MD: University Press of America, 2004.

Hahn, Peter L. *Caught in the Middle East: U.S. Policy toward the Arab–Israeli Conflict, 1945–1961.* Chapel Hill: University of North Carolina Press, 2004.

Hajimu, Masuda. *Cold War Crucible: The Korean Conflict and the Postwar World.* Cambridge, MA: Harvard University Press, 2015.

Halberstam, David. *The Best and the Brightest.* New York: Random House, 1972.

Halpern, Manfred. *The Politics of Social Change in the Middle East and North Africa.* Princeton, NJ: Princeton University Press, 1963.

Hanioğlu, M. Şükrü. *Atatürk: An Intellectual Biography.* Princeton, NJ: Princeton University Press, 2011.

Harmer, Tanya. *Allende's Chile and the Inter-American Cold War.* Chapel Hill: University of North Carolina Press, 2011.

Hart, Parker T. *Saudi Arabia and the United States: Birth of a Security Partnership.* Bloomington: Indiana University Press, 1998.

Harootunian, Harry. *Overcome by Modernity: History, Culture, and Community in Interwar Japan.* Princeton, NJ: Princeton University Press, 2001.

Haskell, Thomas. "Modernization on Trial." *Modern Intellectual History* 2 (August 2005): 235–63.

Hathaway, Jane. *The Politics of Households in Ottoman Egypt: The Rise of the Qazdağlıs.* New York: Cambridge University Press, 1997.

Hathaway, Jane with Karl Barbir. *The Arab Lands under Ottoman Rule, 1516–1800.* Harlow, England: Pearson/Longman, 2008.

Heikal, Mohamed. *The Sphinx and the Commissar: The Rise and Fall of Soviet Influence in the Middle East.* New York: Harper & Row, 1978.

Heiss, Mary Ann. *Empire and Nationhood: The United States, Great Britain, and Iranian Oil, 1950–1954.* New York: Columbia University Press, 1997.

Heydemann, Steven, ed. *War, Institutions, and Social Change in the Middle East.* Berkeley: University of California Press, 2000.

Hinnebusch, Raymond A. "The Political Economy of Economic Liberalization in Syria." *International Journal of Middle East Studies* 27 (August 1995): 305–20.

Hogan, Michael J. and Thomas G. Paterson, eds. *Explaining the History of American Foreign Relations.* 2nd ed. New York: Cambridge University Press, 2004.

Holzman, Michael. *James Jesus Angleton, the CIA, and the Craft of Counterintelligence.* Amherst: University of Massachusetts Press, 2008.

Hopkins, Harry. *Egypt, the Crucible: The Unfinished Revolution in the Arab World.* Boston, MA: Houghton Mifflin, 1969.

Howard, Douglas A. "Ottoman Historiography and the Literature of 'Decline' of the Sixteenth and Seventeenth Centuries." *Journal of Asian History* 22 (1988): 52–77.

Hurewitz, J. C. *Middle East Politics: The Military Dimension.* New York: Frederick A. Praeger, 1969.

Ibrahim, Saad Eddin. *The New Arab Social Order: A Study of the Social Impact of Oil Wealth.* Boulder, CO: Westview Press, 1982.

Ihrig, Stefan. *Atatürk in the Nazi Imagination.* Cambridge, MA: Belknap/Harvard University Press, 2014.

Immerwahr, Daniel. *Thinking Small: The United States and the Lure of Community Development.* Cambridge, MA: Harvard University Press, 2015.

İnalcık Halil with Donald Quataert. *An Economic and Social History of the Ottoman Empire, 1300–1914.* New York: Cambridge University Press, 1994.

İslamoğlu, Huri. *Constituting Modernity: Private Property in the East and West.* New York: I. B. Tauris, 2004.

Ismael, Tareq Y. *The Arab Left.* Syracuse, NY: Syracuse University Press, 1976.

——. *The Rise and Fall of the Communist Party of Iraq.* New York: Cambridge University Press, 2008.

Ismael Tareq Y. and Jacqueline S. Ismael. *The Communist Movement in Syria and Lebanon.* Gainesville: University Press of Florida, 1998.

Jacobs, Jane. *The Death and Life of Great American Cities.* New York: Random House, 1961.

Jacobs, Matthew F. *Imagining the Middle East: The Building of an American Foreign Policy, 1918–1967.* Chapel Hill: University of North Carolina Press, 2011.

Jacobsen, Eric. "A Coincidence of Interests: Kennedy, U.S. Assistance, and the 1963 Iraqi Ba'th Regime." *Diplomatic History* 37 (November 2013): 1029–59.

Jeffs, Joseph E., ed. The George C. McGhee Library, *A Catalogue of Books on Asia Minor and the Turkish Ottoman Empire.* Washington, DC: Georgetown University Library, 1984.

Johnson, Ian. *A Mosque in Munich: Nazis, the CIA, and the Rise of the Muslim Brotherhood in the West.* Boston, MA: Houghton Mifflin Harcourt, 2010.

Jones, Toby Craig. *Desert Kingdom: How Oil and Water Forged Modern Saudi Arabia.* Cambridge, MA: Harvard University Press, 2010.

Joyner, Nancy Douglas. *Aerial Hijacking as an International Crime.* Dobbs Ferry, NY: Oceana Publications, 1974.

Kalinovsky, Artemy M. and Craig Daigle, eds. *The Routledge Handbook of the Cold War.* New York: Routledge, 2014.

Kassab, Elizabeth Suzanne. *Contemporary Arab Thought: Cultural Critique in Comparative Perspective.* New York: Columbia University Press, 2010.

Katznelson, Ira. *Fear Itself: The New Deal and the Origins of Our Time.* New York: W. W. Norton, 2013.

Kaufman, Asher. "Between Permeable and Sealed Borders: The Trans-Arabian Pipeline and the Arab–Israeli Conflict." *International Journal of Middle East Studies* 46 (February 2014): 95–116.

Kaufman, Burton I. *The Oil Cartel Case: A Documentary Study of Antitrust Activity in the Cold War Era.* Westport, CT: Greenwood Press, 1978.

——. *Trade and Aid: Eisenhower's Foreign Economic Policy, 1953–1961.* Baltimore, MD: Johns Hopkins University Press, 1982.

Kayalı, Hasan. *Arabs and Young Turks: Ottomanism, Arabism, and Islamism in the Ottoman Empire, 1908–1918.* Berkeley: University of California Press, 1997.

Kepel, Gilles. *Muslim Extremism in Egypt: The Prophet and the Pharaoh.* Berkeley: University of California Press, 1993.

Khadduri, Majid and Herbert J. Liebesny, eds. *Law in the Middle East.* vol. 1: *Origin and Development of Islamic Law.* Washington, DC: Middle East Institute, 1955.

Khalidi, Rashid. *Sowing Crisis: The Cold War and American Dominance in the Middle East.* Boston, MA: Beacon Press, 2009.

Khoury, Philip S. *Syria and the French Mandate: The Politics of Arab Nationalism, 1920–1945.* Princeton, NJ: Princeton University Press, 1987.

Khuri-Makdisi, Ilham. *The Eastern Mediterranean and the Making of Global Radicalism, 1860–1914.* Berkeley: University of California Press, 2010.

Kieser, Hans-Lukas. *Nearest East: American Millennialism and Mission to the Middle East.* Philadelphia: Temple University Press, 2010.

Klimke, Martin. *The Other Alliance: Student Protest in West Germany and the United States in the Global Sixties.* Princeton, NJ: Princeton University Press, 2009.

Koerner, Brendan I. *The Skies Belong to Us: Love and Terror in the Golden Age of Hijacking.* New York: Crown Publishers, 2013.

Krige, John et al. *NASA in the World: Fifty Years of International Collaboration in Space.* New York: Palgrave Macmillan, 2013.

Kwon, Heonik. *The Other Cold War.* New York: Columbia University Press, 2010.

Laron, Guy. *Origins of the Suez Crisis: Postwar Development Diplomacy and the Struggle over Third World Industrialization, 1945–1956.* Baltimore, MD: Johns Hopkins University Press, 2013.

Latham, Michael. *Modernization as Ideology: American Social Science and "Nation Building" in the Kennedy Era.* Chapel Hill: University of North Carolina Press, 2000.

——. *The Right Kind of Revolution: Modernization, Development, and U.S. Foreign Policy from the Cold War to the Present.* Ithaca, NY: Cornell University Press, 2011.

Latner, Teishan A. "Take Me To Havana! Airline Hijacking, U.S.–Cuba Relations, and Political Protest in Late Sixties' America." *Diplomatic History* 39 (January 2015): 16–44.

Lazarowitz, Arlene. "Different Approaches to a Regional Search for Balance: The Johnson Administration, the State Department, and the Middle East, 1964–1967." *Diplomatic History* 32 (January 2008): 25–54.

Lebon, J.H.G. "The New Irrigation Era in Iraq." *Economic Geography* 31(January 1955): 47–59.

Leffler, Melvyn P. and Odd Arne Westad, eds. *Cambridge History of the Cold War.* 3 vols. New York: Cambridge University Press, 2010.

Lerner, Daniel. *The Passing of Traditional Society: Modernizing the Middle East.* New York: The Free Press, 1958.

Lerner, Daniel and Richard D. Robinson. "Swords and Ploughshares: The Turkish Army as a Modernizing Force," *World Politics* 13 (October 1960): 19–44.

Levey, Zach. *Israel in Africa, 1956–1976.* Dordrecht, Netherlands: Martinus Nijhoff /Republic of Letters, 2012.

——. "The United States, Israel, and Nuclear Desalination: 1964–1968." *Diplomatic History* 39 (November 2015): 904–25.

Lévi-Strauss, Claude. *The Savage Mind*. Chicago: University of Chicago Press, 1962.

LeVine, Mark. *Overthrowing Geography: Jaffa, Tel Aviv, and the Struggle for Palestine, 1880–1948*. Berkeley: University of California Press, 2005.

Lewis, Bernard. *The Emergence of Modern Turkey*. London: Oxford University Press, 1961.

——. *Notes and Documents from the Turkish Archives: A Contribution to the History of the Jews in the Ottoman Empire*. Jerusalem: Israel Oriental Society, 1952.

——. *Notes on a Century: Reflections of a Middle East Historian*. New York: Viking, 2012.

——. "Studies in the Ottoman Archives – I." *Bulletin of the School of Oriental and African Studies*, vol. 16, no. 3 (1954): 469–501.

Lewis, Raphaela. *Everyday Life in Ottoman Turkey*. New York: G.P. Putnam's Sons, 1971.

Lebkicher, Roy, George Rentz, Max Steineke, et al. *Aramco Handbook*. Dhahran: Arabian American Oil Company, 1960.

Lippman, Thomas. *Inside the Mirage: America's Fragile Partnership with Saudi Arabia*. Boulder, CO: Westview Press, 2004.

Little, Douglas. *American Orientalism: The United States and the Middle East since 1945*. 3rd ed. Chapel Hill: University of North Carolina Press, 2008.

——. "Mission Impossible: The CIA and the Cult of Covert Action in the Middle East." *Diplomatic History* 28 (November 2004): 663–701.

——. "The New Frontier on the Nile: JFK, Nasser, and Arab Nationalism." *Journal of American History* 75 (September 1988): 501–27.

Lockman, Zachary. *Comrades and Enemies: Arab and Jewish Workers in Palestine, 1906–1948*. Berkeley: University of California Press, 1996.

——. *Contending Visions of the Middle East: The History and Politics of Orientalism*. New York: Cambridge University Press, 2004.

Lockman, Zachary, ed. *Workers and Working Classes in the Middle East: Struggles, Histories, Historiographies*. Albany: State University of New York Press, 1994.

Louër, Laurence. *Transnational Shia Politics: Religious and Political Networks in the Gulf*. London: Hurst & Company, 2008.

Love, Joseph L. *Crafting the Third World: Theorizing Underdevelopment in Rumania and Brazil*. Stanford, CA: Stanford University Press, 1996.

Makdisi, Ussama. "After Said: The Limits and Possibilities of a Critical Scholarship of U.S.–Arab Relations." *Diplomatic History* 38 (June 2014): 657–84.

——. "Anti-Americanism in the Arab World: An Interpretation of a Brief History." *Journal of American History* 89 (September 2002): 538–57.

——. *Artillery of Heaven: American Missionaries and the Failed Conversion of the Middle East*. Ithaca, NY: Cornell University Press, 2008.

——. "Ottoman Orientalism." *American Historical Review* 107 (June 2002): 768–96.

Manalo, Kathleen. "A Short History of the Middle East Institute." *Middle East Journal* 41 (Winter 1987): 64–73.

Manela, Erez. "A Pox on Your Narrative: Writing Disease Control into Cold War History." *Diplomatic History* 34 (April 2010): 299–323.

——. *The Wilsonian Moment: Self-Determination and the International Origins of Anticolonial Nationalism*. New York: Oxford University Press, 2007.

Mardin, Şerif. *The Genesis of Young Ottoman Thought: A Study in the Modernization of Turkish Political Ideas*. Princeton, NJ: Princeton University Press, 1962.

Marr, Phebe. *The Modern History of Iraq.* 3rd ed. Boulder, CO: Westview Press, 2012.

Mart, Michelle. *Eye on Israel: How America Came to View Israel as an Ally.* Albany: State University Press of New York, 2006.

Matar, Dina. *What It Means to Be Palestinian: Stories of Palestinian Peoplehood.* New York: I. B. Tauris, 2011.

Matthews, Weldon C. *Confronting an Empire, Constructing a Nation: Arab Nationalists and Popular Politics in Mandate Palestine.* New York: Palgrave Macmillan, 2006.

——. "The Kennedy Administration, Counterinsurgency, and Iraq's First Ba'thist Regime." *International Journal of Middle East Studies* 43 (November 2011): 635–53.

Matusow, Allen J. *The Unraveling of America: A History of Liberalism in the 1960s.* New York: Harper & Row, 1984.

Maxfield, Sylvia and James H. Nolt. "Protectionism and the Internationalization of Capital: U.S. Sponsorship of Import Substitution Industrialization in the Philippines, Turkey, and Argentina." *International Studies Quarterly* 34 (March 1990): 49–81.

May, Elaine Tyler. *Homeward Bound: American Families in the Cold War Era.* New York: Basic Books, 1988.

Mayer, Thomas. "Arab Unity of Action and the Palestine Question, 1945–48." *Middle Eastern Studies* 22 (July 1986): 331–49.

McAlister, Melani. *Epic Encounters: Culture, Media, and U.S. Interests in the Middle East since 1945.* Rev. ed. Berkeley: University of California Press, 2005.

McCraw, Thomas K. *Prophets of Regulation: Charles Francis Adams, Louis D. Brandeis, James M. Landis, Alfred E. Kahn.* Cambridge, MA: Belknap Press, 1984.

McDougall, Walter A. *The Heavens and the Earth: A Political History of the Space Age.* New York: Basic Books, 1985.

McGhee, George. *The US-Turkish-NATO Middle East Connection: How the Truman Doctrine Contained the Soviets in the Middle East.* New York: St. Martin's, 1990.

Meijer, Roel. *The Quest for Modernity: Secular Liberal and Left-Wing Political Thought in Egypt, 1945–1958.* New York: Routledge Curzon, 2002.

Menoret, Pascal. *Joyriding in Riyadh: Oil, Urbanism, and Road Revolt.* New York: Cambridge University Press, 2014.

Merrill, Karen R. "Texas Metropole: Oil, the American West, and U.S. Power in the Postwar Years." *Journal of American History* 99 (June 2012): 197–207.

Mieczkowski, Yanek. *Eisenhower's Sputnik Moment: The Race for Space and World Prestige.* Ithaca, NY: Cornell University Press, 2013.

Mitchell, Timothy. *Colonising Egypt.* Berkeley: University of California Press, 1988.

——. *Rule of Experts: Egypt, Techno-Politics, Modernity.* Berkeley: University of California Press, 2002.

Monroe, Kristin V. "Automobility and Citizenship in Interwar Lebanon." *Comparative Studies of South Asia, Africa, and the Middle East,* vol. 34, no. 3 (2014): 518–31.

Morgan, Ted. *A Covert Life: Jay Lovestone, Communist, Anti-Communist, and Spymaster.* New York: Random House, 1999.

Mundy, Martha and Richard Saumarez Smith. *Governing Property, Making the Modern State: Law, Administration, and Production in Ottoman Syria.* New York: I. B. Tauris, 2007.

Nasr, Joe and Mercedes Volait, eds. *Urbanism: Imported or Exported?* Hoboken, NJ: Wiley-Academy, 2003.

Nguyen, Lien-Hang T. *Hanoi's War: An International History of the War for Peace in Vietnam.* Chapel Hill: University of North Carolina Press, 2012.

Omar, Saleh. "Arab Nationalism: A Retrospective Evaluation." *Arab Studies Quarterly* 14 (Fall 1992): 23–37.

Oren, Michael. *Six Days of War: June 1967 and the Making of the Modern Middle East.* New York: Oxford University Press, 2002.

Osgood, Kenneth. *Total Cold War: Eisenhower's Secret Propaganda Battle at Home and Abroad.* Lawrence: University Press of Kansas, 2006.

Osterhammel, Jürgen. *The Transformation of the World: A Global History of the Nineteenth Century*, trans. Patrick Camiller. Princeton, NJ: Princeton University Press, 2014.

Owen, Roger. "The Middle East in the Eighteenth Century – An 'Islamic' Society in Decline? A Critique of Gibb and Bowen's Islamic Society and the West." *Bulletin (British Society for Middle Eastern Studies)* vol. 3, no. 2 (1976): 110–17.

Owen, Roger and Şevket Pamuk. *A History of Middle East Economies in the Twentieth Century.* Cambridge, MA: Harvard University Press, 1998.

Paget, Karen M. *Patriotic Betrayal: The Inside Story of the CIA's Secret Campaign to Enroll American Students in the Crusade Against Communism.* New Haven, CT: Yale University Press, 2015.

Painter, David S. *Oil and the American Century: The Political Economy of U.S. Foreign Oil Policy, 1941–1954.* Baltimore, MD: Johns Hopkins University Press, 1986.

Palmer, Scott W. *Dictatorship of the Air: Aviation Culture and the Fate of Modern Russia.* New York: Cambridge University Press, 2006.

Parker, Jason C. *Brother's Keeper: The United States, Race, and Empire in the British Caribbean, 1937–1962.* New York: Oxford University Press, 2008.

Pedersen, Susan. "Getting out of Iraq – in 1932: The League of Nations and the Road to Normative Statehood." *American Historical Review* 115 (October 2010): 975–1000.

Phillips, Sarah T. *This Land, This Nation: Conservation, Rural America, and the New Deal.* New York: Cambridge University Press, 2007.

Podeh, Elie. "The 'Big Lie': Inventing the Myth of British-US Involvement in the 1967 War." *Review of International Affairs* 2 (Autumn 2002): 1–23.

——. *The Decline of Arab Unity: The Rise and Fall of the United Arabic Republic.* Portland, OR: Sussex Academic Press, 1999.

Podeh, Elie and Onn Winckler, eds. *Rethinking Nasserism: Revolution and Historical Memory in Modern Egypt.* Gainesville: University Press of Florida, 2004.

Poggi, Christine. *Inventing Futurism: The Art and Politics of Artificial Optimism.* Princeton, NJ: Princeton University Press, 2009.

Polk, William R. "The Nature of Modernization: The Middle East and North Africa." *Foreign Affairs* 44 (October 1965): 100–10.

——. *The Opening of South Lebanon, 1788–1840: A Study of the Impact of the West on the Middle East.* Cambridge, MA: Harvard University Press, 1963.

——. *The United States and the Arab World.* Cambridge, MA: Harvard University Press, 1965.

Pollard, Lisa. *Nurturing the Nation: The Family Politics of Modernizing, Colonizing, and Liberating Egypt, 1805–1923*. Berkeley: University of California Press, 2005.

Popp, Roland. "An Application of Modernization Theory During the Cold War? The Case of Pahlavi Iran." *International History Review* 30 (2008): 76–98.

Posusney, Marsha Pripstein. *Labor and the State in Egypt: Workers, Unions, and Economic Restructuring*. New York: Columbia University Press, 1997.

Prashad, Vijay. *Arab Spring, Libyan Winter*. Edinburgh: AK Press, 2012.

Primakov, Yevgeny. *Russia and the Arabs: Behind the Scenes in the Middle East from the Cold War to the Present*. Trans. Paul Gould. New York: Basic Books, 2009.

Provence, Michael. *The Great Syrian Revolt and the Rise of Arab Nationalism*. Austin: University of Texas Press, 2005.

Pye, Lucian, ed. *Communications and Political Development*. Princeton, NJ: Princeton University Press, 1963.

Rakove, Robert B. *Kennedy, Johnson, and the Nonaligned World*. New York: Cambridge University Press, 2013.

al-Rasheed, Madawi. *Contesting the Saudi State: Islamic Voices from a New Generation*. New York: Cambridge University Press, 2007.

al-Rasheed, Madawi and Marat Shterin, eds. *Dying for Faith: Religiously Motivated Violence in the Contemporary World*. New York: Palgrave Macmillan, 2009.

El-Rayyes, Riad and Dunia Nahas. *Guerrillas for Palestine*. New York: St. Martin's Press, 1976.

Rist, Gilbert. *The History of Development: From Western Origins to Global Faith*. Trans. Patrick Camiller. Rev. ed. New York: Zed Books, 2002.

Rodgers, Daniel T. *Age of Fracture*. Cambridge, MA: Belknap/Harvard University Press, 2011.

Rogan, Eugene L. *The Arabs: A History*. New York: Basic Books, 2009.

——. *Frontiers of State in the Late Ottoman Empire: Transjordan, 1850–1921*. New York: Cambridge University Press, 1999.

Rogan, Eugene L. and Tariq Tell, eds. *Village, Steppe, and State: The Social Origins of Modern Jordan*. London: British Academic Press, 1994.

Rosenberg, Emily. "Consuming Women: Images of Americanization in the 'American Century'." *Diplomatic History* 23 (Summer 1999): 479–97.

Rosenberg, Emily et al. eds. *A World Connecting: 1870–1945* (A History of the World). Cambridge, MA: Belknap Press, 2012.

Rostow, Walt. *The Stages of Economic Growth: A Non-Communist Manifesto*. Cambridge, England: Cambridge University Press, 1960.

Roubatis, Yiannis P. and Elias Vlanton. "Who Killed George Polk?" *More* 7 (May 1977): 12–32.

Roy, Delwin A. "Egyptian Emigrant Labor: Domestic Consequences." *Middle Eastern Studies* 27 (October 1991): 551–82.

Rupp, Leila. *Worlds of Women: The Making of an International Women's Movement*. Princeton, NJ: Princeton University Press, 1997.

Rustow, Dankwart A. "The Army and the Founding of the Turkish Republic." *World Politics* 11 (July 1959): 513–52.

——. *Turkey: America's Forgotten Ally*. New York: Council on Foreign Relations, 1987.

——. *A World of Nations: Problems of Political Modernization*. Washington, DC: The Brookings Institution, 1967.

Rustow, Dankwart A. and Robert E. Ward, eds. *Political Modernization in Japan and Turkey.* Princeton, NJ: Princeton University Press, 1964.

Saab, Gabriel S. *The Egyptian Agrarian Reform, 1952–1962.* London: Oxford University Press, 1967.

Sackley, Nicole. "Village Models: Etawah, India, and the Making and Remaking of Development in the Early Cold War." *Diplomatic History* 37 (September 2013): 749–78.

Said, Edward. *Culture and Imperialism.* New York: Alfred A. Knopf, 1993.

——. *Orientalism.* New York: Vintage Books, 1979.

Salas, Miguel Tinker. *The Enduring Legacy: Oil, Culture, and Society in Venezuela.* Durham, NC: Duke University Press, 2009.

Satia, Priya. "The Defense of Inhumanity: Air Control and the British Idea of Arabia." *American Historical Review* 111 (February 2006): 16–51.

Satter, Beryl. *Family Properties: Race, Real Estate, and the Exploitation of Black Urban America.* New York: Metropolitan Books, 2009.

Sayigh, Yezid. *Armed Struggle and the Search for State: The Palestinian National Movement, 1949–1993.* New York: Clarendon Press, 1997.

Schayegh, Cyrus. "1958 Reconsidered: State Formation and the Cold War in the Early Postcolonial Arab Middle East." *International Journal of Middle East Studies* 45 (August 2013): 421–43.

——. "The Many Worlds of 'Abud Yasin; or, What Narcotics Trafficking in the Interwar Middle East Can Tell Us about Territorialization." *American Historical Review* 116 (April 2011): 273–306.

Schmitz, David. *Thank God They're on Our Side: The United States and Right-Wing Dictatorships, 1921–1965.* Chapel Hill: University of North Carolina Press, 1999.

Scott, David Meerman and Richard Jurek. *Marketing the Moon: The Selling of the Apollo Lunar Program.* Cambridge: MIT Press, 2014.

Scott, James C. *Seeing Like a State: How Certain Schemes to Improve the Human Condition Have Failed.* New Haven, CT: Yale University Press, 1998.

Scott-Smith, Giles. "The US State Department's Foreign Leader Program in France During the Early Cold War." *Revue Française d'Études Américaines,* 107 (2006): 47–60.

Seale, Patrick. *The Struggle for Arab Independence: Riad el-Solh and the Makers of the Modern Middle East.* New York: Cambridge University Press, 2010.

Seale, Patrick with assistance of Maureen McConville. *Asad of Syria: The Struggle for the Middle East.* Berkeley: University of California Press, 1988.

Seccombe, Ian J. and Richard I. Lawless. *Work Camps and Company Towns: Settlement Patterns and the Gulf Oil Industry.* Durham, UK: University of Durham, Centre for Middle Eastern and Islamic Studies, 1987.

Shaw, R. Paul. "The Political Economy of Inequality in the Arab World." *Arab Studies Quarterly* 6 (Winter/Spring 1984): 124–54.

Sherry, Michael S. *The Rise of American Air Power: The Creation of Armageddon.* New Haven, CT: Yale University Press, 1987.

Simpson, Bradley. *Economists with Guns: Authoritarian Development and U.S.–Indonesian Relations, 1960–1968.* Stanford, CA: Stanford University Press, 2008.

Simpson, Christopher, ed. *Universities and Empire: Money and Politics in the Social Sciences During the Cold War.* New York: The New Press, 1998.

Smith, Charles D. "The 'Crisis of Orientation': The Shift of Egyptian Intellectuals to Islamic Subjects in the 1930s." *International Journal of Middle East Studies* 4 (October 1973): 382–410.

Snow, Peter and David Phillips. *The Arab Hijack War: The True Story of 25 Days in September, 1970.* New York: Ballantine Books, 1971.

Springborg, Robert. "Patrimonialism and Policy Making in Egypt: Nasser and Sadat and the Tenure Policy for Reclaimed Lands." *Middle Eastern Studies* 15 (January 1979): 49–69.

Stadiem, William. *Jet Set: The People, the Planes, the Glamour, and the Romance in Aviation's Glory Years.* New York: Ballantine Books, 2014.

Steele, James. *An Architecture for People: The Complete Works of Hassan Fathy.* New York: Whitney Library of Design, 1997.

Steigerwald, David. *The Sixties and the End of Modern America.* New York: St. Martin's Press, 1995.

Stevens, Georgiana G., ed. *The United States and the Middle East.* Englewood Cliffs, NJ: Prentice-Hall, Inc., 1964.

Suri, Jeremi. *The Global Revolutions of 1968: A Norton Casebook in History.* New York: W.W. Norton, 2007.

Susser, Asher. *On Both Banks of the Jordan: A Political Biography of Wasfi al-Tall.* Portland, OR: Frank Cass, 1994.

Takriti, Abdel Razzaq. *Monsoon Revolution: Republicans, Sultans, and Empires in Oman, 1965–1976.* Oxford: Oxford University Press, 2013.

Talhami, Ghada Hashem. *The Mobilization of Muslim Women in Egypt.* Gainesville: University Press of Florida, 1996.

Thiollet, Hélène. "Migration as Diplomacy: Labor Migrants, Refugees, and Arab Regional Politics in the Oil-Rich Countries." *International Labor and Working-Class History* 79 (Spring 2011): 103–21.

Thompson, Elizabeth. *Colonial Citizens: Republican Rights, Paternal Privilege, and Gender in French Syria and Lebanon.* New York: Columbia University Press, 2000.

——. *Justice Interrupted: The Struggle for Constitutional Government in the Middle East.* Cambridge, MA: Harvard University Press, 2013.

Thornburg, Max, et al. *Turkey: An Economic Appraisal.* New York: Greenwood Press, 1968[1949].

Tinkle, Lon. *Mr. De: A Biography of Everette Lee DeGolyer.* Boston, MA: Little, Brown, 1970.

Toth, James. *Sayyid Qutb: The Life and Legacy of a Radical Islamic Intellectual.* New York: Oxford University Press, 2013.

Trask, Roger R. "The United States and Turkish Nationalism: Investments and Technical Aid during the Atatürk Era." *Business History Review* 38 (Spring 1964): 58–77.

Tribbe, Matthew D. *No Requiem for the Space Age: The Apollo Moon Landings and American Culture.* New York: Oxford University Press, 2014.

Tripp, Charles. *A History of Iraq.* 2nd ed. New York: Cambridge University Press, 2000.

Turner, John G. *Bill Bright and Campus Crusade for Christ: The Renewal of Evangelicalism in Postwar America.* Chapel Hill: University of North Carolina Press, 2008.

Uslu, Nasuh. *The Turkish–American Relationship between 1947 and 2003: The History of a Distinctive Alliance.* New York: Nova Science Publishers, 2003.

Van Vleck, Jenifer. *Empire of the Air: Aviation and the American Ascendancy.* Cambridge, MA: Harvard University Press, 2013.

Vitalis, Robert. *America's Kingdom: Mythmaking on the Saudi Oil Frontier.* Stanford, CA: Stanford University Press, 2007.

Warriner, Doreen. *Land Reform and Development in the Middle East: A Study of Egypt, Syria, and Iraq.* 2nd ed. London: Oxford University Press, 1962.

Waterbury, John. "The Cairo Workshop on Land Reclamation and Resettlement in the Arab World." *Fieldstaff Reports*: Africa: Northeast Africa, series 17 (December 1971): 1–12.

——. *The Egypt of Nasser and Sadat: The Political Economy of Two Regimes.* Princeton, NJ: Princeton University Press, 1983.

Westad, Odd Arne. *The Global Cold War: Third World Interventions and the Making of Our Times.* New York: Cambridge University Press, 2007.

Wickham, Carrie Rosefsky. *Mobilizing Islam: Religion, Activism, and Political Change in Egypt.* New York: Columbia University Press, 2002.

——. *The Muslim Brotherhood: Evolution of an Islamist Movement.* Princeton, NJ: Princeton University Press, 2013.

Wien, Peter. "Coming to Terms with the Past: German Academia and Historical Relations between the Arab Lands and Nazi Germany." *International Journal of Middle East Studies* 42 (May 2010): 311–21.

——. *Iraqi Arab Nationalism: Authoritarian, Totalitarian, and Pro-Fascist Inclinations, 1932–1941.* New York: Routledge, 2006.

Wiener, Tim. *Legacy of Ashes: The History of the CIA.* New York: Doubleday, 2007.

Wilford, Hugh. *America's Great Game: The CIA's Secret Arabists and the Shaping of the Modern Middle East.* New York: Basic Books, 2013.

Wishart, David. "The Breakdown of the Johnston Negotiations over the Jordan Waters." *Middle Eastern Studies* 26 (October 1990): 536–46.

Worringer, Renée. *Ottomans Imagining Japan: East, Middle East, and Non-Western Modernity at the Turn of the Twentieth Century.* New York: Palgrave Macmillan, 2014.

Wu, Judy Tzu-Chun. *Radicals on the Road: Internationalism, Orientalism, and Feminism during the Vietnam Era.* Ithaca, NY: Cornell University Press, 2013.

Yaqub, Salim. *Containing Arab Nationalism: The Eisenhower Doctrine and the Middle East.* Chapel Hill: University of North Carolina Press, 2004.

Yared, Nazik Saba. *Arab Travellers and Western Civilization.* Trans. Sumayya Damluji Shahbandar. Ed. Tony P. Naufal and Jana Gough. London: Saqi Books, 1996.

Yizraeli, Sarah. *Politics and Society in Saudi Arabia: The Crucial Years of Development, 1960–1982.* New York: Columbia University Press, 2012.

Zollner, Barbara. "Prison Talk: The Muslim Brotherhood's Internal Struggle during Gamal Abdel Nasser's Persecution, 1954–1971." *International Journal of Middle East Studies* 39 (August 2007): 411–33.

Theses, Dissertations

al-Kubaisi, Basil Raouf. "The Arab Nationalists Movement, 1951–1971: From Pressure Group to Socialist Party." PhD diss., American University, 1971.

Pyla, Panayiota I. "Ekistics, Architecture and Environmental Politics, 1945–1976: A Prehistory of Sustainable Development." PhD diss., Massachusetts Institute of Technology, 2002.

Qaim-Maqami, Linda Wills. "Max Thornburg and the Quest for a Corporate Foreign Oil Policy: An Experiment in Cooperation." PhD diss., Texas A&M University, 1986.

Said, Elashiq Saad. "The Arab Civil Aviation Council ACAC." LL.M. thesis, McGill University, 1987.

Wolfe-Hunnicutt, Brandon. "The End of the Concessionary Regime: Oil and American Power in Iraq, 1958–1972." PhD diss., Stanford University, 2011.

Zeman, William J. "U.S. Covert Intervention in Iraq, 1958–1963: The Origins of U.S. Supported Regime Change in Modern Iraq." MA thesis, California State Polytechnic University, Pomona, 2006.

Novels, Fiction

Lederer, William J. and Eugene Burdick, *The Ugly American*. New York: Fawcett Crest, 1958.

McGhee, George Crews. *Dance of the Billions: A Novel about Texas, Houston, and Oil*. Austin, TX: Diamond Books, 1990.

Munif, Abdelrahman. *Cities of Salt*. Trans. Peter Theroux. New York: Vintage International, 1989.

Salih, Tayeb. *Season of Migration to the North*. Trans. Denys Johnson-Davies. New York: Michael Kesend Publishing, Ltd., 1989.

al-Shidyaq, Ahmad Faris. *Leg Over Leg, or the Turtle in the Tree, Concerning the Fariyaq, What Manner of Creature Might He Be*. Ed. and Trans. Humphrey Davies. 4 vols. New York: New York University Press, 2013.

Tanpinar, Ahmet Hamdi. *The Time Regulation Institute*. Trans. Maureen Freely and Alexander Dawe. New York: Penguin Books, [1962] 2013.

Web

Bilderberg Group. "The Formation of the Middle East Study Group." October 6, 1957. http://brd-schwindel.org/download/DOKUMENTE/Bilderberg%20Meetings, %201957,%20Official%20Report.pdf Accessed September 18, 2015.

Central Intelligence Agency. FOIA Reading Room. http://www.foia.cia.gov/.

Federal Aviation Administration, Civil Aviation Security Service. "Hijacking Statistics, U.S. Registered Aircraft." April 1, 1975. https://www.ncjrs.gov/pdffiles1/Digitization/28885NCJRS.pdf Accessed September 25, 2015.

Johnson, Lyndon B. "Remarks in New York City at the Dinner of the Weizmann Institute of Science." February 6, 1964. http://www.presidency.ucsb.edu/ws/index.php?pid=26060 Accessed September 24, 2015.

Polk, William R. "Yemen as Vietnam or Afghanistan." April 1, 2015. https://
consortiumnews.com/2015/04/01/yemen-as-vietnam-or-afghanistan/ Accessed
September 24, 2015.

Sa'ada, Antun. *al-Muhadarat al-'ashar.* Syrian Social Nationalist Party. http://
www.ssnp.com/new/library/saadeh/10_lectures/index.htm Accessed September
28, 2015.

Index